TABLE OF CONTENTS

UNIT 4: ESSAY

INTRODUCTION TO THE SAT

Don't be scared of the SAT. Why? Because we know what's on the exam, and we know exactly how you should prepare for it. Kaplan has been teaching students how to succeed on the SAT for more than 75 years—longer than anyone else, period. Students who are working toward top scores know that they need to practice the most advanced concepts. If your goal is to earn a top score, this SAT Advanced Prep book will help you do just that!

SAT Structure

The SAT is 3 hours long, or 3 hours and 50 minutes long if you choose to complete the optional Essay Test. It is made up of mostly multiple-choice questions that test two subject areas: Math and Evidence-Based Reading and Writing. The latter subject area is split into a Reading Test and a Writing & Language Test.

Test	Allotted Time (min.)	Question Count
Reading	65	52
Writing & Language	35	44
Math	80	58
Essay (optional)	50	1
Total	180 OR 230 (w/essay)	154 OR 155 (w/essay)

SAT Scoring

SAT scoring can be pretty complex. You will receive one score ranging from 200 to 800 for Evidence-Based Reading and Writing and another for Math. Your overall SAT score will range from 400 to 1600 and is calculated by adding these two scores together. You will receive a separate score for the Essay Test, if you choose to take it.

In addition to your overall scores, you will receive subscores that provide a deeper analysis of your SAT performance. The SAT also gives you a percentile ranking, which allows you to compare your scores with those of other high school students who took the test. For example, a student with a percentile of 63 has earned a score better than 63 percent of test takers.

Where and When to Take the SAT

As a general rule, students take the SAT at least once in their junior year, often taking it for the first time in March. The SAT is administered on select Saturdays during the year. Sunday testing is available for students who cannot take the Saturday test because of religious observances. Check the official College Board website at www.collegeboard.org for the most up-to-date test dates. Note that you must register for the SAT approximately one month in advance to avoid paying a late fee.

How to Use This Book

This book contains hundreds of practice questions. Each question is an SAT question type you will see on Test Day and provides you with plenty of opportunities to assess and practice your strengths and weaknesses before Test Day. Answering practice questions is important, but just as important is understanding why you got a particular question right or wrong. When you're done answering one or more questions, check out the detailed Answers and Explanations at the end of the book. These thorough explanations provide both the correct answers and strategic advice to help you practice thinking like an expert! In addition, every explanation includes the difficulty level of each question. All of this practice is geared toward one thing: getting you the most points on Test Day!

Follow these steps to get the most out of these practice questions:

1. Read the Test Overviews before beginning practice questions within that unit.

2. Assess your strengths and weaknesses. After you finish one set of practice questions, go to the back of the book to check your answers AND read the explanations for questions you missed as well as for questions on which you guessed.

3. Use the minutes per question or per passage rates for each Test to create timed practice question sets. For Math, you should think about how many minutes per question, while for Reading and Writing & Language, you should think about how many minutes per passage.

Reading

CHAPTER ONE

SAT Reading Test Overview

The SAT Reading Test

The SAT Reading Test will focus on your comprehension and reasoning skills when presented with challenging extended prose passages taken from a variety of content areas.

SAT Reading Test Overview	
Timing	65 minutes
Questions	52 passage-based multiple-choice questions
Passages	4 single passages; 1 set of paired passages
Passage Length	500–750 words per passage or passage set

Passages will draw from U.S. and World Literature, History/Social Studies, and Science. One set of History/Social Studies or Science passages will be paired. History/Social Studies and Science passages can also be accompanied by graphical representations of data such as charts, graphs, tables, and so on.

Reading Test Passage Types	
U.S. and World Literature	1 passage with 10 questions
History/Social Studies	2 passages or 1 passage and 1 paired-passage set with 10–11 questions each
Science	2 passages or 1 passage and 1 paired-passage set with 10–11 questions each

The multiple-choice questions for each passage will be arranged in order from the more general to the more specific so that you can actively engage with the entire passage before answering questions about details.

Skills Tested by Reading Test Questions	
Information and Ideas	Close reading, citing textual evidence, determining central ideas and themes
Summarizing	Understanding relationships, interpreting words and phrases in context
Rhetoric	Analyzing word choice, assessing overall text structure, assessing part-whole relationships, analyzing point of view, determining purpose, analyzing arguments
Synthesis	Analyzing multiple texts, analyzing quantitative information

CHAPTER TWO

U.S. and World Literature Passages

GETTING STARTED

There will be a single **U.S. and World Literature** passage on the SAT. It is different from the other passages because:

- There will be multiple characters and, therefore, multiple opinions.
- The tone will be nuanced and emotion-based, rather than informative or explanatory.

As you read a **U.S. and World Literature** passage, you should make very short notes in the margin, also known as a Passage Map, in order to quickly locate information in the passage.

> ✔ *Remember*
>
> **Remember, you don't need to memorize the characters and themes of the passage, as you might for the passages you read for your English or Literature classes. Instead, you need to know *where* to go in the passage to find either the answers themselves or the evidence to support the answers.**

Focus on including these important ideas in your **U.S. and World Literature** Passage Map:

1. Identify the characters and evaluate how the author describes them
   - What do the characters want?
   - What are the characters doing?
   - What adjectives describe each character?

2. Assess the characters' opinions of each other and themselves
   - Do they like each other? Dislike each other?
   - Why does each character make a particular decision or take a particular course of action?
   - What do these decisions or actions tell you about a character?

> ✔ *Expert Tip*
>
> **Your Passage Map is an essential part of keeping straight who said what. Use abbreviations and symbols (such as "AM likes EB" or "Sam = hard working") to keep track of the most important ideas within the passage.**

3. Identify the themes of the story
   - What are the "turning points" in the passage?
   - Is there a moral to the story?

IMPROVING WITH PRACTICE

Step 1: Compare Your Notes to the Suggested *U.S. and World Literature* Passage Maps

After reading a **U.S. and World Literature** passage, compare your notes to the suggested Passage Maps to be sure you generally included the same important points. Passage mapping is very personal, and it's just fine if your map is different—even very different!—as long as you captured:

- the *location* of the characters
- the *location* of descriptive details
- major events
- themes of the passage

> ✔ *Expert Tip*
>
> **Some paragraphs are longer than others. If you are mapping a very long paragraph, you can write two or three short notes rather than trying to fit everything into just one long note.**

If you missed important information, go back to the **U.S. and World Literature** passage and identify the keywords that you likely overlooked so you can recognize them more quickly next time. The SAT uses keywords to alert you to the important ideas in the passage. Use these keywords to focus your attention and create strong Passage Maps.

Step 2: Answer the Questions

After you've reviewed, and perhaps improved, your **U.S. and World Literature** Passage Map, work through the questions one at a time. Review the Answer and Explanation for every question immediately after completing it. If you got the question correct, congratulate yourself, but take a moment to read the entire explanation to be sure you got the question right for the right reason. The explanation may also point out a more efficient way that you can use on a later question.

Step 3: Review Incorrect Answers

If you get the question incorrect . . . still congratulate yourself! You're about to learn something new that you'll be able to use to improve your performance on Test Day. Don't read the explanation yet; instead, try the question again.

If you get the question correct the second time, read the explanation to see if you solved the question in the most efficient way. Identify the mistake you made the first time, and determine how you're going to avoid making that mistake again.

> ✔ **Expert Tip**
>
> **Many top scoring students have an SAT notebook where they write down what they learn from every question. Doing this can be time-consuming, but it can also help you identify the types of mistakes you tend to make.**

If you get the question incorrect the second time, use the explanation to learn how to get the question correct. Work through the question again while following the explanation, and identify the steps you will need to take to get a similar question correct. Although the passages and questions will change, the concepts being tested will not. When you encounter unfamiliar questions, take note of them for future study sessions.

> ✔ **Remember**
>
> **The SAT is a standardized test. While Hard Reading questions are usually more difficult to answer than Easy or Medium questions, they are often similar in structure and purpose, and the same four skills (listed in Chapter 1) are tested on every Reading Test. You actually can predict the types of questions you will see on Test Day!**

After all that work, it's time to move to the next question. Reviewing in this way will take time. However, improvement doesn't come from just doing lots and lots of questions; it comes from thinking through your approach and improving it with every question.

RAISING YOUR SCORE EVEN MORE

Once your **U.S. and World Literature** Passage Maps are accurate and quickly leading you to the correct answers, it's time to return to completed passages and study which sections of the passages were the source of the correct answers. When studying the source of each answer, look for the keywords the author used to indicate that section was important. Recognizing keywords helps you to know when to slow down and read thoughtfully and when you can speed up and read superficially.

PRACTICE QUESTIONS

The following test-like question sets provide an opportunity to practice reading U.S. and World Literature Passages and answering related questions.

Questions 1-10 are based on the following passage.

The following passage is adapted from Lucy Maud Montgomery's 1908 novel *Anne of Green Gables*. This excerpt details a conversation between Anne, the young protagonist, and Marilla, Anne's guardian.

"And what are your eyes popping out of
your head about now?" asked Marilla, when
Anne had just come in from a run to the post
Line office. "Have you discovered another kindred
(5) spirit?" Excitement hung around Anne like a
garment, shone in her eyes, kindled in every
feature. She had come dancing up the lane, like
a wind-blown sprite, through the mellow sun-
shine and lazy shadows of the August evening.
(10) "No, Marilla, but oh, what do you think? I
am invited to tea at the manse tomorrow afternoon! Mrs. Allan left the letter for me at the
post office. Just look at it, Marilla. 'Miss Anne
Shirley, Green Gables.' That is the first time I
(15) was ever called 'Miss.' Such a thrill as it gave
me! I shall cherish it forever among my choic-
est treasures."

"Mrs. Allan told me she meant to have all
the members of her Sunday-school class to tea
(20) in turn," said Marilla, regarding the wonderful
event very coolly. "You needn't get in such a fever
over it. Do learn to take things calmly, child."

For Anne to take things calmly would have
been to change her nature. All "spirit and fire
(25) and dew," as she was, the pleasures and pains of
life came to her with trebled intensity. Marilla
felt this and was vaguely troubled over it,
realizing that the ups and downs of existence
would probably bear hardly on this impulsive
(30) soul and not sufficiently understanding that
the equally great capacity for delight might
more than compensate. Therefore Marilla

conceived it to be her duty to drill Anne into a
tranquil uniformity of disposition as impossible
(35) and alien to her as to a dancing sunbeam in
one of the brook shallows. She did not make
much headway, as she sorrowfully admitted to
herself. The downfall of some dear hope or
plan plunged Anne into "deeps of affliction."
(40) The fulfillment thereof exalted her to dizzy
realms of delight. Marilla had almost begun to
despair of ever fashioning this waif of the
world into her model little girl of demure
manners and prim deportment. Neither would
(45) she have believed that she really liked Anne
much better as she was.

Anne went to bed that night speechless with
misery because Matthew had said the wind
was round northeast and he feared it would be
(50) a rainy day tomorrow. The rustle of the poplar
leaves about the house worried her, it sounded
so like pattering raindrops, and the full, faraway
roar of the gulf, to which she listened delight-
edly at other times, loving its strange, sonorous,
(55) haunting rhythm, now seemed like a prophecy
of storm and disaster to a small maiden who
particularly wanted a fine day. Anne thought
that the morning would never come.

But all things have an end, even nights be-
(60) fore the day on which you are invited to
take tea at the manse. The morning, in spite of
Matthew's predictions, was fine and Anne's
spirits soared to their highest. "Oh, Marilla,
there is something in me today that makes me
(65) just love everybody I see," she exclaimed as she
washed the breakfast dishes. "You don't know
how good I feel! Wouldn't it be nice if it could
last? I believe I could be a model child if I were
just invited out to tea every day. But oh,
(70) Marilla, it's a solemn occasion too. I feel so

anxious. What if I shouldn't behave properly?
You know I never had tea at a manse before,
and I'm not sure that I know all the rules of
etiquette, although I've been studying the rules
(75) given in the Etiquette Department of the
Family Herald ever since I came here. I'm so
afraid I'll do something silly or forget to do
something I should do. Would it be good
manners to take a second helping of anything
(80) if you wanted to VERY much?"

"The trouble with you, Anne, is that you're
thinking too much about yourself. You should
just think of Mrs. Allan and what would be
nicest and most agreeable to her," said Marilla,
(85) hitting for once in her life on a very sound and
pithy piece of advice. Anne instantly realized
this.

"You are right, Marilla. I'll try not to think
about myself at all."

1. In lines 4-5, what is implied by Marilla's
   question, "'Have you discovered another
   kindred spirit?'"

   A) Anne is deeply spiritual.

   B) Anne is a sociable person.

   C) Anne seeks out adventures.

   D) Anne has a fear of strangers.

2. The author's use of words such as "dancing" and
   "wind-blown" in lines 7-8 implies that Anne is

   A) graceful and rhythmic.

   B) messy and disorganized.

   C) energetic and active.

   D) scatterbrained and confused.

3. As used in line 42, "fashioning" most nearly
   means

   A) preparing.

   B) constructing.

   C) styling.

   D) devising.

4. Which choice best describes the relationship
   between Anne and Matthew?

   A) Anne does not trust Matthew's
      predictions.

   B) Anne is worried about Matthew's safety.

   C) Anne takes Matthew's statements
      seriously.

   D) Anne is uncertain about Matthew's
      intentions.

5. According to the passage, what does Marilla
   think is Anne's greatest challenge in life?

   A) Anne thinks about herself too much.

   B) Anne must learn to take things calmly.

   C) Anne needs to master the rules of etiquette.

   D) Anne worries too much about things she
      cannot control.

6. The fourth paragraph is important to the
   passage's progression of ideas because it

   A) explains the antagonistic relationship
      between Anne and Marilla.

   B) offers background information about
      Marilla's concerns about Anne.

   C) explains how Marilla has systematically
      changed Anne into a model child.

   D) provides a transition from Anne reading
      the letter to the following morning.

7. As used in line 85, "sound" most nearly means

   A) practical.

   B) clamor.

   C) ethical.

   D) secure.

8. It can be inferred that the author

   A) is an omniscient third-person observer.

   B) allows the reader to know only Anne's inner thoughts.

   C) offers an objective perspective from within the story.

   D) is unaware of actions that take place elsewhere in the story.

9. The passage most strongly suggests that which of the following is true of Marilla?

   A) She hopes Anne will soon learn to admire Mrs. Allan.

   B) She believes Anne's "deeps of affliction" are dangerous.

   C) She has come to dislike Anne's overly excitable nature.

   D) She values calm and even-keeled responses to all situations.

10. Which choice provides the best evidence for the answer to the previous question?

    A) Lines 21-22 ("'You needn't . . . child'")

    B) Lines 26-32 ("Marilla felt . . . compensate")

    C) Lines 44-46 ("Neither would . . . as she was")

    D) Lines 81-86 ("The trouble . . . advice")

Questions 11-20 are based on the following passage.

Adapted from "The Red House Mystery" by
A.A. Milne, first published in 1922.

Whether Mark Ablett was a bore or not
depended on the point of view, but it may be
said at once that he never bored his company
Line on the subject of his early life. However, stories
(5) get about. There is always somebody who
knows. It was understood—and this, anyhow,
on Mark's own authority—that his father had
been a country clergyman. It was said that,
as a boy, Mark had attracted the notice, and
(10) patronage, of some rich old spinster of the
neighbourhood, who had paid for his education,
both at school and university. At about the time
when he was coming down from Cambridge,
his father had died; leaving behind him a few
(15) debts, as a warning to his family, and a reputation for short sermons, as an example to his
successor. Neither warning nor example seems
to have been effective. Mark went to London,
with an allowance from his patron, and (it is
(20) generally agreed) made acquaintance with the
money-lenders. He was supposed, by his patron
and any others who inquired, to be "writing";
but what he wrote, other than letters asking for
more time to pay, has never been discovered.
(25) However, he attended the theatres and music
halls very regularly—no doubt with a view to
some serious articles in the "Spectator" on the
decadence of the English stage.

Fortunately (from Mark's point of view) his
(30) patron died during his third year in London,
and left him all the money he wanted. From that
moment his life loses its legendary character,
and becomes more a matter of history. He
settled accounts with the money-lenders,
(35) abandoned his crop of wild oats to the harvest-
ing of others, and became in his turn a patron.
He patronized the Arts. It was not only usurers
who discovered that Mark Ablett no longer

wrote for money; editors were now offered free
(40) contributions as well as free lunches; publish-
ers were given agreements for an occasional
slender volume, in which the author paid all
expenses and waived all royalties; promising
young painters and poets dined with him; and
(45) he even took a theatrical company on tour,
playing host and "lead" with equal lavishness.

He was not what most people call a snob. A
snob has been defined carelessly as a man who
loves a lord; and, more carefully, as a mean
(50) lover of mean things—which would be a little
unkind to the peerage if the first definition
were true. Mark had his vanities undoubtedly,
but he would sooner have met an actor-manager
than an earl; he would have spoken of his
(55) friendship with Dante—had that been
possible—more glibly than of his friendship
with the Duke. Call him a snob if you like, but
not the worst kind of snob; a hanger-on, but to
the skirts of Art, not Society; a climber, but in
(60) the neighbourhood of Parnassus, not Hay Hill.

His patronage did not stop at the Arts. It
also included Matthew Cayley, a small cousin
of thirteen, whose circumstances were as limited as had been Mark's own before his patron
(65) had rescued him. He sent the Cayley cousin to
school and Cambridge. His motives, no doubt,
were unworldly enough at first; a mere repay-
ing to his account in the Recording Angel's
book of the generosity which had been lav-
(70) ished on himself; a laying-up of treasure in
heaven. But it is probable that, as the boy grew
up, Mark's designs for his future were based on
his own interests as much as those of his
cousin, and that a suitably educated Matthew
(75) Cayley of twenty-three was felt by him to be a
useful property for a man in his position; a
man, that is to say, whose vanities left him so
little time for his affairs.

Cayley, then, at twenty-three, looked after
(80) his cousin's affairs. By this time Mark had

bought the Red House and the considerable
amount of land which went with it. Cayley
superintended the necessary staff. His duties,
indeed, were many. He was not quite secretary,
(85) not quite land-agent, not quite business-
adviser, not quite companion, but something
of all four. Mark leant upon him and called
him "Cay," objecting quite rightly in the
circumstances to the name of Matthew. Cay,
(90) he felt was, above all, dependable; a big, heavy-
jawed, solid fellow, who didn't bother you with
unnecessary talk—a boon to a man who liked
to do most of the talking himself.

11. What is most likely true about Mark's father's
successor?

   A) He made more money than Mark's
father had.

   B) He was more popular than Mark's father.

   C) His sermons were long and boring.

   D) He took a great deal of interest in Mark's
life.

12. Which choice provides the best evidence for
the answer to the previous question?

   A) Lines 5-8 ("There is . . . clergyman")

   B) Lines 6-12 ("It was . . . university")

   C) Lines 12-17 ("At about the time . . .
successor")

   D) Lines 17-18 ("Neither . . . been effective")

13. What can be inferred from the author's choice
to place the word "writing" in quotation marks
in line 22?

   A) People doubted that Mark was actually
writing.

   B) Mark's writing was understood by many
to be terrible.

   C) Mark's writing more closely resembled
philosophy than entertainment.

   D) Mark was writing in secret but his acquaintances knew about his talent.

14. Why is the death of Mark's patron "fortunate"
for him (line 29)?

   A) Mark becomes wealthy as a result.

   B) Mark and his patron do not like each
other.

   C) Mark's patron disapproved of his writing.

   D) Mark felt pressure from his patron to
start a career.

15. As used in line 37, "usurer" most nearly
means

   A) employer.

   B) lender.

   C) relative.

   D) supporter.

16. As used in line 46, "lavishness" most nearly means

    A) diplomacy.

    B) enthusiasm.

    C) melodrama.

    D) skill.

17. Mark's acquaintances probably consider stories of his later life

    A) less respectable than when he had to work for his money.

    B) more interesting because of the lessons he has learned.

    C) less exciting than those of his earlier life in London.

    D) more scandalous than he is willing to admit.

18. Which choice provides the best evidence for the answer to the previous question?

    A) Lines 21-24 ("He was . . . discovered")

    B) Lines 31-33 ("From that . . . of history")

    C) Lines 52-57 ("Mark had . . . the Duke")

    D) Lines 57-60 ("Call him . . . Hay Hill")

19. "Parnassus" (line 60) is included in the passage to illustrate the idea of

    A) a place where the wealthy gather.

    B) an artistic community.

    C) a myth to which Mark can be compared.

    D) a place that does not really exist.

20. The tone of the last paragraph serves to

    A) suggest parallels between Matthew and Mark.

    B) surprise the reader with Matthew's capabilities.

    C) demonstrate the dramatic changes in Mark's character.

    D) mock Mark for the way he sees Matthew.

Questions 21-30 are based on the following passage.

This passage is adapted from Jane Austen's *Sense and Sensibility*.

Before the house-maid had lit their fire the next day, or the sun gained any power over a cold, gloomy morning in January, Marianne, Line only half dressed, was kneeling against one of (5) the window-seats for the sake of all the little light she could command from it, and writing as fast as a continual flow of tears would permit her. In this situation, Elinor, roused from sleep by her agitation and sobs, first perceived (10) her; and after observing her for a few moments with silent anxiety, said, in a tone of the most considerate gentleness,

"Marianne, may I ask—?"

"No, Elinor," she replied, "ask nothing; you (15) will soon know all."

The sort of desperate calmness with which this was said, lasted no longer than while she spoke, and was immediately followed by a return of the same excessive affliction. It was (20) some minutes before she could go on with her letter, and the frequent bursts of grief which still obliged her, at intervals, to withhold her pen, were proofs enough of her feeling how more than probable it was that she was writing (25) for the last time to Willoughby.

At breakfast she neither ate, nor attempted to eat any thing; and Elinor's attention was then all employed, not in urging her, not in pitying her, nor in appearing to regard her, but (30) in endeavouring to engage Mrs. Jennings's notice entirely to herself.

As this was a favourite meal with Mrs. Jennings, it lasted a considerable time, and they were just setting themselves, after it, (35) round the common working table, when a letter was delivered to Marianne, which she eagerly caught from the servant, and, turning of a death-like paleness, instantly ran out of the room. Elinor, who saw as plainly by this, as if she had (40) seen the direction, that it must come from Willoughby, felt immediately such a sickness at heart as made her hardly able to hold up her head, and sat in such a general tremour as made her fear it impossible to escape Mrs. Jen-(45)nings's notice. That good lady, however, saw only that Marianne had received a letter from Willoughby, which appeared to her a very good joke, and which she treated accordingly, by hoping, with a laugh, that she would find it (50) to her liking. Of Elinor's distress, she was too busily employed in measuring lengths of worsted for her rug, to see any thing at all; and calmly continuing her talk, as soon as Marianne disappeared, she said,

(55) "Upon my word, I never saw a young woman so desperately in love in my life! MY girls were nothing to her, and yet they used to be foolish enough; but as for Miss Marianne, she is quite an altered creature. I hope, from (60) the bottom of my heart, he won't keep her waiting much longer, for it is quite grievous to see her look so ill and forlorn. Pray, when are they to be married?"

Elinor, though never less disposed to speak (65) than at that moment, obliged herself to answer such an attack as this, and, therefore, trying to smile, replied, "And have you really, Ma'am, talked yourself into a persuasion of my sister's being engaged to Mr. Willoughby? I thought it (70) had been only a joke, but so serious a question seems to imply more; and I must beg, therefore, that you will not deceive yourself any longer. I do assure you that nothing would surprise me more than to hear of their being (75) going to be married."

"For shame, for shame, Miss Dashwood! how can you talk so? Don't we all know that it must be a match, that they were over head and ears in love with each other from the first moment they (80) met? Did not I see them together in Devonshire every day, and all day long; and did not I know that your sister came to town with me on pur-

pose to buy wedding clothes? Come, come, this won't do. Because you are so sly about it your
(85) self, you think nobody else has any senses; but it is no such thing, I can tell you, for it has been known all over town this ever so long. I tell every body of it and so does Charlotte."

"Indeed, Ma'am," said Elinor, very seriously,
(90) "you are mistaken. Indeed, you are doing a very unkind thing in spreading the report, and you will find that you have though you will not believe me now."

21. As used in line 64, "disposed" most nearly means

   A) capable.

   B) inclined.

   C) shed.

   D) permitted.

22. In lines 37-38, the author describes Marianne as "turning of a death-like paleness" in order to emphasize

   A) her comical overreaction to an everyday event.

   B) the anxiety she feels about the letter's contents.

   C) the supernatural elements that surround the house.

   D) her knowledge that the letter contains news of illness.

23. The passage most strongly suggests which of the following about Elinor's feelings toward Marianne?

   A) Elinor feels protective of Marianne.

   B) Elinor is sad that they are not closer.

   C) Elinor is jealous of Marianne's success in life.

   D) Elinor considers them to be rivals in matters of love.

24. Which choice provides the best evidence for the answer to the previous question?

   A) Lines 16-19 ("The sort . . . excessive affliction")

   B) Lines 26-31 ("At breakfast . . . entirely to herself")

   C) Lines 59-62 ("I hope . . . ill and forlorn")

   D) Lines 69-73 ("'I thought . . . any longer'")

25. Which statement does the passage most strongly suggest is true of Mrs. Jennings?

   A) She does not have many people with whom to talk.

   B) She knows the intimate details of Marianne's feelings.

   C) She is not very perceptive about the events around her.

   D) She has spoken to Willoughby more recently than Marianne.

26. Which choice provides the best evidence for the answer to the previous question?

   A) Lines 26-31 ("At breakfast . . . to herself")

   B) Lines 32-38 ("As this was . . . of the room")

   C) Lines 50-52 ("Of Elinor's . . . any thing at all")

   D) Lines 55-56 ("Upon my word . . . in my life")

27. As used in line 68, "persuasion" most nearly means

   A) argument.

   B) belief.

   C) excitement.

   D) joke.

28. According to the passage, Mrs. Jennings believes that

    A) Willoughby intends to marry Marianne.

    B) Elinor is overreacting to Willoughby's letter.

    C) Marianne loves someone other than Willoughby.

    D) Elinor is mistaken about why Marianne is upset.

29. Based on the information in the passage, Marianne's situation can most directly be compared to that of

    A) a stray cat who shows affection to strangers in hopes of being fed.

    B) a person who cultivates charm in order to compensate for a lack of physical beauty.

    C) a scientist working on an ambitious project in which only she has faith.

    D) a worker who has not been hired for a job she was certain she would get.

30. What is the author's most likely purpose in providing the last paragraph of dialogue?

    A) To help readers understand why Marianne is so upset

    B) To demonstrate the degree of Elinor's concern about Marianne

    C) To argue that Mrs. Jennings's understanding of the situation may be accurate

    D) To persuade readers that Marianne is not entirely innocent

Questions 31-40 are based on the following passage.

Adapted from "Young Goodman Brown" by Nathaniel Hawthorne, first published in 1835.

Young Goodman Brown came forth at sunset into the street at Salem village; but put his head back, after crossing the threshold, to ex-
Line change a parting kiss with his young wife. And
(5) Faith, as the wife was aptly named, thrust her own pretty head into the street, letting the wind play with the pink ribbons of her cap while she called to Goodman Brown.

"Dearest heart," whispered she, softly and
(10) rather sadly, when her lips were close to his ear, "prithee put off your journey until sunrise and sleep in your own bed to-night. A lone woman is troubled with such dreams and such thoughts that she's afeard of herself sometimes.
(15) Pray tarry with me this night, dear husband, of all nights in the year."

"My love and my Faith," replied young Goodman Brown, "of all nights in the year, this one night must I tarry away from thee. My
(20) journey, as thou callest it, forth and back again, must needs be done 'twixt now and sunrise. What, my sweet, pretty wife, dost thou doubt me already, and we but three months married?"

(25) "Then God bless you!" said Faith, with the pink ribbons; "and may you find all well when you come back."

"Amen!" cried Goodman Brown. "Say thy prayers, dear Faith, and go to bed at dusk, and
(30) no harm will come to thee."

So they parted; and the young man pursued his way until, being about to turn the corner by the meeting-house, he looked back and saw the head of Faith still peeping after him with a
(35) melancholy air, in spite of her pink ribbons.

"Poor little Faith!" thought he, for his heart smote him. "What a wretch am I to leave her on such an errand! She talks of dreams, too. Methought as she spoke there was trouble in

(40) her face, as if a dream had warned her what work is to be done tonight. But no, no; 't would kill her to think it. Well, she's a blessed angel on earth; and after this one night I'll cling to her skirts and follow her to heaven."

(45) With this excellent resolve for the future, Goodman Brown felt himself justified in making more haste on his present evil purpose. He had taken a dreary road, darkened by all the gloomiest trees of the forest, which barely
(50) stood aside to let the narrow path creep through, and closed immediately behind. It was all as lonely as could be; and there is this peculiarity in such a solitude, that the traveller knows not who may be concealed by the innu-
(55) merable trunks and the thick boughs overhead; so that with lonely footsteps he may yet be passing through an unseen multitude.

Goodman Brown glanced fearfully behind as he said to himself, "What if the devil himself
(60) should be at my very elbow!"

His head being turned back, he passed a crook of the road, and, looking forward again, beheld the figure of a man, in grave and decent attire, seated at the foot of an old tree. He arose
(65) at Goodman Brown's approach and walked onward side by side with him.

"You are late, Goodman Brown," said he. "The clock of the Old South was striking as I came through Boston, and that is full fifteen
(70) minutes agone."

"Faith kept me back a while," replied the young man, with a tremor in his voice, caused by the sudden appearance of his companion, though not wholly unexpected.

(75) It was now deep dusk in the forest, and deepest in that part of it where these two were journeying. As nearly as could be discerned, the second traveller was about fifty years old, apparently in the same rank of life as Goodman
(80) Brown, and bearing a considerable resemblance to him, though perhaps more in expression than features. Still they might have been taken

for father and son. And yet, though the elder person was as simply clad as the younger, and as (85) simple in manner too, he had an indescribable air of one who knew the world, and who would not have felt abashed at the governor's dinner table or in King William's court, were it possible that his affairs should call him thither.

31. As used in line 77, "discerned" most nearly means

A) perceived.

B) tolerated.

C) surmised.

D) procured.

32. The passage most strongly suggests that which of the following is true of Goodman Brown's journey?

A) Goodman Brown does not enjoy traveling alone with so much money and is scared.

B) Brown is hiding the journey's true and sinister purpose from his innocent wife.

C) Goodman Brown does not wish to go on this journey but is pressured to go by his wife.

D) Brown may not return from the journey, and he is beginning to second-guess his actions.

33. Which choice provides the best evidence for the answer to the previous question?

A) Lines 12-14 ("A lone woman . . . sometimes")

B) Lines 39-41 ("Methought as she spoke . . . tonight")

C) Lines 51-57 ("It was all as lonely . . . multitude")

D) Lines 61-64 ("His head being . . . tree")

34. Which of the following is most strongly implied about Goodman Brown's relationship with the man he meets on the road?

A) Goodman Brown is sure he has seen the strange man before but does not know where.

B) The man by the road is helping Goodman Brown plan a crime during the trip.

C) Goodman Brown is unsettled by the presence of the man by the side of the road.

D) Goodman Brown does not know the stranger who joins him on his journey.

35. Which choice provides the best evidence for the answer to the previous question?

A) Lines 64-66 ("He arose . . . him")

B) Lines 71-74 ("Faith kept . . . unexpected")

C) Lines 75-77 ("It was now deep . . . journeying")

D) Lines 83-89 ("And yet, though he . . . thither")

36. The author's use of words such as "dreary," "darkened," and "lonely" in paragraph 8

A) implies that Goodman Brown misses his wife and regrets his journey.

B) creates a sense that Goodman Brown is about to do something wicked.

C) foreshadows Goodman Brown's meeting his nemesis along the roadside.

D) strengthens Faith's foreboding warning about the dangers on the road.

37. In line 59, what is the most likely reason that the author mentions "the devil himself"?

    A) To help the reader better understand that this story is of the fairy-tale genre

    B) To suggest that Goodman is superstitious and that his fears are driving him crazy

    C) To remind readers of Faith's claim that the road is notorious for robberies and disappearances

    D) To suggest that the forest is unsafe and to foreshadow a meeting with a dangerous figure

38. The greeting offered by the man on the road in lines 67-70 serves to support the claim that Goodman Brown

    A) and the man are heading to Boston.

    B) and the man already know one another.

    C) was supposed to wait at the Old South clock tower.

    D) is trying to delay whatever dark task lies ahead.

39. As used in line 87, "abashed" most nearly means

    A) boisterous.

    B) embarrassed.

    C) famished.

    D) frivolous.

40. Based on the passage, which choice offers the strongest possible connection between Goodman Brown and the man he meets?

    A) The man is an older relative of Goodman Brown.

    B) They are both representatives of the king.

    C) The man is Goodman Brown's twin brother.

    D) They are both competitors for Faith's love.

Questions 41-50 are based on the following passage.

This passage is adapted from "Metamorphosis" by Franz Kafka, a famous story that combines elements of fantasy and reality. This excerpt begins with the protagonist realizing he has literally turned into a giant, beetle-like insect.

One morning, when Gregor Samsa woke from troubled dreams, he found himself transformed in his bed into a horrible vermin.
Line He lay on his armor-like back, and if he lifted
(5) his head a little he could see his brown belly, slightly domed and divided by arches into stiff sections. The bedding was hardly able to cover it and seemed ready to slide off any moment. His many legs, pitifully thin compared with the
(10) size of the rest of him, waved about helplessly as he looked.

"What's happened to me?" he thought. It wasn't a dream. His room, a proper human room although a little too small, lay peacefully
(15) between its four familiar walls. A collection of textile samples lay spread out on the table—Samsa was a travelling salesman—and above it there hung a picture that he had recently cut out of an illustrated magazine and housed in a
(20) nice, gilded frame. It showed a lady fitted out with a fur hat and fur boa who sat upright, raising a heavy fur muff that covered the whole of her lower arm towards the viewer.

Gregor then turned to look out the window
(25) at the dull weather. Drops of rain could be heard hitting the pane, which made him feel quite sad. "How about if I sleep a little bit longer and forget all this nonsense," he thought, but that was something he was unable to do
(30) because he was used to sleeping on his right, and in his present state couldn't get into that position. However hard he threw himself onto his right, he always rolled back to where he was. He must have tried it a hundred times,
(35) shut his eyes so that he wouldn't have to look at the floundering legs, and only stopped when

he began to feel a mild, dull pain there that he had never felt before.

He thought, "What a strenuous career it is
(40) that I've chosen! Travelling day in and day out. Doing business like this takes much more effort than doing your own business at home, and on top of that there's the curse of travelling, worries about making train connections,
(45) bad and irregular food, contact with different people all the time so that you can never get to know anyone or become friendly with them." He felt a slight itch up on his belly; pushed himself slowly up on his back towards the
(50) headboard so that he could lift his head better; found where the itch was, and saw that it was covered with lots of little white spots which he didn't know what to make of; and when he tried to feel the place with one of his legs he
(55) drew it quickly back because as soon as he touched it he was overcome by a cold shudder.

He slid back into his former position. "Getting up early all the time," he thought, "it makes you stupid. You've got to get enough
(60) sleep. Other travelling salesmen live a life of luxury. For instance, whenever I go back to the guest house during the morning to copy out the contract, these gentlemen are always still sitting there eating their breakfasts. I ought to
(65) just try that with my boss; I'd get kicked out on the spot. But who knows, maybe that would be the best thing for me. If I didn't have my parents to think about I'd have given in my notice a long time ago, I'd have gone up to the boss and
(70) told him just what I think, tell him everything I would, let him know just what I feel. He'd fall right off his desk! And it's a funny sort of business to be sitting up there at your desk, talking down at your subordinates from up there, es-
(75) pecially when you have to go right up close because the boss is hard of hearing. Well, there's still some hope; once I've got the money together to pay off my parents' debt to him—another five or six years I suppose—that's definitely

(80) what I'll do. That's when I'll make the big
change. First of all though, I've got to get up,
my train leaves at five."

41. According to the passage, Gregor initially
believes his transformation is a

A) curse.

B) disease.

C) nightmare.

D) hoax.

42. As used in line 13, "proper" most nearly
means

A) called for by rules or conventions.

B) showing politeness.

C) naturally belonging or peculiar to.

D) suitably appropriate.

43. The passage most strongly suggests which of
the following about Gregor's attitude toward
his profession?

A) He is resentful.

B) He is diligent.

C) He is depressed.

D) He is eager to please.

44. Which choice provides the best evidence for
the answer to the previous question?

A) Lines 15-20 ("A collection . . . gilded
frame")

B) Lines 24-27 ("Gregor then turned . . .
quite sad")

C) Lines 60-66 ("Other . . . the spot")

D) Lines 72-76 ("And it's . . . hard of hearing")

45. What central idea does the passage communicate through Gregor's experiences?

A) Imagination is a dangerous thing.

B) People are fearful of change.

C) Dreams become our reality.

D) Humankind is a slave to work.

46. The passage most strongly suggests that which
of the following is true of Gregor?

A) He feels a strong sense of duty toward his
family.

B) He is unable to cope with change.

C) He excels in his profession.

D) He is fearful about his transformation.

47. Which choice provides the best evidence for
the answer to the previous question?

A) Lines 12-15 ("What's happened . . .
familiar walls")

B) Lines 24-27 ("Gregor then turned . . .
quite sad")

C) Lines 41-47 ("Doing business . . . with
them")

D) Lines 76-80 ("Well, there's still . . . what
I'll do")

48. As used in line 36, "floundering" most nearly
means

A) thrashing.

B) painful.

C) pitiful.

D) trembling.

49. The author most likely includes a description of Gregor's itch in lines 48-56 to

    A) remind the reader that Gregor has turned into an insect.

    B) emphasize the disconnect between Gregor's thoughts and his actual situation.

    C) give important details about what Gregor's new body looks like.

    D) show that Gregor's thoughts are focused on the changes to his body.

50. The function of the final sentence of the excerpt ("First of all though, I've got to get up, my train leaves at five") is to

    A) provide a resolution to the conflict Gregor faces.

    B) foreshadow the conflict between Gregor and his boss.

    C) illustrate Gregor's resilience and ability to move on.

    D) emphasize Gregor's extreme sense of duty.

ANSWERS AND EXPLANATIONS

CHAPTER 2

Suggested Passage Map notes:

¶1: A excited

¶2: A invited to impt tea

¶3: M not excited for A

¶4: M wants to make A more calm; unsuccessful

¶5: A worried about rain

¶6: A very excited even when doing dishes; but also nervous she might misbehave at the tea

¶7-8: M gives A advice for being proper at the tea

1. B   Difficulty: Easy

Category: Inference

Getting to the Answer: Reread the excerpt for clues that reveal Anne's previous behavior and her personality traits. Marilla specifically asks Anne whether she has found "another" kindred spirit, implying that Anne has previously rushed home excited about having made a new friend. This is a clue that Anne is a sociable, friendly person. Choice (B) is correct.

2. C   Difficulty: Medium

Category: Rhetoric

Getting to the Answer: Read the sentence and determine how the selected words shape the reader's image of Anne; then, select the answer choice that most accurately reflects this tone and image. The passage states that Anne runs home and implies that she is *excited*. The correct answer, choice (C), supports the image of Anne as energetic.

3. B   Difficulty: Hard

Category: Vocab-in-Context

Getting to the Answer: Predict a word that could replace the word in the question stem, then find its closest match among the answer choices. The

passage states that Marilla hopes to *actively change* Anne from her current state and *mold* her into one of her own designs. Thus, of the various uses of the word "fashioning" used in the answer choices, choice (B) is correct.

4. C   Difficulty: Medium

Category: Inference

Getting to the Answer: Read the context clues in the passage that relate to Matthew's and Anne's interactions. Examine what these clues suggest about their relationship. Anne goes to bed "speechless with misery" (lines 47-48) because Matthew predicts it will rain the next day. Anne's reaction shows that she takes Matthew's predictions seriously, so choice (C) is correct.

5. B   Difficulty: Easy

Category: Detail

Getting to the Answer: Marilla explicitly states that Anne's trouble is that she is "thinking too much about [herself]" (line 82), which matches A. However, this advice is intended for the specific situation at hand, the tea party, rather than Anne's greater challenge of learning to take things calmly, which will affect her entire life. This challenge is outlined in lines 23-32; thus, choice (B) is correct.

6. B   Difficulty: Medium

Category: Rhetoric

Getting to the Answer: Reread the paragraph in question and determine what role it plays in the progression of ideas within the passage. Paragraph 4 explains Marilla's feelings about Anne's personality traits, describes how she hoped to temper them, and states that she failed to do so, while also telling the reader that she likes Anne the way she is. Choice (B) best represents these ideas.

7. A   Difficulty: Medium

Category: Vocab-in-Context

Getting to the Answer: Read the sentence and paragraph for context clues and determine which usage of the selected word best fits the author's intention. Predict that Marilla's advice is *useful* or *helpful*. Choice (A) is correct.

8. A   Difficulty: Medium

Category: Rhetoric

Getting to the Answer: Evaluate the depth of the author's participation in the passage and how many perspectives the author introduces. Use this information to determine the correct answer. The author reveals the inner thinking of both Anne and Marilla while taking no active part in the passage, so choice (A) is correct.

9. D   Difficulty: Easy

Category: Inference

Getting to the Answer: Evaluate how Marilla is presented. Throughout the passage, Marilla asks Anne to remain calm, coolly responds to Anne, and hopes to fashion Anne into a demure, model child. Predict that Marilla values being calm and collected. Choice (D) is correct.

10. A   Difficulty: Medium

Category: Command of Evidence

Getting to the Answer: To answer Command of Evidence questions, start by looking at the part of the passage that helped you answer the previous question. Throughout the passage, Marilla asks Anne to remain calm and coolly responds to Anne, and the quotation noted in lines 21-22 shows Marilla doing this; thus, choice (A) is correct.

Suggested Passage Map notes:

¶1: Mark = preacher's son; patron paid for school

¶2: M inherited patron's money & became patron

¶3: interested in art, not nobility

¶4: sent cousin to school

¶5: cousin took care of M

11. C   Difficulty: Medium

Category: Inference

Getting to the Answer: The correct answer will be supported directly by the passage. The passage states that Mark's father left behind "a reputation for short sermons, as an example for his successor" (lines 15-17). However, it then states, "neither warning nor example seems to have been effective" (lines 17-18). Predict that his successor gave long sermons. Choice (C) is correct.

12. D   Difficulty: Medium

Category: Command of Evidence

Getting to the Answer: Carefully review the part of the passage that you used to answer the previous question. The passage discusses Mark's father's successor in the context of his father's death; Mark's father has left an "example" of short sermons for his successor, but "neither warning nor example seems to have been effective" (lines 17-18). This suggests that Mark's father's successor did not follow his example of giving short sermons. Choice (D) is correct.

13. A   Difficulty: Hard

Category: Inference

Getting to the Answer: The word "writing" is quoted in order to underscore the fact that it is dialogue. It is Mark who has used the word. The passage goes on to state that "what he wrote . . . has never been discovered" (lines 23-24). Predict that the only reason to believe that writing has taken place is Mark's word; other people have their doubts. Choice (A) is correct.

14. A   Difficulty: Easy

Category: Detail

Getting to the Answer: The correct answer is directly stated in the passage. The passage states, "his patron died . . . and left him all the money he wanted" (lines 29-31), which directly supports the idea that he is now wealthy. Predict that Mark's patron's death was fortunate for him because it made him wealthy. Choice (A) is correct.

15. B   Difficulty: Medium

Category: Vocab-in-Context

Getting to the Answer: Consider the topic of the paragraph in which the cited word appears. Then, predict a synonym for this word based on the topic and context of the paragraph. Earlier in the paragraph, the passage states, "he settled accounts with the money-lenders" (lines 33-34). The sentence to which the word in question belongs asserts that it was "not only usurers who discovered that Mark Ablett no longer wrote for money" (lines 37-39). "Money-lender," then, seems to be a synonym for "usurer;" predict *money-lender*. Choice (B) is correct.

16. B   Difficulty: Medium

Category: Vocab-in-Context

Getting to the Answer: Consider the usual meaning of "lavish." How might it be applied figuratively here? "Lavish" usually means something like "elaborate" or "sumptuous," depending on the context. Here, it is used to describe how Mark "play[s] host and 'lead'" (line 46). It seems to be used to describe how Mark enjoys his theater company with enthusiasm and relish. Predict that "lavishness" most nearly means *enthusiasm* or *relish*. Choice (B) is correct.

17. C   Difficulty: Medium

Category: Inference

Getting to the Answer: Identify how the passage characterizes Mark's life, then read the answer choices to see how others view it. The passage characterizes Mark's early life in London as an exciting and irresponsible period (lines 18-28). Later, he inherits money, settles his accounts, and becomes financially responsible (lines 29-46). Predict that, compared with his earlier life, his later life (and therefore stories of his later life) was less exciting. Choice (C) is correct.

18. B   Difficulty: Medium

Category: Command of Evidence

Getting to the Answer: Identify the paragraph that most directly supports your answer to the previous question about the different periods of Mark's life. Since lines 29-46 discussed Mark's later life, the best evidence to support your previous answer should come from those lines. The lines quoted in choice (B) make a direct distinction between these two periods of Mark's life: when he inherits money, "his life loses its legendary character, and becomes more a matter of history" (lines 32-33). In other words, his earlier life in London is more like a legend, or myth, and his later life is less exciting. Choice (B) is correct.

19. B   Difficulty: Hard

Category: Inference

Getting to the Answer: Reread the sentence to find the analogy; it will be explicitly stated in the passage. Then, consider why the passage draws the comparison it does. Mark is described as "a hanger-on, but to the skirts of Art, not Society" (lines 58-59). "Art" is being compared with "Parnassus," and "Society" with "Hay Hill." Each appears to be a neighborhood associated with these ideas. Predict that "Parnassus" is an example of Art. Choice (B) is correct.

20. D   Difficulty: Hard

Category: Rhetoric

Getting to the Answer: Identify the narrator's attitude toward Mark in the last paragraph; your Passage Map notes remind you that Matthew took care of Mark. The tone of the last paragraph is one of mock seriousness. On the surface, it appears to take Mark's ideas about himself and his place in the world seriously. But, when read closely, the final sentence characterizes Mark as a pompous and arrogant man who finds Matthew useful because he doesn't steal attention from himself. Matthew "didn't bother you with unnecessary talk—a boon to a man who liked to do most of the talking himself" (lines 91-93). Predict that the last paragraph serves to subtly make fun of Mark; choice (D) is correct.

Suggested Passage Map notes:

¶1-3: M very upset, E concerned

¶4: M having trouble writing to W

¶5: E distracts Mrs. J

¶6: M receives letter from W, W concerned, Mrs. J clueless

¶7: Mrs. J hopes M marries W

¶8: E suggests unlikely

¶9-10: Mrs. J saw love, E says Mrs. J will see she is wrong in time

21. B   Difficulty: Medium

Category: Vocab-in-Context

Getting to the Answer: Consider each word carefully. The most common meaning for a word is not necessarily the correct one. Elinor, "though never less disposed to speak" (line 64), nonetheless speaks in this paragraph. The correct answer should be something like *eager*, since Elinor is not eager to speak. Plugging in each of the answer choices will reveal which fits best. Choice (B) is similar to *eager*, so it is correct.

22. B   Difficulty: Medium

Category: Rhetoric

Getting to the Answer: Read the lines around this phrase. Look for clues that suggest what is making her react as she does. Marianne is clearly expecting bad news in the letter, as she runs out of the room before even opening it. Choice (B) is correct: she is driven by her anxiety.

23. A   Difficulty: Easy

Category: Inference

Getting to the Answer: Look for clues about Elinor's behavior toward Marianne. What does this suggest about their relationship? Elinor seems almost as upset by what is upsetting Marianne as Marianne herself is. The sisters are clearly very close, and Elinor's words to Mrs. Jennings make clear that

Elinor is trying to prevent Mrs. Jennings from doing further damage to Marianne by spreading rumors. Choice (A) is correct, as it reflects the sisters' close relationship.

24. B   Difficulty: Medium

Category: Command of Evidence

Getting to the Answer: Review the answer to the previous question. Consider which of the answer choices provides the clearest sense of Elinor's feelings toward Marianne. Elinor's feelings toward Marianne are protective. This is demonstrated by the lines that show Elinor's trying to distract Mrs. Jennings from noticing Marianne's distress. Choice (B) is correct; it is a clear illustration of Elinor's protective feelings.

25. C   Difficulty: Easy

Category: Inference

Getting to the Answer: Determine what Mrs. Jennings thinks is happening. Does it differ in any way from what is actually happening? Mrs. Jennings appears not to have noticed Marianne's distress over Willoughby. She remarks on how much the two of them seem to be in love, despite Marianne's altered behavior. Choice (C) is correct because it shows that Mrs. Jennings is not perceptive enough to notice what is happening.

26. C   Difficulty: Medium

Category: Command of Evidence

Getting to the Answer: Review the answer to the previous question. Notice what Mrs. Jennings says or does to support your conclusion about her. Mrs. Jennings is not very perceptive. The passage states that she "was too busily employed . . . to see any thing at all" (lines 50-52) and then observes that Marianne and Willoughby are likely to be married. Choice (C) is correct, as it offers an instance of Mrs. Jennings's failure to notice the events around her.

27. B   Difficulty: Medium

Category: Vocab-in-Context

Getting to the Answer: Consider the context of this line. Notice what Elinor is suggesting about Mrs. Jennings. Elinor is surprised that Mrs. Jennings has "talked [herself] into a persuasion" (line 68) that Marianne and Willoughby are to be married. Other context clues make clear that this is what Mrs. Jennings believes will happen, so the correct answer will mean something like *belief*. Choice (B), therefore, is correct.

28. A   Difficulty: Easy

Category: Detail

Getting to the Answer: Read the passage closely to find the answer stated explicitly. Both Elinor and Mrs. Jennings state that Mrs. Jennings believes Willoughby and Marianne are to be married soon. Choice (A) is correct.

29. D   Difficulty: Hard

Category: Inference

Getting to the Answer: In your own words, describe Marianne's situation. Marianne is upset because of a letter that has come from a man everybody believes she will marry. Then, read the answer choices to see what situation is analogous. The correct answer should relate to unexpected disappointment. Choice (D) is correct: it conveys a sense of disappointment after high expectations have not been met.

30. B   Difficulty: Medium

Category: Inference

Getting to the Answer: Consider what would be lost from the passage if this paragraph were not included. Elinor and Mrs. Jennings have argued over the events taking place. The final paragraph shows Elinor trying to convince Mrs. Jennings that she is "doing a very unkind thing" (lines 90-91) by spreading rumors of Marianne's marriage, rumors that will

likely humiliate her. Elinor is not simply explaining why she believes Mrs. Jennings is wrong, but trying to stop her from causing Marianne additional pain. Choice (B) is correct because it is the only answer choice that conveys this meaning.

Suggested Passage Map notes:

¶1: GB about to depart from his faithful wife
¶2: F to GB: don't leave!
¶3: GB: I must go tonight
¶4-6: F sad to see him go
¶7: GB is up to something, hiding it from F
¶8: dark deeds in a dark setting; danger ahead?
¶9: GB scared of whom he might meet
¶10: a man suddenly appears
¶11: man seems to know GB
¶12: GB startled, but expected the man
¶13: GB and man look similar, man is more sophisticated

31. A   Difficulty: Hard

Category: Vocab-in-Context

Getting to the Answer: Read the sentence for context clues to understand the author's intention. Then replace the author's word with those in the answer choices to see which word's definition correctly reflects the sentence's meaning. "Perceived" is the best match for "discerned," as both words reflect Goodman Brown's observing the stranger's appearance and making judgments based on these observations. Thus, choice (A) is correct.

32. B   Difficulty: Medium

Category: Inference

Getting to the Answer: Review your Passage Map to assess how Goodman Brown feels about his journey, particularly compared to what he tells his wife about the trip. Goodman Brown wonders if his wife had a dream about his trip's true "evil purpose" (line 47) but he is relieved to discover she hasn't. This means she knows nothing of the truth of his journey. Therefore, choice (B) is correct.

33. B   Difficulty: Easy

Category: Command of Evidence

Getting to the Answer: Review each answer choice to assess its purpose in the passage and determine which best supports the correct answer to the previous question. Goodman Brown is hiding the true purpose of the journey from his wife and, as stated in choice (B), he fears that a dream told her of his purpose. He is later relieved when he discovers this is not true. Therefore, choice (B) is correct.

34. C   Difficulty: Medium

Category: Inference

Getting to the Answer: Review your Passage Map for clues to assess how Goodman Brown feels about the man who joins him. Then, determine which answer choice accurately depicts the relationship between the two. Goodman Brown's voice trembles when he speaks to the man who appears by the side of the road, but the appearance is described as "not wholly unexpected" (line 74), meaning Brown knows the man but is still unsettled. While Brown describes his trip as having an "evil purpose," no crime is discussed. Therefore, choice (C) is correct.

35. B   Difficulty: Easy

Category: Command of Evidence

Getting to the Answer: Review each of the cited lines to determine what they reflect about Goodman's relationship with the man on the road and ascertain which answer choice best supports the correct answer from the previous question. Choice (B) is correct as it shows Goodman Brown's trembling in reply to the man's greeting while also acknowledging that the strange man's appearance was not wholly unexpected.

36. B   Difficulty: Medium

Category: Rhetoric

Getting to the Answer: Review how the words in paragraph 8 help the reader understand the author's intention. Compare that intention to what you learned in the rest of the passage to determine which answer choice correctly describes why the author used those specific words. Goodman Brown is clearly hiding the journey's "evil purpose" from his wife, so the dark description of the forest he passes through helps heighten the feeling that Brown is about to do something wicked. Thus, choice (B) is correct.

37. D   Difficulty: Medium

Category: Rhetoric

Getting to the Answer: Review the purpose of the cited lines in relation to the rest of the passage. Then, determine which answer choice correctly describes the author's intention in using those words. The author already describes the forest as a dark and foreboding place, but he also mentions specific figures that would frighten Goodman Brown, hinting at other possible entities waiting in the forest. Choice (D) is correct because the work is not a fairy tale as mentioned in choice A, the author doesn't mention Goodman's going crazy as stated in choice B, and there is no mention of any robberies by Faith, as stated in C.

38. B   Difficulty: Hard

Category: Rhetoric

Getting to the Answer: Review the cited lines and determine what claim about Goodman Brown this detail supports, especially in relation to what you already know about Brown. The man says he passed through Boston, but there is no other detail to support a claim that the two men are going there now, as noted in A. No evidence is provided to indicate that Brown was supposed to wait at the clock tower either, as is stated in C. And, while Brown is late, he has never hinted at any intended delay, as D implies. The only claim that is supported by the greeting is that the man and Brown know one another, as the man calls out Brown's name. Thus, choice (B) is correct.

39. B   Difficulty: Medium

Category: Vocab-in-Context

Getting to the Answer: Read the sentence for clues to understand the author's intention. Predict a synonym to replace the selected word and see which of the answer choices best matches your synonym. "Embarrassed" and "abashed" both mean to feel out of place in a certain setting, which the stranger would not feel according to the sentence; choice (B) is correct.

40. A   Difficulty: Easy

Category: Inference

Getting to the Answer: Review the passage for statements relating to Goodman's relationship with the man on the road and determine which answer choice offers the most logical statement. The man is described as older than Goodman, with a greater aura of wisdom. His expressions bear "a considerable resemblance" (line 80) to Goodman's, enough that "they might have been taken for father and son" (lines 82-83). It is logical to assume that the man could be related to Brown; therefore, choice (A) is correct.

    Suggested Passage Map notes:

        ¶1: Gregor woke up not himself

        ¶2: description of Gregor's room, job

        ¶3: thought sleep would make him normal, couldn't roll over

        ¶4: thought job stress was to blame for how he was

        ¶5: thinks he needs more sleep, wants more luxury but has to help parents

41. C   Difficulty: Easy

Category: Detail

Getting to the Answer: Skim the passage to locate Gregor's first reaction to his transformation. The passage states that Gregor woke "from troubled dreams."

He only realizes "it wasn't a dream" after he has examined his new body and looked around his room to orient himself. Choice (C) is the correct answer. "Nightmare" describes a dream that is "troubled."

42. D   Difficulty: Hard

Category: Vocab-in-Context

Getting to the Answer: Use context clues and tone to help determine the meaning of the word. Use the surrounding text to paint a mental picture of descriptive words. Finally, make sure the answer choice does not alter the meaning of the sentence when inserted. The paragraph in which the word appears describes an average room appropriate for a person. Therefore, choice (D) is the correct answer. "Proper" means "suitably appropriate" in this context.

43. A   Difficulty: Medium

Category: Inference

Getting to the Answer: Look for Gregor's thoughts and statements about work. Use this as evidence of his attitude. Paragraphs 4 and 5 are essentially rants about Gregor's dissatisfaction with his job. He dislikes traveling, feels that he works much harder than others and expresses anger toward his boss. Gregor feels that it is unfair that other salesmen have a life of "luxury" while he has to wake up early. Choice (A) is the correct answer. Gregor is resentful and bitter about his job.

44. C   Difficulty: Medium

Category: Command of Evidence

Getting to the Answer: Review your answer to the previous question. Decide which lines of text give clues to how Gregor feels about his job. Choice (C) offers the best support. These lines describe Gregor's bitterness and the unfairness he perceives. He feels he works much harder than the other salesmen, but that he would be fired if he asked for better treatment or less work.

45. D **Difficulty:** Hard

Category: Global

Getting to the Answer: Ask yourself what purpose the author has in writing the passage. What main point does the majority of the excerpt support? The events in the passage show that despite a dramatic physical transformation, Gregor still plans to go to work. Gregor consistently expresses unhappiness and bitterness about his job but ignores his transformation into an insect because he feels he must still go to work or he will be fired. In this situation, choice (D) is the correct answer. Gregor's duty to his job overrides reason and sense when he plans to attend work despite the physical transformation that has left him inhuman and helpless.

46. A **Difficulty:** Medium

Category: Inference

Getting to the Answer: Reread the text, looking for evidence to support each of the answer choices. Examine Gregor's thoughts and statements for clues about his personality. Based on Gregor's statements about his work, it is clear that he continues to work at a job he dislikes in order to support his parents. He largely ignores his physical transformation, and there is no evidence as to whether he excels at his work. Choice (A) is the correct answer.

47. D **Difficulty:** Medium

Category: Command of Evidence

Getting to the Answer: Review your answer to the previous question. Read each choice and figure out which one provides specific support for that answer. Choice (D) provides the best support. These lines show that Gregor thinks it may be best to quit the job he hates, but he will continue to work until he can pay off his parents' debt.

48. A **Difficulty:** Medium

Category: Vocab-in-Context

Getting to the Answer: Use context clues from the target sentence and surrounding sentence. Predict the meaning of the word and look for a match in the answer choices. Gregor is attempting to turn over in his bed, but finds his legs and body are useless and unable to turn him over into his preferred position. Choice (A) is the nearest match to the meaning of "floundering" in this context.

49. B **Difficulty:** Medium

Category: Rhetoric

Getting to the Answer: Think about where the description of Gregor's itch is placed in the story. Look at the lines before and after it, and consider why the author chose to include it at that particular point in the narrative. The description of the itch comes in the middle of Gregor's thoughts about his job. After attempting and failing to relieve the itch, Gregor immediately goes back to thinking about his job-related concerns. This shows that Gregor is so preoccupied with his job that he is unable to recognize the seriousness—and absurdity—of his situation. The correct answer is choice (B).

50. D **Difficulty:** Medium

Category: Rhetoric

Getting to the Answer: Contrast Gregor's thoughts with the dark tone of the rest of the excerpt. Think about how this phrase adds to or supports the interpretations you made in previous questions. The author ends the excerpt with Gregor completely disregarding the fact that he is now an insect. Gregor plans to go to work as he always does, and the author draws attention to the absurdity of this decision. Choice (D) is the correct choice. The author uses the matter-of-fact tone in the sentence to emphasize that Gregor will ignore his physical condition and go to work because he has such a strong sense of duty to his family.

History/Social Studies Passages

GETTING STARTED

The **History/Social Studies** portion of the SAT Reading Test will consist of either two single **History/Social Studies** passages or one single History/Social Studies passage and one **History/Social Studies** paired-passage set. **History/Social Studies** passages are different from other passage types because:

- The passage will have a clearly stated topic, a well-defined scope, and a specific purpose.
- There will be at least one primary source passage that uses antiquated language.

History/Social Studies passages are often packed with names and dates. In order to read the passage as quickly as possible without missing any information, you should make very short notes in the margin, also known as a Passage Map. Your Passage Map should be designed to help you quickly locate information in the passage when you answer questions.

Focus on including these important ideas in your **History/Social Studies** Passage Map:

1. Identify the topic and scope of the passage
   - The topic is the broad subject of the passage.
   - The scope narrows the topic to the aspect that is of interest to the author.
   - Always read the "blurb"—the italicized introduction at the top of the passage. The blurb will frequently describe the topic and the scope.
   - If they are not in the blurb, the topic and scope are usually found in the first paragraph. Read carefully until you identify them.

2. Identify the topic sentence of each succeeding paragraph
   - What does this paragraph accomplish? Does it provide evidence to support a previous statement? Or does it introduce questions about an earlier claim?
   - If the passage is using unfamiliar language, focus on the main idea of the paragraph. You will likely be able to figure out the meaning of unfamiliar terms from the context.

3. Summarize the purpose of the passage
    - Some common purposes include: to inform, to refute, to promote, to explore.
    - Note the author's tone. Were there any positive or negative keywords? If not, the author's tone is neutral.

> ✔ *Expert Tip*
>
> Some paragraphs are longer than others. If you are mapping a very long paragraph, you can write two or three short notes rather than trying to fit everything into just one long note.

IMPROVING WITH PRACTICE

Step 1: Compare Your Notes to the Suggested *History/Social Studies* Passage Maps

Although every Passage Map is unique, you should compare your notes to the suggested Passage Maps to be sure you generally included the same important points from the **History/ Social Studies** passages. Abbreviations and symbols are both very useful when creating Passage Maps. No matter how you record them, the ideas you should include in your Passage Map include:

- the main idea of each paragraph
- any opinions, especially the author's
- the *location* of descriptive details and examples
- the *reason* the author included details and examples. Is the author using the information to support, modify, or refute the preceding idea?
- any emphasis or "emotional" keywords. Keywords such as "remarkable," "unfortunate," "unprecedented," and "crucial" are important indicators of the author's tone.

If you missed important information, go back to the **History/Social Studies** passage and identify the keywords that you likely overlooked so you can recognize them more quickly next time. Remember these keywords for next time so you can focus your attention and create strong Passage Maps.

> ✔ *Remember*
>
> Resist the temptation to reread large portions of the passage when answering questions. Your Passage Map should help you predict and answer questions correctly without having to dive completely back into the text. Doing this will save you time on Test Day *and* help you get more questions correct!

Step 2: Answer the Questions

Once you have a strengthened **History/Social Studies** Passage Map, complete the questions one at a time. Review the Answer and Explanation for every question immediately after completing it. If you got the question correct, congratulate yourself, but take a moment to read the entire explanation to be sure you got the question right for the right reason. The explanation may even point out a more efficient way that you can use on a later question.

Step 3: Review Incorrect Answers

If you get the question incorrect . . . still congratulate yourself! You're about to learn something new that you'll be able to use to improve your performance on Test Day. Don't read the explanation yet; instead, try the question again.

If you get the question correct the second time, read the explanation to see if you solved the question in the most efficient way. Identify the mistake you made the first time, and determine how you're going to avoid making that mistake again.

> ✔ *Expert Tip*
>
> **Many top scoring students have an SAT notebook where they write down what they learn from every question. Doing this can be time-consuming, but it can also help you identify the types of mistakes you tend to make.**

If you get the question incorrect the second time, use the explanation to learn how to get the question correct. Work through the question again while following the explanation, and identify the steps you will need to take to get a similar question correct. Although the passages and questions will change, the concepts being tested will not. When you encounter unfamiliar questions, take note of them for future study sessions.

> ✔ *Remember*
>
> **The SAT is a standardized test. While Hard Reading questions are usually more difficult to answer than Easy or Medium questions, they are often similar in structure and purpose, and the same four skills (listed in Chapter 1) are tested on every Reading Test. You actually can predict the types of questions you will see on Test Day!**

After all that work, it's time to move to the next question. Reviewing in this way will take time. However, improvement doesn't come from just doing lots and lots of questions; it comes from thinking through your approach and improving it with every question.

RAISING YOUR SCORE EVEN MORE

As soon as you've learned to consistently create accurate **History/Social Studies** Passage Maps that quickly lead you to the correct answers, it's time to look at passages you have already completed to study which sections of the passages were the source of the correct answers. While you search for the source of each answer, look for the keywords the author uses to show that a particular section of the text is important. Recognizing keywords throughout the passage helps you to know when to slow your pace and read carefully, such as when reading an introductory paragraph, and when you can speed up and read superficially, such as when you reach the middle of a body paragraph.

> ✔ *Expert Tip*
>
> **Prove your answer from the passage before you pick it! You can be as confident of your Reading answers as you are of your Math answers because you will always be able to support the correct answer from the passage.**

PRACTICE QUESTIONS

The following test-like question sets provide an opportunity to practice reading History/Social Studies Passages and answering related questions.

Questions 1-11 are based on the following passage and supplementary material.

The following passage describes the discovery of gold in California and the effects of that discovery on the United States.

People around the world unanimously agree that gold is a valuable mineral. Gold has been seen as a precious commodity by many cultures
Line throughout time, and Americans of the 1840s
(5) were no different. When James W. Marshall, a carpenter and sawmill owner, discovered a gold nugget in the American River, California was forever changed. News of his discovery attracted thousands of immigrants from other
(10) parts of California, as well as other places around the United States and the world.

In the Sierra Nevada, a mountain range that runs 400 miles through California, years of erosion caused by rainfall and the downhill
(15) flow of mountain streams loosened pieces of gold that had been embedded in the solid rock formed over 100 million years ago. California is largely made of quartz previously found at the bottom of the Pacific Ocean. Underwater
(20) volcanoes melted the quartz into magma and pushed it up towards the surface, sometimes forming islands. Due to the movements of the Earth's tectonic plates, these islands were pushed together and against the West Coast.
(25) This movement and accumulation of land over millions of years formed the area known as California. The gold that was dispersed across the sea floor became concentrated and redistributed throughout the veins of quartz in the
(30) Sierra Nevada Mountains.

Marshall's discovery was quickly verified and publicized by the New York Herald in August of 1848. Current California residents of the time were able to get to the gold fields
(35) first. Soon after, President James Polk confirmed the discovery in an address to Congress. His address prompted many Americans to move west, as well as other fortune-seekers from around the world to immigrate to the
(40) United States. This influx of people caused California's population to increase, as well as experience a change in demographics. The particular geologic makeup made California the prime location for mining gold. The
(45) Northern California city of San Francisco grew from 1,000 people in 1848 to more than 20,000 people in just two years. Because of the rapid population increase, the United States government incorporated the territory into the
(50) Union. California became the Union's 31st state in 1850, though it had only been acquired from Mexico two short years before. This was the fastest any new territory has ever been given statehood in the history of the United States.
(55) Americans from places east of California migrated via two very long and often dangerous paths. Some endured a six-month boat voyage, which departed from New York City and sailed south as far as the tip of South
(60) America before heading north to California. The trip was so perilous that most Americans relocating to California opted to travel the famous Oregon Trail. Riding in covered wagons through dangerous conditions, travelers who
(65) opted to move by land also had a six-month trip to endure. By 1850, the sheer number of people attempting the voyage inspired the creation of the Panama Railway. Built specifically to reduce travel time to California, the first

(70) transcontinental railroad decreased the length of the trip by several months.

Forty-Niners came to California from many different countries around the globe, including China, Germany, Mexico, Turkey, France, and (75) Ireland. The largest group of people to successfully immigrate to California from abroad was the Chinese. Many did not intend to settle in the United States, but instead planned to return home with their fortunes. While many (80) did so, when gold grew scarce and the Chinese Exclusion Act was passed in 1882, prohibiting Chinese immigration for 10 years, many immigrants instead put down roots in California. The result was the most ethnically (85) diverse state in the Union by the middle of the 19th century.

Though the gold in California didn't last long after its discovery, the effects that it had on the population, including the number of people (90) in the state, their ethnicities, and the way they travelled, have lasted to the modern day.

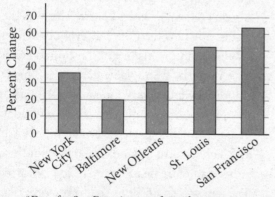

Percent Population Change, 1850–1860

*Data for San Francisco are from the state census in 1852. The 1850 census data were destroyed in a fire.

Data from the *United States Bureau of the Census*.

1. The author includes the second paragraph primarily to

    A) illustrate why gold is such a valuable metal.

    B) show why California was a prime location for gold mining.

    C) explain why California became a state so rapidly.

    D) give scientific information about how gold is formed over time.

2. According to the passage, which of the following was a main cause of westward migration?

    A) President Polk's speech about the gold rush

    B) California's acceptance into the union as a state

    C) The development of new gold extraction techniques

    D) New immigration restrictions passed by the federal government

3. As used in line 40, "influx" most nearly means

    A) assault.

    B) movement.

    C) news.

    D) rush.

4. The passage suggests that which of the following was unusual about California's entry into the Union, as compared to that of other new states?

   A) It had more natural resources.

   B) It had a smaller population.

   C) It had less wealth.

   D) It had spent less time as a territory.

5. Which choice provides the best evidence for the answer to the previous question?

   A) Lines 31-33 ("Marshall's discovery . . . August 1848")

   B) Lines 37-40 ("His address . . . United States")

   C) Lines 52-54 ("This was . . . United States")

   D) Lines 79-84 ("While many . . . in California")

6. According to the passage, what was one result of the presence of many dangers on the journey to California?

   A) Expansion of the population across the entire country

   B) Increased wealth for those living along the Oregon Trail

   C) Decreased immigration to other parts of the country

   D) Improved transportation options between the East Coast and California

7. What can be inferred about immigrants who came to California?

   A) They were forbidden from returning home once California became a state.

   B) Migrating to California was more attractive for them than for other Americans.

   C) They came from more nations than did immigrants to other states.

   D) Most were escaping difficult political conditions at home rather than seeking fortune.

8. Which choice provides the best evidence for the answer to the previous question?

   A) Lines 72-75 ("Forty-Niners . . . and Ireland")

   B) Lines 75-77 ("The largest . . . the Chinese")

   C) Lines 79-84 ("While many . . . in California")

   D) Lines 84-86 ("The result . . . the 19th century")

9. As used in line 61, "perilous" most nearly means

   A) boring.

   B) exotic.

   C) dangerous.

   D) expensive.

10. The overall structure of the passage can be described as

    A) a history of gold in California, followed by a discussion of why gold is valuable.

    B) an analysis of why gold is important, followed by criticism of the politics surrounding gold.

    C) a list of the causes of a gold rush, followed by an analysis of the effects of gold on a region.

    D) a discussion of the benefits of the gold rush in California, followed by a list of consequences.

11. Based on the chart, which conclusion is best supported?

    A) The United States grew greatly from 1850 to 1860.

    B) San Francisco was the largest city in the United States in 1860.

    C) From 1850 to 1860, cities in the East lost population, while San Francisco gained population.

    D) Of all five cities, San Francisco gained the largest total number of people from 1850 to 1860.

Questions 12-22 are based on the following passage.

This passage is adapted from Carrie Chapman Catt's 1917 "Address to the United States Congress." Catt served as president of the National American Woman Suffrage Association; the closing arguments of her speech are excerpted below.

Your party platforms have pledged woman suffrage. Then why not be honest, frank friends of our cause, adopt it in reality as your
Line own, make it a party program and "fight with
(5) us"? As a party measure—a measure of all parties—why not put the amendment through Congress and the Legislatures? We shall all be better friends, we shall have a happier nation, we women will be free to support loyally the
(10) party of our choice, and we shall be far prouder of our history.

"There is one thing mightier than kings and armies"—aye, than Congresses and political parties—"the power of an idea when its time
(15) has come to move." The time for woman suffrage has come. The woman's hour has struck. If parties prefer to postpone action longer and thus do battle with this idea, they challenge the inevitable. The idea will not perish; the party
(20) which opposes it may. Every delay, every trick, every political dishonesty from now on will antagonize the women of the land more and more, and when the party or parties which have so delayed woman suffrage finally let it
(25) come, their sincerity will be doubted and their appeal to the new voters will be met with suspicion. This is the psychology of the situation. Can you afford the risk? Think it over.

We know you will meet opposition. There
(30) are a few "woman haters" left, a few "old males of the tribe," as Vance Thompson calls them, whose duty they believe it to be to keep women in the places they have carefully picked out for them. Treitschke, made world famous
(35) by war literature, said some years ago:

"Germany, which knows all about Germany and France, knows far better what is good for Alsace-Lorraine than that miserable people can possibly know." A few American
(40) Treitschkes we have who know better than women what is good for them. There are women, too . . . But the world does not wait for such as these, nor does Liberty pause to heed the plaint of men and women with a grouch.
(45) She does not wait for those who have a special interest to serve, nor a selfish reason for depriving other people of freedom. Holding her torch aloft, Liberty is pointing the way onward and upward and saying to America, "Come."

(50) To you the supporters of our cause, in Senate and House, and the number is large, the suffragists of the nation express their grateful thanks. This address is not meant for you. We are more truly appreciative of all you have
(55) done than any words can express. We ask you to make a last, hard fight for the amendment during the present session. Since last we asked a vote on this amendment your position has been fortified by the addition to suffrage terri-
(60) tory of Great Britain, Canada, and New York.

Some of you have been too indifferent to give more than casual attention to this question. It is worthy of your immediate consideration—a question big enough to
(65) engage the attention of our Allies in war time, is too big a question for you to neglect. . .

Gentlemen, we hereby petition you, our only designated representatives, to redress our grievances by the immediate passage of the in-
(70) fluence to secure its ratification in your own state, in order that the women of our nation may be endowed with political freedom that our nation may resume its world leadership in democracy.

(75)   Woman suffrage is coming—you know it. Will you, Honorable Senators and Members of the House of Representatives, help or hinder it?

12. What is Carrie Chapman Catt's purpose in giving this speech?

   A)   To assert that women will vote for the party that supports their cause

   B)   To demand more women candidates on political party tickets

   C)   To persuade lawmakers to pass a law for women's right to vote

   D)   To rally support for women's equal representation in Congress

13. What is the explicit meaning of the phrase in line 75 ("Woman suffrage . . . know it")?

   A)   All women support woman suffrage.

   B)   States have already approved woman suffrage.

   C)   Women have always had the right to vote.

   D)   Women will eventually gain the right to vote.

14. The phrase in lines 23-27 ("when the party . . . with suspicion") most nearly implies that

   A)   women voters will not support lawmakers who do not support suffrage.

   B)   women will not run for office because they do not trust politicians.

   C)   women will vote more women into political office.

   D)   women's influence on Congress will be minimal and is not a threat.

15. As used in line 68, "redress" most nearly means

   A)   appeal.

   B)   communicate.

   C)   implement.

   D)   remedy.

16. Catt most likely concludes her speech with a question in order to

   A)   challenge lawmakers to investigate her claims.

   B)   make clear that she is fair-minded and open to reason.

   C)   open the matter of suffrage to debate.

   D)   put responsibility for the choice on each lawmaker.

17. As used in line 22, "antagonize" most nearly means

   A)   dishearten.

   B)   embitter.

   C)   humiliate.

   D)   inhibit.

18. What counterclaim does Catt offer to the argument that some men and women still oppose suffrage?

   A)   They are not voicing their opinions in Congress.

   B)   They cannot stop the inevitable.

   C)   They do have just cause for opposition.

   D)   They have no legal basis for their claims.

19. Which choice provides the best evidence for the answer to the previous question?

    A) Lines 7-11 ("We shall all . . . our history")

    B) Lines 50-53 ("To you . . . grateful thanks")

    C) Lines 57-60 ("Since last . . . New York")

    D) Lines 63-66 ("It is worthy . . . to neglect")

20. Which choice most clearly reflects the inference expressed in lines 71-74 ("in order that . . . in democracy")?

    A) No citizen in our democracy is free as long as women cannot vote.

    B) Other nations have demanded that our government grant woman suffrage.

    C) A nation needs more women in positions of leadership.

    D) Woman suffrage is essential to true democracy.

21. The stance that Catt takes is best described as that of

    A) a historian reflecting on historical events.

    B) an official campaigning for political office.

    C) an activist advocating for legislative reform.

    D) a reporter investigating a current controversy.

22. Which choice provides the best evidence for the answer to the previous question?

    A) Lines 12-15 ("There is one thing . . . to move")

    B) Lines 29-31 ("There are a few . . . calls them")

    C) Lines 57-60 ("Since last we . . . New York")

    D) Lines 67-71 ("Gentlemen, we hereby . . . own state")

Questions 23-32 are based on the following passage.

This passage is adapted from Hillary Rodham Clinton's speech titled "Women's Rights Are Human Rights," addressed to the U.N. Fourth World Conference on Women in 1995.

If there is one message that echoes forth from this conference, it is that human rights are women's rights. . . . And women's rights are
Line human rights.
(5)   Let us not forget that among those rights are the right to speak freely and the right to be heard.

Women must enjoy the right to participate fully in the social and political lives of their
(10) countries if we want freedom and democracy to thrive and endure.

It is indefensible that many women in non-governmental organizations who wished to participate in this conference have not been
(15) able to attend—or have been prohibited from fully taking part.

Let me be clear. Freedom means the right of people to assemble, organize, and debate openly. It means respecting the views of those
(20) who may disagree with the views of their governments. It means not taking citizens away from their loved ones and jailing them, mistreating them, or denying them their freedom or dignity because of the peaceful expres-
(25) sion of their ideas and opinions.

In my country, we recently celebrated the seventy-fifth anniversary of women's suffrage. It took one hundred and fifty years after the signing of our Declaration of Independence
(30) for women to win the right to vote. It took seventy-two years of organized struggle on the part of many courageous women and men.

It was one of America's most divisive philo-sophical wars. But it was also a bloodless war.
(35) Suffrage was achieved without a shot fired.

We have also been reminded, in V-J Day ob-servances last weekend, of the good that comes when men and women join together to combat the forces of tyranny and build a better world.
(40)   We have seen peace prevail in most places for a half century. We have avoided another world war. But we have not solved older, deeply-rooted problems that continue to diminish the potential of half the world's population.
(45)   Now it is time to act on behalf of women everywhere.

If we take bold steps to better the lives of women, we will be taking bold steps to better the lives of children and families too. Families
(50) rely on mothers and wives for emotional sup-port and care; families rely on women for labor in the home; and increasingly, families rely on women for income needed to raise healthy children and care for other relatives.
(55)   As long as discrimination and inequities re-main so commonplace around the world—as long as girls and women are valued less, fed less, fed last, overworked, underpaid, not schooled and subjected to violence in and out
(60) of their homes—the potential of the human family to create a peaceful, prosperous world will not be realized.

Let this conference be our—and the world's—call to action.
(65)   And let us heed the call so that we can cre-ate a world in which every woman is treated with respect and dignity, every boy and girl is loved and cared for equally, and every family has the hope of a strong and stable future.

23. What is the primary purpose of the passage?

    A) To chastise those who have prevented women from attending the conference

    B) To argue that women continue to experience discrimination

    C) To explain that human rights are of more concern than women's rights

    D) To encourage people to think of women's rights as an issue important to all

24. Which choice provides the best evidence for the answer to the previous question?

    A) Lines 5-7 ("Let us . . . be heard")

    B) Lines 12-16 ("It is indefensible . . . taking part")

    C) Lines 42-44 ("But we have . . . population")

    D) Lines 49-54 ("Families . . . other relatives")

25. As used in line 33, "divisive" most nearly means

    A) conflict-producing.

    B) carefully watched.

    C) multi-purpose.

    D) time-consuming.

26. Based on the speech, with which statement would Clinton most likely agree?

    A) More men should be the primary caregivers of their children in order to provide career opportunities for women.

    B) Women do not need the support and cooperation of men as they work toward equality.

    C) Solutions for global problems would be found faster if women had more access to power.

    D) The American movement for women's suffrage should have been violent in order to achieve success more quickly.

27. Which choice provides the best evidence for the answer to the previous question?

    A) Lines 8-11 ("Women . . . endure")

    B) Line 35 ("Suffrage . . . shot fired")

    C) Lines 49-54 ("Families . . . relatives")

    D) Lines 55-62 ("As long . . . realized")

28. As used in line 31, "organized" most nearly means

    A) arranged.

    B) cooperative.

    C) hierarchical.

    D) patient.

29. Which claim does Clinton make in her speech?

    A) The conference itself is a model of nondiscrimination toward women.

    B) Democracy cannot prosper unless women can participate fully in it.

    C) Women's rights are restricted globally by the demands on them as parents.

    D) Women are being forced to provide income for their families as a result of sexism.

30. Clinton uses the example of V-J Day observations to support the argument that

    A) campaigns succeed when they are nonviolent.

    B) historical wrongs against women must be corrected.

    C) many tragedies could have been avoided with more female participation.

    D) cooperation between men and women leads to positive developments.

31. According to lines 40-44, problems that affect women

    A) harm half of the world's women.

    B) are worldwide and long-standing.

    C) could be eliminated in half a century.

    D) are isolated to a few less developed countries.

32. The fifth paragraph (lines 17-25) can be described as

    A) a distillation of the author's main argument.

    B) an acknowledgment of a counterargument.

    C) a veiled criticism of a group.

    D) a defense against an accusation.

Questions 33-42 are based on the following passage.

This passage is adapted from Martin Luther King, Jr.'s "Letter from Birmingham Jail."

. . . I think I should give the reason for my being in Birmingham, since you have been in-fluenced by the argument of "outsiders coming
Line in." I have the honor of serving as president of
(5) the Southern Christian Leadership Confer-ence, an organization operating in every Southern state with headquarters in Atlanta, Georgia. We have some eighty-five affiliate or-ganizations all across the South, one being the
(10) Alabama Christian Movement for Human Rights. Whenever necessary and possible we share staff, educational, and financial resources with our affiliates. Several months ago our lo-cal affiliate here in Birmingham invited us to
(15) be on call to engage in a nonviolent direct ac-tion program if such were deemed necessary. We readily consented and when the hour came we lived up to our promises. So I am here, along with several members of my staff,
(20) because we were invited here. I am here be-cause I have basic organizational ties here. Beyond this, I am in Birmingham because injustice is here. . . .

Moreover, I am cognizant of the interrelated-
(25) ness of all communities and states. I cannot sit idly by in Atlanta and not be concerned about what happens in Birmingham. Injustice any-where is a threat to justice everywhere. We are caught in an inescapable network of mutuality,
(30) tied in a single garment of destiny. Whatever affects one directly affects all indirectly. Never again can we afford to live with the narrow, pro-vincial "outside agitator" idea. Anyone who lives inside the United States can never be considered
(35) an outsider anywhere in this country. . . .

You may well ask, "Why direct action? Why sit-ins, marches, etc.? Isn't negotiation a better path?" You are exactly right in your call for negotiation. Indeed, this is the purpose
(40) of direct action. Nonviolent direct action seeks to create such a crisis and establish such creative tension that a community that has constantly refused to negotiate is forced to confront the issue. It seeks so to dramatize the
(45) issue that it can no longer be ignored. I just re-ferred to the creation of tension as a part of the work of the nonviolent resister. This may sound rather shocking. But I must confess that I am not afraid of the word tension. I have
(50) earnestly worked and preached against violent tension, but there is a type of constructive nonviolent tension that is necessary for growth. Just as Socrates felt that it was neces-sary to create a tension in the mind so that
(55) individuals could rise from the bondage of myths and half-truths to the unfettered realm of creative analysis and objective appraisal, we must see the need of having nonviolent gad-flies to create the kind of tension in society
(60) that will help men rise from the dark depths of prejudice and racism to the majestic heights of understanding and brotherhood. So the pur-pose of the direct action is to create a situation so crisis-packed that it will inevitably open the
(65) door to negotiation. We, therefore, concur with you in your call for negotiation. Too long has our beloved Southland been bogged down in the tragic attempt to live in monologue rather than dialogue. . . .

(70) My friends, I must say to you that we have not made a single gain in civil rights without determined legal and nonviolent pressure. History is the long and tragic story of the fact that privileged groups seldom give up their
(75) privileges voluntarily. Individuals may see the moral light and voluntarily give up their unjust posture; but as Reinhold Niebuhr has reminded us, groups are more immoral than individuals.

(80) We know through painful experience that freedom is never voluntarily given by the oppressor; it must be demanded by the oppressed. . . . For years now I have heard the word "Wait!" It rings in the ear of every *(85)* African American with a piercing familiarity. This "wait" has almost always meant "never." It has been a tranquilizing thalidomide, relieving the emotional stress for a moment, only to give birth to an ill-formed infant of frustration. *(90)* We must come to see with the distinguished jurist of yesterday that "justice too long delayed is justice denied." We have waited for more than three hundred and forty years for our constitutional and God-given rights. *(95)* The nations of Asia and Africa are moving with jet-like speed toward the goal of political independence, and we still creep at horse and buggy pace toward the gaining of a cup of coffee at a lunch counter. . . .

33. King's purpose for writing this letter is

   A) to explain why he came to Birmingham to protest.

   B) to launch a nonviolent protest movement in Birmingham.

   C) to open an affiliate of the Southern Christian Leadership Conference in Birmingham.

   D) to support fellow civil rights activists in Birmingham.

34. Which choice provides the best evidence for the answer to the previous question?

   A) Lines 1-2 ("I think . . . in Birmingham")

   B) Lines 4-8 ("I have . . . Atlanta, Georgia")

   C) Lines 8-11 ("We have some . . . Rights")

   D) Lines 27-28 ("Injustice anywhere . . . everywhere")

35. The passage most strongly suggests that which of the following statements is true?

   A) King was warmly welcomed when he arrived in Birmingham.

   B) King received criticism for his decision to come to Birmingham.

   C) King did not want to cause a disruption by coming to Birmingham.

   D) King was abandoned by his supporters when he arrived in Birmingham.

36. As used in lines 24-25, "interrelatedness of all communities and states" most nearly means that

   A) King has personal connections to people in the town.

   B) the Southern Christian Leadership Conference needs national support.

   C) events in one part of the country affect everyone in the nation.

   D) local civil rights groups operate independently of one another.

37. Based on paragraph 3, it can be reasonably inferred that King believed circumstances in Birmingham at the time

   A) were unfair and wrong.

   B) constituted an isolated event.

   C) justified his arrest.

   D) required federal intervention.

38. Which choice provides the best evidence for the answer to the previous question?

    A) Lines 24-25 ("Moreover, . . . states")

    B) Lines 27-28 ("Injustice anywhere . . . everywhere")

    C) Lines 28-30 ("We are caught . . . destiny")

    D) Lines 31-33 ("Never again . . . idea")

39. As used in line 44, "dramatize" most nearly means

    A) cast events in an appealing light.

    B) draw attention to significant events.

    C) exaggerate events to seem more important.

    D) turn events into a popular performance.

40. Which choice most clearly paraphrases a claim made by King in paragraph 4?

    A) A failure to negotiate in the South has provoked secret action by civil rights activists.

    B) A focus on dialogue blinds reformers to the necessity for direct action to promote change.

    C) Direct action is necessary to motivate people to talk about prejudice and racism.

    D) Nonviolent protest encourages a sense of brotherhood and understanding among citizens.

41. Paragraph 4 best supports the claims made in paragraph 3 by

    A) arguing that nonviolent pressure is most likely to spur just action by individuals.

    B) clarifying that throughout history, privileged classes have been reluctant to let go of privilege.

    C) drawing a distinction between the morality of individuals and of groups.

    D) pointing out that few gains in civil rights have been made without nonviolent pressure.

42. King refers to "the gaining of a cup of coffee at a lunch counter" (lines 98-99) primarily to

    A) call attention to the sedative effect of delaying civil rights reform in the United States.

    B) emphasize that white Americans will not willingly end oppression against black Americans.

    C) describe the progress made toward the winning of equal rights in other countries.

    D) underscore the contrast between progress made in other countries and the United States.

Questions 43-53 are based on the following passage and supplementary material.

This passage details the history of Eleanor Roosevelt and how she changed the role of the First Lady of the United States.

Eleanor Roosevelt, wife of president Franklin Delano Roosevelt (FDR), forever altered the role of American First Lady and women in

Line U.S. politics in general. Dedicated, humble,

(5) and brave, Eleanor Roosevelt powerfully shouldered the nation's burdens during the longest and arguably most difficult presidency America has yet seen. Her sustained commitment to social justice began long before her

(10) husband's presidency and endured through the end of her life.

Born in 1884 to the brother of president Theodore Roosevelt, Eleanor's upbringing acquainted her with both politics and hardship.

(15) Having lost her parents in childhood, Eleanor was cared for by her grandmother in New York and was later sent to London for secondary schooling. After this education, Roosevelt returned to the States and became involved in

(20) humanitarian work, which would prove to be a lifelong engagement. At twenty years old she married her distant cousin, Franklin Delano, with whom she would parent six children.

While Mrs. Roosevelt was a committed wife

(25) and mother, she was also heavily involved with the national and international crises that plagued her generation. During World War I she volunteered in hospitals while supporting and partnering in her husband's political

(30) career. When FDR contracted polio in the early 1920s, she assumed much of his political responsibility, as he held a number of high-profile government positions before his presidency. This quickly afforded her an increasing

(35) national influence. Eleanor Roosevelt fought diligently for women's empowerment and numerous other human rights issues. Her husband's presidency (1933 to 1945) also oversaw both the Great Depression and World War II,

(40) two major national dilemmas with which Eleanor Roosevelt was intimately involved in addressing.

Before Eleanor Roosevelt, U.S. First Ladies had less political voice. Never before had a

(45) First Lady hosted press conferences, let alone assumed significant portions of the public responsibilities of the presidency. But due to FDR's lasting illness and his wife's wisdom, eloquence, and powerful political presence, all of

(50) this was possible, and in many ways essential, for his effective leadership.

Eleanor Roosevelt's concern for human rights aided her husband in his development of the New Deal, which was his legislative

(55) effort to alleviate the Great Depression. Mrs. Roosevelt catalyzed, advocated for, oversaw, and in many ways sustained much of the New Deal programming. Through these programs she sought to equip and employ youth, protect

(60) labor rights, and mend racial injustices.

Eleanor travelled extensively, speaking publicly, taking reports on relief programs, and visiting troops in wartime. Outside of direct political involvements, she taught and lec-

(65) tured in educational settings, aggressively fundraised for charitable causes, hosted countless social functions, and even spearheaded a small furniture business to employ the jobless.

Many remember Eleanor Roosevelt best for

(70) her power with words. Ever an advocate for the rights of the disadvantaged, Roosevelt spoke and wrote extensively. She published several books and even maintained a daily newspaper column for nearly thirty years.

(75) FDR's declining health prevented him from completing his fourth elected presidential term. He died in April of 1945, one month before the official end of Europe's involvement in World War II. This marked the end of (80) Eleanor's time as First Lady, and in her grief she indicated an intent to absent herself from politics altogether. Yet her dedication to the pursuit of world peace and human rights would prevail. Toward the end of that year she (85) accepted President Truman's invitation to help represent the U.S. at the newly forming United Nations.

In serving the UN, Roosevelt drafted the Universal Declaration of Human Rights. This (90) document still holds paramount importance today; it sets a standard against which international justice is still principally measured. She soon became chair of the UN Human Rights Commission. Stateside, Roosevelt actively bol-(95) stered the Civil Rights movement. She visited those imprisoned for nonviolent protest, spoke publicly for the cause, served on the boards of various organizations, and helped to catalyze the Justice Department's Civil Rights Division. (100) Roosevelt's work toward labor justice and women's equality in America also continued into her final years.

Eleanor Roosevelt died in 1962 at the age of 78 years old. Over a half-century later, this (105) woman's legacy remains. Her wise words are cherished in American hearts, her impact echoes throughout national and international human rights legislation, and her strength still empowers the powerless to continue their ef-(110) forts toward equality and justice. Roosevelt's perseverance, integrity, and accomplishments forever render her one of the most well-loved and revered women in American history.

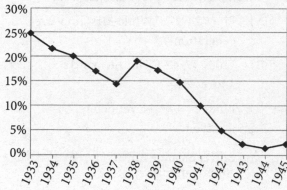

Unemployment Rates Over the Course of FDR's "New Deal" Programs

Adapted from HERB: Resources for Teachers and Bureau of Labor Statistics, "Graph of U.S. Unemployment Rate 1930-1945." ©2011 by American Social History Productions, Inc.

43. As used in line 6, "shouldered" most nearly means

A) arranged.

B) handled.

C) refused.

D) endured.

44. The passage most clearly reflects the author's

A) admiration for Eleanor Roosevelt.

B) regard for the accomplishments of Franklin D. Roosevelt.

C) support for the expansion of women's roles in politics.

D) uncertainty regarding the official role of the First Lady.

45. Which choice provides the best evidence for the answer to the previous question?

    A) Lines 24-27 ("While Mrs. Roosevelt . . . generation")

    B) Lines 37-42 ("Her husband's . . . addressing")

    C) Lines 44-47 ("Never before . . . presidency")

    D) Lines 110-113 ("Roosevelt's perseverance . . . American history")

46. The passage most strongly suggests that Eleanor Roosevelt

    A) modeled her political service on that of the women who had come before her.

    B) proved pivotal to the success of Franklin D. Roosevelt's presidency.

    C) was instrumental in winning suffrage and equal rights for women.

    D) would not have had such a lasting legacy had she not been First Lady.

47. Based on the passage, which choice best describes the focus of Eleanor Roosevelt's work?

    A) Expansion of health care and medical research

    B) Human rights and social justice

    C) Support for small business and entrepreneurship

    D) Wartime economic and political reform

48. The author most likely includes the detail in lines 27-28 ("During World War I . . . hospitals") to

    A) demonstrate Eleanor Roosevelt's expansion of the role of First Lady.

    B) prove the influence of Roosevelt in developing international human rights standards.

    C) show how Roosevelt worked closely with her husband on his policy agenda.

    D) support the idea that humanitarian work was a lifelong pursuit for Roosevelt.

49. The data in the graph most clearly support which conclusion related to the passage?

    A) Labor and other social unrest occurred in direct response to wartime economic cuts.

    B) President Roosevelt's policies helped ease hardship during the Great Depression.

    C) Volunteer efforts undertaken by Eleanor Roosevelt lessened suffering in cities.

    D) Women played a crucial role in the economic recovery of the nation during the war.

50. The passage suggests that Eleanor Roosevelt would most likely engage in what activity?

    A) Volunteer disaster response

    B) Political party campaigning

    C) Legal challenges to corporate monopolies

    D) Protests for tighter environmental regulations

51. Which choice provides the best evidence for the answer to the previous question?

    A) Lines 8-11 ("Her sustained commitment . . . end of her life")

    B) Lines 18-21 ("After this education . . . engagement")

    C) Lines 47-51 ("But due to . . . leadership")

    D) Lines 84-87 ("Toward the end . . . United Nations")

52. As used in line 67, "spearheaded" most nearly means

    A) invested in.

    B) advertised for.

    C) led development of.

    D) worked for.

53. Paragraph 9 most clearly supports the purpose of the whole passage by

    A) applauding the advances made in civil and human rights during Eleanor Roosevelt's lifetime.

    B) distinguishing Eleanor Roosevelt's legacy as independent from her husband's.

    C) emphasizing the importance of Eleanor Roosevelt's skills as an orator and a writer.

    D) showing the relationship between Eleanor Roosevelt's roles as First Lady and as diplomat.

ANSWERS AND EXPLANATIONS

CHAPTER 3

Suggested Passage Map notes:

¶1: topic = CA gold in 1940s
¶2: how CA & gold came to be
¶3: pop. explosion; why CA became a state
¶4: 2 ways to CA
¶5: not just Amer.
¶6: CA gold effects today

1. B   Difficulty: Medium

Category: Rhetoric

Getting to the Answer: Look at your notes for the second paragraph. Why does the author include it? The passage provides geological information to make a point about why gold was so easily mined in California. Choice (B) correctly identifies this information.

2. A   Difficulty: Easy

Category: Detail

Getting to the Answer: One main cause of migration is listed in the passage. Review your notes to find the answer. The passage states that President Polk's "address to Congress . . . prompted many Americans to move west" (lines 36-38). Choice (A) conveys this meaning.

3. D   Difficulty: Medium

Category: Vocab-in-Context

Getting to the Answer: Read the referenced line and the sentences around it. Then, use context clues to determine the word's meaning. The passage suggests that there was an overwhelming increase in population. Choice (D), "rush," conveys this meaning.

4. D   Difficulty: Hard

Category: Inference

Strategic Advice: Note what the passage states about California's statehood: California entered into the Union despite a surprising fact. The passage states that "California became the Union's 31st state in 1850, though it had only been acquired from Mexico two short years before" (lines 50-52). It can be inferred, then, that most states had spent longer as territories before being admitted into the Union. Choice (D) is correct.

5. C   Difficulty: Medium

Category: Command of Evidence

Getting to the Answer: Carefully reread the part of the passage that addresses statehood. Identify the specific claims it makes. The passage states that the United States incorporated California "though it had only been acquired from Mexico two short years before" (lines 51-52). Choice (C) is correct because it explicitly identifies what was unusual about California's statehood process.

6. D   Difficulty: Medium

Category: Inference

Getting to the Answer: Skim quickly to find the information describing the cause stated in the question. Then, read closely to locate the effects of that cause. The passage states explicitly that the creation of the Panama Railway was built in response to the needs of migrants to California. Choice (D) is correct.

7. C   Difficulty: Hard

Category: Inference

Getting to the Answer: Determine what the passage states about immigrant groups. Consider what can be concluded with certainty about them. The passage notes that California was very ethnically diverse by the middle of the 19th century. This suggests that immigrants to California came from more places than did immigrants to other states. Choice (C) is correct.

8.   D   Difficulty: Medium

Category: Command of Evidence

Getting to the Answer: Review your answer to the previous question. Look for information about California immigration from the passage. The passage states that California was "the most ethnically diverse state in the Union by the middle of the 19th century" (lines 84-86). This provides evidence for the assertion that immigrants to California came from more nations than did immigrants to other states. Choice (D), therefore, provides the strongest evidence and is correct.

9.   C   Difficulty: Easy

Category: Vocab-in-Context

Getting to the Answer: Consider the structure of the sentence. What is the relationship between the nature of the voyage and the choice to travel the Oregon Trail? The passage states that both routes to California were "very long and often dangerous" (lines 56-57). "Perilous," therefore, is likely to mean "dangerous." Choice (C) is correct.

10.   C   Difficulty: Hard

Category: Rhetoric

Getting to the Answer: Review each paragraph and try to identify its main point. Then, assess the answer choices. The initial paragraphs discuss why gold is important and why it was concentrated in California. It then analyzes the effects of its discovery there. Choice (C) accurately assesses the structure of the passage.

11.   A   Difficulty: Medium

Category: Synthesis

Getting to the Answer: Read the chart carefully. Pay particular attention to what the *y*-axis represents. The population change of all cities for the period from 1850 to 1860 was positive. In other words, all cities gained population, though some gained more than others. Choice (A) is correct, as it correctly identifies that all cities gained in population during this period.

Suggested Passage Map notes:

- **¶1:** aud = congress; auth: give suff. now
- **¶2:** ideas > parties; give suffrage or lose votes
- **¶3:** haters gonna hate! Am. will not wait for haters to catch up
- **¶4:** thanks suffragists for their work
- **¶5:** suffrage = major issue
- **¶6:** call to action
- **¶7:** suff. will happen with or without gov't

12.   C   Difficulty: Medium

Category: Rhetoric

Getting to the Answer: The correct answer will be clearly stated within the text and will reflect the tone and intent of the author. The introduction to the passage states that Carrie Chapman Catt speaks on behalf of the National American Woman Suffrage Association. In the first paragraph, she asks lawmakers to support a constitutional amendment. The context of the surrounding paragraph makes clear that the amendment would grant women suffrage, rendering choice (C) correct.

13.   D   Difficulty: Easy

Category: Detail

Getting to the Answer: The correct answer will clearly restate or have the same meaning as the excerpted line. The excerpted line states, "woman suffrage is coming" (line 75), which means that women will gain the right to vote, eventually, as expressed in choice (D).

14.   A   Difficulty: Medium

Category: Inference

Getting to the Answer: The correct answer will reflect the underlying or implied meaning of the excerpted line and the context of the surrounding text. The excerpted line states that suffrage will happen and women will gain the vote. It goes on to explain that as voters, women will not trust those who practiced dishonest and devious tactics (as expressed in the previous line). The concluding lines of the paragraph suggest a threat to the politicians' power. Taken together, these lines imply that women voters, when they gain the vote, will not vote for politicians who opposed their right to suffrage, as stated in choice (A).

15.   D   Difficulty: Medium

Category: Vocab-in-Context

Getting to the Answer: The correct answer will correctly replace the original word and retain the meaning of the original sentence. The text states that Catt and her supporters want congressional lawmakers to "redress our grievances" (lines 68-69), meaning to set right—or to remedy—the ills committed against women. Choice (D) reflects this meaning.

16.   D   Difficulty: Hard

Category: Rhetoric

Getting to the Answer: The correct answer will relate directly to the meaning of the question that Catt poses and to the main purpose of the passage as a whole. Catt's speech aims to win support for a constitutional amendment granting woman suffrage. Throughout the speech, she tries to persuade lawmakers to choose suffrage. She concludes by asking lawmakers whether they will help or hinder suffrage. Her final question puts responsibility on each lawmaker for his personal, individual choice on the matter, making choice (D) correct.

17.   B   Difficulty: Medium

Category: Vocab-in-Context

Getting to the Answer: The correct answer will reflect the specific meaning of the word in context of the surrounding sentence and text. The text states that "every delay, every trick, every political dishonesty from now on will antagonize the women of the land more and more" (lines 20-23). The surrounding text suggests that women will only become more resolved to their purpose as a result of delay, as well as more angry—or bitter—with politicians who forestall them, making choice (B) correct.

18.   B   Difficulty: Medium

Category: Rhetoric

Getting to the Answer: The correct answer will be supported by evidence within the text. Catt acknowledges that opposition to woman suffrage remains, but she dismisses the opposition as "woman haters" (line 30) and "old males of the tribe" (lines 30-31), suggesting that they are dated and ineffectual. She goes on to state that the world will not slow down for this opposition and that the cause of liberty will continue, implying that suffrage will happen despite the opposition. In the previous paragraph, Catt even refers to suffrage as "inevitable" (line 19). The suggestion is that suffrage is unavoidable, as stated in choice (B).

19.   C   Difficulty: Medium

Category: Command of Evidence

Getting to the Answer: The correct answer will provide evidence, either in reasoning or in fact, to support the claim in the answer to the previous question. The answer to the previous question asserts that woman suffrage is inevitable. Evidence to support this claim would show that suffrage is advancing, as demonstrated by choice (C).

20.   D   Difficulty: Medium

Category: Inference

Getting to the Answer: The correct answer will reflect the implied meaning of the excerpted line without assuming too much or distorting the context of the text. The excerpted line states that once women have the political freedom granted by suffrage, then the nation will resume its leadership in democracy. The implication is that the nation is not a leader in democracy as long as it denies women the right to vote. Therefore, choice (D) is correct.

21. C   Difficulty: Easy

Category: Rhetoric

Getting to the Answer: The correct answer will reflect both the position of the author and the purpose expressed in the text. In the passage, Catt gives a speech in which she appeals to legislators to enact a constitutional amendment, or legislative reform, to grant women suffrage. She is speaking as a political activist. The correct answer is choice (C).

22. D   Difficulty: Medium

Category: Command of Evidence

Getting to the Answer: The correct answer will provide evidence, either in reasoning or in fact, to support the specific position of the answer to the previous question. The answer to the previous question states that Catt is an activist appealing for legislative reform. Choice (D) is correct because in this line, Catt directly appeals to legislators to secure passage of the reform to which she refers earlier in the speech.

Suggested Passage Map notes:

¶1-3: women are equal and deserve to be treated as such
¶4: what freedom is
¶5-6: history of women fighting for equality
¶7-8: men and women do great things when they work together
¶9-14: must help women in other countries achieve equality and fight discrimination

23. D   Difficulty: Easy

Category: Rhetoric

Getting to the Answer: Consider the word choices Clinton uses throughout her speech. Notice any recurring themes. Choice (D) is the correct answer. Clinton says that working to improve the lives of women will improve others' lives as well.

24. D   Difficulty: Medium

Category: Command of Evidence

Getting to the Answer: Beware of answer choices that are only vaguely related to Clinton's point. The correct answer will follow her purpose closely. Clinton indicates that women's rights issues affect more than just women. Choice (D) is the best fit. These lines from the text provide concrete examples of how improving the lives of women improves their families' lives as well.

25. A   Difficulty: Medium

Category: Vocab-in-Context

Getting to the Answer: Sometimes you can recognize similarities between the word in question and a more familiar word. "Divisive" is similar to "divide" and "division," both of which have to do with things being split or made separate. Clinton is saying that though suffrage produced great conflict and divided people more than other philosophical wars, it was "bloodless." Choice (A) is correct; "divisive" means "conflict-producing."

26. C   Difficulty: Hard

Category: Inference

Getting to the Answer: You're being asked to decide which statement Clinton is most likely to agree with. Because the statement isn't explicitly mentioned in the speech, you must infer, or make a logical guess, based on information in the speech. Clinton states that the world would be improved if women were able to contribute more. She provides specific examples of her vision for an improved world. Choice (C) is correct, as it suggests that if women did not experience discrimination and had more power, the world would be better off.

27. D   Difficulty: Medium

Category: Command of Evidence

Getting to the Answer: Try paraphrasing the answer you chose for the previous test item. Then decide which quote from the speech supports this idea. Choice (D) provides the best evidence. This quote notes that women are discriminated against and that it is not just women who suffer from this discrimination; there are global problems that could benefit from women's ideas.

28. B   Difficulty: Hard

Category: Vocab-in-Context

Getting to the Answer: A word like "organized" can have several meanings, depending on the context. Beware of choosing the most common meaning, as it may not fit this situation. Choice (B) successfully conveys the idea of the women's suffrage movement being one in which many different people worked together over a long period of time.

29. B   Difficulty: Hard

Category: Rhetoric

Getting to the Answer: Be careful to assess not only what topics are mentioned but also how Clinton discusses them. Choice (B) is supported by the passage, which claims that "women must enjoy the right to participate fully in the social and political lives of their countries if we want freedom and democracy to thrive and endure."

30. D   Difficulty: Medium

Category: Rhetoric

Getting to the Answer: Notice how the stem of the question doesn't ask you to find evidence for an argument; it instead gives you the evidence (the example of V-J Day) and then asks you to figure out what argument this evidence supports. Choice (D) is correct. Clinton mentions V-J Day as an example of something that resulted from cooperation between men and women.

31. B   Difficulty: Medium

Category: Detail

Getting to the Answer: Pay close attention to the words Clinton uses in the cited lines to describe problems that affect women. Clinton states that the problems that "diminish the potential" (lines 43-44)

of women are "older" (line 42) and "deeply-rooted" (lines 42-43), making choice (B) the correct answer.

32. C   Difficulty: Medium

Category: Rhetoric

Getting to the Answer: Notice how the question is asking you to figure out how the paragraph functions in relation to other parts of the speech. Clinton goes into specific detail in this paragraph to provide examples of freedom. She very specifically states what she means by freedom and accuses some of failing to respect others' freedom. Therefore, choice (C) is the correct answer.

Suggested Passage Map notes:

¶1: MLK states why he is Birmingham, history of SCLC, in Birmingham due to injustice
¶2: MLK cannot let injustice continue, we are one people
¶3: MLK explains why peaceful protests are needed, benefits of tension to open negotiations
¶4: non-violent pressure only way to enact change
¶5: justice must be demanded by the oppressed

33. A   Difficulty: Medium

Category: Rhetoric

Getting to the Answer: Avoid answer choices that deal with related issues but do not address the main purpose of the letter. The passage as a whole addresses why King came to Birmingham, and then builds on his explanation for being in Birmingham to explore his cause. Choice (A) is correct.

34. A   Difficulty: Easy

Category: Command of Evidence

Getting to the Answer: Choose the answer that relates directly to the purpose you identified in the previous question. King begins the letter by stating "I think I should give the reason for my being in Birmingham," which clearly explains his purpose for writing the letter from the jail. Choice (A) is correct.

35. B   Difficulty: Medium

Category: Inference

Getting to the Answer: Determine whether the details in the passage and its title, which relate to how King was treated when he arrived in Birmingham, indicate a positive or negative reception. The title of the passage, "Letter from Birmingham Jail," indicates that King was incarcerated after his arrival in Birmingham. Furthermore, he is writing to an audience that considered him an "[outsider] coming in" (lines 3-4). It is reasonable to infer from these details that King received criticism for his decision to come to Birmingham; therefore, choice (B) is correct.

36. C   Difficulty: Easy

Category: Vocab-in-Context

Getting to the Answer: Read the complete sentence and the surrounding paragraph to best understand the meaning of the phrase within its greater context. In the paragraph, King goes on to explain that events in Birmingham must necessarily concern him. He states that an injustice in one place threatens justice everywhere, and even writes, "Whatever affects one directly affects all indirectly" (lines 30-31). This suggests that events in Birmingham affect people throughout the nation. Choice (C) is correct, as it explains that the "interrelatedness of all communities and states" refers to the idea that events in one part of the country affect the entire nation.

37. A   Difficulty: Easy

Category: Inference

Getting to the Answer: Predict King's opinions before reviewing the answer choices. The correct answer can be inferred directly from King's views as expressed in the paragraph. In this paragraph, King refers specifically to injustice and how it affects people everywhere. From this, you can most clearly infer that King considered circumstances in Birmingham to be unfair and wrong. Choice (A) is correct.

38. B   Difficulty: Easy

Category: Command of Evidence

Getting to the Answer: Review the answer to the previous question. Read the answer choices to identify the one whose rhetoric provides clear support for the inference. Although the entire paragraph provides general support and context for the inference, only choice (B) suggests that circumstances in Birmingham were unjust—that is, unfair and wrong.

39. B   Difficulty: Medium

Category: Vocab-in-Context

Getting to the Answer: Before viewing the answer choices, think about the purpose of the word in the sentence, and form an alternate explanation of the word. Then, identify the answer choice that best reflects that meaning and intent. King says that direct action in Birmingham aims to "dramatize the issue that it can no longer be ignored." This suggests that the issue, or events, in Birmingham are of great significance and demand attention that they have not received. Therefore, choice (B) is correct.

40. C   Difficulty: Hard

Category: Rhetoric

Getting to the Answer: Consider the overall thrust of King's argument in this paragraph. Choose the answer that encapsulates this idea. In paragraph 4, King responds to charges that activists should focus on negotiation, not direct action. He argues that direct action is needed to spur negotiations. King reasons that nonviolent protests create the tension between forces in society needed to bring people to the table to discuss the relevant issues of prejudice and racism. His claim in the paragraph is that direct action is needed to spur negotiation, making choice (C) correct.

41. D   Difficulty: Hard

Category: Rhetoric

Getting to the Answer: Identify an idea in paragraph 4 that provides clear support to the claim made in the previous paragraph. In paragraph 3, King claims that nonviolent direct action is needed to prompt negotiations on civil rights. In paragraph 4, he supports that argument by explaining that no gains have been made in civil rights without such nonviolent action, as choice (D) states.

42. D   Difficulty: Medium

Category: Rhetoric

Getting to the Answer: Read the complete paragraph to best understand the context and purpose of the cited line. The correct answer will identify what the phrase helps achieve in the paragraph. At the start of the paragraph, King argues that oppressors do not willingly give more freedom to the people whom they oppress. He goes on to explain the delay tactics that have kept African Americans from winning equal rights, and concludes that oppressed peoples in other nations are winning independence while African Americans still cannot get a cup of coffee at a lunch counter. The phrase helps King underscore the contrast between these two scenarios, so choice (D) is the correct answer.

Suggested Passage Map notes:

¶1: ER = v. important
¶2: early life; political involvement
¶3: nat'l and int'l work
¶4: ER changed role of 1st Lady
¶5: New Deal
¶6: many accomplishments
¶7: power with words
¶8: FDR died; ER joined UN
¶9: work at UN
¶10: accomplished beyond role of 1st Lady

43. B   Difficulty: Easy

Category: Vocab-in-Context

Getting to the Answer: The correct answer will flow naturally in place of the original word or phrase and maintain the meaning of the sentence. The text states that Eleanor Roosevelt "shouldered the nation's burdens" (lines 5-6). This means that she took responsibility for addressing, or handling, those burdens, as reflected by choice (B).

44. A   Difficulty: Medium

Category: Rhetoric

Getting to the Answer: Consider the author's point of view throughout the passage. The correct answer will be supported by the central idea of the text as well as by the passage's supporting details. The central idea of the passage focuses on Roosevelt's many achievements both as First Lady and in supporting human rights. The final paragraph summarizes her impact and showcases the respect that the author has for Roosevelt, as indicated in choice (A).

45. D   Difficulty: Medium

Category: Command of Evidence

Getting to the Answer: The correct answer will provide information and use rhetoric to support the central idea and tone of the answer to the previous question. The answer to the previous question asserts that the author holds admiration for Eleanor Roosevelt. Choice (D) identifies Eleanor Roosevelt as the object of love and reverence, and identifies the attributes (perseverance, integrity, and accomplishments) that merit admiration.

46. B   Difficulty: Hard

Category: Inference

Getting to the Answer: The correct answer will make sense in the larger context of the passage and will be supported by specific textual evidence. The passage notes that Eleanor Roosevelt "aided her husband in his development of the New Deal" (lines 53-54), Franklin Roosevelt's key legislative

CHAPTER THREE: HISTORY/SOCIAL STUDIES PASSAGES

policy. Further evidence asserts that Eleanor Roosevelt's contributions were "essential" (line 50) to President Roosevelt's "effective leadership" (line 51), as indicated in choice (B).

47. B   Difficulty: Medium

Category: Detail

Getting to the Answer: The correct answer will be clearly stated in one or more lines from the text. The text repeatedly discusses Roosevelt's advocacy for social justice work and human rights reform, as indicated in choice (B).

48. D   Difficulty: Hard

Category: Rhetoric

Getting to the Answer: The correct answer will reflect the direct intent of the information in the passage and will be supported by evidence throughout the text. Although the passage as a whole explores various contributions made by Eleanor Roosevelt, the excerpted line focuses on her humanitarian efforts during World War I, prior to her husband's rise to the presidency and her ascent to the role of First Lady. Therefore, choice (D) is correct, as it demonstrates that her humanitarian efforts began early in her life, a point argued throughout the passage.

49. B   Difficulty: Hard

Category: Synthesis

Getting to the Answer: The correct answer will be supported by and will connect information shown in the graph and expressed in the passage. The data in the graph show declining unemployment during the Great Depression following the passage of President Roosevelt's New Deal policies. The passage suggests that the New Deal policies made up President Roosevelt's signature effort to ease the troubles of the Great Depression, as stated in choice (B). The passage further suggests that Eleanor Roosevelt proved crucial to this important effort.

50. A   Difficulty: Medium

Category: Inference

Getting to the Answer: The correct answer will reflect Eleanor Roosevelt's ideas, actions, and sentiments as expressed in the passage. The passage focuses largely on the social justice, human rights, and humanitarian efforts of Eleanor Roosevelt, which would make her most likely to engage in choice (A).

51. B   Difficulty: Easy

Category: Command of Evidence

Getting to the Answer: The correct answer will provide direct support for the answer to the previous question by connecting central ideas or themes. The answer to the previous question states that Eleanor Roosevelt would be most likely to volunteer in a disaster response effort, a humanitarian undertaking. Choice (B) is correct, as it states that Eleanor Roosevelt made humanitarian work a lifelong pursuit.

52. C   Difficulty: Easy

Category: Vocab-in-Context

Getting to the Answer: The correct answer will reflect the specific meaning of the original word or phrase in the larger context of the sentence. The text states that Eleanor Roosevelt "spearheaded a small furniture business" (lines 67-68). This suggests that she led the growth of the business, as reflected by choice (C).

53. B   Difficulty: Hard

Category: Rhetoric

Getting to the Answer: The correct answer will reflect the main idea of the paragraph and will identify its role within the larger passage. The paragraph examines the contributions of Eleanor Roosevelt not only as First Lady but also as an individual before, during, and after her husband's presidency. Choice (B) emphasizes the accomplishments that Eleanor Roosevelt made following her husband's presidency.

CHAPTER FOUR

Science Passages

GETTING STARTED

The SAT Reading Test will contain either two single **Science** passages or one single Science passage and one set of paired **Science** passages. **Science** passages differ from other passage types because:

- They often contain a lot of jargon and technical terms.
- They can utilize unfamiliar terms and concepts.

While **Science** passages can be tricky due to unfamiliar language, you will never need to employ knowledge outside of the passage when answering questions.

Science passages are full of details and uncommon terminology. As you read a **Science** passage, you should make very short notes in the margin, also known as a Passage Map, so you can quickly locate information in the passage. Here is an effective strategy to identify the information that should be in your **Science** Passage Map:

1. Locate the central idea in the first paragraph
2. Note how each paragraph relates to the central idea. Does the paragraph . . .
   - Explain?
   - Support?
   - Refute?
   - Summarize?
3. Don't be distracted by jargon or technical terms
   - Unfamiliar terms will generally be defined within the passage or in a footnote.
4. Don't try to learn or thoroughly understand complicated scientific ideas
   - Note the *location* of detailed examples/explanations in your Passage Map.
   - Return to the location in the passage if you need the information for a question.

5. Summarize the purpose of the passage

- Some common purposes include: to inform, to refute, to promote, to explore, to compare.

- Note the author's tone. Were there any positive or negative keywords? If not, the author's tone is neutral.

- Pay particular attention to emphasis and opinion keywords. Science passages may discuss how newer studies have modified older theories or different views on a discovery. Keep careful track of the opinions, and be sure to identify the author's opinion.

> ✔ **Remember**
>
> **When you encounter more than one theory or idea, paraphrase each in as few words as possible in your Passage Map.**

IMPROVING WITH PRACTICE

Step 1: Compare Your Notes to the Suggested *Science* Passage Maps

Your **Science** Passage Maps may look different—even very different!—from the suggested Passage Maps. However, you should always compare your notes to the suggested Passage Maps to be sure you generally included the same important points. Some of the points you should include in your map are:

- the central idea/theory discussed
- the relationship of each paragraph to the central idea. Is the paragraph explaining, supporting, criticizing, modifying, or applying the central idea?
- any opinions, especially the author's
- the *location* of descriptive details and examples
- the *reason* the author included details and examples. Is the author using the information to support, modify, or refute the preceding idea?
- any emphasis or "emotional" keywords. Keywords such as "remarkable," "unfortunate," "unprecedented," and "crucial" are important indicators of the author's tone.

> ✔ **Expert Tip**
>
> **Note the location of explanations and examples so you can find them quickly if needed for a question.**

If your map is missing important information, or if you included far too much detail in your map, go back to the **Science** passage and identify the keywords and phrases that you likely overlooked the first time. Strong writing uses keywords to focus your attention as a reader, so use these keywords to create strong Passage Maps.

> ✔ *Remember*
>
> **Everything you need to answer the questions will be in the passage.**

Step 2: Answer the Questions

Now that you have a strong **Science** Passage Map, answer the questions one at a time, reviewing the Answer and Explanation for each question immediately after completing it. If you got the question correct, congratulate yourself; then, take a moment to read the entire explanation to be sure you got the question right for the right reason. You may even discover a more efficient way to answer a similar question in the future!

Step 3: Review Incorrect Answers

If you get the question incorrect . . . still congratulate yourself! You're about to learn something new that you'll be able to use to improve your performance on Test Day. Don't read the explanation yet; instead, try the question again.

If you get the question correct the second time, read the explanation to see if you solved the question in the most efficient way. Identify the mistake you made the first time, and determine how you're going to avoid making that mistake again.

> ✔ *Expert Tip*
>
> **Many top scoring students have an SAT notebook where they write down what they learn from every question. Doing this can be time-consuming, but it can also help you identify the types of mistakes you tend to make.**

If you get the question incorrect the second time, use the explanation to learn how to get the question correct. Work through the question again while following the explanation, and identify the steps you will need to take to get a similar question correct. Although the passages and questions will change, the concepts being tested will not. When you encounter unfamiliar questions, take note of them for future study sessions.

> ✔ *Remember*
>
> **The SAT is a standardized test. While Hard Reading questions are usually more difficult to answer than Easy or Medium questions, they are often similar in structure and purpose, and the same four skills (listed in Chapter 1) are tested on every Reading Test. You actually can predict the types of questions you will see on Test Day!**

After all that work, it's time to move to the next question. Reviewing in this way will take time. However, improvement doesn't come from just doing lots and lots of questions; it comes from thinking through your approach and improving it with every question.

RAISING YOUR SCORE EVEN MORE

Reading strategically is crucial in **Science** passages. You can lose a lot of time if you try to learn unfamiliar scientific ideas presented in a passage and then discover that there are no questions asking about those ideas. The only reason you're reading these passages is to answer the questions correctly, and by far, most of the questions will ask about the main ideas and the organization of the passage. Reviewing and studying the questions to learn which parts of the passage were tested, and how they were tested, will help you to learn to read **Science** passages strategically.

PRACTICE QUESTIONS

The following test-like question sets provide an opportunity to practice reading Science Passages and answering related questions.

Questions 1-11 are based on the following passage.

This passage is adapted from an article about treating paralysis.

According to a study conducted by the Christopher and Dana Reeve Foundation, more than six million people in the United
Line States suffer from debilitating paralysis. That's
(5) close to one person in every fifty who suffers from a loss of the ability to move or feel in areas of his or her body. Paralysis is often caused by illnesses, such as stroke or multiple sclerosis, or injuries to the spinal cord. Research
(10) scientists have made advances in the treatment of paralysis, which means retraining affected individuals to become as independent as possible. Patients learn how to use wheelchairs and prevent complications that are caused by
(15) restricted movement. This retraining is key in maintaining paralytics' quality of life; however, an actual cure for paralysis has remained elusive—until now.

In 2014, surgeons in Poland collaborated
(20) with the University College London's Institute of Neurology to treat a Polish man who was paralyzed from the chest down as a result of a spinal cord injury. The scientists chose this patient for their study because of the countless
(25) hours of physical therapy he had undergone with no signs of progress. Twenty-one months after their test subject's initial spinal cord injury, his condition was considered complete as defined by the American Spinal Injury Asso-
(30) ciation (ASIA)'s Impairment Scale. This meant that he experienced no sensory or motor function in the segments of his spinal cord nearest to his injury.

The doctors used a technique refined during
(35) forty years of spinal cord research on rats. They removed one of two of the patient's olfactory bulbs, which are structures found at the top of the human nose. From this structure, samples of olfactory ensheathing cells,
(40) responsible for a portion of the sense of smell, were harvested. These cells allow the olfactory system to renew its cells over the course of a human life. It is because of this constant regeneration that scientists chose these particular
(45) cells to implant into the patient's spinal cord. After being harvested, the cells were reproduced in a culture. Then, the cells were injected into the patient's spinal cord in 100 mini-injections above and below the location
(50) of his injury. Four strips of nerve tissue were then placed across a small gap in the spinal cord.

After surgery, the patient underwent a tailor-made neurorehabilitation program. In
(55) the nineteen months following the operation, not only did the patient experience no adverse effects, but his condition improved from ASIA's class A to class C. Class C is considered an incomplete spinal cord injury, meaning that
(60) motor function is preserved to a certain extent and there is some muscle activity. The patient experienced increased stability in the trunk of his body, as well as partial recovery of voluntary movements in his lower extremities. As a
(65) result, he was able to increase the muscle mass in his thighs and regain sensation in those areas. In late 2014, he took his first steps with the support of only a walker.

These exciting improvements suggest that
(70) the nerve grafts doctors placed in the patient's

spinal cord bridged the injured area and prompted the regeneration of fibers. This was the first-ever clinical study that showed beneficial effects of cells transplanted into the spinal (75) cord. The same team of scientists plans to treat ten more patients using this "smell cell" transplant technique. If they have continued success, patients around the world can have both their mobility and their hope restored.

1. The passage is primarily concerned with

   A) how various diseases and injuries can cause permanent paralysis.

   B) ways in which doctors and therapists work to improve patients' quality of life.

   C) one treatment being developed to return mobility to patients suffering paralysis.

   D) methods of physical therapy that can help patients with spinal cord injuries.

2. The author includes a description of retraining paralytics in lines 9-15 primarily to

   A) describe how people with paralysis cope with everyday tasks.

   B) appeal to the reader's sympathies for people with paralysis.

   C) show that most research scientists do not believe a cure can be found.

   D) help readers appreciate the significance of research that may lead to a cure.

3. Based on the information in the passage, it can be inferred that the author

   A) believes more research should be done before patients with paralysis are subjected to the treatment described in the passage.

   B) feels that increased mobility will have a positive impact on patients suffering from all levels of paralysis.

   C) thinks that more scientists should study paralysis and ways to improve the quality of life for patients with limited mobility.

   D) was part of the research team that developed the new method of treating paralysis described in the passage.

4. Which choice provides the best support for the answer to the previous question?

   A) Lines 7-9 ("Paralysis is . . . spinal cord")

   B) Lines 19-23 ("In 2014 . . . injury")

   C) Lines 61-64 ("The patient . . . extremities")

   D) Lines 77-79 ("If they . . . restored")

5. As used in line 15, "restricted" most nearly means

   A) confidential.

   B) dependent.

   C) increased.

   D) limited.

6. In line 54, the author's use of the word "tailor-made" helps reinforce the idea that

   A) the injected cells were from the patient and were therefore well-suited to work in his own body.

   B) spinal cord cells were replaced during the transplant portion of the individualized treatment.

   C) olfactory bulbs were removed from rats and placed in the patient's spinal cord during surgery.

   D) the method used by doctors to locate the damaged area required expertise and precision.

7. It can reasonably be inferred from the passage that

   A) the patient's treatment would have been more successful if scientists had used cells from another area of his body instead of from his olfactory bulbs.

   B) cells from olfactory bulbs will be used to cure diseases that affect areas of the body other than the spinal cord.

   C) the patient who received the experimental treatment using cells from olfactory bulbs would not have regained mobility without this treatment.

   D) soon doctors will be able to treat spinal injuries without time-consuming and demanding physical therapy.

8. Which choice provides the best evidence for the answer to the previous question?

   A) Lines 9-13 ("Research scientists . . . possible")

   B) Lines 23-26 ("The scientists . . . progress")

   C) Lines 36-38 ("They removed . . . nose")

   D) Lines 69-72 ("These exciting . . . fibers")

9. As used in line 34, "refined" most nearly means

   A) advanced.

   B) improved.

   C) experienced.

   D) treated.

10. The success of the patient's treatment was due in large part to

    A) studies done on other patients.

    B) research conducted by other doctors in Poland.

    C) many experiments performed on rats.

    D) multiple attempts on various types of animals.

11. The procedure described in which cells from olfactory bulbs are injected into a damaged area of the spinal cord is most analogous to which of the following?

    A) Replacing a diseased organ in a patient with an organ from a donor who has the same tissue type

    B) Giving a patient with a high fever an injection of medication to bring the core body temperature down

    C) Placing a cast on a limb to hold the bone in place to encourage healing after suffering a break

    D) Grafting skin from a healthy area of the body and transplanting it to an area that has suffered severe burns

Questions 12-22 are based on the following passage.

The following passage details the antibody that produces peanut allergies and how scientists are using this information to develop a peanut that does not cause allergic reactions.

Peanuts can cause deadly allergic reactions in some people, and there is no real cure for peanut allergies. However, scientists may be
Line working on the next best thing to a cure:
(5) peanuts that do not cause allergic reactions.

Allergic reactions start with the immune system, which normally works to keep us healthy. The immune system recognizes dangerous materials, such as poisons and viruses,
(10) and reacts to keep the materials from harming the rest of the body. Some of these reactions, such as swelling of nose and throat tissues, keep the materials from moving farther through the body. Other reactions, such as
(15) producing mucus and coughing, help expel the foreign materials. Unfortunately, too much swelling, mucus, or coughing make it hard to breathe and can even be life-threatening.

People who are allergic to peanuts produce
(20) an antibody called IgE that combines with a specific part of the peanut protein. The IgE-protein complex then alerts the immune system and the reactions begin. Once the allergic person's throat starts swelling, that person
(25) will need immediate medical treatment to reduce the risk of injury or death.

People who are allergic to peanuts must avoid them, and avoiding peanuts can be very hard to do. Many popular fast foods contain
(30) peanuts or peanut oil, or have been made using machines that also handle peanuts. Some very sensitive people cannot even be in the same room where peanuts are being eaten. This can be very difficult for children, and
(35) many allergic children cannot safely eat lunch in their own school cafeteria.

Some scientists wondered if they could find a way to change the allergen, the part of the peanut protein that causes the allergic reac-
(40) tion, to keep IgE from combining with it. They first needed to measure the amount of reaction caused by untreated peanuts. Measuring how much of an allergic reaction the peanuts caused in people would not be safe, so they in-
(45) stead measured how much IgE combined with the peanut protein in a laboratory test. They found that frying and boiling peanuts reduced the amount of reaction, as compared to raw peanuts. However, frying and boiling do not
(50) reduce the amount of antibody reaction to a safe amount, so scientists tried other treatments. Some of the treatments, such as high heat for long periods of time, changed the taste of the peanuts too much.
(55) One treatment that showed promise was exposing the peanuts to very strong light. The light used by the scientists is similar to normal sunlight, but thousands of times stronger. By "pulsing" the light, or producing the light in
(60) short bursts, the scientists hoped to avoid heating the peanuts to the point where the taste changed while still deactivating the allergens in the peanuts.

In one experiment, the scientists exposed
(65) the peanuts to 3 pulses of light per second for different amounts of time. They then extracted the protein from the peanuts. To measure the amount of allergens left in the peanut protein, they coated a special plastic plate with the
(70) extracted protein. Next, they added blood plasma that contained the IgE antibodies. When they washed the plasma off the plate, the IgE antibodies that combined with the allergen part of the protein remained stuck to
(75) the plate. They then added other chemicals that combined with the IgE antibodies and

produced a dark blue color; the darker the blue, the more IgE antibodies remained. Blood also contains very small amounts of other
(80) antibodies that will stick to the plate, so the same test on blood from a non-allergic person would still produce a small amount of blue color. To account for this, the scientists used blood plasma that did not have any IgE
(85) antibodies as a negative control. They then compared the darkness of all of the samples to the darkness of the negative control.

From the results, it appears that the scientists can change the peanut allergens so that
(90) the reaction in an allergic person is about the same as in a non-allergic person. The next steps will be to test the peanuts on humans: first by testing for reactions on the skin of allergic people, and then by having allergic peo-
(95) ple eat the peanuts while being monitored for any reaction. Eventually, the scientists hope, they will have a treatment that will make a safe peanut, which will make eating a much safer and simpler experience for many.

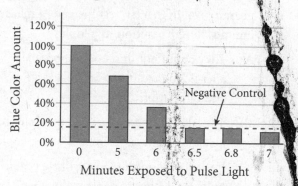

Results of allergen measurements for peanuts exposed to pulsed light for different amounts of time.

Adapted from Xingyu Zhao, "Effect of Pulsed Light on Allergenic Proteins of Shelled Whole Peanuts." ©2013.

12. As used in line 15, "expel" most nearly means

A) dismiss.

B) eject.

C) emit.

D) separate.

13. The passage most strongly suggests that

A) exposure to peanut proteins can be potentially fatal for almost anyone.

B) a peanut allergy is caused by a compromised or weakened immune system.

C) anyone who wishes to avoid developing a peanut allergy should avoid all peanut products.

D) the body of a person allergic to peanuts sees the peanut protein as a dangerous invader.

14. Which choice provides the best evidence for the answer to the previous question?

A) Lines 6-11 ("Allergic reactions . . . body")

B) Lines 27-29 ("People who are . . . hard to do")

C) Lines 37-40 ("Some scientists . . . combining with it")

D) Lines 96-99 ("Eventually . . . for many")

15. Based on the information in the passage, how does an allergic reaction compare to a normal immune system response to a dangerous material?

A) An allergic reaction is milder than a normal immune system response and is usually shorter in duration.

B) A normal immune system response is characterized by the body's producing mucus and coughing, while an allergic reaction makes it difficult to breathe.

C) A normal immune system response is milder than an allergic response, but the allergic response is triggered by a material that is dangerous.

D) An allergic reaction is similar to a normal immune system response, but the response can be stronger and cause life-threatening symptoms.

16. According to paragraph 4, people with peanut allergies

    A) will likely encounter peanut allergens on a daily basis.

    B) are more likely to have other allergies than people without a peanut allergy.

    C) will prefer the taste of peanuts with deactivated allergens.

    D) have a difficult time avoiding peanut allergens.

17. Which choice provides the best evidence for the answer to the previous question?

    A) Lines 3-5 ("However, scientists . . . allergic reactions")

    B) Lines 34-36 ("This can be . . . school cafeteria")

    C) Lines 52-54 ("Some of the treatments . . . too much")

    D) Lines 88-91 ("From the results . . . a non-allergic person")

18. As used in line 62, "deactivating" most nearly means

    A) restricting.

    B) hindering.

    C) disabling.

    D) arresting.

19. It can be reasonably inferred from both the evidence in the passage and the data in the graph that

    A) of the peanuts tested, those exposed to pulses of light for the shortest periods of time contained the lowest amounts of the protein that acts as an allergen.

    B) of the peanuts tested, those exposed to pulses of light for the longest periods of time contained the lowest amounts of the protein that acts as an allergen.

    C) of the peanuts tested, those exposed to pulses of light for the longest periods of time contained the highest amounts of the protein that acts as an allergen.

    D) the amount of time a peanut was exposed to pulses of light had little to no effect on the amounts of the protein that acts as an allergen.

20. According to the passage, why did scientists measure how much IgE combined with peanut protein in a lab test instead of measuring the allergic reaction in people?

    A) They could not find enough people allergic to peanuts to create a large enough sample.

    B) The lab tests gave more accurate and reliable data than experiments with people.

    C) It would be unsafe to provoke a potentially fatal allergic response in a person.

    D) The scientists conducted tests on people before the lab tests began.

21. Paragraphs 6 and 7 can best be described as

    A) a suggestion for how scientists can more productively study how people who are allergic to peanuts are affected by the IgE antibodies.

    B) a description of how some treatments of peanuts aimed at deactivating the allergens in peanuts affect the taste of the peanut.

    C) a summary of one method of treating peanuts scientists hope can reduce the allergic response in people who are allergic to peanuts.

    D) an explanation of how the chemical structure of peanuts can be altered by small genetic changes to the plant.

22. The purpose of the last paragraph is to

    A) describe the next steps scientists might take toward creating a safer environment for peanut allergy sufferers.

    B) persuade the reader to learn more about peanut allergies and how scientists are working to help those who suffer from allergies.

    C) explain how future experiments on peanut proteins could provide clues to helping people who suffer from other food allergies.

    D) summarize the results of the experiments on peanuts described in detail throughout the passage.

Questions 23-33 are based on the following passage.

The following passage is adapted from an article about the Spinosaurus, a theropod dinosaur that lived during the Cretaceous period.

At long last, paleontologists have solved a century-old mystery, piecing together information discovered by scientists from different
Line times and places.
(5)   The mystery began when, in 1911, German paleontologist Ernst Stromer discovered the first evidence of dinosaurs having lived in Egypt. Stromer, who expected to encounter fossils of early mammals, instead found bones
(10) that dated back to the Cretaceous period, some 97 to 112 million years prior. His finding consisted of three large bones, which he preserved and transported back to Germany for examination. After careful consideration, he an-
(15) nounced that he had discovered a new genus of sauropod, or a large, four-legged herbivore with a long neck. He called the genus Aegyptosaurus, which is Greek for Egyptian lizard. One of these Aegyptosaurs, he claimed, was
(20) the Spinosaurus. Tragically, the fossils that supported his claim were destroyed during a raid on Munich by the Royal Air Force during World War II. The scientific world was left with Stromer's notes and sketches, but no hard
(25) evidence that the Spinosaurus ever existed.
It was not until 2008, when a cardboard box of bones was delivered to paleontologist Nizar Ibrahim by a nomad in Morocco's Sahara desert, that a clue to solving the mystery was re-
(30) vealed. Intrigued, Ibrahim took the bones to a university in Casablanca for further study. One specific bone struck him as interesting, as it contained a red line coursing through it. The following year, Ibrahim and his colleagues at
(35) Italy's Milan Natural History Museum were looking at bones that resembled the ones delivered the year before. An important clue

was hidden in the cross-section they were examining, as it contained the same red line
(40) Ibrahim had seen in Morocco. Against all odds, the Italians were studying bones that belonged to the very same skeleton as the bones Ibrahim received in the desert. Together, these bones make up the partial skeleton of the very
(45) first Spinosaurus that humans have been able to discover since Stromer's fossils were destroyed.
Ibrahim and his colleagues published a study describing the features of the dinosaur,
(50) which point to the Spinosaurus being the first known swimming dinosaur. At 36 feet long, this particular Spinosaurus had long front legs and short back legs, each with a paddle-shaped foot and claws that suggest a carnivorous diet.
(55) These features made the dinosaur a deft swimmer and excellent hunter, able to prey on large river fish.
Scientists also discovered significant aquatic adaptations that made the Spinosaurus unique
(60) compared to dinosaurs that lived on land but ate fish. Similar to a crocodile, the Spinosaurus had a long snout, with nostrils positioned so that the dinosaur could breathe while part of its head was submerged in water. Unlike pred-
(65) atory land dinosaurs, the Spinosaurus had powerful front legs. The weight of these legs would have made walking upright like a Tyrannosaurus Rex impossible, but in water, its strong legs gave the Spinosaurus the
(70) power it needed to swim quickly and hunt fiercely. Most notable, though, was the discovery of the Spinosaurus's massive sail. Made up of dorsal spines, the sail was mostly meant for display.
(75)   Ibrahim and his fellow researchers used both modern digital modeling programs and Stromer's basic sketches to create and mount a life-size replica of the Spinosaurus skeleton.

The sketches gave them a starting point, and
(80) by arranging and rearranging the excavated
fossils they had in their possession, they were
able to use technology to piece together hypothetical bone structures until the mystery of
this semiaquatic dinosaur finally emerged
(85) from the murky depths of the past.

23. Which of the following best summarizes the
    central idea of this passage?

    A) Paleontologists were able to identify a
       new genus of dinosaur after overcoming
       a series of obstacles.

    B) Most dinosaur fossils are found in pieces
       and must be reconstructed using the lat-
       est technology.

    C) The first evidence of the Spinosaurus was
       uncovered by German paleontologist
       Ernst Stromer.

    D) Fossils of an aquatic dinosaur called the
       Spinosaurus were first found in Egypt in
       the early twentieth century.

24. According to the passage, the fossils Stromer
    found in the Egyptian desert were

    A) younger and smaller than he expected.

    B) younger and larger than he expected.

    C) older and smaller than he expected.

    D) older and larger than he expected.

25. Based on the information in the passage, the
    author would most likely agree that

    A) aquatic dinosaurs were more vicious than
       dinosaurs that lived on land.

    B) too much emphasis is placed on creating
       realistic models of ancient dinosaurs.

    C) most mysteries presented by randomly
       found fossils are unlikely to be solved.

    D) the study of fossils and ancient life pro-
       vides important scientific insights.

26. Which choice provides the best evidence for
    the answer to the previous question?

    A) Lines 14-17 ("After careful . . . long neck")

    B) Lines 58-61 ("Scientists also . . . ate fish")

    C) Lines 64-66 ("Unlike . . . front legs")

    D) Lines 79-85 ("The sketches . . . past")

27. As used in lines 40-41, the phrase "against all
    odds" most nearly means

    A) by contrast.

    B) at the exact same time.

    C) to their dismay.

    D) despite low probability.

28. The author uses the phrases "deft swimmer"
    and "excellent hunter" in lines 55-56 to

    A) produce a clear visual image of the
       Spinosaurus.

    B) show how the Spinosaurus searched for
       prey.

    C) create an impression of a graceful but
       powerful animal.

    D) emphasize the differences between
       aquatic and land dinosaurs.

29. The information presented in the passage
    strongly suggests that Ibrahim

    A) chose to go into the field of paleontology
       after reading Stromer's work.

    B) was familiar with Stromer's work when
       he found the fossils with the red lines.

    C) did not have the proper training to solve
       the mystery of the Spinosaurus on his
       own.

    D) went on to study other aquatic dinosaurs
       after completing his research on the
       Spinosaurus.

30. Which choice provides the best evidence for the answer to the previous question?

    A) Lines 26-30 ("It was . . . revealed")

    B) Lines 48-51 ("Ibrahim . . . swimming dinosaur")

    C) Lines 58-61 ("Scientists . . . ate fish")

    D) Lines 75-78 ("Ibrahim and his fellow researchers . . . skeleton")

31. As used in lines 82-83, "hypothetical" most nearly means

    A) imaginary.

    B) actual.

    C) possible.

    D) interesting.

32. Which statement best describes the relationship between Stromer's and Ibrahim's work with fossils?

    A) Stromer's work was dependent on Ibrahim's work.

    B) Stromer's work was contradicted by Ibrahim's work.

    C) Ibrahim's work built on Stromer's work.

    D) Ibrahim's work copied Stromer's work.

33. Which of the following is most similar to the methods used by Ibrahim to create a life-size replica of the Spinosaurus?

    A) An architect using computer software and drawings to create a scale model of a building

    B) A student building a model rocket from a kit in order to demonstrate propulsion

    C) A doctor using a microscope to study microorganisms unable to be seen with the naked eye

    D) A marine biologist creating an artificial reef in an aquarium to study fish

Questions 34-44 are based on the following passage and supplementary material.

The following passage discusses the interactions between sickle cell disease and malaria and their implications.

Sickle cell disease affects millions of people throughout the world, and it affects about 1 in 500 African Americans. It is the most common
Line inherited blood disorder in America. The dis-
(5) ease causes severe illness and shortens a person's life span if not treated. However, it is much more common than other disorders because it also has a surprising helpful side effect.

Sickle cell disease is caused by a small muta-
(10) tion in a gene that carries the instructions to make hemoglobin, the protein in red blood cells that helps carry oxygen. Hemoglobin, like all proteins, is made from amino acids strung together like a chain in a certain sequence. The
(15) gene's instructions indicate which amino acids to include and their sequence in the hemoglobin chain. The mutation in the gene changes the instructions and substitutes a different amino acid at one point in the sequence,
(20) thereby changing the properties of the hemoglobin protein. The hemoglobin then tends to stick together and form long, thin structures. The structures grow long enough to push the red blood cell out of shape, forming a curved
(25) sickle-like shape that gives the disease its name.

The sickle-shaped red blood cells wear out faster than normal red blood cells, so a person with the disease often has a low red blood cell
(30) count. With fewer red blood cells, that person does not get enough oxygen in the blood, causing weakness and exhaustion. The cells also tend to get stuck in the smaller blood vessels, causing pain and tissue damage.

(35) We each receive two copies of the hemoglobin gene, one from each parent. A person with sickle cell disease receives the sickle cell gene

from both parents and consequently produces no normal hemoglobin. A person who receives
(40) only one sickle cell gene will produce both normal and abnormal hemoglobin. This person will not have sickle cell disease but will carry the gene for it. Red blood cells in people who carry the gene do not normally form the
(45) sickle shape. Carriers turn out to have an unusual advantage over people who have two normal copies of the gene: they are better able to survive malaria.

Malaria is a disease caused by a parasite that
(50) invades red blood cells. It can be deadly, especially in young children. People who survive malaria infections gain a certain amount of immunity against future infections. After a few infections, their immune system is able to
(55) recognize and destroy the parasites. When a parasite invades a red blood cell of a carrier, the cell forms the sickle shape. Since the sickle-shaped cells wear out rapidly, the parasite is destroyed with the cell soon after invad-
(60) ing. The immune system removes the worn out cells and recognizes the parasite, so it starts to attack the parasite even before it invades the red blood cells. The carrier is then more likely to survive the infection and also gains resis-
(65) tance to future infections.

It is therefore not surprising that the gene for sickle cell anemia is found mainly in people whose ancestors come from parts of the world in which malaria is common. People living in
(70) these areas have an increased chance of survival if they are carriers of the sickle cell gene and so are more likely to live long enough to pass the gene on to their children. Therefore, although people with two copies of the gene
(75) were likely to die of the disease before they could pass it on, the gene still became common because of the benefit to the carriers. Because modern medicine has treatments for

both malaria and sickle cell disease, neither
(80) disease is as dangerous as it once was. Scientists hope to wipe out malaria in the future. The gene for sickle cell disease, however, being a part of the human gene pool, will persist.

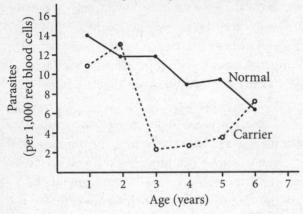

Malaria Parasites in Blood of Children Living in a High-Malaria Area

Adapted from Lucio Luzzatto, "Sickle Cell Anemia and Malaria."

34. The central idea of the passage is that sickle cell disease and malaria are

    A) both serious conditions that are untreatable.

    B) likely to be wiped out in the future.

    C) related in an unexpected way.

    D) similar to one another in the way they develop.

35. The passage most strongly suggests that which of the following is true?

    A) Malaria is often the result of poor nutrition.

    B) Sickle cell disease can be caught through exposure to it.

    C) Malaria is found in the southern states of the United States.

    D) Sickle cell disease is a major threat for African Americans.

36. Which choice provides the best evidence for the answer to the previous question?

    A) Lines 1-3 ("Sickle cell . . . African Americans")

    B) Lines 9-12 ("Sickle cell . . . carry oxygen")

    C) Lines 27-30 ("The sickle-shaped red . . . cell count")

    D) Lines 49-51 ("Malaria . . . young children")

37. As used in lines 9-10, "mutation" most nearly means

    A) failure.

    B) change.

    C) structure.

    D) process.

38. According to the passage, which of the following is most likely true?

    A) It is better to have one sickle cell gene than to have two.

    B) It is difficult to understand the relationship between sickle cell disease and malaria.

    C) People who suffer from malaria are also sickle cell gene carriers.

    D) People who have sickle cell disease have higher rates of malaria.

39. Which choice provides the best evidence for the answer to the previous question?

    A) Lines 6-8 ("However, it is . . . side effect")

    B) Lines 23-26 ("The structures . . . its name")

    C) Lines 41-45 ("This person . . . sickle shape")

    D) Lines 36-43 ("A person . . . gene for it")

40. Which claim in the passage is supported by the graphic?

A) Children are more likely to develop malaria than adults are.

B) Carriers of the sickle cell gene are prone to getting other diseases.

C) Children should receive treatment for sickle cell disease as early as three years old.

D) Carriers of the sickle cell gene are less likely to get malaria.

41. As used in line 83, "pool" most nearly means

A) puddle.

B) lake.

C) group.

D) team.

42. According to the passage, why do people with sickle cell disease often have a low red blood cell count?

A) They are more easily exposed to the malaria parasite.

B) They have two copies of the hemoglobin gene.

C) Sickle cell blood cells are inherited from parents.

D) Sickle cell blood cells wear out faster than normal red blood cells.

43. Why does the author use the word "surprising" in line 8?

A) To suggest that malaria is an unpredictable disease

B) To pique the interest of the reader

C) To give an insight into the author's point of view

D) To help the reader better understand what malaria is

44. The purpose of this passage is to

A) instruct the reader about the connection between sickle cell disease and malaria.

B) explain how red blood cells are affected by sickle cell disease.

C) show that malaria and sickle cell disease are usually diagnosed easily.

D) discuss the differences in treatment for sickle cell disease and malaria.

Questions 45-54 are based on the following passage and supplementary material.

The following passage is adapted from an essay about mercury in fish.

Mercury is an unusual element; it is a metal but is liquid at room temperature. It is also a neurotoxin and a teratogen, as it causes nerve
Line damage and birth defects. Mercury can be
(5) found just about everywhere; it is in soil, in air, in household items, and even in our food. Everyday objects, such as thermometers, light switches, and fluorescent light bulbs, contain mercury in its elemental form. Batteries can
(10) also contain mercury, but they contain it in the form of the inorganic compound mercury chloride. Mercury can also exist as an organic compound, the most common of which is methylmercury. While we can take steps to
(15) avoid both elemental and inorganic mercury, it is much harder to avoid methylmercury.

Most of the mercury in the environment comes from the emissions of coal-burning power plants; coal contains small amounts of
(20) mercury, which are released into the air when coal burns. The concentration of mercury in the air from power plants is very low, so it is not immediately dangerous. However, the mercury is then washed out of the air by rain-
(25) storms and eventually ends up in lakes and oceans.

The mercury deposited in the water does not instantaneously get absorbed by fish, as elemental mercury does not easily diffuse
(30) through cell membranes. However, methyl-mercury diffuses into cells easily, and certain anaerobic bacteria in the water convert the elemental mercury to methylmercury as a byproduct of their metabolic processes.
(35) Methylmercury released into the water by the bacteria diffuses into small single-celled

organisms called plankton. Small shrimp and other small animals eat the plankton and ab-sorb the methylmercury in the plankton dur-
(40) ing digestion. Small fish eat the shrimp and then larger fish eat the smaller fish; each time an animal preys on another animal, the preda-tor absorbs the methylmercury. Because each animal excretes the methylmercury much
(45) more slowly than it absorbs it, methylmercury builds up in the animal over time and is passed on to whatever animal eats it, resulting in a process called bioaccumulation.

As people became aware of the bioaccumu-
(50) lation of mercury in fish, many reacted by eliminating seafood from their diet. However, seafood contains certain omega-3 fatty acids that are important for good health. People who do not eat enough of these fatty acids, espe-
(55) cially eicosapentaenoic acid (EPA) and doco-sahexaenoic acid (DHA), are more likely to have heart attacks than people who have enough EPA and DHA in their diet. Because fish and shellfish, along with some algae, are
(60) the only sources of these fatty acids, eliminat-ing them from our diet might have worse health effects than consuming small amounts of mercury.

Scientists have studied the effects of mer-
(65) cury by conducting tests on animals and by studying various human populations and re-cording the amount of mercury in their blood. By determining the levels of mercury con-sumption that cause any of the known symp-
(70) toms of mercury poisoning, they were able to identify a safe level of mercury consumption. The current recommendation is for humans to take in less than 0.1 microgram of mercury for every kilogram of weight per day. This means
(75) that a 70-kilogram person (about 155 pounds)

could safely consume 7 micrograms of mercury per day. Because haddock averages about 0.055 micrograms of mercury per gram, that person could safely eat 127 grams (about
(80) 4.5 ounces) of haddock per day. On the other hand, swordfish averages about 0.995 micrograms of mercury per gram of fish, so the 70-kilogram person could safely eat only about 7 grams (about one-quarter of an ounce) of
(85) swordfish per day.

Nutritionists recommend that, rather than eliminate fish from our diet, we try to eat more of the low-mercury fish and less of the high-mercury fish. Low-mercury species tend to be
(90) smaller omnivorous fish while high-mercury species tend to be the largest carnivorous fish. Awareness of the particulars of this problem, accompanied by mindful eating habits, will keep us on the best course for healthy eating.

Species	Average Weight Range (grams)	Average Mercury Concentration (parts per billion)
Alaskan Pollock	227–1,000	31
Atlantic Haddock	900–1,800	55
Atlantic Herring	100–600	84
Chub Mackerel	100–750	88
Cod	800–4,000	111
Skipjack Tuna	2,000–10,000	144
Black-Striped Bass	6,820–15,900	152
Albacore Tuna	4,540–21,364	358
Marlin	180,000	485

45. The author of the passage would most likely agree with which of the following statements?

A) Mercury poisoning is only one of many concerns that should be considered when choosing which fish to add to one's diet.

B) More should be done by scientists and nutritionists to inform people about the dangers of mercury poisoning.

C) Fish is an essential part of a healthy diet and can be eaten safely if recommendations for mercury consumption are kept in mind.

D) The mercury present in the air is more dangerous to people than the mercury consumed by eating fish with high mercury levels.

46. Which choice provides the best evidence for the answer to the previous question?

A) Lines 17-19 ("Most of . . . plants")

B) Lines 35-37 ("Methylmercury released . . . plankton")

C) Lines 64-67 ("Scientists . . . their blood")

D) Lines 92-94 ("Awareness . . . eating")

47. In addition to the levels of mercury in a specific species of fish, people should also consider which of the following when determining a safe level of consumption?

A) Their own body weight

B) Where the fish was caught

C) The other meats they are eating

D) What they ate the day before

48. As used in line 21, "concentration" most nearly means

   A) focus.

   B) application.

   C) density.

   D) awareness.

49. The passage most strongly suggests which of the following statements is accurate?

   A) It is not possible to completely avoid environmental exposure to mercury.

   B) Inorganic mercury is more dangerous to humans than organic mercury.

   C) Most of the exposure to mercury experienced by humans comes from fish consumption.

   D) Mercury is one of the most abundant elements found in nature.

50. Which choice provides the best evidence for the answer to the previous question?

   A) Lines 1-2 ("Mercury is an unusual . . . temperature")

   B) Lines 4-6 ("Mercury . . . our food")

   C) Lines 21-23 ("The concentration . . . dangerous")

   D) Lines 30-34 ("However, methylmercury . . . processes")

51. The main purpose of paragraph 3 is to explain

   A) the reasons why mercury deposited in water is not harmful to fish.

   B) the relationships between predators and prey in aquatic animals.

   C) how the largest fish accumulate the greatest amounts of mercury.

   D) the difference between methylmercury and other types of mercury.

52. Which of the following pieces of evidence would most strengthen the author's line of reasoning?

   A) More examples in paragraph 1 of places mercury is found

   B) Details in paragraph 2 about the levels of mercury found in the air

   C) An explanation in paragraph 4 of how to treat mercury poisoning

   D) More examples in paragraph 5 of how many micrograms of mercury people of different weights could eat

53. As used in line 92, "particulars" most nearly means

   A) data.

   B) specifics.

   C) points.

   D) evidence.

54. Based on the information in the passage and the graphic, which of the following statements is true?

   A) The fish with the lowest average weight is the safest to eat.

   B) A person can safely eat more marlin than albacore tuna in one day.

   C) Eating large fish carries a lower risk of mercury poisoning than eating small fish.

   D) A person can safely eat more Alaskan pollock than black striped bass in one day.

ANSWERS AND EXPLANATIONS

CHAPTER 4

Suggested Passage Map notes:

¶1: six million US people paralyzed; causes of paralysis

¶2: patient in Poland became subject of study

¶3: spinal cord research on rats, now used to develop treatment

¶4: patient responded well to treatment

¶5: future benefits of treatment

1. C Difficulty: Easy

Category: Global

Getting to the Answer: Keep in mind that the correct answer will be supported by all of the information in the text rather than just a few details. The passage is concerned with one experimental treatment that doctors are exploring to help paralyzed patients regain mobility. Choice (C) is the correct answer.

2. D Difficulty: Medium

Category: Rhetoric

Getting to the Answer: Review the cited lines to determine how the information they present affects the reader's perception of the information that follows in the passage. Just after describing how the treatment of paralytics consists of retraining, the author informs the reader that a cure may be in sight. The description of retraining helps the reader understand that finding a cure is a significant leap forward. Choice (D) is correct.

3. B Difficulty: Medium

Category: Inference

Getting to the Answer: Consider the main points the author makes throughout the passage. The correct answer will be directly related to these points, even if it is not directly stated in the passage. Choice (B) is the

correct answer. It can be inferred that the author feels that increased mobility will have a positive impact on patients suffering from all levels of paralysis.

4. D Difficulty: Easy

Category: Command of Evidence

Getting to the Answer: Locate each answer choice in the passage. Decide which one provides the best support for the answer to the previous question. In the last line of the passage, the author says that paralyzed patients "can have both their mobility and their hope restored" (lines 78-79). This answer, choice (D), offers the strongest support for the answer to the previous question.

5. D Difficulty: Easy

Category: Vocab-in-Context

Getting to the Answer: The correct answer will not only be a synonym for "restricted" but will also make sense in the context of the sentence in the passage. Eliminate answers, such as A, that are synonyms for "restricted" but do not make sense in context. Here, the author is explaining that patients in wheelchairs must learn to prevent complications from restricted movement. In this context, "restricted" most nearly means "limited," answer choice (D).

6. A Difficulty: Hard

Category: Rhetoric

Getting to the Answer: Locate line 54 in the passage, and then read the paragraph that comes before it. This will help you identify why the author chose "tailor-made" to describe the patient's treatment. The patient received his own cells during the treatment, meaning that the treatment was tailored to his own body. Choice (A) fits this situation and is therefore the correct answer.

7. C   Difficulty: Hard

Category: Inference

Getting to the Answer: Remember that when a question is asking you to infer something, the answer is not stated explicitly in the passage. In paragraph 2, the author explains that the patient who received the experimental treatment had not seen an increase in mobility despite "countless hours" (lines 24-25) of physical therapy. Therefore, it is logical to infer that the patient would not have regained mobility without this experimental treatment. Choice (C) is the correct answer.

8. B   Difficulty: Medium

Category: Command of Evidence

Getting to the Answer: Think about how you selected the correct answer for the previous question. Use that information to help you choose the correct answer to this question. In paragraph 2, the author explains that the patient selected for the experimental treatment had not regained mobility despite intensive physical therapy. This provides the strongest support for the answer to the previous question, so choice (B) is correct.

9. B   Difficulty: Easy

Category: Vocab-in-Context

Getting to the Answer: Substitute each of the answer choices for "refined." Select the one that makes the most sense in context and does not change the meaning of the sentence. In this context, "refined" most nearly means "improved." Choice (B) is the correct answer.

10. C   Difficulty: Easy

Category: Inference

Getting to the Answer: Skim the passage and look for details about how doctors came to use the treatment described. In paragraph 3, the author explains that the doctors used a technique that was developed during years of research on rats. Therefore, choice (C) is the correct answer.

11. D   Difficulty: Medium

Category: Connections

Getting to the Answer: Compare and contrast each answer choice with the procedure described in the passage. As in the procedure described in the passage, skin transplants for burn victims involve taking tissue containing healthy cells from one area of the body and using it to repair damage done to another area. Choice (D) is the correct answer.

Suggested Passage Map notes:

¶1: scientists working on peanut that won't cause allergic reaction (central idea)
¶2: why allergic response = immune system; regular v. allergic responses
¶3: peanut allergy antibody IgE
¶4: difficult to avoid peanuts
¶5: change peanut allergen?; experiments
¶6: light tests showed promise
¶7: details of light experiment
¶8: promising results; test people next

12. B   Difficulty: Easy

Category: Vocab-in-Context

Getting to the Answer: Read the sentence again and predict another word that could substitute for "expel" in context. Predict that "expel" in this context means to get rid of. Choice (B) is correct because in this context, "eject" means almost the same thing as "expel."

13. D   Difficulty: Medium

Category: Inference

Getting to the Answer: It will be difficult to make predictions for a few questions. In that case, review each answer choice systematically to determine which one is correct. Avoid answers that go too far or are not supported by direct evidence in the passage. In paragraph 2, the author describes how a typical immune system response looks when the body recognizes a dangerous material. The author goes on to explain in paragraph 3 that a particular protein found in peanuts is responsible for triggering the immune system response in people allergic to peanuts. Choice (D) is correct.

14. A   Difficulty: Hard

Category: Command of Evidence

Getting to the Answer: Find each of the answer choices in the passage. The correct answer should provide direct support for the answer to the previous question. In paragraph 2, the author describes what causes a reaction in the immune system. Choice (A) is correct because this sentence describes what causes the immune system to react—a material it considers dangerous.

15. D   Difficulty: Medium

Category: Inference

Getting to the Answer: Use your Passage Map to find the paragraph that describes the normal immune system response and an allergic reaction. Summarize each in your head and use those summaries to make a prediction. Paragraph 2 includes information about what a normal immune system response looks like, as well as details about allergic reactions and what makes them dangerous. Choice (D) is correct because it accurately summarizes the differences between a normal immune system response and an allergic reaction. Choices A, B, and C may be tempting, but there are specific reasons why each is incorrect. Choice A is incorrect because an allergic reaction is stronger than a normal reaction. Choice B is incorrect because both a normal immune response and an allergic response could produce mucus and coughing. Choice C is incorrect because the allergic response is triggered by a material that the body incorrectly considers dangerous.

16. D   Difficulty: Medium

Category: Detail

Getting to the Answer: Review your notes for paragraph 4 to predict an answer to the question. In paragraph 4, the author explains that people who have peanut allergies must simply avoid allergens. The author also describes how difficult it is to avoid peanut allergens. Choice (D) is correct. Choice A may be tempting, but while avoidance is difficult, the examples given do not justify A's statement that the allergens will be encountered "daily."

17. B   Difficulty: Medium

Category: Command of Evidence

Getting to the Answer: Locate each quote to determine which provides the best support for the previous answer: people with peanut allergies have a difficult time avoiding the allergens. The correct evidence tells you that allergens are so common that children cannot avoid them, even at school. Choice (B) is correct.

18. C   Difficulty: Medium

Category: Vocab-in-Context

Getting to the Answer: Read the sentence again and replace "deactivating" with a prediction based on the sentence's context. Predict that scientists want to stop the allergens. Therefore, choice (C) is correct. In this context, "disabling" means almost the same thing as "deactivating."

19. B   Difficulty: Medium

Category: Synthesis

Getting to the Answer: Carefully evaluate the data in the graph. Use your Passage Map to find where the author discusses the information presented in the graph. In paragraph 7, the author describes the experiment that produced the data presented in the graph. According to lines 77-78, "the darker the blue, the more IgE antibodies remained." Use this information to interpret the graph. The lower the percentage of "Blue Color Amount," the longer the peanuts were "Exposed to Pulse Light." Choice (B) correctly expresses this relationship.

20. C **Difficulty:** Easy

Category: Detail

Getting to the Answer: Use your Passage Map to find the paragraph that describes the lab tests. Eliminate answer choices that are not explicitly stated in the text. In line 44, the author states that it would "not be safe" to measure allergic reactions caused in people. Choice (C) is correct.

21. C **Difficulty:** Medium

Category: Rhetoric

Getting to the Answer: Refer to your Passage Map to identify the purposes of paragraphs 6 and 7. Paragraph 6 introduces the method used by scientists to conduct the experiment described in paragraph 7. Paragraphs 6 and 7 are a summary of this method, and therefore choice (C) is correct.

22. A **Difficulty:** Medium

Category: Rhetoric

Getting to the Answer: Refer to your Passage Map. Think about the central idea of the paragraph and how it relates to the central idea of the entire passage. In the preceding paragraphs, the author describes experiments that have already taken place. In the final paragraph, the author describes what scientists might do next. Choice (A) is correct.

Suggested Passage Map notes:

¶1: new info discovered

¶2: Stromer discovered dinosaur fossils in Egypt, new genus, fossils destroyed in WWII, notes and sketches survived

¶3: Ibrahaim rediscovered similar fossils, able to make partial skeleton

¶4: description of spinosaurus

¶5: spino unique—lived on land, hunted in water

¶6: Ibrahaim used digital model and Stromer sketches to create replica

23. A **Difficulty:** Easy

Category: Global

Getting to the Answer: Look for the answer choice that describes an important idea that is supported throughout the text rather than a specific detail. The passage is mostly about how the mystery of the Spinosaurus fossils was decoded. Choice (A) is the best summary of the central idea of the passage.

24. D **Difficulty:** Medium

Category: Detail

Getting to the Answer: Locate the information about the fossils Stromer expected to find and the fossils he actually found, particularly those fossils' sizes and ages. The passage explains that Stromer expected to find fossils of early mammals, but instead found fossils that "dated back to the Cretaceous period" (line 10). This indicates that the fossils were older than he expected. Eliminate choices A and B. Because the Spinosaurus was larger than any mammal, choice (D) is correct.

25. D **Difficulty:** Medium

Category: Inference

Getting to the Answer: Think about the overall message of the passage and consider why the author would choose to write about this topic. The author's tone, or attitude, toward the topic of the passage demonstrates the point of view that the study of fossils and ancient life has value. Choice (D) is the correct answer. The evidence in the passage supports the idea that the author thinks the study of fossils and ancient life is important.

26. B **Difficulty:** Medium

Category: Command of Evidence

Getting to the Answer: Some answer choices may seem important. However, if they don't support your answer to the previous question, they aren't what you should choose. Choice (B) is correct. The author's use of the word "significant" in this quote shows that he or she thinks the study of fossils and ancient life is important.

27. D   Difficulty: Medium

Category: Vocab-in-Context

Getting to the Answer: Though more than one answer choice might seem acceptable, one comes closest to meaning the same as the phrase in question. Earlier in the paragraph, the author explains that two different bones gathered at different times both had a red line coursing through them. This means that the bones were from the same animal. Choice (D) fits best. "Against all odds" most nearly means "despite low probability."

28. C   Difficulty: Medium

Category: Rhetoric

Getting to the Answer: Be careful to avoid answers that don't make sense in the context of the paragraph. These phrases help the author describe the animal in a generally positive way. Choice (C) is the correct answer.

29. B   Difficulty: Hard

Category: Inference

Getting to the Answer: Be careful of answers that make sense but are not implied by the information presented in the passage. Choice (B) is correct. The passage does not explicitly state how Ibrahim became familiar with Stromer's work, but it is implied that he was familiar with Stromer's work when he found the fossils with the red lines and used Stromer's sketches to aid with the modern digital models as mentioned in the last paragraph.

30. D   Difficulty: Hard

Category: Command of Evidence

Getting to the Answer: Eliminate any answer choices that have nothing to do with your answer to the previous question. Choice (D) is correct. It directly supports the inference that Ibrahim was familiar with Stromer's work, showing that he used

Stromer's sketches to aid in creating his life-size replica of the Spinosaurus.

31. C   Difficulty: Easy

Category: Vocab-in-Context

Getting to the Answer: Ibrahim and his fellow researchers didn't know how the bones went together. They were making an educated guess with the help of technology and Stromer's sketches. Choice (C) is correct. "Hypothetical" in this sentence means "possible."

32. C   Difficulty: Easy

Category: Connections

Getting to the Answer: Think about the order in which Stromer and Ibrahim's work with the fossils occurred. Choice (C) is correct. Ibrahim used Stromer's sketches to create his models of the Spinosaurus. He built on Stromer's work to complete his own.

33. A   Difficulty: Hard

Category: Connections

Getting to the Answer: Think about the process described in each answer choice and compare it to how Ibrahim went about building his replica of the Spinosaurus. Choice (A) is the right choice. An architect creating a model of a building would use tools and methods similar to those used by Ibrahim, such as drawings and digital technologies.

Suggested Passage Map notes:

¶1: sickle cell: causes disease, but has + side effects

¶2: cause: mutation in hem. gene; hem. sticks together, deforms cells

¶3: cells wear out faster

¶4: genes come from both parents; one copy = carrier, have advantage

¶5: resistant to malaria

¶6: sickle cell assoc. w/malaria; carriers likely to survive, though victims likely to die; malaria gone, SC remains

34. C   Difficulty: Medium

Category: Global

Getting to the Answer: Think about the central idea of the passage. Ask what the author's main point is. Eliminate answer choices that contain incorrect or incomplete information, such as B or D. The correct answer will reflect the overall message of the passage. The passage is mostly about how sickle cell disease and malaria interact, or choice (C).

35. D   Difficulty: Hard

Category: Inference

Getting to the Answer: Use your Passage Map to look for specific clues that could support each of the answer possibilities. Determine which answer choice can be inferred from the information in the passage. Choice (D) is the only answer choice that is supported by the passage.

36. A   Difficulty: Medium

Category: Command of Evidence

Getting to the Answer: Review your answer to the previous question. Then, determine which quotation directly supports that answer. Choice (A) is correct. It supports the inference that sickle cell disease is a major threat for African Americans.

37. B   Difficulty: Easy

Category: Vocab-in-Context

Getting to the Answer: Read the sentence again and substitute all of the answer choices for the word "mutation." Determine which word makes the most sense and is the best substitution. Choice (B) is correct. The meaning of "mutation" is explained through context, specifically through the use of the words "changes" (line 17) and "changing" (line 20).

38. A   Difficulty: Hard

Category: Inference

Getting to the Answer: Avoid answer choices that go too far or are not supported by direct evidence in the passage, such as C and D. The passage states that carriers of sickle cell disease have only one gene, but the presence of this one gene helps protect them from malaria. People with two genes have sickle cell disease, and they do not have extra protection from malaria. When considered together, these details lead to the inference that having one sickle cell gene is better than having two of the genes. Choice (A) is correct.

39. D   Difficulty: Medium

Category: Command of Evidence

Getting to the Answer: Review your answer to the previous question. Check to see which answer choice relates to your answer and directly supports it with details. Choice (D) supports the inference that it is better to be a carrier of the sickle cell gene than to have the disease itself. This is the case for people who have one sickle cell gene.

40. D   Difficulty: Medium

Category: Synthesis

Getting to the Answer: Study the graphic and summarize what information is being presented. Review the part of the passage where the benefits of being a sickle cell carrier are discussed. Determine where these ideas connect. Based on the information in the text and the graphic, choice (D) is the correct answer. The graph shows that children who are carriers of the sickle cell gene have fewer parasites in their blood, which suggests protection against malaria.

41. C   Difficulty: Medium

Category: Vocab-in-Context

Getting to the Answer: Substitute each answer choice for the word "pool" in the sentence. While all the words are synonyms of "pool," only one has the connotation that fits into the sentence. After trying each word in its place, it is clear that the meaning of "pool" is "group." The phrase "human gene pool" refers to the overall group of available human genes. Choice (C) is correct.

42. D   Difficulty: Easy

Category: Detail

Getting to the Answer: Remember, you can locate the answer directly in the passage in a Detail question. According to the passage, "sickle-shaped red blood cells wear out faster than normal red blood cells" (lines 27-28). The correct answer is choice (D). Choices A–C are all distortions and are not supported by the passage.

43. B   Difficulty: Medium

Category: Rhetoric

Getting to the Answer: Make sure to read the text closely and decide why the author used this word. What effect was the author attempting to achieve? The correct answer will describe the author's purpose. The author is hoping to interest the reader by introducing this topic in an unexpected manner—one would not expect a terrible condition to have a helpful side effect. This matches choice (B).

44. A   Difficulty: Medium

Category: Rhetoric

Getting to the Answer: Focus on *why* rather than *what* to figure out the author's purpose. Your Passage Map can help here. Paragraph after paragraph, the author seems to have a clear purpose: to instruct the reader about the connection between sickle cell disease and malaria, or choice (A). While the structure of red blood cells is mentioned, it is only detailed briefly in a portion of paragraph 2, making choice B incorrect. Diagnosis and treatment are not the focus either, eliminating answer choices C and D, as well.

Suggested Passage Map notes:

¶1: what mercury is, uses for mercury

¶2: causes of mercury pollution

¶3: water affected by mercury, issue for many organisms

¶4: consumption of mercury-laden seafood, risks and benefits

¶5: explanation of safe levels of mercury based on body weight and fish type

¶6: nutritionists' recommendations

45. C   Difficulty: Medium

Category: Inference

Getting to the Answer: The correct answer will be directly supported by the evidence in the passage. Avoid answers like A and B that go beyond what can logically be inferred about the author. The author explains how mercury gets into the fish that humans eat and goes on to say that it is possible to eat fish that contain mercury without getting mercury poisoning. Choice (C) is the correct answer because it is directly supported by the evidence in the passage.

46. D   Difficulty: Medium

Category: Command of Evidence

Getting to the Answer: The correct answer will provide direct support for the answer to the previous question. Avoid answers like B that include relevant details but do not provide direct support. In the last paragraph, the author says that nutritionists recommend eating low-mercury fish instead of eliminating fish altogether, adding that an awareness of the issues with mercury can help us make healthy eating choices. This statement supports the answer to the previous question, so choice (D) is the correct answer.

47. A   Difficulty: Easy

Category: Detail

Getting to the Answer: Review the details provided in the passage about how to determine a safe level of mercury consumption. In paragraph 5, the author explains that humans should consume less than 0.1 microgram of mercury for every kilogram of their own weight. Therefore, choice (A) is the correct answer.

48. C   Difficulty: Easy

Category: Vocab-in-Context

Getting to the Answer: Eliminate answer choices that are synonyms for "concentration" but do not make sense in context. In this sentence, the author is describing the amount of mercury in the air from power plants. "Concentration" most nearly means "density" in this context, so choice (C) is the correct answer.

49. A   Difficulty: Medium

Category: Inference

Getting to the Answer: Eliminate any answer choices that are not directly supported by information in the passage. The passage strongly suggests that it is impossible to avoid exposure to mercury completely. Therefore, choice (A) is the correct answer.

50. B   Difficulty: Easy

Category: Command of Evidence

Getting to the Answer: Locate each of the answer choices in the passage. The correct answer should provide support for the answer to the previous question. In paragraph 1, the author explains that mercury can be found in many places. This supports the conclusion that it is impossible to avoid mercury completely. Choice (B) is the correct answer.

51. C   Difficulty: Hard

Category: Rhetoric

Getting to the Answer: Think about how the process paragraph 3 describes relates to the rest of the passage. Paragraph 3 describes the process by which larger organisms absorb mercury by eating smaller organisms. This information is necessary to understanding why larger fish have the highest mercury levels. Choice (C) is correct.

52. D   Difficulty: Hard

Category: Rhetoric

Getting to the Answer: Consider one of the central ideas of the passage. The correct answer would help provide additional support for this idea. One central idea in the passage is that people can eat fish if they know what mercury levels are safe for human consumption. The author states that scientists have determined safe mercury levels by studying at what point symptoms of mercury poisoning occur. However, the author only provides one example weight of how many micrograms of mercury a person could eat. Therefore, choice (D) is the correct answer.

53. B   Difficulty: Easy

Category: Vocab-in-Context

Getting to the Answer: Reread the sentence and replace "particulars" with each answer choice. Though the answer choices are similar in meaning to a certain degree, one of them makes the most sense when substituted for "particulars." In this context, "particulars" most nearly means "specifics"; therefore, choice (B) is the correct answer.

54. D   Difficulty: Hard

Category: Synthesis

Getting to the Answer: Remember that the correct answer will be supported by information in both the passage and the graphic. Refer to the passage to draw conclusions about the information in the graphic. The passage states that it is safe to eat fish that contain mercury as long as certain guidelines are followed regarding daily consumption. The graphic shows that Alaskan pollock has the lowest concentration of mercury of the fish listed. Therefore, choice (D) is the correct answer; a person can safely eat more Alaskan pollock than black-striped bass in one day.

Paired Passages

GETTING STARTED

There will be exactly one set of **Paired Passages** on the SAT Reading Test. These passages will be either History/Social Studies passages or Science passages. Together, the two passages will be about the same length as the other single passages.

The Kaplan Strategy for **Paired Passages** helps you attack each set of paired passages you face by dividing and conquering rather than processing two different passages and then 10-11 questions all at once:

- Read and map Passage 1, then answer its questions
- For the moment, "forget" what you just read in Passage 1
- Read and map Passage 2, then answer its questions
- Review your map for Passage 1, then identify the relationship between the passages. Possible relationships include: two complementary views, two opposing views, one view modifying the other, one passage applying an idea discussed in the other, etc.
- Answer questions about both passages

By reading Passage 1 and answering its questions before moving on to Passage 2, you avoid falling into wrong answer traps that reference the text of Passage 2. Furthermore, by addressing each passage individually, you will have a better sense of the central idea and purpose of each passage. This will help you answer questions that ask you to synthesize information about both passages.

> ✔ *Remember*
>
> Even though the individual passages are shorter in a **Paired Passage** set, you should still map both of them. Overall, there is still too much information to remember effectively in your head. Your Passage Maps will save you time by helping you locate key details.

Fortunately, questions in a **Paired Passage** set that ask about only one of the passages will be no different from questions you've seen and answered about single passages. Use the same methods and strategies you've been using to answer these questions.

Questions in a **Paired Passage** set that ask about both passages are called Synthesis questions. You may be asked to identify similarities or differences between the passages or how the author of one passage may respond to a point made by the author of the other passage.

✔ *Expert Tip*

The toughest questions in the **Paired Passages** are usually the Synthesis questions that ask you about both passages. Thinking through, and noting at the end of your Passage Map, the relationship between the passages *before* working on these questions will improve your accuracy.

IMPROVING WITH PRACTICE

Step 1: Compare Your Notes to the Suggested *Paired Passage* Passage Maps

After reading the first passage, compare your notes to the suggested Passage Map and note the ways your map was both similar and different. Because Synthesis questions require you to answer questions about both passages, your Passage Maps for **Paired Passages** are even more important than usual. As usual, the exact notes you will take depend on the genre of the passages.

For History/Social Studies passages, take note of:

- the main idea of each paragraph
- any opinions, especially the author's
- the *location* of descriptive details and examples
- the *reason* the author included details and examples. Is the author using the information to support, modify, or refute the preceding idea?
- any emphasis or "emotional" keywords. Keywords such as "remarkable," "unfortunate," "unprecedented," and "crucial" are important indicators of the author's tone.

For Science passages, take note of:

- the central idea/theory discussed
- the relationship of each paragraph to the central idea. Is the paragraph explaining, supporting, criticizing, modifying, or applying the central idea?
- any opinions, especially the author's
- the *location* of descriptive details and examples
- the *reason* the author included details and examples. Is the author using the information to support, modify, or refute the preceding idea?
- any emphasis or "emotional" keywords. Keywords such as "remarkable," "unfortunate," "unprecedented," and "crucial" are important indicators of the author's tone.

If you missed important information, go back to the passage with the above bullet points in mind. Reread the passage, connecting each part of the suggested Passage Map to the text in the passage and determining what made you overlook or ignore this text the first time. Keywords are often extremely important when identifying key information, so use them to focus your attention and create strong Passage Maps.

After you've checked your Passage Map for Passage 1, move on to Step 2 without looking at Passage 2. Since you should always tackle the passages one at a time, you should practice them one at a time!

> ✔ **Remember**
>
> When answering **Paired Passage** questions, first, read and answer questions about Passage 1. Then, read and answer questions about Passage 2. Finally, answer the questions about both passages.

Step 2: Answer the Questions

Review the Answer and Explanation for each Passage 1 question as soon as you complete it. If you got the question correct, congratulate yourself! Then, take a moment to read the entire explanation to make sure you got the question correct for the right reason. Sometimes, the explanation may even help you notice a more efficient way to identify the correct answer next time.

Step 3: Review Incorrect Answers

If you got the question incorrect . . . still congratulate yourself! You're about to learn something new that you'll be able to use to improve your performance on Test Day. Don't read the explanation yet; instead, try the question again.

If you get the question correct the second time, read the explanation to see if you solved the question in the most efficient way. Identify the mistake you made the first time, and determine how you're going to avoid making that mistake again.

If you get the question incorrect the second time, use the explanation to learn how to get the question correct. Work through the question again while following the explanation, and identify the steps you will need to take to get a similar question correct. Although the passages and questions will change, the concepts being tested will not. When you encounter unfamiliar questions, take note of them for future study sessions.

After all that work, it's time to move to the next question. Once you have answered and reviewed every Passage 1 question, it's time to move on to Passage 2! Go back to Step 1, and follow these steps again for Passage 2 questions. Finally, go back to Step 2, and follow steps 2 and 3 for the questions that ask about both passages.

Reviewing in this way will take time. However, improvement doesn't come from just doing lots and lots of questions; it comes from thinking through your approach and improving it with every question.

RAISING YOUR SCORE EVEN MORE

Questions that ask about one author's response to another will hinge on the emphasis/opinion keywords used by that author. Be sure to circle, underline, or note them in some other way. For example, the author may be "dismayed" or may identify an opposing view as "mistaken." Strong opinion keywords justify strong, definite answer choices. In the absence of emphatic keywords, a more neutral answer choice will be correct.

PRACTICE QUESTIONS

The following test-like question sets provide an opportunity to practice reading Paired Passages and answering related questions.

Questions 1-11 are based on the following passages.

The following passages discuss acidity. Passage 1 describes the effect of acid rain on the environment, while Passage 2 focuses on how the human body responds to abnormal acidity levels.

Passage 1

In the past century, due to the burning of fossil fuels in energy plants and cars, acid rain has become a cause of harm to the environ-
Line ment. However, rain would still be slightly
(5) acidic even if these activities were to stop. Acid rain would continue to fall, but it would not cause the problems we see now. The environment can handle slightly acidic rain; it just cannot keep up with the level of acid rain
(10) caused by burning fossil fuels.

A pH of 7 is considered neutral, while pH below 7 is acidic and pH above 7 is alkaline, or basic. Pure rain water can have a pH as low as 5.5. Rain water is acidic because carbon
(15) dioxide gas in the air reacts with the water to make carbonic acid. Since it is a weak acid, even a large amount of it will not lower the pH of water much.

Soil, lakes, and streams can tolerate slightly
(20) acidic rain. The water and soil contain alkaline materials that will neutralize acids. These include some types of rocks, plant and animal waste, and ashes from forest fires. Altogether, these materials can easily handle the slightly
(25) acidic rain that occurs naturally. The alkaline waste and ashes will slowly be used up, but more will be made to replace it.

Anthropomorphic causes of acid rain, such as the burning of fossil fuels, release nitrogen
(30) oxide and sulfur oxide gases. These gases react with water to make nitric acid and sulfuric acid. Since these are both strong acids, small amounts can lower the pH of rain water to 3 or less. Such a low pH requires much more
(35) alkaline material to neutralize it. Acid rain with a lower pH uses up alkaline materials faster, and more cannot be made quickly enough to replace what is used up. Soil and water become more acidic and remain that way, as they are
(40) unable to neutralize the strong acid.

Passage 2

In humans, keeping a constant balance between acidity and alkalinity in the blood is essential. If blood pH drops below 7.35 or rises above 7.45, all of the functions in the body are
(45) impaired and life-threatening conditions can soon develop. Many processes in the body produce acid wastes, which would lower the pH of blood below the safe level unless neutralized. Several systems are in place to keep pH constant
(50) within the necessary range. Certain conditions, however, can cause acids to be made faster than these systems can react.

Most of the pH control involves three related substances: carbon dioxide, carbonic acid, and
(55) bicarbonate ions. Carbonic acid is formed when carbon dioxide reacts with water. Bicarbonate ions are formed when the carbonic acid releases a hydrogen ion. Excess carbonic acid lowers the pH, while excess bicarbonate ions raise it.
(60) The kidneys store bicarbonate ions and will release or absorb them to help adjust the pH of

the blood. Breathing faster removes more carbon dioxide from the blood, which reduces the
amount of carbonic acid; in contrast, breathing
(65) more slowly has the opposite effect. In a
healthy body, these systems automatically
neutralize normal amounts of acid wastes and
maintain blood pH within the very small range
necessary for the body to function normally.

(70)   In some cases, these systems can be overwhelmed. This can happen to people with diabetes if their blood sugar drops too low for too
long. People with type 1 diabetes do not make
enough insulin, which allows the body's cells
(75) to absorb sugar from the blood to supply the
body with energy. If a person's insulin level
gets too low for too long, the body breaks
down fats to use for energy. The waste produced from breaking down fats is acidic, so the
(80) blood pH drops. If the kidneys exhaust their
supply of bicarbonate ions, and the lungs cannot remove carbon dioxide fast enough to
raise pH, other functions in the body begin to
fail as well. The person will need medical treat-
(85) ment to support these functions until the pH
balancing system can catch up. The system will
then keep the blood pH constant, as long as
the production of acid wastes does not exceed
the body's capacity to neutralize them.

1. Passage 1 most strongly suggests that
   A) the environment will be damaged
      seriously if people do not reduce the
      burning of fossil fuels.
   B) scientists must find a way to introduce
      more alkaline materials into the water
      supply to combat acid rain.
   C) acid rain will not be a problem in the fu-
      ture as we move away from fossil fuels
      and toward alternative energy sources.
   D) acidic rain water is more of a problem
      than acidic soil because soil contains
      more alkaline materials.

2. Which choice provides the best evidence for
   the answer to the previous question?
   A) Lines 7-10 ("The environment . . . fuels")
   B) Lines 14-16 ("Rain water . . . acid")
   C) Lines 19-20 ("Soil, lakes . . . rain")
   D) Lines 28-30 ("Anthropomorphic . . . gases")

3. According to the information in Passage 1,
   which pH level for rain water would cause the
   most damage to the environment?
   A) 2.25
   B) 4
   C) 5
   D) 9.1

4. As used in line 19, "tolerate" most nearly
   means
   A) accept.
   B) endure.
   C) acknowledge.
   D) distribute.

5. Passage 2 most strongly suggests that
   A) a pH of 7.35 is ideal for blood in the
      human body.
   B) acid wastes in the blood multiply if not
      neutralized.
   C) the normal range of blood pH narrows as
      a person ages.
   D) small amounts of acid wastes in the blood
      are a normal condition.

6. Which choice provides the best evidence for the answer to the previous question?

    A) Lines 43-46 ("If blood pH . . . develop")

    B) Lines 50-52 ("Certain conditions . . . react")

    C) Lines 65-69 ("In a healthy . . . normally")

    D) Lines 73-76 ("People with . . . energy")

7. As used in line 80, "exhaust" most nearly means

    A) fatigue.

    B) consume.

    C) deplete.

    D) dissolve.

8. Which of the following plays a role in the environment most similar to the role played by excess bicarbonate ions in the blood?

    A) Acid rain

    B) Ashes from a forest fire

    C) Sulfur oxide gases

    D) Fossil fuels

9. Based on the information in Passage 2, which of the following can cause the body to break down fats to use for energy?

    A) An excess of carbonic acid

    B) Low blood pH

    C) A drop in blood sugar

    D) Not enough insulin

10. Which of the following best describes a shared purpose of the authors of both passages?

    A) To encourage readers to care for delicate systems such as the environment and human body

    B) To explain how the human body neutralizes acid wastes that it produces and deposits in the blood

    C) To describe systems that can neutralize small amounts of acids but become overwhelmed by large amounts

    D) To persuade readers to work toward reducing acid rain by cutting consumption of fossil fuels

11. Both passages support which of the following generalizations?

    A) The human body and the environment are delicate systems that require balance to function properly.

    B) There are many similarities between the systems that make up the human body and the water cycle.

    C) Acid rain is an important issue that will continue to impact the environment until we reduce the use of fossil fuels.

    D) Medical treatment is necessary when the pH of a person's blood drops below 7.35 or rises above 7.45.

Questions 12-22 are based on the following passages and supplementary material.

Passage 1 is about how scientists use radioisotopes to date artifacts and remains. Passage 2 discusses the varying problems with radioactive contaminants.

Passage 1

Archaeologists often rely on measuring the amounts of different atoms present in an item from a site to determine its age. The identity of
Line an atom depends on how many protons it has
(5) in its nucleus; for example, all carbon atoms have 6 protons. Each atom of an element, however, can have a different number of neutrons, so there can be several versions, or isotopes, of each element. Scientists name the isotopes by
(10) the total number of protons plus neutrons. For example, a carbon atom with 6 neutrons is carbon-12 while a carbon atom with 7 neutrons is carbon-13.

Some combinations of protons and neutrons
(15) are not stable and will change over time. For example, carbon-14, which has 6 protons and 8 neutrons, will slowly change into nitrogen-14, with 7 protons and 7 neutrons. Scientists can directly measure the amount of carbon-12 and
(20) carbon-14 in a sample or they can use radiation measurements to calculate these amounts. Each atom of carbon-14 that changes to nitrogen-14 emits radiation. Scientists can measure the rate of emission and use that to calculate
(25) the total amount of carbon-14 present in a sample.

Carbon-14 atoms are formed in the atmosphere at the same rate at which they decay. Therefore, the ratio of carbon-12 to carbon-14
(30) atoms in the atmosphere is constant. Living plants and animals have the same ratio of carbon-12 to carbon-14 in their tissues because they are constantly taking in carbon in the form of food or carbon dioxide. After the

(35) plant or animal dies, however, it stops taking in carbon and so the amount of carbon-14 atoms in its tissues starts to decrease at a predictable rate.

By measuring the ratio of carbon-12 to carbon-14 in a bone, for example, a scientist
(40) can determine how long the animal the bone came from has been dead. To determine an object's age this way is called "carbon-14 dating." Carbon-14 dating can be performed on any material made by a living organism, such as
(45) wood or paper from trees or bones and skin from animals. Materials with ages up to about 50,000 years old can be dated. By finding the age of several objects found at different depths at an archeological dig, the archeologists can
(50) then make a timeline for the layers of the site. Objects in the same layer will be about the same age. By using carbon dating for a few objects in a layer, archeologists know the age of other objects in that layer, even if the layer
(55) itself cannot be carbon dated.

Passage 2

Radioactive materials contain unstable atoms that decay, releasing energy in the form of radiation. The radiation can be harmful to living tissue because it can penetrate into cells and
(60) damage their DNA. If an explosion or a leak at a nuclear power plant releases large amounts of radioactive materials, the surrounding area could be hazardous until the amount of radioactive material drops back to normal levels.
(65) The amount of danger from the radiation and the amount of time until the areas are safe again depends on how fast the materials emit radiation.

Scientists use the "half-life" of a material to
(70) indicate how quickly it decays. The half-life of a material is the amount of time it takes for half of a sample of that material to decay. A material with a short half-life decays more quickly than a material with a long half-life.

(75) For example, iodine-131 and cesium-137 can both be released as a result of an accident at a nuclear power plant. Iodine-131 decays rapidly, with a half-life of 8 days. Cesium-137, however, decays more slowly, with a half-life (80) of 30 years.

If an accident releases iodine-131, therefore, it is a short-term concern. The amount of radiation emitted will be high but will drop rapidly. After two months, less than one percent (85) of the original iodine-131 will remain. An accidental release of cesium-137, however, is a long-term concern. The amount of radiation emitted at first will be low but will drop slowly. It will take about 200 years for the amount of (90) cesium-137 remaining to drop below one percent. The total amount of radiation emitted in both cases will be the same, for the same amount of initial material. The difference lies in whether the radiation is all released rapidly (95) at high levels in a short time, or is released slowly at low levels, over a long time span.

Decay of Carbon-14

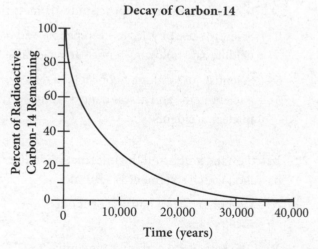

This data is from the *Journal of Research of the National Bureau of Standards*, Vol. 64, No. 4, April 1951, pp. 328 – 333.

12. Based on the information in Passage 1, which of the following could be dated using carbon-14 dating?

A) An iron pot found in a cave

B) A rock at the bottom of a quarry

C) An arrowhead made from bone

D) The remains of a house made from stone

13. Which choice provides the best evidence for the answer to the previous question?

A) Lines 10-13 ("For example . . . carbon-13")

B) Lines 30-34 ("Living plants . . . dioxide")

C) Lines 34-37 ("After the plant . . . rate")

D) Lines 43-46 ("Carbon-14 dating . . . animals")

14. As used in line 28, "decay" most nearly means

A) yield.

B) deteriorate.

C) discharge.

D) circulated.

15. Which statement best describes the relationship between carbon-12 and carbon-14 in living tissue?

A) There is more carbon-14 than carbon-12.

B) There is more carbon-12 than carbon-14.

C) The ratio of carbon-12 to carbon-14 is constant.

D) The ratio of carbon-12 to carbon-14 fluctuates greatly.

16. Which choice provides the best evidence for the answer to the previous question?

    A) Lines 14-15 ("Some combinations . . . time")

    B) Lines 27-28 ("Carbon-14 atoms . . . decay")

    C) Lines 30-34 ("Living plants . . . carbon dioxide")

    D) Lines 34-37 ("After the plant . . . rate")

17. In Passage 2, the author refers to an accident that results in the release of iodine-131 as a "short-term concern" (line 82) because the initial amount of radiation released is

    A) low but will drop slowly.

    B) high but will drop quickly.

    C) low and will drop quickly.

    D) high and will drop slowly.

18. Based on the information in Passage 2, living tissue exposed to radioactive material can

    A) be destroyed by high levels of heat caused by the radiation.

    B) become radioactive itself and damage surrounding tissue.

    C) suffer injury when the cells' components are damaged.

    D) be killed by extra protons released by the radioactive material.

19. As used in line 85, "original" most nearly means

    A) earliest.

    B) unique.

    C) unusual.

    D) critical.

20. According to Passage 2, scientists use the half-life of radioactive material to determine the

    A) amount of danger posed by radiation immediately following a nuclear accident.

    B) likelihood of a nuclear accident involving the release of radioactive material at any given location.

    C) amount of radiation contained in a sample of iodine-131 or cesium-137 used in nuclear reactions.

    D) length of time that must pass until an area is safe after the release of radioactive material.

21. Which generalization about the study of physics is supported by both passages?

    A) The study of atomic and nuclear physics can have many applications in a variety of fields.

    B) The study of physics has helped revolutionize how archaeologists study artifacts.

    C) Scientists use physics to keep people and wildlife safe following a nuclear accident.

    D) Scientists use different concepts to date ancient items and assess danger from nuclear accidents.

22. Based on the graph and the information in the passages, which statement is accurate?

    A) Carbon-14 has a half-life of about 5,400 years.

    B) The half-life of carbon-14 is similar to that of cesium-137.

    C) The half-life of iodine-131 is greater than that of cesium-137.

    D) All radioactive materials have a half-life of 30 to 5,400 years.

Questions 23-33 are based on the following passages and supplementary material.

The idea of a World Bank became a reality in 1944, when delegates to the Bretton Woods Conference pledged to "outlaw practices which are agreed to be harmful to world prosperity." Passage 1 discusses the benefits of the World Bank, while Passage 2 focuses on the limited lifespan of the Bretton Woods system.

Passage 1

In 1944, 730 delegates from forty-four Allied nations met in Bretton Woods, New Hampshire, just as World War II was ending.
Line They were attending an important conference.
(5) This mostly forgotten event shaped our modern world because delegates at the Bretton Woods Conference agreed on the establishment of an international banking system.

To ensure that all nations would prosper, the
(10) United States and other allied nations set rules for a postwar international economy. The Bretton Woods system created the International Monetary Fund (IMF). The IMF was founded as a kind of global central bank from
(15) which member countries could borrow money. The countries needed money to pay for their war costs. Today, the IMF facilitates international trade by ensuring the stability of the international monetary and financial system.

(20) The Bretton Woods system also established the World Bank. Although the World Bank shares similarities with the IMF, the two institutions remain distinct. While the IMF maintains an orderly system of payments and
(25) receipts between nations, the World Bank is mainly a development institution. The World Bank initially gave loans to European countries devastated by World War II, and today it lends money and technical assistance specifically to
(30) economic projects in developing countries.

For example, the World Bank might provide a low-interest loan to a country attempting to improve education or health. The goal of the World Bank is to "bridge the economic divide
(35) between poor and rich countries." In short, the organizations differ in their purposes. The Bank promotes economic and social progress so people can live better lives, while the IMF represents the entire world in its goal to foster
(40) global monetary cooperation and financial stability.

These two specific accomplishments of the Bretton Woods Conference were major. However, the Bretton Woods system particu-
(45) larly benefited the United States. It effectively established the U.S. dollar as a global currency. A global currency is one that countries worldwide accept for all trade, or international transactions of buying and selling. Because
(50) only the U.S. could print dollars, the United States became the primary power behind both the IMF and the World Bank. Today, global currencies include the U.S. dollar, the euro (European Union countries),
(55) and the yen (Japan).

The years after Bretton Woods have been considered the golden age of the U.S. dollar. More importantly, the conference profoundly shaped foreign trade for decades to come.

Passage 2

(60) The financial system established at the 1944 Bretton Woods Conference endured for many years. Even after the United States abrogated agreements made at the conference, the nation continued to experience a powerful position in
(65) international trade by having other countries tie their currencies to the U.S. dollar. The world, however, is changing.

In reality, the Bretton Woods system lasted only three decades. Then, in 1971, President
(70) Richard Nixon introduced a new economic

policy by ending the convertibility of the dollar to gold. It marked the end of the Bretton Woods international monetary framework, and the action resulted in worldwide financial (75) crisis. Two cornerstones of Bretton Woods, however, endured: the International Monetary Fund (IMF) and the World Bank.

Since the collapse of the Bretton Woods system, IMF members have been trading using (80) a flexible exchange system. Namely, countries allow their exchange rates to fluctuate in response to changing conditions. The exchange rate between two currencies, such as the Japanese yen and the U.S. dollar, for example, (85) specifies how much one currency is worth in terms of the other. An exchange rate of 120 yen to dollars means that 120 yen are worth the same as one dollar.

Even so, the U.S. dollar has remained the (90) most widely used money for international trade, and having one currency for all trade may be better than using a flexible exchange system.

This seems to be the thinking of a powerful group of countries. The Group of Twenty (95) (G20), which has called for a new Bretton Woods, consists of governments and leaders from 20 of the world's largest economies including China, the United States, and the European Union. In 2009, for example, the (100) G20 announced plans to create a new global currency to replace the U.S. dollar's role as the anchor currency. Many believe that China's yuan, quickly climbing the financial ranks, is well on its way to becoming a major world (105) reserve currency.

In fact, an earlier 1988 article in *The Economist* stated, "30 years from now, Americans, Japanese, Europeans, and people in many other rich countries and some relatively poor (110) ones will probably be paying for their shopping with the same currency."

The article predicted that the world supply of currency would be set by a new central bank of the IMF. This prediction seems to be coming (115) to fruition since the G20 indicated that a "world currency is in waiting." For an international construct such as the original Bretton Woods to last some 26 years is nothing less than amazing. But move over, Bretton Woods; a new world (120) order in finance could be on the fast track.

Top 10 International Currencies						
(Percent Shares of Average Daily Currency Trading)						
	2007		2010		2013	
	Share	*Rank*	*Share*	*Rank*	*Share*	*Rank*
U.S. Dollar (USD)	85.6%	1	84.9%	1	87.0%	1
Euro (EUR)	37.0%	2	39.1%	2	33.4%	2
Japanese Yen (JPY)	17.2%	3	19.0%	3	23.0%	3
UK Pound (GBP)	14.9%	4	12.9%	4	11.8%	4
Australian Dollar (AUD)	6.6%	6	7.6%	5	8.6%	5
Swiss Franc (CHF)	6.8%	5	6.3%	6	5.2%	6
Canadian Dollar (CAD)	4.3%	7	5.3%	7	4.6%	7
Mexican Peso (MXN)	1.3%	12	1.3%	14	2.5%	8
Chinese Yuan (CNY)	0.5%	20	0.9%	17	2.2%	9
New Zealand Dollar	1.9%	11	1.6%	10	2.0%	10

Adapted from Mauldin Economics; Bank for International Settlements, September 2013 Triennial Central Bank Survey.

23. Based on Passage 1, it can reasonably be inferred that

    A) world leaders recognized the need for markets to function independently.

    B) Bretton Woods increased U.S. economic influence around the world.

    C) the IMF and the World Bank work closely together to ensure prosperity.

    D) the conclusion of World War II had little influence on events at Bretton Woods.

24. Which choice provides the best evidence for the answer to the previous question?

    A) Lines 9-11 ("To ensure . . . economy")

    B) Lines 11-13 ("The Bretton . . . Fund")

    C) Lines 49-52 ("Because only . . . World Bank")

    D) Lines 58-59 ("More importantly . . . to come")

25. As used in line 39, "foster" most nearly means

    A) publicize.

    B) rear.

    C) stabilize.

    D) encourage.

26. Which statement best explains the difference between the purposes of the IMF and the World Bank?

    A) The IMF provides money to pay for war costs, while the World Bank offers assistance to rebuild countries recovering from war across the globe.

    B) The IMF encourages stability in the global financial system, while the World Bank promotes economic development in relatively poor nations.

    C) The IMF supports the U.S. dollar in international markets, while the World Bank provides low-interest loans to many nations around the world.

    D) The IMF offers governments advice about participation in global markets, while the World Bank encourages monetary cooperation between nations.

27. Based on the second paragraph in Passage 2, it can be reasonably inferred that

    A) the United States did not support the goals of the IMF and the World Bank.

    B) Bretton Woods was originally intended to last for three decades.

    C) President Nixon acted to reinforce the decisions made at Bretton Woods.

    D) some U.S. policy decisions differed from international consensus over Bretton Woods.

28. Which choice provides the best evidence for the answer to the previous question?

    A) Lines 68-69 ("In reality . . . three decades")

    B) Lines 69-72 ("Then, in 1971 . . . to gold")

    C) Lines 75-77 ("Two cornerstones . . . World Bank")

    D) Lines 78-80 ("Since the collapse . . . exchange system")

29. As used in line 102, "anchor" most nearly means

   A) key.

   B) fastening.

   C) rigid.

   D) supporting.

30. It can reasonably be inferred from both Passage 2 and the graphic that

   A) international markets are increasingly comfortable using the yuan as trade currency.

   B) the United States favors using the yuan as one of the world's reserve currencies.

   C) the G20 wants to replace the yuan and other currencies with a new global currency.

   D) the IMF continues to support the yuan and other currencies in a flexible exchange system.

31. The last paragraph of Passage 2 can be described as

   A) a refutation of opponents' criticisms.

   B) an indication of the author's opinion.

   C) a summary of the author's main points.

   D) an introduction of a contradictory position.

32. Which statement most effectively compares the authors' purposes in both passages?

   A) Passage 1's purpose is to contrast the functions of the IMF and World Bank, while Passage 2's purpose is to outline the benefits of a flexible trade system to the United States.

   B) Passage 1's purpose is to describe the history of international trade in the 20th century, while Passage 2's purpose is to explain why the Bretton Woods system collapsed.

   C) Passage 1's purpose is to describe Bretton Woods' effect on the global economy, while Passage 2's purpose is to suggest that a new currency for global trade may soon be implemented.

   D) Passage 1's purpose is to promote the economic benefits of the IMF and World Bank, while Passage 2's purpose is to encourage the reestablishment of the Bretton Woods system.

33. Both passages support which generalization about the global economy?

   A) U.S. influence on global trade has continued under a flexible exchange system.

   B) The purposes of the International Monetary Fund and the World Bank are indirectly related.

   C) The Group of Twenty represents the financial interests of the world's largest economies.

   D) International institutions such as the IMF continue to influence economic trade and development.

Questions 34-44 are based on the following passages.

Passage 1 discusses possible uses of video games in designing educational materials. Passage 2 explores how elements of video games can be used in combating deteriorating cognition in older adults.

Passage 1

Many teenagers have heard from their parents that playing too many video games can negatively affect their learning and socialization.

Line Studies performed in the 1990s supported this
(5) claim. Scientists evaluated the content of popular video games and the amount of time children and teenagers were allowed to spend playing them. They eventually connected video games to anger issues, obesity, and addiction.

(10) Studies showed that violent video games played for long periods of time inadvertently mimic the same type of repetition used by teachers to reinforce subject matter. The method of advancement in many violent video
(15) games involves winning a contest of some kind. This is also an approach used in the classroom and other settings familiar to children and teenagers. This method makes the content of the video games, including
(20) overall aggressive themes, easy to absorb.

Until recently, the only positive effect of playing video games seemed to be an improvement in manual dexterity and computer literacy. These important upsides
(25) didn't seem to outweigh the negatives. A 2013 study by the National Academy of Sciences shows that the playing of fast-paced video games can actually improve performance in many areas, such as attention span, spatial
(30) navigation, cognition, reasoning, and memory. Researchers tested small pools of gamers and found that those who had a history of playing action-packed video games were better at tasks such as pattern discrimination. They also found

(35) that the gamers excelled at conceptualizing 3-D objects.

This new information could change the form that educational materials take. Content developers hope that the new materials may
(40) inspire interest in the fields of engineering, math, and technology. Educators can transform these data into classroom experiences that will not only cater to the current interests of students, but also use old patterns of teaching in a new
(45) and more modern way.

Passage 2

As adults age, certain brain functions deteriorate. Two of these important functions are cognition and memory. This kind of decline can lead to an associated loss of well-being.
(50) The number of adults affected by Alzheimer's disease or dementia is also on the rise. Researchers are racing to find ways for people to maintain brain health while aging. A recent study examined the effects of non-action
(55) video-game training on people experiencing cognitive decline.

The study worked with small sample sizes of aging participants. Researchers found that the use of video games can allow the adult
(60) brain to maintain some plasticity. Test subjects trained their memories with games that featured patterned blocks, jigsaw puzzles, facial recognition, and other iterations requiring the recall of patterns. Test subjects
(65) who completed as few as twenty training sessions with these video games showed an increase in attention span, alertness, and visual memory. They also showed a decrease in distraction. These results are encouraging, as
(70) they suggest that there may be ways to stave off mental decline and to help the elderly maintain functions needed for safe driving and other activities of daily living.

More tests need to be done in order to
(75) understand the full potential of video games
in the anti-aging market. There are several
companies currently capitalizing on the success
of these studies, and increasingly more games
that promise increased cognitive function are
(80) sure to find their way to retailers soon.

34. The central idea of Passage 1 is

    A) the effects of video games on teenagers
    who play popular violent video games.

    B) outdated methods used by teachers and
    content developers to interest students in
    science and engineering.

    C) how research about the effects of video
    games on gamers is being used to develop
    new teaching methods.

    D) how the impact that video games have
    had on children and teenagers has
    changed over the past few decades.

35. Which choice provides the best evidence for
the answer to the previous question?

    A) Lines 5-8 ("Scientists evaluated . . .
    them")

    B) Lines 18-20 ("This method . . . absorb")

    C) Lines 21-24 ("Until recently . . . literacy")

    D) Lines 41-45 ("Educators . . . modern way")

36. Based on the information in the passage,
studies performed in the 1990s support the
claim that

    A) excessive video game playing can have a
    negative effect on teenagers.

    B) children who play video games are
    more likely to be interested in math and
    science.

    C) video games can improve performance in
    many areas related to success in education.

    D) teenagers who spend too much time
    playing violent video games become
    violent criminals.

37. As used in line 11, "inadvertently" most nearly
means

    A) hastily.

    B) impulsively.

    C) unintentionally.

    D) imprudently.

38. According to the information presented in
Passage 1, the content of video games is easily
absorbed by teenagers because

    A) games are played for many hours a day
    on a daily basis.

    B) the games utilize methods used in the
    classroom to encourage retention.

    C) playing video games improves memory
    and increases cognitive functions.

    D) teenagers are predisposed to absorb
    material to which they are repeatedly
    exposed.

39. Based on the information in Passage 2, the reader can infer that

    A) elderly people who are able to ward off or reverse dementia may be able to live longer independently.

    B) video games could completely cure dementia and other age-related cognitive problems.

    C) playing board games for extended periods of time could have the same effect as playing video games.

    D) too much time spent playing video games would likely have a negative effect on cognition in aging populations.

40. Which choice provides the best evidence for the answer to the previous question?

    A) Lines 50-51 ("The number of . . . rise")

    B) Lines 53-56 ("A recent study . . . decline")

    C) Lines 69-73 ("These results . . . living")

    D) Lines 74-76 ("More tests . . . market")

41. As used in lines 46-47, "deteriorate" most nearly means

    A) adapt.

    B) restrict.

    C) transform.

    D) diminish.

42. The author of Passage 2 supports the central claim of the passage in paragraph 2 by

    A) explaining the results of preliminary research involving the elderly and video games.

    B) describing the physiological causes of memory loss and declining cognitive functions.

    C) listing ways that the elderly can reduce the cognitive effects of aging and Alzheimer's disease.

    D) giving details about the research methods used to study dementia in elderly populations.

43. The purpose of Passage 2 is to

    A) describe the potential of video games to help combat the deterioration of brain function in aging populations.

    B) explain how companies are reaching out to the elderly to increase video game markets.

    C) encourage the reader to play video games as a way to increase memory and attention span.

    D) support research that will increase the quality of life of people as they age and lose brain function.

44. Which generalization about video games does the evidence presented in both passages support?

   A) People who have trouble with memory loss and are easily distracted should avoid video games.

   B) Initial research conducted in the 1990s failed to uncover some of the benefits of playing video games.

   C) Video games could be part of a comprehensive approach to helping people cope with the effects of aging.

   D) Researchers in a diverse range of fields are looking to video games for solutions to problems.

Questions 45-55 are based on the following passages and supplementary material.

The following passages discuss the history and traditions associated with tea.

Passage 1

Europe was a coffee-drinking continent before it became a tea-drinking one. Tea was grown in China, thousands of miles away.
Line The opening of trade routes with the Far East
(5) in the fifteenth and sixteenth centuries gave Europeans their first taste of tea.

However, it was an unpromising start for the beverage, because shipments arrived stale, and European tea drinkers miscalculated the
(10) steeping time and measurements. This was a far cry from the Chinese preparation techniques, known as a "tea ceremony," which had strict steps and called for steeping in iron pots at precise temperatures and pouring into
(15) porcelain bowls.

China had a monopoly on the tea trade and kept their tea cultivation techniques secret. Yet as worldwide demand grew, tea caught on in Europe. Some proprietors touted tea as a cure
(20) for maladies. Several European tea companies formed, including the English East India Company. In 1669, it imported 143.5 pounds of tea—very little compared to the 32 million pounds that were imported by 1834.

(25) Europeans looked for ways to circumvent China's monopoly, but their attempts to grow the tea plant (Latin name *Camellia sinensis*) failed. Some plants perished in transit from the East. But most often the growing climate
(30) wasn't right, not even in the equatorial colonies that the British, Dutch, and French controlled. In 1763, the French Academy of Sciences gave up, declaring the tea plant unique to China and unable to be grown anywhere else.
(35) Swedish and English botanists grew tea in

botanical gardens, but this was not enough to meet demand.

After trial and error with a plant variety discovered in the Assam district of India, the
(40) British managed to establish a source to meet the growing demands of British tea drinkers. In May 1838, the first batch of India-grown tea shipped to London. The harvest was a mere 350 pounds and arrived in November. It sold
(45) for between 16 and 34 shillings per pound. Perfecting production methods took many years, but ultimately, India became the world's largest tea-producing country. By the early 1900s, annual production of India tea
(50) exceeded 350 million pounds. This voluminous source was a major factor in tea becoming the staple of European households that it is today.

Passage 2

In Europe, there's a long tradition of taking afternoon tea. Tea time, typically four o'clock,
(55) means not just enjoying a beverage, but taking time out to gather and socialize. The occasion is not identical across Europe, though; just about every culture has its own way of doing things.

(60) In France, for example, black tea is served with sugar, milk, or lemon and is almost always accompanied by a pastry. Rather than sweet pastries, the French prefer the savory kind, such as the *gougère*, or puff pastry,
(65) infused with cheese.

Germans, by contrast, put a layer of slowly melting candy at the bottom of their teacup and top the tea with cream. German tea culture is strongest in the eastern part of the
(70) country, and during the week tea is served with cookies, while on the weekend or for special events, cakes are served. The Germans think of tea as a good cure for headaches and stress.

(75)   Russia also has a unique tea culture, rooted in the formalism of its aristocratic classes. Loose leaf black tea is served in a glass held by a *podstakannik*, an ornate holder with a handle typically made from silver or chrome—though (80) sometimes it may be goldplated. Brewed separately, the tea is then diluted with boiled water and served strong. The strength of the tea is seen as a measure of the host's hospitality. Traditionally, tea is taken by the entire family and (85) served after a large meal with jams and pastries.

Great Britain has a rich tradition of its own. Prior to the introduction of tea into Britain, the English had two main meals, breakfast and a second, dinner-like meal called "tea," which (90) was held around noon. However, during the middle of the eighteenth century, dinner shifted to an evening meal at a late hour; it was then called "high tea." That meant the necessary introduction of an afternoon snack to tide one (95) over, and "low tea" or "tea time" was introduced by British royalty. In present-day Britain, your afternoon tea might be served with scones and jam, small sandwiches, or cookies (called "biscuits"), depending on whether you're in (100) Ireland, England, or Scotland. Wherever they are and however they take it, Europeans know the value of savoring an afternoon cup of tea.

Average Annual Tea Consumption (Pounds per Person)

Country	Pounds
Turkey	6.961
Ireland	4.831
United Kingdom	4.281
Russia	3.051
New Zealand	2.629
Japan	2.133
Netherlands	1.714
Germany	1.524
China	1.248
Switzerland	0.971
India	0.715
Finland	0.539

Data from Euromonitor International and World Bank.

45. Based on the information provided in Passage 1, it can be inferred that

A) European nations tried to grow tea in their colonies.

B) European tea growers never learned Chinese cultivation techniques.

C) Europeans' purpose in opening trade routes with the Far East was to gain access to tea.

D) Europeans believed tea was ineffective as a treatment against illness.

46. Which choice provides the best evidence for the answer to the previous question?

A) Lines 7-10 ("However . . . measurements")

B) Lines 19-20 ("Some . . . maladies")

C) Lines 29-31 ("But . . . French controlled")

D) Lines 43-45 ("The harvest . . . per pound")

47. Based on the information in Passage 1, what would have been the most likely result if the British had not been able to grow tea in India?

A) Tea would have decreased in price across Europe.

B) The British would have learned to grow tea in Europe.

C) Europeans would have saved their tea for special occasions.

D) China would have produced more tea for the European market.

48. As used in line 25, "circumvent" most nearly means

A) destroy.

B) get around.

C) ignore.

D) compete with.

49. It can be inferred from both Passage 1 and the graphic that

    A) English botanical gardens helped make the United Kingdom one of the highest tea-consuming countries in the world.

    B) if the French Academy of Sciences hadn't given up growing tea in 1763, France would be one of the highest tea-consuming countries in the world.

    C) Britain's success at growing tea in India in the 1800s helped make the United Kingdom one of the highest tea-consuming nations in the world.

    D) China's production of tea would be higher if Britain hadn't discovered a way to grow tea in India in the 1800s.

50. It is reasonable to infer, based on Passage 2, that

    A) serving tea is an important part of hosting guests in Russia.

    B) Germans generally avoid medicine for stress.

    C) drinking tea in modern Britain is confined to the upper classes.

    D) the usual hour for drinking tea varies across Europe.

51. Which choice provides the best evidence for the answer to the previous question?

    A) Lines 54-56 ("Tea time . . . socialize")

    B) Lines 72-74 ("The Germans . . . stress")

    C) Lines 82-83 ("The strength . . . hospitality")

    D) Lines 93-96 ("That meant . . . royalty")

52. As used in line 76, "aristocratic" most nearly means

    A) culinary.

    B) political.

    C) rigid.

    D) noble.

53. Compared with France's tradition of tea-drinking, having tea in Germany

    A) is more formal.

    B) involves sweeter food.

    C) requires greater solitude.

    D) is more of a meal than a snack.

54. Which statement is the most effective comparison of the two passages' purposes?

    A) Passage 1's purpose is to describe the early history of tea in Europe, while Passage 2's purpose is to compare European cultural practices relating to tea.

    B) Passage 1's purpose is to argue against the Chinese monopoly of tea, while Passage 2's purpose is to argue that Europeans perfected the art of tea drinking.

    C) Passage 1's purpose is to express admiration for the difficult task of tea cultivation, while Passage 2's purpose is to celebrate the rituals surrounding tea.

    D) Passage 1's purpose is to compare Chinese and European relationships with tea, while Passage 2's purpose is to describe the diffusion of tea culture in Europe.

55. Both passages support which generalization about tea?

    A) Tea drinking in Europe is less ritualized than in China.

    B) Coffee was once more popular in Europe than tea was.

    C) India grows a great deal of tea.

    D) Tea is a staple of European households.

ANSWERS AND EXPLANATIONS

CHAPTER 5

Suggested Passage Map notes:

Passage 1

¶1: acid rain is a problem
¶2: explain pH scale
¶3: slightly acidic rain ok
¶4: human-made problems make bad acid rain

Passage 2

¶1: human blood needs controlled pH
¶2: pH controlled in body
¶3: kidneys aid in maintaining pH
¶4: uncontrolled pH causes problems - ex: diabetes

1. A   Difficulty: Medium

Category: Inference

Getting to the Answer: Consider what the author of Passage 1 is saying in the first paragraph about the causes and consequences of acid rain. Avoid answers like C that go too far and are not directly supported by the evidence in the passage. The author clearly states that acid rain, largely caused by the burning of fossil fuels, is bad for the environment. It is reasonable to conclude that if the burning of fossil fuels is not reduced, the environment will be damaged. Therefore, choice (A) is correct.

2. A   Difficulty: Medium

Category: Command of Evidence

Getting to the Answer: Look back at your answer to the previous question. Think about the information you found in the passage that helped you choose this answer. The last sentence in the first paragraph provides the strongest evidence for the idea that burning fossil fuels will seriously damage the environment. Therefore, choice (A) is correct.

3. A   Difficulty: Easy

Category: Detail

Getting to the Answer: Find where Passage 1 discusses the pH of rain water. Determine whether lower or higher pH levels indicate that rain water is dangerously acidic. The passage states that the pH of pure rain water can be as low as 5.5, and a pH level of 3 can cause soil and water to become too acidic. A pH level of 2.25 is less than 3, meaning it is even more dangerously acidic; therefore, the correct answer is choice (A).

4. B   Difficulty: Easy

Category: Vocab-in-Context

Getting to the Answer: Remember that some answer choices might be synonyms for "tolerate" but do not reflect the meaning of the word in this context. In this context, "tolerate" most nearly means "endure." Choice (B) is the correct answer.

5. D   Difficulty: Hard

Category: Inference

Getting to the Answer: Reread the text, looking for evidence to support each of the answer choices. The first paragraph of Passage 2 states: "Many processes in the body produce acid wastes" (lines 46-47), from which you can infer that it's normal to have acid wastes in the blood. Choice (D), therefore, is the correct answer.

6. C   Difficulty: Medium

Category: Command of Evidence

Getting to the Answer: Look for evidence that supports the inference you made in the previous question. In lines 65-69, the author explains how normal amounts of acid are neutralized in the blood. Choice (C) is correct.

7. C   Difficulty: Medium

Category: Vocab-in-Context

Getting to the Answer: Eliminate any answer choices that don't make sense in the context of the sentence. In this context, "exhaust" means "to use up" or "deplete." Therefore, choice (C) is the correct answer.

8. B   Difficulty: Hard

Category: Inference

Getting to the Answer: Read paragraph 2 of Passage 2 again, and determine the role of excess bicarbonate ions in the blood. Each answer choice is mentioned in Passage 1. Determine how each acts in the environment. Choice (B) is the correct answer. In Passage 2, the author explains that excess bicarbonate ions raise the pH of the blood, neutralizing acid wastes. In paragraph 3 of Passage 1, the author explains that alkaline materials in the environment, such as ashes from a forest fire, neutralize acid in the water supply.

9. D   Difficulty: Medium

Category: Connections

Getting to the Answer: You are looking for a cause-and-effect relationship to answer this question. Skim Passage 2, looking for an explanation of what causes the body to break down fats for energy. In paragraph 4 of Passage 2, the author explains that low insulin will cause the body to break down fats for energy. Therefore, choice (D) is the correct answer.

10. C   Difficulty: Medium

Category: Synthesis

Getting to the Answer: Consider the main topic and purpose of each passage. Decide what the passages have in common. Each passage describes a different system, the environment and the human body respectively, and how each system deals with acid. In each passage, the author describes how acid can be introduced into the system and neutralized in small amounts but also describes the ways in which large amounts of acid can damage or overwhelm each system, making choice (C) the correct answer.

11. A   Difficulty: Easy

Category: Synthesis

Getting to the Answer: The question is asking you about both passages. Eliminate answers that only address the information found in one of the passages. Although Passage 1 is about the environment and Passage 2 is about the human body, both passages are about delicate systems that need balance to remain healthy, so choice (A) is correct.

Suggested Passage Map notes:

Passage 1

¶1: (central idea): use atoms to date things; isotopes def. & exs.

¶2: isotopes unstable; measure C-14

¶3: C-14 decay = predictable

¶4: C-14 dating; materials; timeline based on layers

Passage 2

¶1: def. radioactive; why dangerous; danger = radiation rate

¶2: half-life def. = decay rate; exs.

¶3: long half-life = long problem

12. C   Difficulty: Hard

Category: Inference

Getting to the Answer: Use your Passage Map to locate the paragraph that explains carbon-14 dating. This paragraph will contain the description of what materials can be dated using this method. In paragraph 4, the author states that carbon-14 dating can be used on materials made by a living organism. An arrowhead made from a bone is constructed of such material, choice (C).

13. D   Difficulty: Hard

Category: Command of Evidence

Getting to the Answer: Locate each of the answer choices in the passage. The correct answer should provide direct support for the answer to the previous question: the bone arrowhead can be dated using carbon-14 dating. In paragraph 4, the author describes the process for carbon-14 dating. Choice (D) is correct because this sentence provides a direct description of the materials that can be dated using carbon-14 dating.

14. B   Difficulty: Medium

Category: Vocab-in-Context

Getting to the Answer: Pretend that the word "decay" is a blank. Reread around the cited word to predict a word that could substitute for "decay" in context. The previous paragraph discusses how scientists measure the rate of emission to calculate the amount of carbon-14 in a sample. "Emission" means release; therefore, the amount of carbon-14 is becoming smaller if the atoms are releasing it. In this sentence, therefore, predict "decay" means to *decrease*, which matches "deteriorate," choice (B).

15. C   Difficulty: Easy

Category: Inference

Getting to the Answer: Look at your notes for paragraph 3. Summarize the ratio of carbon-12 to carbon-14 in living tissue in your own words. Look for the answer choice that most closely matches your prediction. In paragraph 3, the author explains that the ratio of carbon-12 to carbon-14 for living things is the same as the ratio in the atmosphere: constant. Choice (C) is correct.

16. C   Difficulty: Medium

Category: Command of Evidence

Getting to the Answer: Review what part of the passage you used to predict an answer for the previous question: the ratio is constant for living things.

Of the answer choices, only lines 30-34 explain the ratio of carbon-12 to carbon-14 in living things. Choice (C) is correct.

17. B   Difficulty: Medium

Category: Detail

Getting to the Answer: Read around the cited lines. The author directly states why a release of iodine-131 is not cause for long-term concern. In paragraph 3, the author explains that the initial release of radiation from an accident involving iodine-131 will be high, but the level of radiation will drop quickly (line 82-84). Choice (B) is correct.

18. C   Difficulty: Medium

Category: Detail

Getting to the Answer: Use your Passage Map to find the information about why exposure to radiation is dangerous. In paragraph 1, lines 58-60, the author explains that radiation is harmful to living tissue because it can cause damage to the cells' DNA, which matches choice (C).

19. A   Difficulty: Easy

Category: Vocab-in-Context

Getting to the Answer: Pretend that the word "original" is a blank. Reread around the cited word to predict a word that could substitute for "original" in context. The previous paragraph explains how scientists use "half-life" to determine how quickly material decays. If the material is decaying, then predict "original" refers to the *first* material. Choice (A) matches your prediction.

20. D   Difficulty: Medium

Category: Detail

Getting to the Answer: Review your notes for Passage 2. Try to put into your own words how scientists use half-life calculations of radioactive materials. Look for the answer that most closely matches your idea. In paragraph 1, the author explains that the level of danger posed by radiation released during a nuclear accident depends on how quickly radiation is released (lines 65-68). In paragraph 2, the author discusses how the half-life of radioactive material is used to determine how long a material will emit radiation. Paragraph 3 then explains how different half-lives translate into short-term or long-term radiation concerns. Choice (D) is correct because it most clearly paraphrases the information in the passage about how scientists use half-life calculations.

21. A   Difficulty: Hard

Category: Synthesis

Getting to the Answer: The central idea will be supported by all of the evidence presented in both passages. Review the central idea you identified for each passage in your Passage Maps. Passage 1 discusses the application of atomic and nuclear physics in archaeology while Passage 2 details how scientists apply atomic and nuclear physics to studies of radioactivity in nuclear power plant accidents. Choice (A) is correct.

22. A   Difficulty: Hard

Category: Synthesis

Getting to the Answer: Analyze the graph to see that it describes the decay of carbon-14 over time. Think about how this data relates to the texts. The graph portrays the decay of carbon-14 as described in Passage 1. The definition of "half-life" is given in Passage 2. The half-life of a material is the amount of time it takes for half of that material to decay. The graph shows that about 50 percent of carbon-14 remains after 5,400 years. Choice (A) is correct.

Suggested Passage Map notes:

Passage 1

¶1: background of Bretton Woods
¶2: created IMF to facilitate international trade
¶3: created World Bank to give loans to war affected countries, bridge rich and poor countries, BW made US dollar global currency

¶4: shaped foreign trade
¶5: BW made US powerful

Passage 2:

¶1: BW only lasted 3 decades, Nixon changed economic policy
¶2: BW collapsed, IMF began flexible exchange system for currency
¶3: US dollar still widely used
¶4: G20 wants to create global currency
¶5-6: predicts worldwide currency, new world order in finance coming

23. B   Difficulty: Medium

Category: Inference

Getting to the Answer: Remember that you are being asked to choose an inference suggested by Passage 1, not a statement of fact. The passage notes that the U.S. dollar became a global currency that nations around the world accept for trade, leaving the United States in a stronger position to influence international markets. Choice (B) is the correct answer.

24. C   Difficulty: Medium

Category: Command of Evidence

Getting to the Answer: The correct choice should support your answer to the previous question. Consider which choice best shows a clear relationship with your answer to the item above. Choice (C) explicitly states the United States became the "primary power" behind the institutions established at Bretton Woods.

25. D   Difficulty: Medium

Category: Vocab-in-Context

Getting to the Answer: Predict an answer based on the context of the passage. The correct answer should not alter the meaning of the sentence in the passage. Then choose the option that best fits your prediction. The passage states that the IMF gives loans to member countries to ensure their continued stability. Choice (D) is correct because it most closely reflects the IMF's goals of proactively promoting global economic growth and stability.

26. B   Difficulty: Medium

Category: Connections

Getting to the Answer: Locate information in the passage that accurately summarizes the purposes of both institutions. Then ask yourself how these purposes differ. Both institutions encourage economic growth. However, Passage 1 notes that the IMF maintains payments and receipts between nations. The World Bank, on the other hand, focuses on "economic and social progress" (line 37) in individual countries. Choice (B) is the correct answer.

27. D   Difficulty: Hard

Category: Inference

Getting to the Answer: Eliminate any answer choices that are not suggested in the passage. The paragraph states that President Nixon's decision broke with the Bretton Woods framework. It can be reasonably inferred that the decision differed from the consensus of other nations, given the fact that many nations had agreed to Bretton Woods. Choice (D) is correct.

28. B   Difficulty: Medium

Category: Command of Evidence

Getting to the Answer: The answer choice should support your answer to the previous question. The paragraph states that President Nixon's decision "marked the end" of the Bretton Woods framework, which best supports the inference that the United States did not have the support of other nations. The correct answer is choice (B).

29. A   Difficulty: Medium

Category: Vocab-in-Context

Getting to the Answer: Reread the sentence in which the word appears and decide which meaning makes the most sense in context. The sentence is referring to a new global currency that might take the place of the U.S. dollar as the major, or key, currency. Therefore, choice (A) is the correct definition of "anchor" in this context.

30. A   Difficulty: Hard

Category: Synthesis

Getting to the Answer: Study the yuan's percent share of use in daily trading relative to other currencies in the graphic over time. What does this suggest about global views of the yuan? Passage 2 explicitly states that the yuan is "becoming a major world reserve currency" (lines 104-105). This is supported by the data in the chart, which shows the yuan's percent share of use in daily trading climbing from 0.5% in 2007 to 2.2% in 2013. Choice (A) is correct.

31. B   Difficulty: Medium

Category: Rhetoric

Getting to the Answer: Determine what purpose the final paragraph of Passage 2 serves in relation to the rest of the passage. Passage 2 is mostly about the changes to the world's financial system since the 1944 Bretton Woods Conference. The last paragraph of Passage 2 discusses a prediction about that system with which the author appears to agree. This is an opinion rather than a fact; therefore, choice (B) is correct.

32. C   Difficulty: Medium

Category: Synthesis

Getting to the Answer: Identify the overall purpose of each passage. Then consider which answer choice accurately describes these purposes. Choice (C) is the correct answer. Passage 1 focuses on the effects of Bretton Woods, while Passage 2 focuses on the reasons why the international economy may transition to a new global currency.

33. D   Difficulty: Medium

Category: Synthesis

Getting to the Answer: Keep in mind that the correct answer will be a statement that is evident in both passages. The role of the IMF is mentioned prominently in both passages. Therefore, choice (D) is the correct answer.

Suggested Passage Map notes:

Passage 1

¶1: neg. effects of video games
¶2: violent games similar to teaching methods
¶3: newer studies show positive effects
¶4: can shape future ed. techniques

Passage 2

¶1: brain deterioration in old age
¶2: studies show video games slow deterioration
¶3: need more research

34. C   Difficulty: Medium

Category: Global

Getting to the Answer: Review your notes about the passage's central ideas. The correct answer will include an idea that is supported by all of the evidence presented in the passage. Avoid answer choices like A that refer to only one idea presented in the passage. All of the details presented in the passage are related to the idea that research about the effects of video games on those who play them is being used to develop new educational tools and methods. Choice (C) is correct.

35. D   Difficulty: Medium

Category: Command of Evidence

Getting to the Answer: Locate each answer choice in the passage. Consider which lines from the passage most directly support the central idea of the passage, which you identified in the previous question. The central idea of the passage is related to how

research about video games is affecting the development of new methods of teaching. Choice (D) provides the most direct support for the answer to the previous question.

36. A   Difficulty: Easy

Category: Detail

Getting to the Answer: Use your Passage Map to find the paragraph that discusses studies performed in the 1990s. The correct answer will be stated explicitly in the passage. In paragraph 1, the author states that studies performed in the 1990s confirmed what parents had long said: that too many video games can have a negative impact on learning and socialization in teenagers. Choice (A) is correct.

37. C   Difficulty: Medium

Category: Vocab-in-Context

Getting to the Answer: Treat the tested word as a blank. Replace it with a synonym that makes sense in the context of the sentence, paragraph, and passage. In paragraph 2, the author explains that certain video games simulate a repetition method used in the classroom but indicates that this was *not intentional* on the part of the game developers. Choice (C) is correct because "inadvertently" most nearly means "unintentionally" in this context.

38. B   Difficulty: Medium

Category: Connections

Getting to the Answer: Review your Passage Map notes from paragraph 2. Identify the cause-and-effect relationship the author describes. In paragraph 2, the author explains that when played for extended periods of time, video games mimic methods used in the classroom to teach children information. This is what makes it easier for game players to absorb the content of the games. Choice (B) is correct.

39. A   Difficulty: Hard

Category: Inference

Getting to the Answer: The correct answer will not be stated directly in the text but should be supported by the evidence presented. Avoid answers like B and D that go too far. In paragraph 2, the author asserts that the findings of the research described suggest that those elderly persons who are able to prevent mental decline could better maintain the functions they need to operate independently, such as driving. Choice (A) is correct.

40. C   Difficulty: Medium

Category: Command of Evidence

Getting to the Answer: The answer to the previous question will not be directly stated in the answer choice to this question. Rather, the correct answer to this question will provide the strongest support for your answer to the previous question. In the previous question, you inferred from the information in the passage that people who are able to put off the cognitive effects of aging might be able to live longer independently. Choice (C) provides the strongest support for this connection.

41. D   Difficulty: Medium

Category: Vocab-in-Context

Getting to the Answer: Reread the target sentence and predict your own definition for the cited word. Then, evaluate the answer choices to find the closest match to your prediction. In this context, "deteriorate" most nearly means *get worse* or *weaken*. Choice (D) is correct.

42. A   Difficulty: Medium

Category: Rhetoric

Getting to the Answer: Review your notes from paragraph 2. Consider how the information presented in this paragraph supports the central claim presented by the author in the overall passage. Passage 2 is mostly about how researchers are considering the potential of video games in treating

brain deterioration; paragraph 2 focuses on the studies that show video games slow deterioration. Choice (A) is correct.

43. A   Difficulty: Medium

Category: Rhetoric

Getting to the Answer: Consider the overall message the author is conveying through the information presented in the passage. The author's purpose will not be directly stated but will be supported by the evidence presented. You determined the central claim to help you solve the previous question: Passage 2 is mostly about how researchers are considering the potential of video games in treating brain deterioration. Use this claim to help you determine the purpose of the passage: to describe how video games can potentially help elderly people who are experiencing brain deterioration. Choice (A) is correct.

44. D   Difficulty: Medium

Category: Synthesis

Getting to the Answer: The correct answer will be supported by the information in both passages. Think generally to predict what both passages agree on; avoid answers like B and C that refer only to information presented in one of the passages. Both passages discuss how video games are being used by researchers in different fields. Choice (D) is correct.

Suggested Passage Map notes:

Passage 1

¶1: history of tea, Europe and China
¶2: tea not received well in Europe at first
¶3: China controlled tea production
¶4: Europe wanted to produce tea
¶5: finally had tea growing success in India

Passage 2

¶1: history of tea time in Europe
¶2: tea in France served with savory
¶3: tea in Germany served with sweet
¶4: tea in Russia sign of class
¶5: tea in GB

45. A   Difficulty: Medium

Category: Inference

Getting to the Answer: Be careful to choose an answer that is clearly supported by the information in the passage. The passage states that the climate was not right for growing tea "even in the equatorial colonies" (line 30). Choice (A) is the correct answer. Clearly, European tea-drinking nations tried to grow tea in their equatorial colonies; that's how they learned that the climate there wasn't right.

46. C   Difficulty: Medium

Category: Command of Evidence

Getting to the Answer: The correct answer will be the reason you were able to make the inference in the previous question. Choice (C) works logically. Europeans knew that tea would not grow well in their colonies; this leads to the conclusion that they tried.

47. C   Difficulty: Medium

Category: Inference

Getting to the Answer: When a question refers to only one of the Paired Passages, be sure to focus on the correct passage. Find where Passage 1 discusses Great Britain's attempts to grow tea in India. Eliminate any answer choices that are not supported by information in this section of the passage. The last sentence of Passage 1 states that the large quantities of tea imported from India allowed tea to become a "staple" (line 52) in European households. You can infer that if the British had not succeeded in growing tea in India, Europeans would have had tea less often. Choice (C) is correct.

48. B   Difficulty: Medium

Category: Vocab-in-Context

Getting to the Answer: You should be able to replace the original word with the correct answer in the sentence. The passage states that in order to

"circumvent" the monopoly, European growers tried growing their own tea. It makes sense that Europeans' attempt at growing their own tea was a way to "get around" the Chinese monopoly. Therefore, choice (B) is the best choice.

49. C   Difficulty: Hard

Category: Synthesis

Getting to the Answer: Keep in mind that the graphic focuses on tea consumption, not tea production. The last paragraph of Passage 1 describes Britain's great success growing tea in India, which resulted in great increases in the amount of tea arriving in London. Therefore, choice (C) is a reasonable conclusion that may be drawn by synthesizing information in Passage 1 and the graphic.

50. A   Difficulty: Hard

Category: Inference

Getting to the Answer: Be careful to deduce only information that can reasonably be inferred from the passage. It can logically be inferred that hosting guests in Russia generally involves tea. Passage 2 emphasizes that Russian hosts are judged based on the strength of their tea, and that Russians have elaborate tea-making equipment. Choice (A) is the correct answer.

51. C   Difficulty: Medium

Category: Command of Evidence

Getting to the Answer: Identify the country associated with the correct answer to the previous question and see what evidence fits. The passage states that Russian tea ceremonies are highly formal and that hosts are judged on their tea-making. Choice (C) is the correct answer. The referenced lines support the conclusions about Russia.

52. D   **Difficulty:** Medium

Category: Vocab-in-Context

Getting to the Answer: Look for other words in this sentence that offer clues to the word's meaning. A noble, or high-ranking, class is likely to have associations with formalism, so choice (D) is the correct answer.

53. B   **Difficulty:** Easy

Category: Connections

Getting to the Answer: Make sure to compare only the two countries being asked about. The passage notes that cookies and cakes are served with tea in Germany, while foods served with tea in France are "savory" and include puff pastry with cheese. Choice (B) is correct.

54. A   **Difficulty:** Easy

Category: Synthesis

Getting to the Answer: Look for true statements about Passage 1. Then do the same for Passage 2. Passage 1 focuses on an earlier period in European history, while Passage 2 compares different cultures within Europe. Choice (A) is correct.

55. D   **Difficulty:** Medium

Category: Synthesis

Getting to the Answer: For this question, you're looking for a statement that is reflected in both passages. Choice (D) is the only choice supported by both passages.

Writing & Language

CHAPTER SIX

SAT Writing & Language Test Overview

The SAT Writing & Language Test

The SAT Writing & Language Test will focus on your ability to revise and edit text from a range of content areas.

SAT Writing & Language Test Overview	
Timing	35 minutes
Questions	44 passage-based multiple-choice questions
Passages	4 single passages with 11 questions each
Passage Length	400–450 words per passage

The SAT Writing & Language Test will contain four single passages, one from each of the following subject areas: Careers, Humanities, History/Social Studies, and Science.

Writing & Language Passage Types	
Careers	Hot topics in "major fields of work" such as information technology and health care
Humanities	Texts about literature, art, history, music, and philosophy pertaining to human culture
History/Social Studies	Discussion of historical or social sciences topics such as anthropology, communication studies, economics, education, human geography, law, linguistics, political science, psychology, and sociology
Science	Exploration of concepts, findings, and discoveries in the natural sciences including Earth science, biology, chemistry, and physics

Passages will also vary in the "type" of text. A passage can be an argument, an informative or explanatory text, or a nonfiction narrative.

Writing & Language Passage Text Type Distribution	
Argument	1–2 passages
Informative/Explanatory Text	1–2 passages
Nonfiction Narrative	1 passage

Some passages and/or questions will refer to one or more informational graphics that represent data. Questions associated with these graphical representations will ask you to revise and edit the passage based on the data presented in the graphic.

The most prevalent question format on the SAT Writing & Language Test will ask you to choose the best of three alternatives to an underlined portion of the passage or to decide that the current version is the best option. You will be asked to improve the development, organization, and diction in the passages to ensure they conform to conventional standards of English grammar, usage, and style.

Skills Tested by Writing & Language Test Questions	
Expression of Ideas (24 questions)	Development, organization, and effective language use
Standard English Conventions (20 questions)	Sentence structure, conventions of usage, and conventions of punctuation

Organization and Development

GETTING STARTED

Study the **Organization** and **Development** question types below to learn how to approach them and the concepts that these questions test. Knowing the information that you'll need to answer the questions helps you identify the important clues in the passage that will lead you to the correct answers.

Organization

Organization questions require you to assess the logic and coherence of a Writing & Language passage. These questions differ in scope; you might be asked to organize the writing at the level of the sentence, the paragraph, or even the entire passage.

There are two kinds of **Organization** questions:

1. Logical Sequence

- These questions ask you to reorder the sentences in a paragraph or paragraphs in a passage to ensure that information and ideas are logically conveyed.

- When rearranging sentences or paragraphs, begin by determining which sentence or paragraph most logically introduces the paragraph or the passage, respectively.

2. Introductions, Conclusions, And Transitions

- These questions task you with improving the beginning or ending of a passage or paragraph, making sure that the transition words, phrases, or sentences are being used effectively not only to connect information and ideas but also to maintain logical structure.

- While introductions and conclusions focus on the beginning and ending of a passage or paragraph, respectively, transitions are a bit more complicated. It's important to identify what two ideas the transition is linking and how it is doing so. Common types and examples of transitions are listed in the following chart.

Contrast Transitions	Cause-and-Effect Transitions	Continuation Transitions
although but despite even though however in contrast nonetheless on the other hand rather than though unlike while yet	as a result because consequently since so therefore thus	**Providing an example** for example for instance
		Showing emphasis certainly in fact indeed that is
		Showing a parallel relationship also furthermore in addition and moreover

✔ **Remember**

Organization questions require you not only to improve grammar and style but also to ensure that these elements accurately express the author's logic and reasoning.

Development

Proposition

Proposition questions ask about how well a writer uses language—arguments, information, and ideas—to express the central purpose of a passage or part of a passage.

You will be asked to add, revise, or retain portions of the passage to communicate key ideas, claims, counterclaims, and topic sentences most clearly and effectively.

To answer Proposition questions, you need to identify the topic and purpose of the passage and focus on the writer's point of view. Ask questions such as:

- What is the central idea of the passage?
- Why did the author write the passage?
- What does the author think about the subject?
- What is the author's tone?

> ✔ *Expert Tip*
>
> **The writer's point of view will be consistent throughout the passage. If the writer supports a certain issue, the correct answer choices will reflect this support and how the author effectively communicates it.**

Support

Support questions test issues related to information and ideas presented by the writer. You will be asked to evaluate the effectiveness of the facts and details employed by the writer to support claims made in the passage.

Support questions may ask you to keep, change, or add a detail or example. A Support question could ask about an example used to support a central argument or simply a minor detail used to weaken a point made by the author.

To answer Support questions, look around the underlined portion for a clue indicating what kind of support is required. If the example supports a central idea or claim, ask whether the example strengthens the author's central idea. Eliminate answer choices that don't fit the context or have a negative or trivial effect on the central idea.

Focus

Focus questions require you to assess whether portions of the passage include only the information and ideas relevant to the author's topic and purpose. You may be asked to add, change, or omit text.

When answering Focus questions, identify whether the text in question fits the topic, scope, and purpose of the entire passage.

> ✔ *Remember*
>
> *Topic* is what the passage is about. *Scope* is the aspect of the broader topic that is the center of the author's focus. *Purpose* is the author's reason for writing.

IMPROVING WITH PRACTICE

Step 1: Read Until You Can Identify the Issue

Always read the entire Writing & Language passage. This is particularly important for **Organization** and **Development** questions because the best clues for the correct answers may be before or after the underlined segment or the question marker. Be sure you identify:

- the main idea of each paragraph
- the author's opinion/tone
- any keywords, especially transition and timing keywords

You may have to read well after the underlined segment or question marker to be able to identify the issue. If you're not sure there's an issue, keep reading and then return to the question.

Step 2: Answer the Questions

As you're practicing, refer back to the tips in the "Getting Started" section and answer questions one at a time. Review the Answer and Explanation for every question immediately after completing it. If you got the question correct, congratulate yourself, but take a moment to read the entire explanation to be sure you got the question right for the right reason. The explanation may also point out a more efficient way that you can use on a later question.

Step 3: Review Incorrect Answers

If you get the question incorrect . . . still congratulate yourself! You're about to learn something new that you'll be able to use to improve your performance on Test Day. Don't read the explanation yet; instead, try the question again.

If you get the question correct the second time, read the explanation to see if you solved the question in the most efficient way. Identify the mistake you made the first time, and determine how you're going to avoid making that mistake again.

> ✔ *Expert Tip*
>
> **Many top scoring students have an SAT notebook where they write down what they learn from every question. Doing this can be time-consuming, but it can also help you identify the types of mistakes you tend to make.**

If you get the question incorrect the second time, use the explanation to learn how to get the question correct. Work through the question again while following the explanation, and identify the steps you will need to take to get a similar question correct. Although the passages and questions will change, the concepts being tested will not. When you encounter unfamiliar questions, take note of them for future study sessions.

> ✔ *Remember*
>
> **The SAT is a standardized test. While Hard Writing & Language questions are usually more difficult to answer than Easy or Medium questions, they are often similar in structure and purpose, and the same six skills (listed in Chapter 6) are tested on every Writing & Language Test. You actually can predict the types of questions you will see on Test Day!**

After all that work, it's time to move to the next question. Reviewing in this way will take time. However, improvement doesn't come from just doing lots and lots of questions; it comes from thinking through your approach and improving it with every question.

RAISING YOUR SCORE EVEN MORE

Here is one of the "secrets" to conquering the Writing & Language section: because the SAT is a standardized test, there will always be clues that make one choice definitely correct and the other choices completely wrong. It's never a matter of opinion.

For **Organization** and **Development** questions, these clues include:

- transition keywords, such as those listed above
- timing keywords, such as "first," "then," "finally"
- underlined pronouns, such as "this" or "these." Always ask yourself, "What is 'this'?" and substitute that idea back into the sentence. The idea to which the pronoun refers must immediately precede the sentence containing the pronoun.

> ✔ *Expert Tip*
>
> **Time spent identifying the clues not only saves time evaluating the choices but also improves your accuracy. Always find the clues first!**

For questions asking about introductions, evaluate each choice by reading it strictly on its own. If any part of the sentence is unclear when you read the sentence in isolation, it is not a good introductory sentence.

For questions asking about conclusions, the correct choice will not bring in any new ideas, but it will effectively summarize the paragraph or the passage.

PRACTICE QUESTIONS

The following test-like question sets provide an opportunity to practice reading Organization and Development questions. While many of the questions pertain to Organization and Development, some touch on other concepts tested on the Writing & Language Test to ensure that your practice is test-like, with a variety of question types per passage.

Questions 1-11 are based on the following passage and supplementary material.

Putting Microbes to Work for Us

[1]

The decline of the world's supply of fossil fuels is a growing concern. With increasingly more countries becoming dependent on fossil fuels for transportation, heating homes, and powering engines, the **1** <u>failing</u> of this finite resource has the potential to cause major disruption around the globe. To combat this issue, scientists are researching alternative energy sources. **2** <u>Used to produce biofuel are living things or the waste of living things, and biofuel is one such alternative.</u>

[2]

3 <u>Until recently, the primary focus of biofuel development has been ethanol.</u> Ethanol is created from plants such as corn, sugarcane, soybeans, and rice. While ethanol is a viable energy

1. A) NO CHANGE
   B) wilting
   C) depletion
   D) obstruction

2. A) NO CHANGE
   B) Biofuel is produced from living things or the waste of living things, and is one such alternative.
   C) Living things or the waste of living things are used in producing the one such alternative known as biofuel.
   D) One such alternative is biofuel, produced from living things or from the waste of living things.

3. Which choice most effectively establishes the central idea of this paragraph?
   A) NO CHANGE
   B) A variety of food crops can be used to produce ethanol.
   C) Many farmers have begun to grow corn for ethanol rather than food.
   D) Converting corn to ethanol is a complicated and expensive process.

[4] source, its use has been met with several challenges. These have limited its development as a quality alternative to traditional fossil fuels. One roadblock is that ethanol is expensive to produce. The plant must be first broken down into sugars and then fermented by microbes into a final useable product. It cannot be distributed by pipeline because it can pick up impurities along the way, so it must be transported by truck, train, or barge. Additionally, very large areas of cropland must be dedicated to growing these plants in order to produce enough ethanol to be designated for commercial use. This raises ethical questions because it means farmers are growing food sources earmarked solely for fuel when there are many people around the world in [5] horrible need of food. [6] In recent years, the price of corn has increased as the percentage of corn produced for ethanol has stayed the same. In addition, countries such as Brazil are decimating rain forests in order to grow sugarcane for ethanol production.

[3]

Once ethanol is produced, it is limited in its use as a commercial fuel. Therefore, it must be heavily refined and then blended with petroleum-based fuels in order to be used. [7] Standard internal combustion engines, such as those in cars, cannot run on ethanol alone.

[4]

The fossil fuels we rely on today for energy are finite. By researching alternate energy resources,

4. A) NO CHANGE
    B) source, its'
    C) source, it's
    D) source, it is

5. A) NO CHANGE
    B) dire
    C) grim
    D) grieving

6. Which choice best supports the paragraph with relevant and accurate information based on the graph?
    A) NO CHANGE
    B) In recent years, the price of corn has stayed the same as the percentage of corn produced for ethanol has decreased.
    C) In recent years, the price of corn has increased as the percentage of corn produced for ethanol has increased.
    D) In recent years, the price of corn has decreased as the percentage of corn produced for ethanol has increased.

7. Which choice best supports the central idea of the paragraph?
    A) NO CHANGE
    B) Most fuel sold for automobiles in the United States contains a blend of ethanol and gasoline.
    C) Ethanol has been used as an energy source in the United States for over 200 years.
    D) Although most often used to power automobiles, ethanol can also be used to power other engines.

including fuel produced by bacteria and other microbes, we can become less dependent on nonrenewable sources.

[5]

Researchers in the United Kingdom **8** had been developing a new kind of biofuel that addresses several of the issues hindering ethanol use. They have extracted genes from different species of bacteria and inserted them into *E. coli* bacteria. Once this process is complete, the *E. coli* can then perform the same metabolic functions as the donor **9** bacteria, this enables it to absorb fat molecules, convert these molecules to hydrocarbons, and then excrete the hydrocarbons as a waste product. The hydrocarbons produced by the genetically modified *E. coli* are the same as those found in commercial fossil fuels. **10** Finally, the newly created hydrocarbon molecules are interchangeable with the hydrocarbon molecules found in petroleum-based diesel fuels. This allows them to be used in a typical diesel engine, without any blending or refining.

8. A) NO CHANGE
   B) have developed
   C) had developed
   D) were developing

9. A) NO CHANGE
   B) bacteria; and this enables it
   C) bacteria. This enables it
   D) bacteria this enables it

10. A) NO CHANGE
    B) Therefore,
    C) For example,
    D) Also,

Think about the previous passage as a whole as you answer question 11.

11. To make the passage most logical, paragraph 4 should be placed
    A) where it is now.
    B) before paragraph 2.
    C) before paragraph 3.
    D) after paragraph 5.

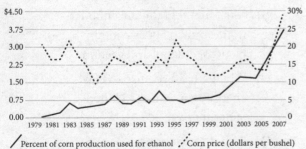

Percentage of U.S. Corn Used to Produce Ethanol and Price per Bushel, 1980-2007

/ Percent of corn production used for ethanol   .·´ Corn price (dollars per bushel)

Adapted from United States Department of Agriculture–Economic Research Service and United States Energy Information Administration, "Percentage of U.S. Corn Used to Produce Ethanol and Price per Bushel, 1980-2007."

Questions 12-22 are based on the following passage.

The Power of the PA

[12] Today, physician assistants are vital members of any health care system, but it hasn't always been that way. In 1960s America, there were not enough doctors to meet the primary care needs of patients nationwide. Due to the shortage, and in hopes of improving health care and its accessibility, educators sought to establish alternatives to medical school that would effectively equip other health care workers to share more of the physicians' workload. Their project altered health care history: the physician assistant (PA) was born. In 1967, the first PA program [13] launched at Duke University, notable for its education degrees and sports teams. The coming decades saw the field develop into what is considered today to be one of the most desirable and quickly growing careers in the country.

[1] Becoming a PA is simpler than becoming a physician, which usually takes over nine years of higher education and training. [2] Those seeking acceptance into PA programs typically study science or health as undergraduates. [3] Once practicing, PAs are required to maintain proficiency through continued education and a recertification exam every ten years. [4] They also usually [14] obtain some health-related work experience before applying. [5] [15] Once accepted to a program,

12. Which choice most effectively establishes the main topic of the paragraph?
   A) NO CHANGE
   B) For many years, doctors and educators struggled to find a role for the high number of incoming medical students.
   C) The difference between physician assistants and nurse practitioners was often hard to quantify, but then came a shift in health care needs.
   D) Physician assistants had long played a vital role in the medical field, but the PA career didn't become popular until the mid-20th century.

13. A) NO CHANGE
   B) launched at Duke University, noted for its education degrees.
   C) launched at the renowned Duke University.
   D) launched at Duke University.

14. A) NO CHANGE
   B) accrue
   C) perceive
   D) formulate

15. A) NO CHANGE
   B) Once accepted,
   C) Once they begin,
   D) Once programs accept them,

most students will be in their programs for about twenty-seven months. [6] Schooling involves both classroom and field study, and students undergo hundreds of hours in clinical training rotations in order to gain a breadth of supervised experience. [7] Today there are over one hundred and seventy accredited PA programs, most of which award masters degrees to graduates. [8] After graduation, **16** graduates must complete one final step: passing the national licensure exam. **17**

While physicians can work **18** anonymously, PAs always work under the supervision of physicians. But like nurse practitioners, another primary care alternative that emerged in the 1960s, PAs can do much of the work commonly expected of a physician. PAs are trained and qualified to meet with, examine, treat, diagnose, and counsel patients. They can prescribe medication, interpret lab data, and help physicians with surgical procedures. **19** In many ways, PAs lighten the workload for physicians on their teams. This enables clinics, hospitals, and other health care systems to run more efficiently and meet patient needs with greater accuracy and timeliness.

Physician assistants enjoy various options in terms of where they can practice. Almost every field of medicine has positions for those PAs who specialize accordingly. Also, depending on the needs of the physicians **20** under which PAs work, as well as the particular limitations that might be

16. A) NO CHANGE
   B) physicians
   C) PAs
   D) candidates

17. To make this paragraph most logical, sentence 3 should be placed
   A) where it is now.
   B) after sentence 5.
   C) after sentence 6.
   D) after sentence 8.

18. A) NO CHANGE
   B) defensively,
   C) autonomously,
   D) fundamentally,

19. A) NO CHANGE
   B) On the other hand,
   C) For example,
   D) First of all,

20. A) NO CHANGE
   B) where PAs work,
   C) under whom PAs work,
   D) who work under PAs,

imposed by a specific state, the requirements and responsibilities of the job can vary.

The past half-century saw the career of physician assistant rise from nascence to become a highly sought-after and still rapidly growing addition to American health care. Projections indicate that within the next decade, the number of employed PAs should increase significantly. 21 I believe PAs are an ever-increasing presence in health care and a powerful influence on the medical world for the better. 22

21. A) NO CHANGE

    B) PAs are an ever-increasing presence

    C) Doctors believe PAs are an ever-increasing presence

    D) You can believe that PAs are an ever-increasing presence

22. Which detail, if added to the paragraph, would best support the writer's claims?

    A) The number of PAs hired over the last half-century

    B) The expected PA-to-patient ratio over the next decade

    C) The number of PA positions compared to the number of nurse practitioner positions

    D) The specific rate at which PAs will be employed over the next decade

Questions 23-33 are based on the following passage.

The UK and the Euro

[1] The United Kingdom is a longstanding member of the European Union (EU), a multinational political organization and economic world leader **23** elected over the course of the past half-century. [2] However, there is one key feature of the EU in which the UK does not **24** participate; the monetary union known as the Eurozone, consisting of countries that share the euro as currency. [3] While the nation's public opinion has remained generally supportive of that decision, evidence suggests that the euro's benefits for the UK might, in fact, outweigh the risks. [4] When the EU first implemented the euro in 1999, intending to strengthen collective economy across the union, Britain was permitted exclusion and continued using the pound instead. [5] This, UK leaders hoped, would shield Britain from financial dangers that the euro might suffer. **25**

Proponents for avoiding the euro point **26** to faltering economies in the Eurozone region throughout the Eurozone. To join a massive, multinational economy would involve surrendering taxable wealth from one's own region to aid impoverished countries that may be some thousands of miles away. If a few economies in the Eurozone suffer, all of the participating nations suffer, too. Other proponents point to details of

23. A) NO CHANGE
    B) determined
    C) advanced
    D) built

24. A) NO CHANGE
    B) participate: the monetary
    C) participate, the monetary
    D) participate. The monetary

25. To make this paragraph most logical, sentence 3 should be placed
    A) where it is now.
    B) after sentence 1.
    C) after sentence 4.
    D) after sentence 5.

26. Which choice best completes the sentence?
    A) NO CHANGE
    B) to financial dangers that the euro might suffer.
    C) to faltering economies in most if not all Eurozone countries.
    D) to financial dangers and faltering economies in Eurozone countries throughout Europe.

financial policy such as interest rates and territory responsibilities, fearing loss of agency and political traction. **27** The UK's taxable wealth would decrease if it assisted impoverished countries.

But complications loom: the UK's current EU status may be untenable. In recent years, EU leaders seem to intend to transition all members **28** toward the Eurozone, for many reasons, this action appears necessary for protecting nations involved and ensuring the monetary union's long-term success. These conditions may potentially force the UK to choose either the security of its multidecade EU membership, or the pound and all it entails for Britain's economy. Enjoying both may not remain possible. **29** The UK wants to maintain the pound as its currency.

[1] Regarding Britain's intent to be protected from the Eurozone's economic dangers, this hope never quite materialized. [2] The UK saw economic downturns of its own during the euro's problematic years thus far. [3] Many families in the UK still struggle to pay their bills in the face of higher than normal unemployment rates. [4] It seems that regardless of shared currency, the economies of Britain and its Eurozone neighbors are too closely **30** intertwined

27. Which statement most clearly communicates the main claim of the paragraph?

A) NO CHANGE

B) Economic independence from impoverished countries would still be possible.

C) The UK would take on significant economic risk if it adopted the euro as its currency.

D) Euro adoption would require subsequent economic assistance on the UK's behalf.

28. A) NO CHANGE

B) toward the Eurozone. For many reasons,

C) toward the Eurozone, for many reasons.

D) toward the Eurozone. For many reasons.

29. Which sentence most effectively concludes the paragraph?

A) NO CHANGE

B) All EU members may soon have to accept the euro.

C) The UK faces a difficult decision regarding its EU membership.

D) All member nations want to ensure the success of the EU.

30. A) NO CHANGE

B) disparate

C) identical

D) relevant

for one to remain unscathed by another's crises. **31**

Perhaps this question of economic security has been the wrong one. Due to Britain's location and long-standing trade relationships with its neighbors, economies will persist to be somewhat reliant on each other, euro or not. **32** Furthermore, political security, power, and protection bear more significance for the future. If the UK hopes to maintain and expand its influential presence in world leadership, its association and close involvement with greater Europe are invaluable. Considering that the euro probably offers a lower risk margin than many have supposed, the benefits of euro **33** adoption: to secure EU membership and strengthen its cause, made Britain carefully reconsider.

31. Which sentence is least relevant to the central idea of this paragraph?
    A) Sentence 1
    B) Sentence 2
    C) Sentence 3
    D) Sentence 4

32. A) NO CHANGE
    B) Or,
    C) Also,
    D) However,

33. A) NO CHANGE
    B) adoption—to secure EU membership and strengthen its cause—
    C) adoption: to secure EU membership and strengthen its cause—
    D) adoption; to secure EU membership and strengthen its cause,

Questions 34-44 are based on the following passage.

Coffee: The Buzz on Beans

Americans love coffee. [34] Some days you can find a coffee shop in nearly every American city. But this wasn't always true. How did coffee, which was first grown in Africa over five hundred years ago, come to America?

The coffee plant, from which makers get the "cherries" that [35] is dried and roasted into what we call beans, first appeared in the East African country Ethiopia, in the province of Kaffa. From there, it spread to the Arabian Peninsula, where the coffeehouse, or *qahveh khaneh* in Arabic, was very popular. Like spices and cloth, coffee was traded internationally as European explorers reached far lands and [36] establishing shipping routes. The first European coffeehouse opened in Venice, Italy, in 1683, and not long after London [37] displayed over three hundred coffeehouses.

There is no record of coffee being amongst the cargo of the *Mayflower*, which reached the New World in 1620. It was not until 1668 that the first written reference to coffee in America was made. The reference described a beverage made from roasted beans and flavored with sugar or honey, and cinnamon. Coffee was then chronicled in the New England colony's official records of 1670. In 1683, William Penn, who lived in a settlement on the Delaware River, wrote of buying supplies of

34. A) NO CHANGE
    B) Many
    C) The
    D) These

35. A) NO CHANGE
    B) are being dried and roasted
    C) are dried and roasted
    D) is being dried and roasted

36. A) NO CHANGE
    B) established
    C) having established
    D) was establishing

37. A) NO CHANGE
    B) bragged
    C) highlighted
    D) boasted

coffee in a **38** <u>New York market, he paid</u> eighteen shillings and nine pence per pound. **39**

Coffeehouses like those in Europe were soon established in American colonies, and as America expanded westward, coffee consumption grew. In their settlement days, **40** <u>Chicago St. Louis and New Orleans</u> each had famous coffeehouses. By the mid-twentieth century, coffeehouses were abundant. In places like New York and San Francisco, they became **41** <u>confused</u> with counterculture, as a place where intellectuals and artists gathered to share ideas. In American homes, coffee was a social lubricant, bringing people together to socialize as afternoon tea had done in English society. With the invention of the electric coffee pot, it became a common courtesy to ask a

38. A) NO CHANGE
   B) New York market and William Penn
   C) New York market so he paid
   D) New York market, paying

39. Which choice best establishes a concluding sentence for the paragraph?
   A) Coffee's appearance in the historical record shows it was becoming more and more established in the New World.
   B) The colonies probably used more tea than coffee because there are records of it being imported from England.
   C) William Penn founded Pennsylvania Colony, which became the state of Pennsylvania after the Revolutionary War with England ended.
   D) The Mayflower did carry a number of items that the colonists needed for settlement, including animals and tools.

40. A) NO CHANGE
   B) Chicago, St. Louis, and New Orleans
   C) Chicago, St. Louis, and, New Orleans
   D) Chicago St. Louis and, New Orleans

41. A) NO CHANGE
   B) related
   C) associated
   D) coupled

guest if she wanted "coffee or tea?" **42** "There were many coffee shops in New York and in Chicago."

However, by the 1950s, U.S. manufacturing did to coffee what it had done to **43** other foods; produced it cheaply, mass-marketed it, and lowered its quality. Coffee was roasted and ground in manufacturing plants and freeze-dried for a long storage life, which compromised its flavor. An "evangelism" began to bring back the original bracing, dark-roasted taste of coffee, and spread quickly. **44** In every major city of the world, now travelers around the world, expect to be able to grab an uplifting, fresh, and delicious cup of coffee—and they can.

42. Which choice most effectively concludes the paragraph?
A) NO CHANGE
B) Electric coffee machines changed how people entertained at home.
C) Over time, it was clear that coffee had become a part of everyday American life.
D) People went to coffeehouses to discuss major issues.

43. A) NO CHANGE
B) other foods produced
C) other foods, produced
D) other foods: produced

44. A) NO CHANGE
B) Now travelers, in every major city of the world, around the world expect to be able to grab an uplifting, fresh, and delicious cup of coffee—and they can.
C) Now in every major city of the world, travelers around the world expect to be able to grab an uplifting, fresh, and delicious cup of coffee—and they can.
D) Now travelers around the world expect to be able to grab an uplifting, fresh, and delicious cup of coffee in every major city of the world—and they can.

Questions 45-55 are based on the following passage and supplementary material.

The UN: Promoting World Peace

The United Nations (UN) is perhaps the most important political contribution of the 20th century. Some may argue that the work of the UN [45] ; an international peacekeeping organization— has proven futile, given persisting global conflict. However, the UN's worldwide influence demands a closer look. This organization's global impact is undeniable. The UN is a strong political organization determined to create opportunities for its member nations to enjoy a peaceful and productive world. [46]

[47] Decades ago, provoked by the events of World Wars I and II, world leaders began imagining a politically neutral force for international peace. The UN was born in 1945 with 51 participating nations. It was to be a collective political authority for global peace and security.

45. A) NO CHANGE
    B) —an international peacekeeping organization;
    C) —an international peacekeeping organization—
    D) ; an international peacekeeping organization,

46. Which choice would most clearly end the paragraph with a restatement of the author's claim?
    A) The UN is an organization dedicated to advancing social and political justice around the world.
    B) Those who argue otherwise are not well educated about geopolitical issues in the 20th century or today.
    C) The UN has had its share of corruption over the years, but it has a well-earned reputation of effectively settling international disputes.
    D) A better understanding of the UN suggests that the UN enables far greater peace in today's world than could have been possible otherwise.

47. A) NO CHANGE
    B) Recently,
    C) Consequently,
    D) In other words,

Today, 193 nations are UN members. **48** <u>In keeping with the original hope, the UN still strives toward peaceful international relations.</u>

Understandably, no single organization can perfectly solve the world's countless, complex problems. But the UN has offered consistent relief for many of the past half-century's most difficult disasters and conflicts. It also provides a safe space for international conversation. Moreover, it advocates for issues such as justice, trade, hunger relief, human rights, health, and gender **49** <u>equality, the UN</u> also coordinates care for those displaced by disaster and conflict, **50** <u>dictates</u> environmental protection, and works toward conflict reconciliation.

51 <u>The UN's budget, goals, and personnel count have significantly expanded with time to meet</u>

48. A) NO CHANGE
   B) In having kept with the original hope, the UN still strives toward peaceful international relations.
   C) In keeping with the original hope, the UN still strived toward peaceful international relations.
   D) In keeping with the original hope, the UN still strove toward peaceful international relations.

49. A) NO CHANGE
   B) equality. The UN
   C) equality: the UN
   D) equality, The UN

50. A) NO CHANGE
   B) prefers
   C) promotes
   D) celebrates

51. Which choice provides the most logical introduction to the paragraph?
   A) NO CHANGE
   B) The UN has developed over the years, but critics charge it has met with limited success.
   C) The responsibilities of the UN have expanded in recent years in response to challenging events.
   D) The UN has maintained a quiet but effective voice on the world stage in spite of criticism.

more needs. **52** The year 2014 witnessed the UN peacekeeping force grow to over 100,000 strong. These uniformed, volunteer, civilian personnel represent 128 nations. The UN's budget has also grown over the years to support an international court system, as well as countless agencies, committees, and centers addressing sociopolitical topics. Today's UN does big things, and it functions with remarkable organization and efficiency. Critics highlight shortcomings to discount the UN's effectiveness. But considering the countless disasters to which the UN has responded over its six decades of existence, today's world might enjoy **53** far less peace, freedom, and safety without the UN.

[1] From promoting overarching sociopolitical change to offering food and care for displaced groups, the UN serves to protect human rights. [2] Equally **54** quotable are its initiatives to foster international collaboration, justice, and peace. [3] The UN provided aid to the Philippines after the disastrous 2013 typhoon. [4] Certainly, this work is not finished. [5] But no other organization

52. Which choice best completes the sentence with accurate data based on the graphic?

A) NO CHANGE

B) The year 2010 led to an increase of approximately 100,000 in the UN peacekeeping force.

C) The year 2010 saw the UN peacekeeping force grow to approximately 100,000 strong.

D) The year 2010 saw the UN peacekeeping force decrease to just over 100,000 strong.

53. A) NO CHANGE

B) considerably less peace, less freedom, and less safety

C) much less peace, less freedom, and less safety

D) significantly less peace and freedom, and less safety

54. A) NO CHANGE

B) luminous

C) noteworthy

D) repeatable

compares with the work and influence of the UN. [6] This brave endeavor to insist on and strive for peace, whatever the obstacles, has indeed united hundreds of once-divided nations. [7] Today, with eleven Nobel Peace Prizes to its name, the UN is undoubtedly an irreplaceable and profoundly successful force for peace.

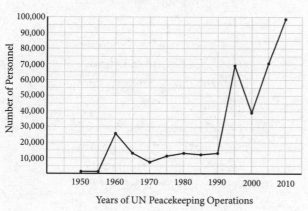

UN Peacekeeping Personnel Numbers Since 1950

55. Which sentence should be removed to improve the focus of the concluding paragraph?

A) Sentence 1

B) Sentence 3

C) Sentence 5

D) Sentence 6

Questions 56-66 are based on the following passage.

Interpreter at America's Immigrant Gateway

[56] Among the many diverse and fascinating possibilities for a career, David Kaufman chose language interpretation. Throughout his career as an interpreter at America's largest immigrant processing station, Kaufman has spent many ferry rides mentally preparing himself for the vivid realities of his job. Although some of his contemporaries might consider his work menial or inconsequential, he cherishes his opportunity to witness and contribute to the unfolding stories of countless immigrants. These immigrant stories, Kaufman knows, hold [57] great significance for his and American history. Most of the brave, sea-worn travelers who disembark at Ellis Island will soon depart as new Americans, [58] lugging all there courage, hope, and worldly possessions into

56. Which choice provides the most appropriate introduction to the passage?

A) NO CHANGE

B) Many people never consider language interpretation as a job, but David Kaufman knows all about it.

C) All jobs come with difficulties, and David Kaufman believes language interpretation is no different.

D) A pale horizon meets the early-morning sky as David Kaufman's commuter ferry crosses the New York Harbor, bound for Ellis Island.

57. A) NO CHANGE

B) great significance for his—and America's—history.

C) great significance for his: and America's history.

D) great significance for his, and America's, history.

58. A) NO CHANGE

B) lugging all they're courage,

C) lugging all their courage,

D) lugging all there are courage,

New York City. Many [59] <u>will remain in the city and some other people will disperse across the</u> nation.

[1] The year is 1907: the busiest year Kaufman, or Ellis Island, has seen. [2] One and a quarter million immigrants have been admitted to the U.S. this year. [3] Only about 2 percent of Ellis Island's immigrants are denied, typically for perceived potential criminal or public health threats. [4] The rest will establish life in America, although not without difficulty and perseverance. [5] At the immigration station, Kaufman regularly sees the range of raw human emotion, from deep, exhausted grief to powerful hope. [6] He has witnessed it all. [60]

[61] <u>Many Ellis Island interpreters were born to European immigrants.</u> [62] <u>His heritage, and surrounding community, enabled him to learn six languages.</u> Fluency in six languages is typical for Ellis Island interpreters, although Kaufman knows some who speak as many as twelve or thirteen. Kaufman knows that in some ways, his ability to listen and translate effectively can impact the course of an immigrant's future. For this reason, he constantly hones his language skills, picking up

59. A) NO CHANGE
     B) will remain in the city, but other people will nonetheless disperse across the
     C) will remain in the city; many others will disperse across the
     D) will remain in the city, though yet others will disperse across the

60. Sentence 1 should be placed
     A) where it is now.
     B) after sentence 2.
     C) after sentence 3.
     D) after sentence 4.

61. Which sentence most effectively establishes the central idea of the paragraph?
     A) NO CHANGE
     B) Like many Ellis Island interpreters, Kaufman was born to European immigrants.
     C) Language ability was especially important among Ellis Island interpreters.
     D) Some accused children of European immigrants of having an unfair advantage in getting jobs at Ellis Island.

62. A) NO CHANGE
     B) His heritage, and surrounding community enabled him to learn six languages.
     C) His heritage and surrounding community, enabled him to learn six languages.
     D) His heritage and surrounding community enabled him to learn six languages.

various 63 shades and dialects in hopes to better help those he serves.

Kaufman assists colleagues at every checkpoint. Ellis Island is equipped with a hospital, dining room, and boarding room, in addition to the more central processing facilities. 64 Kaufman is one of an army of Ellis Island employees spread around the enormous compound. This morning, he helps an Italian family discuss their child's health with nurses. Later, he translates for a Polish woman who expects to meet her brother soon. When Kaufman meets immigrants whose language he cannot speak, he finds another interpreter 65 to help speak to them instead of him doing it.

To some extent, Kaufman sees himself distinctly in the shoes of these immigrants. He intimately knows the reality that almost all Americans, somewhere in their ancestry, were not native to this nation. With every encounter, Kaufman hopes that these immigrants will soon find whatever they crossed oceans to seek. He hopes, as he still does for his own family, that life in America will someday render the 66 advantages of leaving home worthwhile.

63. A) NO CHANGE
    B) meanings
    C) tricks
    D) nuances

64. Which sentence best supports the central idea of the paragraph?
    A) NO CHANGE
    B) From medical screening to records confirmation to inspection, Kaufman interprets as needs arise.
    C) Sometimes, Kaufman feels the stress of being pulled in many different directions, but ultimately he finds his job worthwhile.
    D) Kaufman and his colleagues work, eat, and practically live together, making them feel closer than typical coworkers.

65. A) NO CHANGE
    B) to help speak instead of him.
    C) helping him out with speaking.
    D) to help.

66. A) NO CHANGE
    B) journeys
    C) difficulties
    D) penalties

ANSWERS AND EXPLANATIONS

CHAPTER 7

1. C   Difficulty: Medium

Category: Effective Language Use

Getting to the Answer: Think about the overall meaning of the sentence. Select the answer choice that makes the most sense in context. "Depletion" is the reduction of a resource, so choice (C) is correct.

2. D   Difficulty: Hard

Category: Effective Language Use

Getting to the Answer: The most important element of the sentence is that biofuel is an alternative fuel source. Choice (D) is correct because this sentence places the emphasis on "alternative is biofuel."

3. A   Difficulty: Medium

Category: Development

Getting to the Answer: Look for the answer choice that clearly states the main topic of the paragraph and introduces the central idea supported by all of the details presented. Topic sentences or introductory sentences of body paragraphs should generally introduce that paragraph's topic. While other answer choices address details disclosed in the paragraph, choice (A) is the most general and also uses the transition "until recently" to tie this paragraph to the one that precedes it.

4. A   Difficulty: Medium

Category: Usage

Getting to the Answer: "It" refers to ethanol and is possessive. The possessive form of "it" is "its," so the sentence is correct as written. Choice (A) is correct.

5. B   Difficulty: Medium

Category: Effective Language Use

Getting to the Answer: The underlined word, "horrible," is too casual. Be careful of answer choices that are close in meaning to "horrible" but do not fit the established tone. Replace "horrible" with each of the answer choices. In this context, "dire," which means severe or urgent, best fits the tone and style of the sentence. Choice (B) is correct.

6. C   Difficulty: Medium

Category: Quantitative

Getting to the Answer: Look at the most recent data in the graph. Pay attention to the relationship between the two lines: the solid line represents the percentage of corn production used for ethanol, and the dotted line reflects the price of corn. In the most recent years displayed in the graph, the price of corn and the percentage of corn production used for ethanol have both increased. Choice (C) is correct.

7. A   Difficulty: Hard

Category: Development

Getting to the Answer: Determine the central idea of the paragraph. In this paragraph, the author explains that ethanol is limited as a commercial fuel. Choice (A) describes one way in which ethanol use is limited and is therefore correct.

8. B   Difficulty: Easy

Category: Usage

Getting to the Answer: Read the first few sentences of the paragraph and pay attention to the verb tenses used in the following sentences. As written, the underlined portion is in the past perfect tense. The following sentence, however, uses the present perfect form of the verb "to develop." The underlined portion should also be in the present perfect form; therefore, (B) is correct.

9. C   Difficulty: Medium

Category: Sentence Formation

Getting to the Answer: Check to see if this sentence contains two independent clauses that create a run-on sentence without proper punctuation. This sentence contains two complete thoughts with two independent main clauses and should therefore be separated into two sentences with a period. Choice (C) is correct.

10. B   Difficulty: Medium

Category: Organization

Getting to the Answer: Read the previous sentence in conjunction with this one. Think about the relationship between the ideas in the two sentences. There is a cause-and-effect relationship between the ideas in the previous sentence and this sentence, but the underlined portion contains a concluding transition. "Therefore" is a cause-and-effect transition, so choice (B) is correct.

11. D   Difficulty: Easy

Category: Organization

Getting to the Answer: Read this paragraph in the context of the entire passage to determine its proper placement. This paragraph makes general statements about the central idea of the passage and draws a conclusion. Choice (D) is correct because paragraph 4 is an appropriate concluding paragraph.

12. A   Difficulty: Medium

Category: Development

Getting to the Answer: Reread the paragraph to determine which answer choice best introduces the main point. The correct answer, choice (A), is the only one that accurately explains how the career is now popular and helpful but had to develop over time after a shift in health care needs.

13. D   Difficulty: Easy

Category: Development

Getting to the Answer: Reread the sentence and determine which answer choice creates the most focused sentence. The additional comments about the school's quality and features are unnecessary. Choice (D) creates the most focused sentence.

14. B   Difficulty: Medium

Category: Effective Language Use

Getting to the Answer: Look for nearby context clues and use what you know of each answer choice's definition to determine which word most accurately reflects the intention of the sentence. The intention of the sentence is to state that students should acquire hands-on medical knowledge through work experience. The word with the definition that best describes this acquisition is "accrue," choice (B).

15. B   Difficulty: Easy

Category: Effective Language Use

Getting to the Answer: Read the entire sentence for context clues and determine which answer choice creates a logical sentence without wordiness or redundancies. Only choice (B) correctly eliminates wordiness, as the word "programs" is used later in the same sentence.

16. D   Difficulty: Medium

Category: Effective Language Use

Getting to the Answer: Find context clues and determine which answer choice creates a logical sentence without wordiness or redundancies. Because there is still an exam to pass before these individuals become PAs, and because the repetition of the words "graduates" and "graduation" is redundant, choice (D) is the correct answer.

17. D   Difficulty: Medium

Category: Organization

Getting to the Answer: Review the answer choices to determine which creates a paragraph with the best logical progression of ideas. The paragraph discusses the steps a student must take in order to become a PA and should not discuss maintaining one's license until the end, as it is done only after becoming a PA. Choice (D) is correct.

18. C   Difficulty: Medium

Category: Effective Language Use

Getting to the Answer: Use context clues to determine which answer choice best fits the context of the sentence and paragraph while conveying the author's intended meaning. The sentence suggests that doctors work alone while PAs work under supervision. The word with the definition that best describes a doctor's unsupervised work is "autonomously," choice (C).

19. A   Difficulty: Medium

Category: Organization

Getting to the Answer: Decide which answer choice offers the best transition for an accurate flow of ideas. Choice (A) offers the best transition in order to summarize why the previous information is important and to show the positive effects PAs have on the health care team.

20. C   Difficulty: Hard

Category: Usage

Getting to the Answer: Evaluate whether the subject or object of the sentence is referred to by the pronoun and then determine which answer choice creates a logical and grammatically sound sentence. It is the PA who works under a physician, and because the pronoun refers to the object of the sentence, physicians, the appropriate pronoun to use in this situation is "whom." Therefore, choice (C) is correct.

21. B   Difficulty: Medium

Category: Effective Language Use

Getting to the Answer: Reread the paragraph and decide which answer choice maintains the style and tone of the author's voice. The author has not yet referenced him or herself, the reader, or any third party for an opinion in this passage. This makes the consistent tone found in choice (B) correct.

22. D   Difficulty: Medium

Category: Development

Getting to the Answer: Review the paragraph to determine which claim made by the author is lacking details or supporting evidence that would strengthen the author's case. The second sentence in the paragraph is the only one in which the author makes a claim based on projections, but the author fails to use specific figures. Adding these figures would strengthen this claim, thus choice (D) is correct.

23. D   Difficulty: Medium

Category: Effective Language Use

Getting to the Answer: Read carefully to identify the context of the underlined word. Then, choose the word that best fits the content of the sentence. You're looking for a word that suggests that the organization has developed over time, as is stated in the last part of the sentence. "Built," (D), best fits the context of the sentence.

24. B   Difficulty: Medium

Category: Punctuation

Getting to the Answer: Read the entire sentence to get a better sense for which punctuation would be correct. A colon will introduce an explanation of the "key feature," allowing the rest of the sentence to elaborate on the preceding clause. Choice (B) is correct. In this case, the colon prompts the reader to see that the part of the sentence after the colon defines the phrase "key feature."

25. D   Difficulty: Medium

Category: Organization

Getting to the Answer: Watch out for any choices that would make the sentence seem out of place. Choice (D) is correct. Sentence 3 offers a transition to a specific discussion of those risks in the next paragraph.

26. B   Difficulty: Medium

Category: Effective Language Use

Getting to the Answer: Avoid choices that are redundant, or use more words than necessary to communicate an idea. All of the choices communicate the same idea, but one does so with a greater economy of language. Choice (B) uses a minimal number of well-chosen words to revise the text.

27. C   Difficulty: Hard

Category: Development

Getting to the Answer: Watch out for answer choices that correctly identify supporting points but do not explain the main claim. The paragraph contains evidence, including decreased taxable wealth and decreased control over interest rates, to support the main claim. Choice (C) is correct. It expresses the main claim of the paragraph and is supported by the evidence.

28. B   Difficulty: Medium

Category: Sentence Formation

Getting to the Answer: Read the text carefully. Notice that the existing structure creates a run-on sentence. Then consider which answer choice will create two complete sentences. Choice (B) revises the run-on sentence to create two grammatically complete sentences.

29. C   Difficulty: Medium

Category: Development

Getting to the Answer: Find the main claim in the paragraph and then come back to the question. The statement found in choice (C) best supports the paragraph statements that maintaining the current status may not be an option and moving to the Eurozone may be in the best interest of the UK.

30. A   Difficulty: Easy

Category: Effective Language Use

Getting to the Answer: Watch out for choices that imply little relationship between the EU and the UK. "Intertwined" most accurately reflects the content of the text, because it implies a complex economic relationship between the UK and the Eurozone. Therefore, choice (A) is correct; no change is necessary.

31. C   Difficulty: Hard

Category: Development

Getting to the Answer: Find the central idea of the paragraph and then come back to the question. The central idea in the paragraph is that economic downturns in the Eurozone also affect the UK. Choice (C) is correct.

32. D   Difficulty: Easy

Category: Organization

Getting to the Answer: Decide which transition word makes the most sense in the context of the sentence by reading each choice in the sentence. The correct choice should connect the two sentences as the text transitions from economic concerns to those of "security, power, and protection." The word "however" is the best transition because it provides a logical contrast between the ideas in the passage. Choice (D) is the correct answer.

33. B   Difficulty: Medium

Category: Punctuation

Getting to the Answer: Consider which punctuation will correctly set off the parenthetical information in this sentence. Dashes are often used to offset parenthetical sentence elements. Choice (B) is correct.

34. D   Difficulty: Easy

Category: Usage

Getting to the Answer: Review each answer choice and decide which makes the most sense in terms of what the first sentence says. Choice (D) is the correct answer. "These days" contrasts with the next sentence's use of "this wasn't always true."

35. C   Difficulty: Medium

Category: Usage

Getting to the Answer: Make sure that verbs agree with the subject. Check back and figure out what the subject is and then see if it agrees. The word "cherries" requires a plural verb. Choice (C) is the correct answer.

36. B   Difficulty: Medium

Category: Sentence Formation

Getting to the Answer: Read the complete sentence carefully whenever you see a shift in tense or verb form. Decide whether this change is logically correct in the sentence. The verbs in a sentence need to be in parallel form. Choice (B) is in parallel form with the first verb "reached," so it is the correct answer.

37. D   Difficulty: Medium

Category: Effective Language Use

Getting to the Answer: Beware of some answer choices that may have similar meanings but do not fit into the context of this sentence. The word "boasted" is the best fit for the context of the sentence, so (D) is the correct answer.

38. D   Difficulty: Medium

Category: Sentence Formation

Getting to the Answer: Pay close attention to commas to ensure that they do not create run-on sentences. Notice that this sentence contains two complete thoughts. Choice (D) is the correct answer because it combines the two complete thoughts into one sentence in the best way.

39. A   Difficulty: Hard

Category: Development

Getting to the Answer: To find the best conclusion, look for the choice that summarizes the main points of the paragraph and best completes the paragraph. The paragraph begins by talking about the lack of record of coffee as cargo on the Mayflower and then introduces when it was first referenced. Choice (A) does the best job of retelling what the paragraph is about, therefore providing an effective conclusion.

40. B   Difficulty: Easy

Category: Punctuation

Getting to the Answer: Study the words in the series and see where commas might need to be placed or eliminated. Choice (B) is the correct answer.

41. C   Difficulty: Medium

Category: Effective Language Use

Getting to the Answer: Replace the word with the other answer choices. See which word works best in the context of the sentence. One answer choice indicates the correct relationship between coffeehouses and counterculture, and that is (C). "Associated" works best within the context of the sentence.

42. C   Difficulty: Medium

Category: Development

Getting to the Answer: To find the main topic of a paragraph, identify important details and summarize them in a sentence or two. Then find the answer choice that is the closest to your summary. Choice (C) is the correct answer. The sentence best explains the increasing popularity of coffee in American life, the main topic of the paragraph.

43. D   Difficulty: Medium

Category: Punctuation

Getting to the Answer: Determine the relationship between the two parts of this sentence, and then consider the purpose of the various forms of punctuation. A colon indicates that the rest of the sentence will be a list or an explanation. Choice (D) is the correct answer, as it shows the correct relationship between both parts of the sentence.

44. D   Difficulty: Hard

Category: Sentence Formation

Getting to the Answer: Read the complete sentence carefully and look for sections that do not seem to follow logically. The modifiers need to be in the proper order so the sentence's meaning is clear; choice (D) is correct.

45. C   Difficulty: Medium

Category: Punctuation

Getting to the Answer: Examine the passage to determine whether the current punctuation is incorrect. Then consider which set of punctuation marks correctly emphasizes the selected part of the sentence. The dashes provide emphasis for the idea that the UN is a peacekeeping organization; the dashes help set off this part of the sentence from the remaining content. The correct answer is choice (C).

46. D   Difficulty: Hard

Category: Development

Getting to the Answer: Review the main points made so far. The correct answer should touch on or summarize previous ideas in the paragraph. Choice (D) is correct. This concluding sentence effectively summarizes the ideas that compose the paragraph's main claim.

47. A   Difficulty: Medium

Category: Organization

Getting to the Answer: Read the previous paragraph and identify the word or phrase that is the best transition between the two paragraphs. The previous paragraph describes the UN today, and the paragraph beginning with the phrase in question explains the origins of the UN in the 1940s. Choice (A) indicates the correct shift in time period and provides the most effective transition between paragraphs.

48. A   Difficulty: Medium

Category: Usage

Getting to the Answer: Pay close attention to the context of the previous sentence to help you establish the correct verb tense for this particular sentence. The correct answer is choice (A). It uses the present tense to logically follow the previous sentence that refers to the UN in the present tense, as well.

49. B   Difficulty: Easy

Category: Punctuation

Getting to the Answer: Watch out for choices that create a run-on sentence. The correct answer is choice (B), which provides a clear separation between one complete sentence and the next.

50. C   Difficulty: Easy

Category: Effective Language Use

Getting to the Answer: Substitute each choice in the complete paragraph. The correct answer will most appropriately fit within the context of the sentence and the paragraph. The correct answer is (C). The UN encourages, or promotes, environmental protection.

51. A   Difficulty: Medium

Category: Development

Getting to the Answer: The correct choice should introduce a central idea that is supported by subsequent sentences in the paragraph. The correct answer is choice (A). The expansion of the UN's budget, goals, and personnel numbers connects to specific evidence in the rest of the paragraph.

52. C   Difficulty: Medium

Category: Quantitative

Getting to the Answer: Notice that the graphic gives specific information about the increases and decreases in the UN peacekeeping force over a period of time. Study the answer choices to find the one that best relates to the paragraph while using accurate information from the graphic. The graphic shows data through the year 2010 and does not indicate that personnel levels rose above 100,000. Choice (C) is the correct answer.

53. A   Difficulty: Medium

Category: Effective Language Use

Getting to the Answer: Watch out for unnecessarily wordy choices like choice B. The correct answer is choice (A) because it effectively communicates an idea without additional words that distract from the content.

54. C   Difficulty: Easy

Category: Effective Language Use

Getting to the Answer: Look at the context of the sentence in which the word appears as well as the paragraph itself to choose the answer that works best. Choice (C), "noteworthy," is synonymous with "worth mentioning," which clearly fits within the context of the paragraph and the author's intent to highlight the accomplishments of the UN.

55. B   Difficulty: Medium

Category: Development

Getting to the Answer: Read the entire paragraph. Identify the sentence that is least relevant to the paragraph's topic and purpose. The purpose of this paragraph is to sum up the central ideas of the passage. Choice (B) introduces a detail that, while important, does not summarize the central ideas of the passage and therefore detracts from the paragraph's focus.

56. D   Difficulty: Hard

Category: Development

Getting to the Answer: Read the entire first paragraph. The correct answer should offer descriptive details and introduce David Kaufman as a character. The first paragraph discusses David Kaufman specifically and his relationship to his job. While choices A, B, and C are informative, they do not add beauty or descriptive interest to the paragraph. Only choice (D) sparks the reader's interest with descriptive language and relates directly to the following sentences.

57. B   Difficulty: Medium

Category: Punctuation

Getting to the Answer: Determine whether the information is all one thought or whether the sentence suggests that some part of it is an aside. The sentence is mainly discussing Kaufman, but it also introduces the idea of America's history, almost as an afterthought. By setting this aside within dashes, the sentence will draw attention to its parenthetical relationship to the rest of the sentence. Choice (B) is correct.

58. C   Difficulty: Easy

Category: Usage

Getting to the Answer: Determine whether the underlined word is being used as a place or a possessive. Then, consider which answer choice would be most appropriate here. In this sentence, "there courage" is meant to be describing the courage belonging to these new Americans. It should therefore be changed to the correct possessive form "their," making choice (C) correct.

59. C   Difficulty: Medium

Category: Effective Language Use

Getting to the Answer: Eliminate unnecessary words. Then, reorder the nouns and verbs to achieve the most concise language possible. Choice (C) contains no unnecessary words. It concisely explains the actions taken by the two different groups of people and is, therefore, the correct answer.

60. A   Difficulty: Medium

Category: Organization

Getting to the Answer: Consider the function of this sentence. At what point in the paragraph should this function be employed? The sentence is setting a scene, so it should be placed where it is now, at the beginning of the paragraph. To place it later would cause confusion in the following sentences, as the reader does not have all the information he or she needs. Choice (A), leaving it in its current position, is the correct answer.

61. B   Difficulty: Medium

Category: Development

Getting to the Answer: The correct answer should introduce an idea that is supported by the sentences that follow. Consider whether the current sentence should be revised to do this. The rest of the paragraph discusses the relationship between immigrant communities and language ability, as well as information about Kaufman's position. Therefore, the introductory sentence to this paragraph should tie together these thoughts. Choice (B) is the correct answer, as it ties Kaufman to his background in an immigrant community.

62. D   Difficulty: Easy

Category: Punctuation

Getting to the Answer: Determine whether the information enclosed in commas is separate or should be integrated into the rest of the sentence. The subject of the sentence is a compound noun: "his heritage and surrounding community." Therefore, the nouns making up this compound noun should not be separated by commas. Choice (D) punctuates this sentence correctly.

63. D   Difficulty: Hard

Category: Effective Language Use

Getting to the Answer: Consider the tone of this sentence as well as its meaning. Then review the answer choices to determine which one best matches both the tone and the meaning. The sentence suggests that Kaufman is trying to make his language abilities more refined and precise in order to help the immigrants. While choice C, "tricks," is tempting, it does not match the more formal tone of the passage. Choice (D), "nuances," conveys the fact that Kaufman is trying to understand the subtleties of language; this answer maintains the passage's formal tone.

64. B   Difficulty: Medium

Category: Development

Getting to the Answer: Reread the rest of the paragraph to determine which answer choice would most effectively add specific, relevant detail to this section of the passage. The paragraph notes that Kaufman helps "at every checkpoint," then mentions the variety of facilities Ellis Island possesses. Choice (B) adds detail about the variety of ways Kaufman helps at Ellis Island and is therefore the correct answer.

65. D   Difficulty: Medium

Category: Effective Language Use

Getting to the Answer: Consider whether the sentence's intended meaning can be conveyed in fewer words. All that is really needed in this sentence is "to help." The reader will still understand what is happening without anything extra; as a result, the other options are wordy and awkward. Choice (D) is the correct answer.

66. C   Difficulty: Medium

Category: Effective Language Use

Getting to the Answer: Before looking at the answer choices, identify a word on your own that will convey the correct meaning for the context. The context of the sentence makes clear that the correct word is something that is "rendered . . . worthwhile." In other words, it is a challenging situation that will be made worthwhile by living in America. While both choices (C) and D are negative words, choice (C), "difficulties," specifically connotes something hard or troubling, so it is the correct answer.

Effective Language Use and Sentence Structure

GETTING STARTED

Effective Language Use questions test your knowledge of the correct words to use in different situations. **Sentence Structure** questions assess your ability to construct correct sentences and to recognize poorly structured sentences. Study the question types below to learn how to approach them and the concepts that these questions test. Knowing the information that you'll need to answer the questions helps you identify the important clues in the passage that will lead you to the correct answers.

Effective Language Use

Precision

On the SAT, precision refers to the exactness and accuracy of the author's choice of words, also known as diction. Precision questions will ask you to revise a text as needed to make a vague word more precise or to change a word or phrase so that it makes sense with the rest of the content.

Word choice is important because being precise in language use allows an author to effectively and clearly convey his or her thoughts, including the thesis and central arguments.

Precision questions mostly test your knowledge of correct word choice in context. Although these questions are similar to the Reading Test's Vocab-in-Context questions, Precision questions do not ask about the definition or implication of a word. Instead, Precision questions test the correctness of the word or phrase—is it the right choice of word(s) to convey the author's meaning?

Concision

Remember the third step of the Kaplan Method for Writing & Language: Plug in the remaining answer choices and select the most clear, *concise*, and relevant one. You must use not only the correct words to convey your ideas but also as few words as possible.

Concision questions will require you to revise text to improve the economy of word choice by eliminating wordiness and redundancy. The SAT tests concision by presenting you with unnecessarily long and complex structures or redundant usage—or, sometimes, both.

> ✔ **Expert Tip**
>
> **The shortest answer is often, though not always, the correct one; always substitute the answer choice back into the passage to make sure it is grammatically correct and retains the intended meaning.**

Unnecessarily long and complex structure implies that a sentence uses more words than necessary to make its point, even though it may actually be grammatically correct. Not every long, underlined segment will include a concision issue; sometimes it does take a lot of words to convey meaning. Nevertheless, when a long selection is underlined, you should ask, "Are all of these words necessary, or is there a more concise way to say the same thing?"

Another aspect of concision is redundancy. Redundancy errors occur when two words in the sentence have essentially the same meaning in context or when the meaning of one word is implicit in the meaning of another.

Style and Tone

Elements of an author's style and tone include his or her choices of words, rhetorical devices, and sentence structure. The author might write informally, as if for a friendly, general audience; academically, as if for an expert audience; or forcefully, as if expounding his or her point of view. SAT Style and Tone questions ask you to revise a text to ensure consistency of style and tone or to reflect the author's purpose. You must also confirm that the text's style and tone match the subject and format.

Some Style and Tone questions will have question stems, while others will not. In the case of the latter, you must determine whether the underlined segment matches the general tone of the passage or whether one of the other choices is more appropriate in context.

> ✔ **Expert Tip**
>
> **If you spot a Style and Tone question at the beginning of a passage, read the rest of the passage before answering it so you can first determine the overall tone.**

Syntax

Syntax refers to the arrangement of words and phrases within a sentence. Questions about syntax will ask you to assess whether different sentence structures accomplish an author's intended rhetorical purpose. In narratives or prose, syntax can enhance the intended meaning and contribute toward tone.

Academic texts, such as the passages you'll see on the SAT, employ varied kinds of syntax. One way in which syntax is categorized is by sentence type. The following table describes four sentence types that are classified by the clauses they contain.

 Remember

A clause is a part of a sentence containing a subject and a predicate verb.

Sentence Type	Description	Example
Simple	Contains a single, independent clause	*I applied for a summer job.*
Compound	Contains two independent clauses that are joined by a coordinating conjunction (e.g., *but, or, and, so*)	*I applied for a summer job, and the human resources manager hired me.*
Complex	Contains an independent clause plus one or more dependent clauses (a dependent clause starts with a coordinating conjunction such as *that, because, while, although, where, if*)	*I applied for a summer job at the local hospital because I am interested in gaining experience in the medical field.*
Compound-Complex	Contains three or more clauses (of which at least two are independent and one is dependent)	*I applied for a summer job at the local hospital, and the human resources manager hired me because I am interested in gaining experience in the medical field.*

Sentence Structure

Run-Ons and Fragments

Run-ons and fragments create grammatically incorrect sentences. The SAT requires that you know the specific rules governing sentence construction.

A complete sentence must have a subject and a predicate verb in an independent clause that expresses a complete thought. If any one of these elements is missing, the sentence is a fragment. You can recognize a fragment because the sentence will not make sense as written. A fragment lacks one of the three components. Take a look at some fragment examples:

- *Seth running down the street.* (The fragment lacks a predicate verb.)
- *Because Michaela led the team in assists.* (The fragment is a dependent clause and does not express a complete thought.)
- *Practiced the piano every day.* (The fragment needs a subject.)

> ✔ *Remember*
>
> A **predicate** is the part of the sentence that describes what the **subject** *does* (action), *is* (being), or *has* (condition); the **predicate verb** is the main verb in the sentence.

If a sentence has more than one independent clause, the clauses must be properly joined. Otherwise, the sentence is a run-on. Take a look at an example of a run-on:

- *My friends and I usually walk home from school together, we ride the bus if the weather isn't nice.*

To Correct a Run-On	Example
Use a semicolon.	*My friends and I usually walk home from school together; we ride the bus if the weather isn't nice.*
Make one clause dependent.	***Although** my friends and I usually walk home from school together, we ride the bus if the weather isn't nice.*
Add a FANBOYS conjunction: *For, And, Nor, But, Or, Yet, So.*	*My friends and I usually walk home from school together, **but** we ride the bus if the weather isn't nice.*

Coordination and Subordination

Coordination and subordination questions focus on the relationship between clauses. On the SAT, you will be asked to determine the best way to link clauses to most effectively express the writer's intent.

Coordinate Clauses

Coordinate clauses are independent clauses that can stand on their own and express a complete thought. When two or more independent clauses are properly joined, they form a compound sentence.

Two independent clauses are coordinated by using a comma and the conjunction *and*:

- *The class was interesting, and we prepared thoroughly for each session.* (Equal emphasis on the two ideas suggests that the class would have been interesting whether or not we prepared, and it suggests that we would have prepared whether or not the class was interesting.)

Subordinate Clauses

A subordinate clause cannot stand on its own and still make sense. Combining a subordinate clause with an independent clause by using a connecting word forms a complex sentence in which the independent clause expresses the central idea of the sentence and the subordinate clause provides additional support that modifies or clarifies the central idea.

The central idea of the sentence is changed depending upon which clause is subordinated:

- *Because the class was interesting,* we prepared thoroughly for each session. (The main emphasis is on our preparation. The subordinate clause gives the reason for our thoroughness.)
- The class was interesting *because we prepared thoroughly for each session.* (The main emphasis is on the class. The subordinate clause explains why it was interesting.)

Parallelism

Parallelism questions on the SAT test your ability to revise sentences to create parallel structure. Items in a series, list, or compound must be parallel in form. Series, lists, and compounds may contain nouns, adjectives, adverbs, or verb forms.

Check for parallelism if the sentence contains:

Feature	Example	Parallel Form
A list	*Before you leave, you should **charge your phone**, **clean your room**, and **find your bus pass**.*	3 verb phrases
A compound	***Swimming** and **biking** provide aerobic exercise.*	2 gerund verb forms
A correlative	*The debate coach encouraged the students **to listen** carefully and **to speak** clearly.*	2 infinitive verb forms
A comparison	*Your **practice test sessions** are just as important as your **class sessions**.*	2 nouns
Related nouns	***Students** who complete all of their **homework assignments** are more likely to earn **higher test scores**.*	3 related plural nouns

Modifiers

A modifier is a word or a group of words that describes, clarifies, or provides additional information about another part of the sentence. Modifier questions on the SAT Writing & Language Test require you to identify the part of a sentence being modified and use the appropriate modifier in the proper place.

> ✔ **Expert Tip**
>
> On the SAT, modifiers should be close to the words they modify.

Modifier	Function	Example
Adjective	An adjective is a single word modifier that describes a noun or pronoun.	*Asara bought a **blue** backpack from the **thrift** shop.*
Adverb	An adverb is a single word modifier that describes a verb, an adjective, or another adverb.	*Ian **carefully** walked over the **rapidly** melting ice.*
Modifying phrase	Modifying phrases and clauses must be properly placed to correctly modify another part of the sentence.	***Wanting to do well at the competition**, Sasha devoted extra time to her practice sessions.*

Use context clues in the passage to identify the correct placement of a modifier; a misplaced modifier can cause confusion:

- *The restaurant provides carryout meals to its diners **in recyclable containers**.*

Who or what is in the containers? The context of the sentence suggests that the meals are in the containers; however, because modifiers should be placed near what they modify, the sentence can be grammatically interpreted to suggest that the diners are in the containers! When the modifier is correctly placed near what it modifies, the meaning is clarified:

- *The restaurant provides carryout meals **in recyclable containers** to its diners.*

> ✔ **Expert Tip**
>
> The SAT requires verbs to be modified by adverbs. Adverbs usually end in *-ly*. It has become common usage to modify verbs with adjectives, but this is incorrect on the SAT. Use *"He drives slowly,"* not *"He drives slow."*

Modifier placement can change the meaning of a sentence:

- *The waiter **just** described the dinner specials.* (The sentence is about **when** the action took place.)
- ***Just** the waiter described the dinner specials.* (The sentence is about **who** completed the action.)
- *The waiter described **just** the dinner specials.* (The sentence is about **what** was acted upon.)

Verb Tense, Mood, and Voice

On the SAT Writing & Language Test, you will be asked to identify and replace unnecessary shifts in verb tense, mood, and voice. Because these shifts may occur within a single sentence or among different sentences, you will need to read around the underlined portion to identify the error.

In questions about shifts in construction, the underlined segment must logically match the tense, mood, and voice in other parts of the sentence.

> ✔ **Expert Tip**
>
> The noun closest to the verb may not be the subject of the sentence. Mentally "strip out" the modifiers between the subject and the verb when checking the person and number of the verb.

Verb tense places the action or state of being described by the verb into a place in time: **present**, **past**, or **future**. Each tense has three forms: **simple**, **progressive**, and **perfect**.

	Present	Past	Future
Simple: Actions that simply occur at some point in time	*She studies diligently every day.*	*She studied two extra hours before her math test.*	*She will study tomorrow for her French test.*
Progressive: Actions that are ongoing at some point in time	*She is studying today for her math test tomorrow.*	*She was studying yesterday for a French test today.*	*She will be studying tomorrow for her physics test next week.*
Perfect: Actions that are completed at some point in time	*She has studied diligently every day this semester.*	*She had studied two extra hours before her math test yesterday.*	*She will have studied each chapter before her physics test next week.*

Grammatical **moods** are classifications that indicate the attitude of the speaker.

	Description	Example
Indicative Mood	Used to make a statement or ask a question	*Snow **covered** the moonlit field.*
Imperative Mood	Used to give a command or make a request	*Please **drive** carefully in the snow.*
Subjunctive Mood	Used to express hypothetical outcomes	*If I **were** at the library, I could find the book I need.*

The **voice** of a verb describes the relationship between the action expressed by the verb and the subject.

	Description	Example
Active	The subject is the agent or doer of the action.	*The carpenter **hammered** the nail.*
Passive	The subject is the target of the action.	*The nail **was hammered** by the carpenter.*

✔ *Expert Tip*

On the SAT, the active voice is preferred over the passive voice.

Pronoun, Person, and Number

Pronouns replace nouns in sentences. They must agree with the noun they are replacing in person and number. The SAT will test your ability to recognize and correct inappropriate shifts in pronoun usage.

Person	Refers To	Singular Pronouns	Plural Pronouns
First person	The person speaking	I, me, my	we, us, our
Second person	The person spoken to	you, your	you, your
Third person	The person or thing spoken about	he, she, it, him, her, his, hers, its	they, them, theirs
Indefinite	A nonspecific person or group	anybody, anyone, each, either, everyone, someone, one	both, few, many, several

✔ *Remember*

Do not shift between "you" and "one" unnecessarily. "You" refers to a specific person or group. "One" refers to an indefinite individual or group.

IMPROVING WITH PRACTICE

Step 1: Read Until You Can Identify the Issue

Always read the entire Writing & Language passage. This is particularly important for **Effective Language Use** and **Sentence Structure** questions because the best clues for the correct answers may be before or after the underline or the question marker. Be sure to identify:

- the main idea/purpose of each paragraph
- the author's style/tone

Within the underline, check:

- If a verb is underlined, check the subject. Then check the tense of a nearby non-underlined verb in that same paragraph.
- If a pronoun is underlined, check the noun immediately preceding it.
- If a comma is underlined, check if there are independent clauses before and after it. If so, the sentence is a run-on and must be corrected.
- If a comma is underlined, check if the information preceding the comma is a modifying phrase. If so, the first noun following the comma must be what the modifier describes.

You may have to read well after the underline or question marker to be able to identify the issue. If you're not sure there's an issue, keep reading and then return to the question.

> ✔ *Expert Tip*
>
> **The best clue for the correct answer is frequently found either before or after the underlined segment. A non-underlined verb sets the tense for the entire paragraph, and a non-underlined antecedent determines the correct pronoun.**

Step 2: Answer the Questions

As you're practicing, after identifying the issue, refer back to the topics in the "Getting Started" section and answer questions one at a time. Review the Answer and Explanation for every question immediately after completing it. If you got the question correct, congratulate yourself, but take a moment to read the entire explanation to be sure you got the question right for the right reason. The explanation may also point out a more efficient way that you can use on a later question.

Step 3: Review Incorrect Answers

If you get the question incorrect . . . still congratulate yourself! You're about to learn something new that you'll be able to use to improve your performance on Test Day. Don't read the explanation yet; instead, try the question again.

If you get the question correct the second time, read the explanation to see if you solved the question in the most efficient way. Identify the mistake you made the first time, and determine how you're going to avoid making that mistake again.

> ✔ **Expert Tip**
>
> **Many top scoring students have an SAT notebook where they write down what they learn from every question. Doing this can be time-consuming, but it can also help you identify the types of mistakes you tend to make.**

If you get the question incorrect the second time, use the explanation to learn how to get the question correct. Work through the question again while following the explanation, and identify the steps you will need to take to get a similar question correct. Although the passages and questions will change, the concepts being tested will not. When you encounter unfamiliar questions, take note of them for future study sessions.

> ✔ **Remember**
>
> **The SAT is a standardized test. While Hard Writing & Language questions are usually more difficult to answer than Easy or Medium questions, they are often similar in structure and purpose, and the same six skills (listed in Chapter 6) are tested on every Writing & Language Test. You actually can predict the types of questions you will see on Test Day!**

After all that work, it's time to move to the next question. Reviewing in this way will take time. However, improvement doesn't come from just doing lots and lots of questions; it comes from thinking through your approach and improving it with every question.

RAISING YOUR SCORE EVEN MORE

Here is one of the "secrets" to conquering the Writing & Language section: Because the SAT is a standardized test, there will always be clues that make one choice definitely correct and the other choices completely wrong. It's never a matter of opinion.

Since **Effective Language Use** questions hinge on the correct word, the clue is the intention of the sentence and the author's tone. Always replace the underlined word with the word in the choice and reread the sentence. If the meaning or tone changes, the choice is incorrect.

In addition to the clues for **Sentence Structure** questions described in "Improving With Practice" above, look for:

- semicolons. A non-underlined semicolon preceding an underlined section means the underline must be an independent clause.
- comparison keywords such as "than" or "as." Comparisons require parallel structure.

PRACTICE QUESTIONS

The following test-like question sets provide an opportunity to practice reading Effective Language Use and Sentence Structure questions. While many of the questions pertain to Effective Language Use and Sentence Structure, some touch on other concepts tested on the Writing & Language Test to ensure that your practice is test-like, with a variety of question types per passage.

Questions 1-11 are based on the following passage.

Sorting Recyclables for Best Re-Use

From the time a plastic container is thrown into a recycling bin to the time the plastic **1** are actually recycled, it passes through several sorting cycles. In addition to being separated from the non-plastic items, the plastics themselves must be **2** detached, because not all plastics are alike, making some easier to recycle than others.

3 Special machines have been developed to assist in sorting plastics. During manual sorting,

1. A) NO CHANGE
    B) is
    C) has been
    D) will be

2. A) NO CHANGE
    B) demolished,
    C) flanked,
    D) categorized,

3. Which choice most effectively sets up the information that follows?
    A) NO CHANGE
    B) Sorting by hand is less efficient than using machines to sort plastics.
    C) Classifying plastics can be done manually or by machines.
    D) Plastics are widely used today, so they need to be recycled.

people **4** <u>very thoroughly check</u> the numbers on the bottom of each plastic item. The numbers indicate the type of plastic each is made from. Some sorting can be automated by using machines that can detect the composition of the plastic. The detectors in these machines use infrared light to characterize and sort the plastics, similar to how a human might use visible light to sort materials by their color. By either method, the plastics can eventually be arranged into bins or piles corresponding to the recycling code numbers running from one to seven.

In some cases, plastics are further sorted by the method by which they were manufactured. **5** <u>However,</u> **6** <u>bottles, tubs and, trays</u> are typically **7** <u>made from either PET (polyethylene terephthalate) or HDPE (high density polyethylene), two of the least recovered plastics.</u> Bottles are produced by a process called blow-molding, in which the plastic is heated until soft, then blown up, much like a balloon, while being pushed against a mold. Tubs and trays are usually made by a process called injection molding, in which the plastic is heated until it can be pushed through nozzles into a mold. Different additives are added to the plastics before **8** <u>molding. It depends</u> on the method. Since the additives for injection molding might not be suitable for blow-molding of the recycled plastic, PET and HDPE

4. A) NO CHANGE
    B) completely and thoroughly check
    C) thoroughly check
    D) make sure to thoroughly check

5. A) NO CHANGE
    B) For example,
    C) Consequently,
    D) Similarly,

6. A) NO CHANGE
    B) bottles, tubs, and trays
    C) bottles tubs, and trays,
    D) bottles, tubs, and, trays

7. Which choice completes the sentence with accurate data based on the graphic?
    A) NO CHANGE
    B) made from PET (polyethylene terephthalate) or HDPE (high density polyethylene), the two most recovered plastics after the leading type, LDPE.
    C) made from PP (polypropene) or PS (polystyrene), the two most recovered plastics after the leading type, PVC.
    D) made from PP (polypropene) or PS (polystyrene), the two most recovered plastics after the leading type, EPS.

8. Which choice most effectively combines the sentences at the underlined portion?
    A) molding, however, it depends
    B) molding, depending
    C) molding despite depending
    D) molding, it depends

bottles are often separated out from the other PET and HDPE plastics.

While the numbers 1 through 6 indicate a **9** <u>specific</u> plastic, number 7 indicates that the plastic is either one of many other plastics, or that it is a blend of plastics. These plastics are more difficult to recycle, as different amounts of the various types of number 7 plastics will be sent to recycling each day. They are typically used for products in which the plastic will be mixed with other materials.

Although there are many types of plastics to be found in a typical recycling bin, each one can play a part in a recycled **10** <u>product, the many</u> cycles of sorting guarantee that each piece can be correctly processed and sent off for re-use. **11**

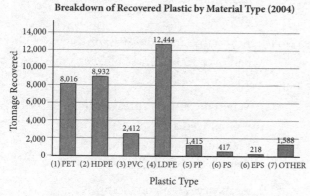

Breakdown of Recovered Plastic by Material Type (2004)

Original graph at http://www.recycle.co.nz/symbols.php.

9. A) NO CHANGE
    B) vague
    C) common
    D) pending

10. A) NO CHANGE
    B) product the many
    C) product. The many
    D) product, so the many

11. Which choice most effectively establishes a concluding sentence for the paragraph?
    A) Sorting ensures that plastics will not linger in the landfills, but continue to be of use.
    B) Sorting different types of plastics is done in many ways, either by hand or machine.
    C) Oftentimes, people are required to sort their own plastics by type.
    D) There are many different kinds of plastics, and each one is useful.

Questions 12-22 are based on the following passage and supplementary material.

The Pony Express: Not a Tame Ride

The 19th century saw the Civil War, the California Gold Rush, and the migration of thousands of people to the West along the Oregon Trail. With these events came **12** the really great and strong need for communication between the original colonies and the new state of California. **13** William H. Russell, Alexander Majors, and William B. Waddell brought about the solution to this need by creating Leavenworth & Pike's Peak Express Company, which later became known as the Pony Express.

The Pony Express was a system of riders that ran 2,000 miles from St. Joseph, Missouri, to Sacramento, California. Riders, who carried mail in leather satchels, changed every 75 to 100 miles. They changed horses every 10 to 15 miles. **14** When the Pony Express was at its largest, it had a lot of riders who were paid for their services.

Riders changed horses or took a short break at relay posts, or stations: small, simple cabins, with dirt floors and a few stalls for the horses. Riders could get small meals at the **15** stations, these meals usually consisted of dried fruit, cured meats, pickles, coffee, and cornmeal. At some bigger stations, known as "home stations," riders were able to enjoy a more relaxed meal, chat with other riders, and get some sleep.

12. A) NO CHANGE
    B) the very strong and real need
    C) the need
    D) the strong and real need

13. A) NO CHANGE
    B) William H. Russell Alexander Majors and William B. Waddell
    C) William H. Russell Alexander Majors, and William B. Waddell
    D) William H. Russell, Alexander Majors, and, William B. Waddell

14. Which choice most effectively revises the underlined sentence?
    A) When the Pony Express was at its largest, it was a very glamorous job.
    B) At its largest, the Pony Express had over 150 riders of all ages and they were paid.
    C) When the Pony Express peaked, it employed a lot of riders and the youngest one was named Bronco Charlie Miller.
    D) At its peak, the Pony Express employed over 180 riders who ranged in age from 11 to 50 years old and earned $50 a month.

15. A) NO CHANGE
    B) stations these meals usually consisted
    C) stations. These meals usually consisted
    D) stations yet these meals usually consisted

The relay posts were also a source of employment. Each housed a station keeper who was responsible for having horses saddled and ready when a rider arrived, as well as for logging [16] accurate records of arrival and departure times. The job of a station keeper was not an easy one. The [17] stations were located in remote areas, had little access to resources, and were being unprotected from attacks by Native Americans.

[18] The riders' routes were fraught with danger of many kinds. Riders often rode through rough, unfamiliar terrain; were exposed to harsh weather; and were susceptible to attack by hostile Native Americans. [19] As a result of these challenges, only one mail delivery was lost during the Pony Express's 19 months of operation.

16. A) NO CHANGE
   B) lengthy
   C) sorrowful
   D) agreeable

17. A) NO CHANGE
   B) stations were located in remote areas, had little access to resources, and were unprotected
   C) stations were being located in remote areas, had little access to resources, and were unprotected
   D) stations were located in remote areas, having little access to resources, and were unprotected

18. Which choice most effectively establishes the main topic of the paragraph?
   A) NO CHANGE
   B) The Pony Express helped tie California with the rest of the country.
   C) The Pony Express was not successful financially.
   D) Some of the riders died while trying to deliver the mail.

19. A) NO CHANGE
   B) Despite
   C) However
   D) For instance

Shortly after the first riders of the Pony Express set out on April 3, 1860, Congress approved a bill [20] <u>funding the construction of a transcontinental telegraph line on March 5, 1860.</u> The result of this bill was the creation of the Overland Telegraph Company of California and the Pacific Telegraph Company of Nevada. Once they were fully [21] <u>invented</u> on October 24, 1861, the Pony Express was no longer needed. Two days later, the Pony Express announced its closure.

Although its existence was a short one, the Pony Express played an important role in the development of [22] <u>the Pacific Coast. It remains</u> an icon of the Wild West.

History of the Pony Express

January-March 1860 ➤	Russell, Majors, and Waddell establish Pony Express mail service.
April 3, 1860 ➤	First riders leave St. Joseph, Missouri, and Sacramento, California.
June 8, 1860 ➤	Congress authorizes building of transcontinental telegraph line.
October 24, 1861 ➤	East and West coasts connected by telegraph line.
October 26, 1861 ➤	Pony Express discontinued.

20. Which choice completes the sentence with accurate data based on the timeline?

A) NO CHANGE

B) funding the construction of a transcontinental telegraph line on June 8, 1860.

C) funding the construction of a transcontinental telegraph line on October 24, 1861.

D) funding the construction of a transcontinental telegraph line on January, 1860.

21. A) NO CHANGE

B) breached

C) operational

D) contrasted

22. Which choice most effectively combines the sentences at the underlined portion?

A) the Pacific Coast, since it remains

B) the Pacific Coast, however, it remains

C) the Pacific Coast, that it remains

D) the Pacific Coast and remains

Questions 23-33 are based on the following passage and supplementary material.

Tesla Lights Up the World

[1] Nikola Tesla, born in 1856, was an Austrian electrical engineer who worked for a telegraph company in Budapest before immigrating to the United States to join Thomas Edison's company in New York. [2] The two engineers did not work well together, and Tesla moved on to work with George Westinghouse, another engineer and inventor, at the Westinghouse Electric & Manufacturing Company in 1885. [3] **23** <u>During his time there, Tesla invented the alternating current system, what we know in our homes as AC power.</u> [4] Several years later, Tesla made the first successful wireless energy transfer. [5] Reportedly, Tesla slept little and often occupied himself with games, such as chess and billiards. **24**

[1] The Westinghouse Electric Company was quick to put Tesla's invention to work. [2] They **25** <u>implemented</u> the use of alternating current during the World Colombian Exposition in **26** <u>1897,</u> with fantastic results. [3] It was more efficient than Edison's earlier energy transfer system, the direct current (DC) system, as well as more effective. [4] Edison knew that the DC system was difficult to transmit over long distances. [5] He didn't, however, believe that Tesla's AC system was a credible threat to the dominance he and his

23. A) NO CHANGE

B) Tesla, while there, invented the AC power system we know in our homes, more formally called the alternating current system.

C) Tesla invented the alternating current system during his time there, also known in our homes as AC power.

D) When he worked there, the alternating current system, or what we know in our homes as AC power, was invented by him.

24. Which sentence should be removed in order to improve the focus of this paragraph?

A) Sentence 1

B) Sentence 2

C) Sentence 4

D) Sentence 5

25. A) NO CHANGE

B) encouraged

C) invoked

D) developed

26. Which choice completes the sentence with accurate data based on the timeline at the end of the passage?

A) NO CHANGE

B) 1882,

C) 1890,

D) 1893,

company held over the electrical market of the time because of his invention of the light bulb. [6] **27 But it is Tesla's system that moves power from a main grid across long distances.**

[1] Tesla went on to develop the technology that is now used in X-rays, as well as radio and remote controls. [2] Some of his inventions even worked together, expanding his influence on the world and history. [3] Tesla paired his AC system with his understanding of physics to invent an electric motor. [4] Developing the AC system was only the beginning for Tesla, though. [5] To do so, he used his knowledge of magnetism to create a closed system in which a motor could turn without disruption or the use of manpower. [6] The motor generated a stable current that had been lacking in earlier attempts to transition industry to AC power. [7] With Tesla's motor, though, AC power systems could be broadly used in manufacturing and beyond. **28**

[1] Tesla's inventions are not only a part of our daily lives; they continue **29 to be expanded upon to create** new advances in science and technology.

27. Which choice most effectively conveys the central idea of the paragraph?

A) NO CHANGE

B) However, bulbs alone do not light our homes; it is Tesla's system that moves power from one grid across long distances to the fixtures we use every day.

C) Later, Tesla developed a system that allows us to use light bulbs every day.

D) We now use Edison's bulbs every day; we can thank Tesla for inventing the system that moves power from one grid across distances to those fixtures.

28. Which sentence provides the best transition from the previous paragraph if placed before sentence 1?

A) Sentence 2

B) Sentence 4

C) Sentence 6

D) Sentence 7

29. Which of the following provides the most concise revision without altering the writer's intended meaning?

A) to necessitate

B) to be developed into

C) to inspire scientists to make

D) to lead to

[2] Tesla's approach to energy transmission, as well as his invention of the radio, including antenna and other recognizable aspects, has allowed leaps and bounds to be made in wireless communications, such as radio broadcasting. [3] Edison may have invented the lightbulb, **30** but Tesla was an inventor bent on bringing electricity to the people, seeking no fame or fortune. [4] The reach of his technology goes even as far as the mobile phone. [5] Although long gone, Tesla remains **31** a pathfinder on the edge of miraculous invention. **32**

30. A) NO CHANGE
    B) but Tesla, seeking no fame or fortune, was an inventor bent on bringing electricity to the people.
    C) but seeking no fame or fortune, Tesla was an inventor bent on bringing electricity to the people.
    D) but Tesla was an inventor bent on seeking no fame or fortune, bringing electricity to the people.

31. A) NO CHANGE
    B) an explorer
    C) a champion
    D) a pioneer

32. Which supporting detail is least essential to sentence 2?
    A) That Tesla invented the radio
    B) That Tesla's invention of the radio included the "antenna and other recognizable aspects"
    C) That Tesla's invention of the radio allowed further innovation in wireless communications
    D) That radio broadcasting is a kind of wireless communication

Tesla's Inventions

1882 ➤ Rotating Magnetic Field—A rotating field that enabled alternating current to power a motor.

1883 ➤ AC Motor—The rotating magnetic field was put into practice in this motor, which spun without a mechanical aid.

1890 ➤ Tesla Coil—A coil that enables transformers to produce extremely high voltages.

1893 ➤ Tesla and Westinghouse display their AC current systems at the Columbian Exposition in Chicago.

1897 ➤ Radio—Tesla invented the radio, including antennae, tuners, and other familiar components.

Think about the previous passage as a whole as you answer question 33.

33. Based on the timeline, "In 1883," would be most appropriately added to the beginning of which of the following sentences?

A) Paragraph 1, sentence 2

B) Paragraph 2, sentence 1

C) Paragraph 3, sentence 3

D) Paragraph 4, sentence 3

Questions 34-44 are based on the following passage and supplementary material.

Predicting Nature's Light Show

One of the most beautiful of nature's displays is the aurora borealis, commonly known as the Northern Lights. As **34** their informal name suggests, the best place to view this phenomenon **35** is the Northern Hemisphere. How far north one needs to be to witness auroras depends not on conditions here on Earth, but on the sun. **36**

As with hurricane season on Earth, the sun **37** observes a cycle of storm activity, called the solar cycle, which lasts approximately 11 years. Also referred to as the sunspot cycle, this period is caused by the amount of magnetic flux that rises to the surface of the sun, causing sunspots, or areas of intense magnetic activity. The magnetic energy is sometimes so great it causes a storm that explodes away from the sun's surface in a solar flare.

These powerful magnetic storms eject high-speed electrons and protons into space. Called a coronal mass ejection, this ejection is far more powerful than the hot gases the sun constantly emits. The speed at which the atoms are shot away from the sun is almost triple that of a normal solar wind. It takes this shot of energy one to three days to arrive at Earth's upper atmosphere. Once it arrives, it is captured by Earth's own magnetic field.

34. A) NO CHANGE
    B) an
    C) its
    D) that

35. A) NO CHANGE
    B) is through the Northern Hemisphere.
    C) is over the Northern Hemisphere.
    D) is in the Northern Hemisphere.

36. Which of the following would most strengthen the passage's introduction?
    A) A statement about the Kp-Index and other necessary tracking tools scientists use
    B) A mention that the National Oceanic and Atmospheric Administration monitors solar flares
    C) An explanation about why conditions on the sun rather than on Earth affect the Northern Lights
    D) A statement about what scientists think people should study before viewing auroras

37. A) NO CHANGE
    B) experiences
    C) perceives
    D) witnesses

It is this newly captured energy that causes the Northern Lights. **38** Scientists and interested amateurs in the Northern Hemisphere **39** use tools readily available to all in order to predict the likelihood of seeing auroras in their location at a specific time. One such tool is the Kp-Index, a number that determines the potential visibility of an aurora. The Kp-Index measures the energy added to Earth's magnetic field from the sun on a scale of 0-9, with 1 representing a solar calm and 5 or more indicating a magnetic storm, or solar flare. The magnetic fluctuations are measured in three-hour intervals (12 AM to 3 AM, 3 AM to 6 AM, and so on) so that deviations can be factored in and accurate data can be presented. **40**

Magnetometers, tools that measure the strength of Earth's magnetic field, are located around the world. When the energy from solar flares reaches Earth, the strength and direction of the energy **41** is recorded by these tools and analyzed by scientists at the National Oceanic and Atmospheric Administration, who calculate the difference between the average strength of the magnetic field and spikes due to solar flares. They plot this information on the Kp-Index and **42** update the public with information on viewing the auroras

38.
A) NO CHANGE
B) Interested scientists and amateurs
C) Scientists and amateurs interested
D) Scientists interested and amateurs

39.
A) NO CHANGE
B) use tools for prediction
C) use specific tools to predict
D) use all tools readily available to predict

40. Which of the following, if added to this paragraph, would best support the author's claims?
A) The speeds of normal solar winds and coronal mass ejections
B) The strength of Earth's magnetic field
C) The temperature of normal solar wind
D) The definition of coronal mass ejection

41.
A) NO CHANGE
B) are
C) will be
D) has been

42.
A) NO CHANGE
B) update aurora viewing information
C) update information on viewing the auroras
D) update aurora viewing information for the public

as well as other impacts solar flares may have on life on Earth. **43** <u>While</u> solar flares can sometimes have negative effects on our communications systems and weather patterns, the most common effect is also the most enchanting: a beautiful light show, such as the solar flare that took place from **44** <u>3 PM to 6 PM on September 11.</u>

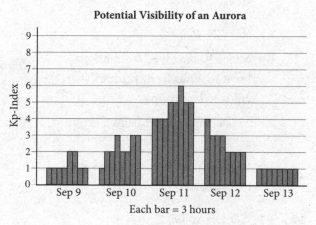

Potential Visibility of an Aurora

Each bar = 3 hours

Data from National Oceanic and Atmospheric Administration.

43. A) NO CHANGE

B) However,

C) Since

D) Whereas

44. Which choice completes the sentence with accurate data based on the graphic?

A) NO CHANGE

B) 12 AM on September 11 to 3 AM on September 12.

C) 9 AM on September 10 to 12 PM on September 12.

D) 9 AM on September 11 to 12 AM on September 12.

Questions 45-55 are based on the following passage.

Musical Enjoyment: Better in Numbers?

Music is many things to many **45** people: a mode of expression, an escape, or a way to understand life experiences. Although its prominence in global culture has stayed the same, music has changed considerably since its prehistoric invention. **46** Music has evolved from a primarily group-enjoyed art form into one consumed mostly on an individual basis.

Researchers have no way of knowing who first invented music, **47** but educated guesses can be made about the purposes it served. It is hypothesized that in the Prehistoric Era, early humans used sounds like hand clapping and foot stomping to create rhythmic repetition. **48** For instance, art in both Stone Age cave paintings and later Persian cave paintings shows examples of people using handmade instruments to create music in a group setting. The sounds produced

45. A) NO CHANGE
    B) people, a mode of expression, an escape, or a way
    C) people; a mode of expression; an escape; or a way
    D) people: a mode of expression or an escape or a way

46. A) NO CHANGE
    B) Music has evolved from an art form that has been primarily enjoyed by groups
    C) Music has evolved from a group art form
    D) Primarily, music as a group art form has evolved

47. A) NO CHANGE
    B) but they can make educated guesses about the purposes it served.
    C) but educated guesses of the purposes it served have been made.
    D) but educated guesses are made about the purposes it served.

48. A) NO CHANGE
    B) Similarly,
    C) For example,
    D) In other words,

were an early form of communication. The use of music as a tool opened early humans **49** up to one another. Advancing social bonding even in an age before common languages.

In ancient Egypt, musicians were appointed to play for specific gods. In addition to enhancing religious ceremonies, music was used in the royal court. Gifted musicians were hired to honor the pharaoh and impress guests of the royal family. In American history, music has been used as a vehicle for storytelling. At the time of the Underground Railroad, music was used to deliver messages to groups of people trying to escape slavery. Directions were embedded **50** in lyrics that were well-known to many. Although these examples are very different, they highlight how music was used to encourage social bonding. **51**

[1] With the **52** advent of headphones in 1910, music was changed from an inherently social experience to a personal one. [2] Based on Thomas Edison's discovery of sound created by electrical signals, Nathaniel Baldwin created the first headset that could amplify sound. [3] This invention has been greatly improved upon since. [4] Instead of music being primarily used in group settings, it became a highly individual form of entertainment. [5] While this is seen as a positive departure, studies link the use of headphones to feelings of isolation and decreased personal satisfaction.

49. Which choice most effectively combines the sentences at the underlined portion?

A) up to one another while advancing

B) up to one another; this advanced

C) up to one another, advancing

D) up to one another, a tool advancing

50. A) NO CHANGE

B) in lyrics that included references to famous abolitionists.

C) in popular lyrics, hiding helpful instructions in plain sight.

D) in lyrics that were typically banned by plantation owners.

51. Which choice creates the most cohesive transition from the previous paragraph?

A) More recent examples show music primarily becoming a source of entertainment.

B) Music became a notable social bonding tool among wealthy and aristocratic circles.

C) Music from Egypt traveled to America and helped convey the importance of social bonding.

D) Further examples throughout history show the development of music as a social bonding tool.

52. A) NO CHANGE

B) enhancement

C) prevalence

D) prohibition

[6] With music becoming more portable than ever, headphones have enabled people to listen to music in almost any situation, including on their way to work, at the workplace, and at home while their families listen to their own choice of music. **53**

54 Psychologists' and sociologists' hypothesize that the shift in music from a social to an individual enjoyment contributes to a high number of people reporting feelings of loneliness in recent studies. While the long-term psychological effects of this shift will take time to analyze, it is already apparent that humans are less connected in their enjoyment of something we have shared throughout history. **55**

53. To make this paragraph most logical, sentence 5 should be placed

A) where it is now.

B) after sentence 2.

C) before sentence 4.

D) after sentence 6.

54. A) NO CHANGE

B) Psychologists and sociologists'

C) Psychologist's and sociologist's

D) Psychologists and sociologists

55. Which choice, if added to this paragraph, would best support the author's claims?

A) The number of people reporting feelings of loneliness in recent studies

B) Which psychologists and sociologists are making these claims

C) The specific differences in the ways humans have shared music over time

D) Which long-term psychological effects may be related to using headphones

Questions 56-66 are based on the following passage.

DNA Analysis in a Day

Jane Saunders, a forensic DNA specialist, arrives at work and finds a request waiting for her: She needs to determine if the DNA of a fingernail with a few skin cells on it **56** match any records in the criminal database.

"Human DNA is a long, double-stranded **57** molecule; each strand consists of a complementary set of nucleotides," she explains. "DNA has four nucleotides: **58** adenine (A), thymine (T), guanine (G), and, cytosine (C). On each strand is a sequence of nucleotides that 'match,' or pair up with the nucleotides on the other, or complementary, strand. **59** On the other hand, when there is an adenine on one strand, there is a thymine on the complementary strand, and where there is guanine on one strand, there is cytosine on the complementary strand."

She begins by **60** moving the DNA from the rest of the sample, transferring it to a

56. A) NO CHANGE
    B) matches
    C) has matched
    D) will be matching

57. A) NO CHANGE
    B) molecule, each strand consists
    C) molecule each strand consists
    D) molecule but each strand consists

58. A) NO CHANGE
    B) adenine (A), thymine (T), guanine (G), and cytosine (C).
    C) adenine (A), thymine (T) guanine (G) and cytosine (C).
    D) adenine (A) thymine (T), guanine (G) and cytosine (C).

59. A) NO CHANGE
    B) Specifically,
    C) However,
    D) Similarly,

60. A) NO CHANGE
    B) reviewing
    C) changing
    D) detaching

[61] reaction tube. She adds a solution of primers, DNA polymerase, and nucleotides. Her goal is to separate the two strands of the DNA molecules and then make complementary copies of each strand.

[62] The process of testing the DNA includes several steps and many changes in temperature. After mixing the primers, DNA polymerase, and nucleotides with the evidence DNA, Saunders closes the reaction tube and puts it in a thermocycler. It is programmed to raise the temperature to 94°C to separate the double strands into single strands, and then lower the temperature to 59°C to attach the primers to the single strands. Finally, it raises the temperature to 72°C for the DNA polymerase to build the complementary strands. The thermocycler holds each temperature for one minute and repeats the cycle of three temperatures for at least 30 cycles. At the end of each cycle, the number of DNA segments containing the sequence marked by the primers doubles. If the original sample contains only 100 DNA strands, [63] the absolute final sample will have billions of segments.

[1] After a short lunch break, Saunders needs to separate and identify the copied DNA segments. [2] She had used primers that bind to 13 specific

61. Which choice most effectively combines the sentences at the underlined portion?
    A) reaction tube since she adds
    B) reaction tube, however, she adds
    C) reaction tube, and adding
    D) reaction tube, she adds

62. Which sentence most effectively establishes the central idea?
    A) NO CHANGE
    B) The object of testing the DNA is to recreate many strands of the DNA in question.
    C) Saunders uses a variety of machines in order to analyze the DNA.
    D) Saunders would be unable to identify the DNA without the thermocycler.

63. A) NO CHANGE
    B) absolutely the final sample
    C) the final sample
    D) the most final sample

sites in human DNA called short tandem repeats, or STRs. [3] The 13 STRs are segments of four nucleotides that repeat, such as GATAGATAGATA. [4] "Now here's where the real magic happens!" Saunders says excitedly. [5] "Most DNA is identical for all humans. [6] But STRs vary greatly. [7] The chances of any two humans—other than identical twins—having the same set of 13 STRs is less than one in one trillion." 64

Saunders knows that the detectives will be 65 <u>prepared</u> to hear her findings, so she sits down at her desk to compare her results with the criminal database in the hopes of finding a match. 66 <u>Is it possible that too much time is spent identifying DNA in cases that are relatively easy to solve?</u>

64. Where should sentence 1 be placed to make the paragraph feel cohesive?

A) Where it is now

B) After sentence 2

C) After sentence 3

D) After sentence 4

65. A) NO CHANGE

B) eager

C) impatient

D) conditioned

66. At this point, the writer wants to add a conclusion that best reflects Jane's feelings conveyed in the passage. Which choice accomplishes that?

A) NO CHANGE

B) It takes a good deal of work and expense to identify DNA in the world of modern forensics.

C) She takes pride in the fact that her scientific expertise plays such a key role in bringing criminals to justice.

D) She marvels at how far science has come in DNA analysis.

ANSWERS AND EXPLANATIONS

CHAPTER 8

1. B   Difficulty: Easy

Category: Usage

Getting to the Answer: Read the sentence and check to see whether the verb agrees with the subject. The verb "are" is in a plural form, but the subject is singular. Choice (B) is correct because it is the singular form of the verb "to be."

2. D   Difficulty: Medium

Category: Effective Language Use

Getting to the Answer: Read the sentences surrounding the word to better understand the context in which the word appears. Then substitute each answer choice into the sentence to see which fits into the context best. The passage states that the plastics are sorted by types. Only (D) has the correct connotation and fits within the context of the sentence.

3. C   Difficulty: Hard

Category: Development

Getting to the Answer: Read the entire paragraph and write down the central idea. Then review the answer choices and look for a close match with your prediction. The paragraph discusses the two methods used to sort plastics. Choice (C) is closest to this summation.

4. C   Difficulty: Easy

Category: Effective Language Use

Getting to the Answer: Watch out for choices like A and B, which use extra words that do not add meaning to the sentence. It is better to be as direct and simple as possible. The word "thoroughly" indicates that the people doing the job are paying attention to every detail. Additional words such as

"very" or "completely" do not add more meaning to this sentence. Choice (C) is the most concise and effective way of stating the information.

5. B   Difficulty: Medium

Category: Organization

Getting to the Answer: Look for the relationship between this sentence and the previous one. This will help you choose the appropriate transition word. Read the sentence using the word you chose to ensure that it makes sense. Choice (B) shows the relationship between the two sentences by giving an example of how the products are manufactured.

6. B   Difficulty: Medium

Category: Punctuation

Getting to the Answer: Study the words in a series to see where a comma might need to be placed or eliminated. Only one answer choice will include the correct punctuation. Choice (B) is correct.

7. B   Difficulty: Hard

Category: Quantitative

Getting to the Answer: The graphic gives specific information about how much of each type of plastic was recovered. Study the graphic in order to select the correct answer choice. Choice (B) accurately reflects the information in the graphic.

8. B   Difficulty: Medium

Category: Effective Language Use

Getting to the Answer: Watch out for choices that may include incorrect transition words. Choice (B) uses the present participle "depending" to join the sentences concisely and correctly.

9. A   Difficulty: Easy

Category: Effective Language Use

Getting to the Answer: Check each answer choice for its connotations, and be sure to pick one that fits with the context of the sentence. Substitute each answer choice for the word to see which works best. Notice that the sentence sets up a contrast between plastics numbered 1 through 6 and plastics with the number 7, which may consist of one of many other plastics or a blend of plastics. Choice (A) is correct because the word "specific" indicates that each of the numbers 1 through 6 is used for only one type of plastic.

10. C   Difficulty: Medium

Category: Sentence Formation

Getting to the Answer: Two complete thoughts should be two separate sentences. Be careful of inappropriate transition words. Choice (C) divides the two thoughts into two complete sentences by adding a period and capitalizing the first word of the second sentence.

11. A   Difficulty: Medium

Category: Development

Getting to the Answer: Read the entire paragraph and then read each of the choices. Decide which one sums up the paragraph best by stating the overall central idea. Choice (A) is the correct answer. It concludes the paragraph by stating the overall central idea of the paragraph and passage.

12. C   Difficulty: Easy

Category: Effective Language Use

Getting to the Answer: Watch out for answer choices, like choice B, that are extremely wordy. It is better to be as direct and simple as possible. Additional adjectives do not add more meaning to this content. Choice (C) is the most concise and effective way of stating the information in the passage.

13. A   Difficulty: Medium

Category: Punctuation

Getting to the Answer: Study the words in a series and see where a comma might need to be inserted or eliminated. Recall that the SAT requires lists of three to have commas after the first two items in the list, not just after the first item. Choice (A) is correct.

14. D   Difficulty: Hard

Category: Development

Getting to the Answer: To find the best answer choice, look for the sentence that has the most relevant details presented in a clear and concise way. Choice (D) has the most relevant details about what the Pony Express was like when it was at its peak.

15. C   Difficulty: Medium

Category: Sentence Formation

Getting to the Answer: Be careful of inappropriate transition words when relating sentences to one another. Choice (C) divides the two complete thoughts into two sentences by adding a period and capitalizing the first word of the second sentence.

16. A   Difficulty: Easy

Category: Effective Language Use

Getting to the Answer: The context of the sentence suggests which word would have the correct connotation. Check each word to see how it fits with the context. Only choice (A) fits with the context of the sentence. The other choices are incorrect in context.

17. B   Difficulty: Medium

Category: Sentence Formation

Getting to the Answer: Verbs within a sentence should be parallel. Check to see if this is true here. The correct answer, choice (B), has all the verbs in the same form.

18. A   Difficulty: Hard

Category: Development

Getting to the Answer: To find the central idea of a paragraph, identify important details and summarize them in a sentence. Then, find the choice that is the closest to your summary. Be careful not to choose a detail instead of a central idea. The paragraph mostly discusses the challenges riders faced, so choice (A) most accurately sums up the central idea of the paragraph.

19. B   Difficulty: Medium

Category: Organization

Getting to the Answer: Look for the relationship between this sentence and the previous one to choose the appropriate transition word. Read the word into the sentence to ensure that it makes sense. Choice (B) shows the relationship between the two sentences by emphasizing that the riders could overcome these challenges.

20. B   Difficulty: Medium

Category: Quantitative

Getting to the Answer: The graphic gives specific information about when events relating to the Pony Express took place. Interpret it to choose the correct answer choice. Choice (B) is the only one that accurately reflects the information in the timeline.

21. C   Difficulty: Medium

Category: Effective Language Use

Getting to the Answer: The context of the sentence suggests which word would have the best fit. Check each word to see how it fits with the context. Choice (C) best fits the context of the sentence.

22. D   Difficulty: Medium

Category: Effective Language Use

Getting to the Answer: Watch out for answer choices that may have incorrect transition words. Choice (D) joins the sentences concisely and correctly by using the conjunction "and."

23. A   Difficulty: Hard

Category: Effective Language Use

Getting to the Answer: Read the complete sentence. The correct answer will flow smoothly from the preceding sentence and place the different phrases of the sentence in a logical order based on their importance. Choice (A) is correct, as the existing sentence arranges the phrases in the most logical order. The sentence begins, "During his time there," smoothly transitioning from the previous sentence and providing nonessential context for the rest of the sentence. The main point is that Tesla invented the alternating current system. This is the first time the alternating current system has been named, so it should be written out fully, and the nonessential information, "what we know in our homes as AC power," should come last, set off by the comma.

24. D   Difficulty: Easy

Category: Development

Getting to the Answer: Identify the sentence that contributes the least relevant information to the focus, or purpose, of the paragraph and the passage as a whole. The paragraph introduces Tesla and his professional activities and accomplishments. The passage as a whole goes on to explore Tesla's scientific legacy. Sentence 5 provides accurate, but irrelevant, information regarding Tesla's personal interests and habits; therefore, the correct answer is choice (D).

25. A   Difficulty: Medium

Category: Effective Language Use

Getting to the Answer: Choose the most contextually appropriate word. Choice (A) is correct because "implemented" most accurately conveys the idea that Westinghouse first carried out the use of alternating current, which had already been developed, during the exposition..

26. D   Difficulty: Easy

Category: Quantitative

Getting to the Answer: The correct answer will reflect the correct data contained in the timeline. The timeline states that Tesla and Westinghouse displayed the AC system at the Columbian Exposition in 1893, so choice (D) is correct.

27. B   Difficulty: Medium

Category: Development

Getting to the Answer: Identify the subject of the paragraph and consider what the author wants to convey about it. That is the central idea. Then, select the answer choice that correctly conveys the central idea of the paragraph as supported by the details in the preceding sentences. The paragraph discusses the importance of Tesla's development of alternating current and its impact on daily life. In particular, it distinguishes the legacy of Tesla relative to the contributions of Edison. For this reason, choice (B) is correct because it is the only answer choice that emphasizes that Tesla's AC system was crucial (not just incidental) to the success of Edison's bulbs as fixtures in everyday life. "However, bulbs alone do not light our homes" makes clear that Edison's invention would not have done so well without Tesla's.

28. B   Difficulty: Medium

Category: Organization

Getting to the Answer: The correct answer will provide a clear, smooth transition of ideas that connects the content of the previous and current paragraphs. It will also place sentences in logical sequence. The previous paragraph discusses the development of Tesla's AC technology, while the current paragraph discusses Tesla's other inventions. Choice (B) is correct because it links Tesla's development of alternating current with his other innovations. Moving sentence 4 to the beginning of the paragraph also provides a logical sequence of ideas.

29. D   Difficulty: Easy

Category: Effective Language Use

Getting to the Answer: The correct answer will demonstrate economy of word choice and retain active voice while preserving the meaning of the sentence. The sentence communicates that Tesla's inventions contributed to the development of future technologies. Choice (D) is correct because it uses minimal verbiage to express that Tesla's inventions led to later inventions.

30. B   Difficulty: Hard

Category: Sentence Formation

Getting to the Answer: The correct answer will align the modifier with its subject without disrupting the syntax of the remainder of the sentence. The sentence begins "Edison may have invented the lightbulb" and proceeds to contrast Edison's achievement with Tesla's. The second part of the sentence is a dependent clause connected with "but" and should lead off with its subject "Tesla," follow with the modifier "seeking no fame or fortune," and then proceed with the rest of the sentence. Choice (B) does so and is therefore correct.

31. D   Difficulty: Medium

Category: Effective Language Use

Getting to the Answer: Choose the most contextually appropriate word. Eliminate A, "pathfinder," because although Tesla was among the first to make advances toward the use of electricity—and the lightbulb—in daily life, he was neither the first nor the only one to do so. Choice (D) is correct because "pioneer" most correctly conveys the idea that Tesla was among the first.

32. B   Difficulty: Medium

Category: Development

Getting to the Answer: Consider other information in the passage. The correct answer will identify and remove the least essential supporting information to streamline the rhetoric. The least essential information will not alter the meaning of the sentence and will most likely be irrelevant or redundant. The sentence communicates Tesla's impact on wireless communications. Choice (B) is correct because it provides examples that, while somewhat relevant, are nonessential.

33. C   Difficulty: Medium

Category: Quantitative

Getting to the Answer: Read the information next to 1883 in the timeline and find the answer choice that matches that content. The correct answer will correspond to the same event in the passage and timeline. According to the timeline, in 1883, Tesla used alternating current to power a motor. This date corresponds to the information in sentence 3 of paragraph 3, making choice (C) correct.

34. C   Difficulty: Medium

Category: Usage

Getting to the Answer: Recall that a pronoun must agree with its antecedent, or the word to which it refers. Begin by identifying the antecedent of the pronoun. Then, check each choice against the antecedent to find the best match. The antecedent for the pronoun "their" is "this phenomenon," which appears in the main clause. The antecedent and its pronoun do not currently agree as "this phenomenon" is singular and "their" is plural. Although the "s" in "Lights" implies many lights, it is still considered a singular phenomenon and so requires a singular pronoun. Choice (C) is the correct answer.

35. D   Difficulty: Medium

Category: Effective Language Use

Getting to the Answer: Ensure the correct choice is accurate without eliminating other possibilities. Some choices, while correct in some context, are limiting and exclude other possible viewing locations. Choice (D) is the correct answer. The Northern Hemisphere is referred to later in the passage; it also provides an accurate, precise location for best viewing the Northern Lights without excluding other possible viewing locations.

36. C   Difficulty: Medium

Category: Development

Getting to the Answer: Choice (C) is the correct answer because it provides additional information regarding how people are able to view auroras.

37. B   Difficulty: Hard

Category: Effective Language Use

Getting to the Answer: When choosing the correct verb, note how it alters the relationship between the subject, the "sun," and the stated action, in this case "storm activity." Choice (B) is correct. The verb "experiences" is the only one that states a direct action upon the subject, the sun, rather than the sun "observing" an action occurring externally, as suggested by the other verbs.

38. B   Difficulty: Easy

Category: Effective Language Use

Getting to the Answer: The placement of the adjective has a great effect upon the intention of the noun. Read the sentence carefully to determine where the adjective makes the most sense. By placing the adjective before the nouns, choice (B) ensures that only those scientists and amateurs interested in the topic at hand use the specific tools mentioned in this passage.

39. C   Difficulty: Hard

Category: Effective Language Use

Getting to the Answer: Generalized statements with inexact definitions that border on opinion have no place in a scientific essay. The tone and style must exhibit a reliance on verifiable statements. Because "readily available" cannot be quantified and implies the author's opinion, using the word "specific" in choice (C) creates a more exact statement that precedes the information on the precise tools used.

40. A   Difficulty: Medium

Category: Development

Getting to the Answer: Reread the paragraph to understand the author's claims. Which answer choice provides a fact that would best support these claims? Make sure the answer choice does not digress from the progression of ideas. The speed of the solar flare is referenced as being three times the speed of normal solar winds, but neither exact speed is given. To make a stronger case for the author's statements, both speeds should be stated. Therefore, choice (A) is the correct answer.

41. B   Difficulty: Medium

Category: Usage

Getting to the Answer: Read closely to find the subject of the verb. Sometimes, the closest noun is not the subject. The subject of the sentence is "strength and direction," not "energy." Choice (B) is the correct answer because it matches the subject in number and maintains a consistent tense with the rest of the passage.

42. B   Difficulty: Hard

Category: Effective Language Use

Getting to the Answer: Eliminate extraneous and redundant information ("the public") and needless prepositions. Then, reorder the verb and nouns to achieve the most efficient language possible. Making adjustments to the passage language, as shown in choice (B), results in the most concise phrasing.

43. A   Difficulty: Hard

Category: Sentence Formation

Getting to the Answer: Consider the meanings of each introductory word carefully. Use the context clues in the rest of the sentence to choose the correct word. The context clues in the rest of the sentence reveal that the Northern Lights can create communication and weather problems and yet is still beautiful. Keeping the word "While" makes the most sense in this context, so choice (A) is the correct answer.

44. D   Difficulty: Hard

Category: Quantitative

Getting to the Answer: Reread paragraph 4 for information that will help you understand how to read the graphic. Use that information to calculate the precise start and end time for the solar flare as indicated in the graphic. The passage states that a solar flare is represented by any Kp-Index of 5 or higher. While there is one three-hour period where the Kp-Index reached 6, there is a consistent period where the chart shows readings of level 5 or higher. Choice (D) is the correct answer. This choice gives the complete time period showing a reading of level 5 or higher, according to the chart.

45. A   Difficulty: Easy

Category: Punctuation

Getting to the Answer: Examine each answer choice and determine which presents the list in a grammatically correct manner with proper punctuation. The list is presented correctly as is, beginning with a colon and featuring the three items separated with commas with no additional information about the topic presented after the listed items. Choice (A) is correct.

46. C   Difficulty: Medium

Category: Effective Language Use

Getting to the Answer: Reread the sentence and select the answer choice that creates the most concise sentence. Minimize wordiness and awkward word combinations to ensure clarity. Choice (C) is correct as it creates the most concise sentence by removing unnecessary and awkward word choices while retaining the meaning of the sentence.

47. B   Difficulty: Hard

Category: Usage

Getting to the Answer: To avoid the passive voice, identify the subject and the object and make sure the subject comes before the verb. The sentence is passive as written, since the object ("educated guesses") should be preceded by the subject's actions. The verb "make" should come first and should be in the present tense. Choice (B) shows the correct construction of the sentence and eliminates the passive voice.

48. B   Difficulty: Medium

Category: Organization

Getting to the Answer: Study the surrounding sentences for context clues to determine which of the answer choices creates a logical flow of ideas. The preceding sentence discusses early humans using hands and feet to create music, and the following sentence discusses humans using tools to create music. The progression of ideas is a comparison of shared intentions and traits, so "Similarly," or choice (B), is correct.

49. C   Difficulty: Medium

Category: Sentence Formation

Getting to the Answer: Read the two underlined sentences and determine which answer choice best creates a logical and grammatically correct sentence. A grammatically correct sentence must contain a complete idea, utilizing both a subject and a predicate. Choice (C) is correct because it creates a logical, grammatically correct sentence with a subject and predicate.

50. C   Difficulty: Hard

Category: Development

Getting to the Answer: Reread the sentence and select the answer choice that clearly conveys the author's full meaning. Sometimes adding a detail or two can improve a sentence and strengthen an author's claims. The author claims that directions for escape were embedded in well-known lyrics, implying that some people listening to the music may not have discovered the lyrics' true meaning. Choice (C) is correct as it makes this statement clear and direct for the reader and strengthens the author's claim in a concise manner.

51. D   Difficulty: Medium

Category: Organization

Getting to the Answer: Assess the central idea of both paragraphs and determine which answer choice creates an effective and logical transition from the previous idea while summarizing the next. The passage states music has affected all global cultures, and the noted paragraph explores two more examples showing how music is a social bonding tool. The correct answer, (D), is the only answer that creates a cohesive, logical transition while not limiting the number of cultures affected by music.

52. A   Difficulty: Medium

Category: Effective Language Use

Getting to the Answer: Review the rest of the sentence. Look for context clues that can help you determine which answer choice makes the most sense based on the information provided. The sentence states that as of 1910, headphones created a shift in how we listen to music, implying that headphones are a relatively new invention. Since "advent" is the only word meaning the headphones first appeared at a specific point in time, (A) is correct.

53. D   Difficulty: Easy

Category: Organization

Getting to the Answer: Read the entire paragraph for context. Then test the placement given in each answer choice to determine which one creates a paragraph with a logical progression of ideas. Choice (D) is correct because this sentence creates a transition into the subject discussed in the next paragraph.

54. D   Difficulty: Easy

Category: Punctuation

Getting to the Answer: The placement or lack of apostrophes can alter a noun's possessive meaning. Read the entire sentence to understand the author's intention. Which answer choice uses the correct punctuation to convey this idea? The nouns "Psychologists and sociologists" are not in possession of anything in this circumstance. Choice (D) correctly reflects this.

55. A   Difficulty: Medium

Category: Development

Getting to the Answer: Review the paragraph to assess areas in which the author may have left out facts or may have provided only partial information. Then determine which answer choice will have the greatest benefit to the reader. The author specifically mentions "recent studies" but does not cite any figures. Doing so will strengthen the importance of these studies, thus (A) is correct.

56. B   Difficulty: Easy

Category: Usage

Getting to the Answer: Read the sentence and notice that the verb in question is in a clause with intervening prepositional phrases that come between the subject and the verb. Check to see what the subject is and whether the verb agrees with the subject. The verb "match" is in a plural form, but the subject is "DNA," not one of the other nouns in the prepositional phrases. "DNA" is singular. Choice (B) is the correct answer because it is the singular form of the verb "to match."

57. A   Difficulty: Medium

Category: Punctuation

Getting to the Answer: Read the sentence to determine whether the two clauses separated by the semicolon are independent or not. If they are both independent, a semicolon is the appropriate punctuation. Be careful of answer choices with inappropriate transition words. A semicolon is the correct way to separate two independent but related clauses, so (A) is the correct answer.

58. B   Difficulty: Easy

Category: Punctuation

Getting to the Answer: Study the words in a series and see where a comma might need to be inserted or eliminated. Choice (B) is correct.

59. B   Difficulty: Hard

Category: Organization

Getting to the Answer: When you see an underlined transition, identify how the sentence relates to the previous one to determine what kind of transition is appropriate. Choice (B) is correct because the sentence to which the transition belongs provides more detail about a general statement that preceded it.

60. D   Difficulty: Easy

Category: Effective Language Use

Getting to the Answer: Imagine that the sentence has a blank where the word in question is. Read the entire paragraph for context and predict what word could complete the blank. Review the answer choices to find the word closest in meaning to your prediction. The paragraph later states that Jane Saunders's goal is to separate the two strands of DNA. Only answer choice (D) has the correct connotation and fits within the context of the sentence.

61. C   Difficulty: Medium

Category: Effective Language Use

Getting to the Answer: It is important to combine sentences in order to vary sentence structures. But the correct choice should not only be the most effective way to combine the two sentences; it must also be in parallel construction with the first sentence. Watch out for choices that may have incorrect transition words as well. Choice (C) is the correct answer. It joins the sentences concisely and correctly because the verb "adding" is in parallel construction with the earlier verbs "detaching" and "transferring." The subject in both sentences is the same, "she," so it can be dropped when combining the two sentences.

62. A   Difficulty: Medium

Category: Development

Getting to the Answer: Read the entire paragraph and then put each answer choice at the beginning. Choose the one that makes the most sense and is further explained by subsequent details in the paragraph. The paragraph discusses the process of identifying DNA, which is lengthy and involves changing the temperature of the DNA several times. Choice (A) is closest to this summation of what is to follow and is the correct answer.

63. C   Difficulty: Easy

Category: Effective Language Use

Getting to the Answer: Watch out for choices that are wordy or redundant. Choice (C) is the most concise and effective way of stating the information in the passage.

64. A   Difficulty: Medium

Category: Organization

Getting to the Answer: Consider the function of this sentence. At what point in the paragraph should this function be employed? The sentence is setting the scene, so it should be placed where it is now, at the beginning of the paragraph. To place it later would make the meaning of the paragraph unclear. Choice (A) is the correct answer.

65. B   Difficulty: Easy

Category: Effective Language Use

Getting to the Answer: Think about the connotations of each answer choice, and be sure to pick the one that fits with the context of the sentence. Substitute each answer choice for the word to see which word works best. "Eager" best reflects how the detectives would be feeling while waiting for important test results. They would be eagerly anticipating this important information and would want it as quickly as possible. Choice (B) is the correct answer.

66. C   Difficulty: Hard

Category: Development

Getting to the Answer: Decide which sentence sounds like the most appropriate way to conclude the passage. The rhetorical question currently in the passage (choice A) introduces an opinion that the passage never reveals; there is no sign that Jane Saunders would feel this way. Likewise, there is no indication in the passage of how expensive modern DNA analysis is (choice B), nor that Saunders marvels about how far science has come in DNA analysis (choice D). Choice (C) is the correct answer; it presents a fairly natural way for Saunders to feel given her accomplishments for the day.

CHAPTER NINE

Conventions of Usage and Punctuation

GETTING STARTED

Conventions of Usage and **Punctuation** questions test your knowledge of pronouns, agreements, frequently misused words, comparatives, idioms, and a variety of punctuation marks. Study the question types below to learn how to approach them and the concepts that these questions test. Knowing the information that you'll need to answer the questions helps you identify the important clues in the passage that will lead you to the correct answers.

Conventions of Usage

Pronouns

A pronoun is ambiguous if the noun to which it refers (its antecedent) is either missing or unclear. On the SAT, you must be able to recognize either situation and make the appropriate correction. When you see an underlined pronoun, make sure you can find the specific noun to which it refers.

Missing Antecedent

- *When the flight arrived, **they** told the passengers to stay seated until the plane reached the gate.* (The pronoun "they" does not have an antecedent in this sentence.)
- *When the flight arrived, **the flight crew** told the passengers to stay seated until the plane reached the gate.* (Replacing the pronoun with a specific noun clarifies the meaning.)

Unclear Antecedent

- *Kayla asked Mia to drive Sree to the airport because **she** was running late.* (The pronoun "she" could refer to any of the three people mentioned in the sentence.)
- *Because Kayla was running late, **she** asked Mia to drive Sree to the airport.* (The pronoun "she" now unambiguously refers to Kayla.)

✔ **Remember**

The **antecedent** is the noun that the pronoun replaces or stands in for elsewhere in the sentence. To identify the **antecedent** of a pronoun, check the nouns near the pronoun. Substitute those nouns for the pronoun to see which one makes sense.

Agreement

Pronoun-Antecedent Agreement

Pronouns must agree with their antecedents not only in person and number but also in gender. Only third-person pronouns make distinctions based on gender.

Gender	Example
Feminine	Because Yvonne had a question, **she** raised her hand.
Masculine	Since **he** had lots of homework, Rico started working right away.
Neutral	The rain started slowly, but then **it** became a downpour.
Unspecified	If a traveler is lost, **he or she** should ask for directions.

Pronoun-Case Agreement

There are three pronoun cases:

1. Subjective case: The pronoun is used as the subject
2. Objective case: The pronoun is used as the object of a verb or a preposition
3. Possessive case: The pronoun expresses ownership

Case	Example
Subjective Case	I, you, she, he, it, we, you, they, who
Objective Case	me, you, her, him, it, us, you, them, whom
Possessive Case	my, mine, your, yours, his, her, hers, its, our, ours, their, theirs, whose

✔ **Remember**

Use "who" when a sentence refers to "she," "he," or "I." (*Quynh was the person* **who provided** *the best answer.*) Use "whom" when a sentence refers to "her," "him," or "me." (*With* **whom** *did Aaron attend the event?*)

Subject-Verb Agreement

A verb must agree with its subject in person and number:

- Singular: *The* **apple tastes** *delicious.*
- Plural: **Apples taste** *delicious.*

The noun closest to a verb may not be its subject: *The **chair** with the cabriole legs **is** an antique.* The noun closest to the verb in this sentence ("is," which is singular) is "legs," which is plural. However, the verb's subject is "chair," so the sentence is correct as written.

Only the conjunction *and* forms a compound subject requiring a plural verb form:

- *Saliyah **and** Taylor **are** in the running club.*
- ***Either** Saliyah **or** Taylor **is** in the running club.*
- ***Neither** Saliyah **nor** Taylor **is** in the running club.*

> ✔ **Expert Tip**
>
> When there are two pronouns or a noun and a pronoun in a compound structure, drop the other noun to confirm which pronoun case to use. For example: *Leo and me walk into town.* Would you say, "Me walk into town"? No, you would say, "I walk into town." Therefore, the correct case is subjective and the original sentence should read *Leo and I walk into town.*

Noun-Number Agreement

Related nouns must be consistent in number:

- ***Students** applying for college must submit their **applications** on time.* (The sentence refers to multiple students, and they all must submit applications.)

Comparisons

The SAT will test your ability to recognize and correct improper comparisons. There are three rules governing correct comparisons:

1. Compare Logical Things

    *The **price of tea** has risen sharply, while **coffee** has remained the same.*

    This sentence incorrectly compares *the price of tea* to *coffee*. The sentence should read: *The **price of tea** has risen sharply, while the **price of coffee** has remained the same.*

2. Use Parallel Structure

    *On a sunny day, I enjoy **hiking** and **to read** outside.*

    This sentence incorrectly uses the gerund verb form (*hiking*) and then switches to the infinitive verb form (*to read*). To correct the sentence, make sure the verb forms are consistent: *On a sunny day, I enjoy **hiking** and **reading** outside.*

3. Structure Comparisons Correctly

    *Some animals are **better** at endurance running **than** they are at sprinting.*

    *Others are **as** good at endurance running **as** they are at sprinting.*

    Both of these sentences are correctly structured: the first with the use of *better . . . than,* and the second with the use of *as . . . as.*

When comparing like things, use adjectives that match the number of items being compared. When comparing two items or people, use the comparative form of the adjective. When comparing three or more items or people, use the superlative form.

Comparative	Superlative
Use when comparing two items.	Use when comparing three or more items.
better	best
more	most
newer	newest
older	oldest
shorter	shortest
taller	tallest
worse	worst
younger	youngest

Idioms

An **idiom** is a combination of words that must be used together to convey either a figurative or literal meaning. Idioms are tested in four ways on the SAT:

1. Proper Preposition Usage in Context

    *The three finalists will compete **for** the grand prize: an all-inclusive cruise to Bali.*
    *Roger will compete **against** Rafael in the final round of the tournament.*
    *I will compete **with** Deborah in the synchronized swimming competition.*

2. Verb Forms

    *The architect likes **to draft** floor plans.*
    *The architect enjoys **drafting** floor plans.*

3. Idiomatic Expressions

    Idiomatic expressions refer to words or phrases that must be used together to be correct.
    *Simone will **either** continue sleeping **or** get up and get ready for school.*
    ***Neither** the principal **nor** the teachers will tolerate tardiness.*
    *This fall, Shari is playing **not only** soccer **but also** field hockey.*

4. Implicit Double Negatives

    Some words imply a negative and therefore cannot be paired with an explicit negative.
    *Janie **cannot hardly** wait for summer vacation.*

This sentence is incorrect as written. It should read: *Janie **can hardly** wait for summer vacation.*

Frequently Tested Prepositions	Idiomatic Expressions	Words That Can't Be Paired with Negative Words
at	as . . . as	barely
by	between . . . and	hardly
for	both . . . and	scarcely
from	either . . . or	
of	neither . . . nor	
on	just as . . . so too	
to	not only . . . but also	
with	prefer . . . to	

Punctuation

End-Of-Sentence and Within-Sentence Punctuation

The SAT Writing & Language Test will require you to identify and correct inappropriate use of ending punctuation that deviates from the intent implied by the context. You will also have to identify and correct inappropriate colons, semicolons, and dashes when used to indicate breaks in thought within a sentence.

You can recognize Punctuation questions because the underlined portion of the text will include a punctuation mark. The answer choices will move that punctuation mark around or replace it with another punctuation mark.

Use **commas** to:

- Separate independent clauses connected by a FANBOYS conjunction (*For, And, Nor, But, Or, Yet, So*)

  Jess finished her homework earlier than expected, so she started on a project that was due the following week.

- Separate an introductory or modifying phrase from the rest of the sentence

  Knowing that soccer practice would be especially strenuous, Tia filled up three water bottles and spent extra time stretching beforehand.

- Set off three or more items in a series or list

  Jeremiah packed a sleeping bag, a raincoat, and a lantern for his upcoming camping trip.

✔ *Expert Tip*

The SAT requires a comma after the final item in a list and before the final "and."

- Separate nonessential information from the rest of the sentence

  Professor Mann, who was the head of the English department, was known for including a wide variety of reading materials in the curriculum.

- Separate an independent and dependent clause

  Tyson arrived at school a few minutes early, which gave him time to clean his locker before class.

✔ **Expert Tip**

When you see an underlined comma, ask yourself, "Can the comma be replaced by a period or a semicolon?" If yes, the comma is grammatically incorrect and needs to be changed.

Use **semicolons** to:

- Join two independent clauses that are not connected by a FANBOYS conjunction

  Gaby knew that her term paper would take at least four more hours to write; she got started in study hall and then finished it at home.

- Separate items in a series or list if those items already include commas

  The team needed to bring uniforms, helmets, and gloves; oranges, almonds, and water; and hockey sticks, pucks, and skates.

✔ **Expert Tip**

When you see an underlined semicolon, ask yourself, "Can the semicolon be replaced by a comma?" If yes, the semicolon is grammatically incorrect and needs to be changed. If the semicolon is separating two independent clauses and can be replaced with a period, it is grammatically correct.

Use **colons** to:

- Introduce and/or emphasize a short phrase, quotation, explanation, example, or list

  Sanjay had two important projects to complete: a science experiment and an expository essay.

Use **dashes** to:

- Indicate a hesitation or a break in thought

  Going to a history museum is a good way to begin researching prehistoric creatures—on second thought, heading to the library will likely be much more efficient.

✔ **Expert Tip**

When you see an underlined colon or dash, ask yourself, "Has the author included a new idea by introducing or explaining something, or by breaking his or her thought process?" If yes, the punctuation is often grammatically correct.

Possessive Nouns and Pronouns

Possessive nouns and pronouns indicate who or what possesses another noun or pronoun. Each follows different rules, and the SAT will test both. These questions require you to identify both the singular and plural forms.

You can spot errors in possessive noun and pronoun construction by looking for:

- Two nouns in a row
- Context clues
- Pronouns with apostrophes
- Words that sound alike

Possessive Nouns		
Singular	sister's	My oldest **sister's** soccer game is on Saturday.
Plural	sisters'	My two older **sisters'** soccer games are on Saturday.

Questions about possessive pronouns often require you to watch out for contractions and sound-alike words.

Possessive Pronouns and Words to Watch Out For	
its = possessive	it's = it is/it has
their = possessive	there = location/place
whose = possessive	who's = who is/who has

✔ Expert Tip

"It's" always means "it is" or "it has." Use "its" to indicate possession.

Parenthetical/Nonrestrictive Elements and Unnecessary Punctuation

Use **commas**, **dashes**, or **parentheses** to set off parenthetical or nonrestrictive information in a sentence.

✔ Remember

Parenthetical or nonrestrictive information includes words or phrases that aren't essential to the sentence structure or content. Sometimes, however, this information is explanatory.

The SAT will also ask you to recognize instances of unnecessary punctuation, particularly **commas**.

Do not use a comma to:

- Separate a subject from its predicate
- Separate a verb from its object or its subject, or a preposition from its object
- Set off restrictive elements
- Precede a dependent clause that comes after an independent clause
- Separate adjectives that work together to modify a noun

> ✔ *Expert Tip*
>
> To determine whether information is nonessential, read the sentence without the information. If the sentence still makes sense without the omitted words, then those words need to be set off with punctuation.

IMPROVING WITH PRACTICE

Step 1: Read Until You Can Identify the Issue

Always read the entire Writing & Language passage. This is particularly important for **Conventions of Usage** and **Punctuation** questions because the best clues for the correct answers may be before or after the underline or the question marker. Be sure to identify the issue by checking:

- any underlined punctuation mark
- any underlined pronouns
- any comparison keywords
- any of the "Frequently Confused Words" from the list above.

You may have to read well after the underline or question marker to be able to identify the issue. If you're not sure there's an issue, keep reading and then return to the question.

Step 2: Answer the Questions

As you're practicing, after identifying the issue, refer back to the tips in the "Getting Started" section and answer questions one at a time. Review the Answer and Explanation for every question immediately after completing it. If you got the question correct, congratulate yourself, but take a moment to read the entire explanation to be sure you got the question right for the right reason. The explanation may also point out a more efficient way that you can use on a later question.

Step 3: Review Incorrect Answers

If you get the question incorrect . . . still congratulate yourself! You're about to learn something new that you'll be able to use to improve your performance on Test Day. Don't read the explanation yet; instead, try the question again.

If you get the question correct the second time, read the explanation to see if you solved the question in the most efficient way. Identify the mistake you made the first time, and determine how you're going to avoid making that mistake again.

> ✔ *Expert Tip*
>
> **Many top scoring students have an SAT notebook where they write down what they learn from every question. Doing this can be time-consuming, but it can also help you identify the types of mistakes you tend to make.**

If you get the question incorrect the second time, use the explanation to learn how to get the question correct. Work through the question again while following the explanation, and identify the steps you will need to take to get a similar question correct. Although the passages and questions will change, the concepts being tested will not. When you encounter unfamiliar questions, take note of them for future study sessions.

> ✔ *Remember*
>
> **The SAT is a standardized test. While Hard Writing & Language questions are usually more difficult to answer than Easy or Medium questions, they are often similar in structure and purpose, and the same six skills (listed in Chapter 6) are tested on every Writing & Language Test. You actually can predict the types of questions you will see on Test Day!**

After all that work, it's time to move to the next question. Reviewing in this way will take time. However, improvement doesn't come from just doing lots and lots of questions; it comes from thinking through your approach and improving it with every question.

RAISING YOUR SCORE EVEN MORE

Here is one of the "secrets" to conquering the Writing & Language section: because the SAT is a standardized test, there will always be clues that make one choice definitely correct and the other choices completely wrong. It's never a matter of opinion.

The most important clues for **Conventions and Usage** and **Punctuation** questions are listed in the "Improving With Practice" section above. To raise your score even more:

- memorize the uses of a comma listed above, and check the list systematically whenever a comma is underlined.

- mentally "strip out" modifying phrases, especially prepositional phrases, when checking subject-verb agreement. Ask yourself, "Who or what is performing the action of the verb?"

- check underlined pronouns to be sure there is only one antecedent, and that the antecedent is the noun closest to the pronoun.

- check modifiers to be sure they are as close as possible to the word they're modifying.

- "than" and "as" indicate comparisons. Check to be sure the items being compared are logical, and that the grammatical structure is parallel.

- use the comparative (-*er*) when comparing two people or items, use the superlative (-*est*) when comparing three or more. *"Mary is the taller of the twins." "John is the tallest singer in the chorus."*

PRACTICE QUESTIONS

The following test-like question sets provide an opportunity to practice reading Conventions of Usage and Punctuation questions. While many of the questions pertain to Conventions of Usage and Punctuation, some touch on other concepts tested on the Writing & Language Test to ensure that your practice is test-like, with a variety of question types per passage.

Questions 1-11 are based on the following passage and supplementary material.

Edgard Varèse's Influence

Today's music, from rock to jazz, has many **1** influences. And perhaps none is as unique as the ideas from French composer Edgard Varèse. Called "the father of electronic music," he approached compositions from a different theoretical perspective than classical composers such as Bartók and Debussy. He called his **2** works "organized sound"; they did not **3** endear melodies but waged assaults of percussion, piano, and human voices. He thought of sounds as having intelligence and treated music spatially, as "sound objects floating in space."

His unique vision can be credited to his education in science. Born in 1883 in France, Varèse was raised by a great-uncle and grandfather in the Burgundy region. He was interested in classical music and composed his first opera as a teenager. While the family lived **4** in Italy he studied engineering in Turin, where he learned math and science and was inspired by the work of the artist Leonardo da Vinci.

1. A) NO CHANGE
   B) influences, and perhaps none is as
   C) influences, but perhaps none is as
   D) influences. Or perhaps none is as

2. A) NO CHANGE
   B) works "organized sound": They
   C) works "organized sound," they
   D) works—"organized sound"—they

3. A) NO CHANGE
   B) amplify
   C) deprive
   D) employ

4. A) NO CHANGE
   B) in Italy, he studied engineering in Turin, where he
   C) in Italy he studied engineering in Turin where he
   D) in Italy, he studied engineering in Turin; where he

In 1903, he returned to France to study music at the Paris Conservatory. There, he composed the radical percussion performance piece *Ionisation*, which featured cymbals, snares, bass drum, xylophone, and sirens wailing. Later compositions were scored for the theremin, a new electronic instrument controlled by **5** <u>the player's hands</u> waving over its antennae, which sense their position. No composer had ever scored any music for the theremin before.

In his thirties, Varèse moved to New York City, where he played piano in a café and conducted other composers' works until his own compositions gained success. His piece *Amériques* was performed in Philadelphia in 1926. Varèse went on to travel to the western United States, where he recorded, lectured, and collaborated with other musicians. By the 1950s, he was using tape recordings in **6** <u>contention</u> with symphonic performance. His piece *Déserts* was aired on a radio program amid selections by Mozart and Tchaikovsky but was received by listeners with hostility. **7**

5. A) NO CHANGE
   B) the players' hands
   C) the players hands
   D) the player's hands'

6. A) NO CHANGE
   B) conjunction
   C) appropriation
   D) supplication

7. If added to the paragraph, which fact would best support the author's claims?
   A) The critical response to his 1926 performance in Philadelphia
   B) The selections by Mozart and Tchaikovsky that were played on the radio
   C) Which specific states he traveled to in the western United States
   D) The cities in which the radio program was aired

Varèse's ideas were more forward-thinking than could be realized. One of his most ambitious scores, called *Espace*, was a choral symphony with multilingual lyrics, which was to be sung simultaneously by choirs in Paris, Moscow, Peking, and New York. He wanted the timing to be orchestrated by radio, but radio technology did not support worldwide transmission. If only Varèse **8** had had the Internet!

Although many of **9** their written compositions were lost in a fire in 1918, many modern musicians and composers have been influenced by Varèse, including Frank Zappa, John Luther Adams, and John Cage, who wrote that Varèse is "more relevant to present musical necessity than even the Viennese masters."

10 Despite being less famous than Stravinsky or Shostakovich, his impact is undeniable. **11** Varèse's love of science and mathematics is shown in his later compositions, but less so in his early works.

Composer	Number of Surviving Works
Edgard Varèse	14
Benjamin Britten	84
Charles Ives	106
Igor Stravinsky	129
Arnold Schoenberg	290
Dmitri Shostakovich	320

8.
   A) NO CHANGE
   B) would have had
   C) would have
   D) have had

9.
   A) NO CHANGE
   B) its
   C) our
   D) his

10. Which choice most accurately and effectively represents the information in the graph?
   A) NO CHANGE
   B) Despite having fewer surviving works than his contemporaries, his impact is undeniable.
   C) Even though he wrote pieces using a wider range of instruments than other composers, his impact is undeniable.
   D) Even though far fewer of his works are now performed compared with those of his contemporaries, his impact is undeniable.

11. Which sentence best summarizes the central idea?
   A) NO CHANGE
   B) In contrast with his newfound popularity, Varèse's early works have long been ignored due to increasing critical hostility.
   C) Varèse and his innovative compositions became an inspiration for artists seeking to challenge traditional musical beliefs.
   D) Though Varèse's contemporary critics failed to call him a "Viennese master," this distinction is changing.

Questions 12-22 are based on the following passage and supplementary material.

The Brooklyn Bridge: The Eighth Wonder of the World

As one of New York City's most iconic landmarks, the Brooklyn Bridge spans 5,989 feet across the East River. Connecting the boroughs of Brooklyn (Kings County) and Manhattan, this bridge was a fantastic marvel of engineering **12** when it was completed in 1883, just years after the Golden Gate Bridge. The Brooklyn Bridge was the longest suspension bridge of **13** its time. It was dubbed the "8th Wonder of the World." Its construction, **14** consequently, was riddled with problems from the very start.

12. Which choice most accurately completes the sentence based on the table?

A) NO CHANGE
B) when it was completed in 1883, several years before the Tower Bridge in London, England, was built.
C) when it was completed in 1883, two years after the Tower Bridge in London, England, was built.
D) when it was completed in 1883, the same year that the Golden Gate Bridge was built.

13. Which choice most effectively combines the sentences at the underlined portion?

A) its time, however, it was dubbed
B) its time, and it was dubbed
C) its time, was dubbed
D) its time, it was dubbed

14. A) NO CHANGE
B) as a result,
C) for example,
D) however,

Residents of Brooklyn had **15** watched for a bridge to connect them with Manhattan, as the frozen East River was **16** absolutely so impossible to cross during the winter. The dream would finally come to fruition when New York legislators approved John Augustus Roebling's plan for a suspension bridge over the East River. Roebling had a successful reputation as a designer of suspension bridges, and the Brooklyn Bridge would be **17** their biggest feat yet, as both the suspension bridge with the longest span (1,600 feet from tower to tower) and as the first steel-cabled suspension bridge.

Roebling would never see his design completed; in fact, he would never even see construction begin. Just before construction was about to start in 1867, Roebling was the victim of **18** a special accident; a boat **19** was smashing into his foot, and he succumbed to tetanus. His son, Washington Roebling, took over the project.

15. A) NO CHANGE
    B) longed
    C) fought
    D) went

16. A) NO CHANGE
    B) absolutely impossible
    C) impossible
    D) so impossible

17. A) NO CHANGE
    B) its
    C) her
    D) his

18. A) NO CHANGE
    B) an exceptional
    C) a common
    D) a freak

19. A) NO CHANGE
    B) smashing
    C) smashed
    D) was smashed

20 <u>Designs for the Brooklyn Bridge included a promenade above the traffic.</u> The first task was for workers to excavate the riverbed in order to anchor the two towers of the bridge to the bedrock below. To accomplish this, bottomless wooden boxes called caissons were sunk into the depths of the river. Once inside, workers would begin the laborious task of removing mud and boulders. To get down into the caissons, workers traveled in airlocks filled with compressed air, which prevented water **21** <u>from entering, if the workers ascended</u> to the surface and left the compressed air too quickly, they would suffer from the debilitating condition known as "caisson disease," or "the bends." Over 100 workers experienced caisson disease, and many others died or were injured from construction-related accidents. The cement-filled caissons remain under the towers of the bridge today.

20. Which choice most effectively establishes the central idea of the paragraph?

A) NO CHANGE

B) The conditions inside the caissons were so terrible that workmen could stay there only for two hours.

C) The towers were built of limestone, granite, and cement that came from a village called Rosendale in upstate New York.

D) The building of the bridge was a monumental and often dangerous undertaking.

21. A) NO CHANGE

B) from entering. If the workers ascended

C) from entering if the workers ascended

D) from entering, since if the workers ascended

Washington Roebling himself suffered from the bends and was partially paralyzed for the rest of his life. Determined to remain part of the project now supervised by his wife, Emily, he watched the construction continue with a telescope. [22] <u>In May, 1883, more than a dozen years after construction began, Emily Roebling was given the first ride over the completed Brooklyn Bridge.</u> She was followed by 150,300 people on that opening day. Despite the setbacks, Manhattan and Brooklyn were finally connected.

Bridges of the World			
Bridge Name & Location	Date Completed	Length	Largest Single Span
Akashi Kaikyo Bridge, Japan	1998	12,828 feet	6,527 feet
Brooklyn Bridge, New York	1883	5,989 feet	1,595 feet
Golden Gate Bridge, San Francisco	1937	8,981 feet	4,200 feet
Tower Bridge, London	1894	880 feet	200 feet

22. Which choice most effectively revises the underlined sentence?

A) In 1883, many years after construction began, Emily Roebling was given a ride over the completed Brooklyn Bridge.

B) In May 1883, many years after construction began, Emily Roebling was given the first ride over the completed Brooklyn Bridge.

C) On May 24, 1883, 14 years after construction began, Emily Roebling was given the first ride over the completed Brooklyn Bridge.

D) In 1883, 14 years after construction began, Emily Roebling was given a ride over the completed Brooklyn Bridge.

Questions 23-33 are based on the following passage.

Murals: The Large-Scale Paintings Remain Symbols of Hope

A mural is a painting done on a wall or ceiling in such a way that it becomes a part of the architecture of the building on which it is painted. Murals are distinct from all other types of pictorial art, or art in which the artist **23** attempts to create a picture of something. The addition of a mural to a building renders the artwork three-dimensional. Murals are still as popular an art form as they were in ancient civilizations, although the techniques for painting them have evolved over time. **24**

Cave paintings are considered the **25** worlds first murals. The earliest prehistoric examples can be found in caves throughout France and Spain, where the paintings show several different species of animals depicted on the walls. Like most early cave paintings, humans were not **26** entailed in these paintings. Artists preferred to use the medium to present things surrounding them. This is still common today.

23. A) NO CHANGE
    B) attempt
    C) are attempting
    D) have attempted

24. Which sentence should be added to the beginning of paragraph 1 to best state the passage's central idea?

    A) Murals are often referred to as the "art of the common man," as they were used exclusively in public places.

    B) A once-ignored art form, murals have recently found a home in many buildings and monuments around the world.

    C) Murals have changed over time, but one thing has remained the same—the inclusion of human figures accomplishing great feats.

    D) Murals have been used across civilizations and centuries to share ideas and messages with the masses in an artistic manner.

25. A) NO CHANGE
    B) world is
    C) worlds'
    D) world's

26. A) NO CHANGE
    B) patronized
    C) depicted
    D) transposed

Murals were also the artwork of choice **27** in ancient classical civilizations such as Ancient Egypt. Murals were painted on the inside of tombs in Egypt, depicting the life of the entombed. Ancient **28** Romans nearly used murals on the walls of all of their buildings, and remnants of these murals can be seen in **29** towns, like Pompeii and Ostia in Italy. The Romans used murals to decorate the insides of their buildings, depicting columns and landscaped patios as a way of artificially opening the interiors of their homes and public houses. Murals remained a popular art form through the Renaissance as well as the Baroque period.

[1] In the times of the ancient Greeks and Romans, color pigments were mixed into hot beeswax and applied to walls or ceilings while the color mixture was still hot. [2] This was called encaustic painting. [3] It was not until the 16th century that oil paints were used for murals, though this proved problematic as oil paints **30** decline easily under certain conditions. [4] In other areas, egg yolks or egg whites were used instead of beeswax in a technique called tempera painting. **31**

27. A) NO CHANGE
    B) in the classical civilization
    C) prior to classical civilizations
    D) in classical civilizations

28. A) NO CHANGE
    B) Romans used murals on the walls of nearly all their buildings
    C) Romans used murals on the walls of all their buildings nearly
    D) Romans used murals nearly on the walls of all their buildings

29. A) NO CHANGE
    B) towns like Pompeii and Ostia in Italy
    C) towns, like Pompeii and Ostia, in Italy
    D) towns—like Pompeii and Ostia in Italy

30. A) NO CHANGE
    B) provoke
    C) deteriorate
    D) permeate

31. For the sake of cohesion of this paragraph, sentence 4 should be placed
    A) where it is now.
    B) before sentence 1.
    C) before sentence 2.
    D) after sentence 2.

The uses of murals have also evolved over time. Murals were once used as educational tools, [32] painting on church walls to educate illiterate attendees. This form of visual art remains an important form of communication, and is sometimes used for political purposes, drawing attention to social issues or supporting various ideals. In Mexico, murals were painted to give hope to those in downtrodden communities after the Mexican Revolution. The common thread seems to be that murals serve to bring people together, offering a common message that all community members can understand and support. [33]

32. A) NO CHANGE
    B) painted
    C) paint
    D) paints

33. Which of these details would best support the author's claims in this paragraph?
    A) The rate of decline in the use of murals to spread political ideas
    B) An instance of a politician opposing the use of murals in public spaces
    C) The names of artists who created murals in Mexico during the revolution
    D) A specific example of a church wall mural that helped educate the masses

Questions 34-44 are based on the following passage.

From Here to the Stars

Gene Kranz hadn't slept in ages. **34** <u>The flight director, pacing</u> between rows of monitors in NASA's Mission Control Center, an impossible problem weighing heavy in his weary mind: Three astronauts were operating a crippled spacecraft nearly 200,000 miles from Earth. And time was running out.

Kranz was no stranger to **35** <u>issues.</u> After losing his father at an early age, Kranz turned to the stars for guidance—and found inspiration. His high school thesis was about the possibility of **36** <u>space travel; an idea</u> that prompted Kranz to set a path for the stars. Kranz pursued a degree in aeronautical engineering after high school graduation. After the Wright brothers had pioneered powered, controlled flight only half a century earlier, aviation milestones like breaking the sound barrier changed the future of flight. Aeronautical engineering required a thorough understanding of **37** <u>physics—like lift and drag on wings—as well as proficiency</u> in mathematics to determine maximum weight on an aircraft. After graduating from Saint Louis University's Parks College of Engineering, Aviation, and Technology, Kranz piloted jets for the Air Force Reserve before performing research and development on missiles and rockets. Kranz

34. A) NO CHANGE
    B) The flight director paced
    C) The pacing flight director
    D) The flight director pacing

35. A) NO CHANGE
    B) adversity.
    C) deadlines.
    D) maladies.

36. A) NO CHANGE
    B) space travel: an idea
    C) space travel, an idea
    D) space travel. An idea

37. A) NO CHANGE
    B) physics; like lift and drag on wings, as well as proficiency
    C) physics like lift and drag on wings, as well as proficiency
    D) physics: like lift and drag on wings—as well as proficiency

later joined NASA and directed the successful *Apollo 11* mission to the moon in 1969.

38 Without his unusual vest, no one would have noticed Kranz in the crowd. One year after the launch, the mood had drastically changed; there were no cheers, no celebratory pats on the back or teary-eyed congratulations. Coffee and adrenaline fueled the scientists and engineers communicating with the astronauts on *Apollo 13*. **39** Kranz was easy to spot among the avalanche of moving bodies and shifting papers. He was dressed, as ever, in his signature handmade vest. **40** The engineers looked to the calm man in the homemade vest.

38. Which sentence would serve as the most effective introduction to the paragraph?
    A) NO CHANGE
    B) During the mission, Kranz stood out as a pillar of strength in the chaos of the command center.
    C) Kranz earned the badges of honor that now adorned his vest.
    D) Kranz possessed more years of experience than anyone in the control center.

39. A) NO CHANGE
    B) Among the avalanche of moving bodies and shifting papers, it is easy to spot Kranz.
    C) Kranz easily spotted the avalanche of moving bodies and shifting papers.
    D) Kranz is easy to spot among the avalanche of moving bodies and shifting papers.

40. Which sentence provides effective evidence to support the main focus of the paragraph?
    A) NO CHANGE
    B) Many of the men in the Mission Control Center had lengthy military careers.
    C) Kranz's thoughts returned to the many tribulations he had experienced.
    D) Several engineers joined together as a bastion of calm in a sea of uncertainty.

Kranz's wife, Marta, had begun making vests at his request in the early '60s. **41** <u>Their was</u> power in a uniform, something Kranz understood from his years serving overseas. The vests served not as an authoritative mark or **42** <u>sartorial</u> flair but as a defining symbol for his team to rally behind. During the effort to save the *Apollo 13* crew, Kranz wore his white vest around the clock like perspiration-mottled battle armor.

43 <u>Among</u> meetings and calculations, Kranz and the NASA staff hatched a wild plan. By using the gravitational force of the moon, **44** <u>it</u> could slingshot the injured spacecraft back on an earthbound course. It was a long shot, of course, but also their best and only one. And, due to the tireless efforts of support staff on Earth and the intrepid spirit of the *Apollo 13* crew, it worked. Six days after takeoff, all three astronauts splashed down safely in the Pacific Ocean.

41. A) NO CHANGE
    B) They're was
    C) There was
    D) They were

42. A) NO CHANGE
    B) sanguine
    C) military
    D) martial

43. A) NO CHANGE
    B) In spite of
    C) Despite
    D) Between

44. A) NO CHANGE
    B) he
    C) they
    D) one

Questions 45-55 are based on the following passage and supplementary material.

Batteries Out in the Cold

Many people have trouble starting their cars on a cold winter morning. In a cold car, the engine turns over more slowly, **45** <u>since</u> it sometimes does not turn over at all. Car owners may **46** <u>credit</u> their cold engines, but the real problem is a cold battery.

[1] A motor is generally connected to its circuit through a battery. [2] When a motor is hooked up in a circuit with a battery, electrons move through the circuit, creating a current. [3] Likewise, decreasing the number of electrons moving decreases the current, which then decreases the amount of power available. [4] Increasing the number of electrons moving increases the current, which then increases the amount of power available to the motor. **47**

45. A) NO CHANGE
    B) and
    C) but
    D) yet

46. A) NO CHANGE
    B) criticize
    C) accuse
    D) blame

47. To make this paragraph most logical, sentence 3 should be placed
    A) where it is now.
    B) before sentence 1.
    C) before sentence 2.
    D) after sentence 4.

48 Electrons move through a battery as a result of two chemical reactions occurring within the battery, one at each pole. **49** A typical car battery, uses lead, and sulfuric acid. At the negative pole, lead reacts with sulfate ions in the solution around it to form lead sulfate, giving off electrons. At the positive pole, lead oxide **50** would have reacted with sulfate ions, hydrogen ions, and electrons in the same solution to also form lead sulfate, taking in electrons. The electrons produced at the negative pole flow through the **51** boundary to the positive pole, providing an electric current in the circuit.

48. Which choice most effectively establishes the main topic of the paragraph?

A) NO CHANGE

B) Sulfuric acid can cause burns to the skin, eyes, lungs, and digestive tract, and severe exposure can result in death.

C) In a direct current circuit, one pole is always negative, the other pole is always positive, and the electrons flow in one direction only.

D) Lead sulfate is toxic by inhalation, ingestion, and skin contact; repeated exposure may lead to anemia, kidney damage, and other serious health issues.

49. A) NO CHANGE

B) A typical car battery uses lead, and sulfuric acid.

C) A typical car battery, uses lead and sulfuric acid.

D) A typical car battery uses lead and sulfuric acid.

50. A) NO CHANGE

B) did react

C) reacts

D) reacted

51. A) NO CHANGE

B) cycle

C) circuit

D) path

A battery charger uses the same reactions, but in reverse. As the current flows in the opposite direction, supplied by house current or a generator, the lead sulfate at the positive pole reacts to change back to lead oxide. 52

Temperature affects the speed of chemical reactions in two ways. For a chemical reaction to happen, the reactants must collide with enough energy to get the reaction going. As the temperature increases, the motion of the reactants increases. The increased motion of the reactants increases the 53 practicality that they will collide and therefore increases the rate of reaction. The amount of energy in the reactants also increases as temperature increases.

This makes it more likely that any two colliding reactants in a battery will have enough energy to react, and so 54 its rate of reaction increases.

Low temperatures have the opposite effect from high temperatures. The chemicals in the battery react more slowly at low temperatures, due both to fewer collisions and less energetic collisions, so fewer electrons move through the circuit. A cold battery takes longer to charge and often cannot provide enough energy to start a car.

52. At this point, the writer wants to add information that supports the main topic of the paragraph. Which choice most effectively accomplishes this goal?
A) Lead oxide, sometimes called litharge, is an inorganic compound with a formula including lead and oxygen.
B) At the same time, the lead sulfate at the negative pole reacts to change back to lead metal.
C) The difference between a house current and a generator is that the generator converts mechanical energy to electrical energy for use in an external circuit.
D) Using a battery charger incorrectly can be dangerous since a car battery contains chemicals that produce hydrogen, a potentially volatile gas.

53. A) NO CHANGE
B) way
C) question
D) probability

54. A) NO CHANGE
B) it's
C) their
D) they're

A cold car that will not start will need either additional power from another car to get the motor moving or a source of heat to warm up the battery and speed up the chemical reactions. Research conducted by FleetCarma in Waterloo, Ontario, demonstrates that **55** <u>colder temperatures negatively affect the distance electric cars can travel.</u>

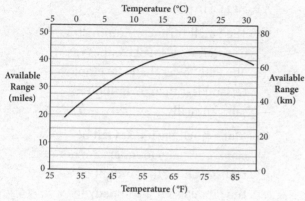

Average Range of Electric Cars as a Function of Temperature

Adapted from research published by FleetCarma, Waterloo, Ontario.

55. Which choice most accurately represents the information in the graph?

A) NO CHANGE

B) the number of kilometers an electric car can travel declines as the outside temperature increases.

C) temperatures below 15°C make it extremely difficult to start an electric car.

D) once the electric car's battery has an alternate heat source by which to start, the distance the car can travel is greatly increased.

Questions 56-66 are based on the following passage.

Will Your Start-Up Succeed?

According to research from Harvard Business School, the majority of small businesses [56] <u>fail in fact</u> the success rate for a first-time company owner is a meager 18 percent. With odds so dismal, why would anyone become a business entrepreneur?

[57] <u>Veteran entrepreneurs achieve a higher 30 percent success rate, so the most predictive factor for success appears to be the number of innovations that a person has "pushed out."</u> More specifically, the people who succeed at building a robust start-up are the ones who have previously tried. Finally, many entrepreneurs [58] <u>grab</u> the idea for their business by solving practical problems, and it's more than luck; 320 new entrepreneurs out of 100,000 *do* succeed by starting a company at the right time in the right industry.

Mitch Gomez is evidence of this data. He [59] <u>did graduate</u> from college with a degree in accounting. "I quickly realized that I have too big of a personality to be content practicing accounting," he laughs. He first built a successful

56. A) NO CHANGE
    B) fail, in fact,
    C) fail; in fact,
    D) fail: in fact

57. Which sentence most effectively establishes the central idea?
    A) NO CHANGE
    B) The Small Business Administration defines a small business as one with fewer than 500 employees and less than $7 million in sales annually.
    C) Many small businesses fail because company founders are not realistic about the amount of time it takes for a company to become profitable.
    D) Running a small business can take up a lot more time than punching a clock for someone else and might not be enjoyable for everyone.

58. A) NO CHANGE
    B) derive
    C) achieve
    D) grasp

59. A) NO CHANGE
    B) has graduated
    C) graduated
    D) would have graduated

insurance claims **60** <u>service, and next</u> founded his own independent insurance agency. "I continually employ my accounting skills, but I've ascertained that I'm an even more effective salesperson."

Similarly, Barbara Vital, the woman behind Vital Studio, explains, "I love spending as much time with my family as possible." Vital saw an opportunity to **61** <u>launch</u> a monogramming business when her two young sons started school, so she founded a company that offers monogrammed backpacks and water bottles for kids, as well as **62** <u>totes, rain boots; and</u> baseball caps for college students. What is the secret to Vital's success? "I'm always learning how to incorporate social media and add functionality to my product website to keep customers happy," she says.

Finally, Chris Roth is an entrepreneur who can step out of his comfort zone. Always seeking a new **63** <u>challenge his company</u> designed and manufactured technology to keep the nozzles of water misting systems clean. Roth has also established a corporate travel agency and a truck customization company, most recently claiming he has become an innovator who beat the odds by "striving to serve customers better than my competition." **64** <u>Large companies often employ corporate travel agencies to arrange travel for their employees and clients.</u>

60. A) NO CHANGE
    B) service. And next
    C) service and next
    D) service; and next

61. A) NO CHANGE
    B) present
    C) propel
    D) impact

62. A) NO CHANGE
    B) totes; rain boots; and
    C) totes, rain boots, and,
    D) totes, rain boots, and

63. A) NO CHANGE
    B) challenge: his company
    C) challenge; his company
    D) challenge, his company

64. Which sentence would best support the central idea?
    A) NO CHANGE
    B) Savvy entrepreneurs know which risks are worth taking and which risks can tank their business before their doors open.
    C) Now Roth's small business installs water misters on restaurant patios and even sets up misting stations at outdoor music festivals.
    D) Many new small businesses fail because company founders fail to do market research and identify the needs of their community.

Gomez, Vital, and Roth [65] agrees that although being an entrepreneur can be a formidable challenge, exceptionally skillful entrepreneurs have important strategies for success, including stretching [66] his personal boundaries and recovering from failures. "And nothing beats being your own boss," adds Gomez.

65. A) NO CHANGE
    B) agree
    C) should agree
    D) had agreed

66. A) NO CHANGE
    B) their
    C) our
    D) her

ANSWERS AND EXPLANATIONS

CHAPTER 9

1. C   Difficulty: Medium

Category: Sentence Formation

Getting to the Answer: Read the two sentences connected by the underlined portion, and decide which answer choice creates a grammatically correct and logical sentence. Using the coordinating conjunction "but" with a comma to combine the sentences shows that the second portion, which mentions Varèse as being unique, stands in contrast to the first portion, which mentions many influential artists. Choice (C) is correct. The other options, featuring "and" and "or," do not show this necessary contrast.

2. A   Difficulty: Hard

Category: Punctuation

Getting to the Answer: Reread the entire sentence to assess how the punctuation in the answer choices affects how each portion of the sentence relates to the others. The correct answer is choice (A). The semicolon correctly links the two independent clauses that have a direct relationship with one another.

3. D   Difficulty: Medium

Category: Effective Language Use

Getting to the Answer: Read the sentence for context clues, and think about the author's intention. Then determine which answer provides the most appropriate word choice. "Employ" is the only word that matches the meaning of the sentence, which states that Varèse did not use traditional melodies. Thus, choice (D) is correct.

4. B   Difficulty: Medium

Category: Punctuation

Getting to the Answer: Reread the sentence to determine how each portion relates to the others. Then examine how the punctuation in the answer choices affects these relationships. The portion of the sentence discussing the family's move to Italy is an introductory element and needs a comma to offset it from the rest of the sentence. The portion discussing what Varèse learned in Turin is a parenthetical element and also requires a comma. Therefore, choice (B) is correct.

5. A   Difficulty: Medium

Category: Punctuation

Getting to the Answer: Review the sentence for context clues and to assess the subject's ownership of the objects in the sentence. Then determine which form of the possessive noun correctly reflects this ownership. The hands in the sentence belong to a single player using a single theremin; therefore, the correct answer will use the singular possessive noun "player's." Choice (A) is correct.

6. B   Difficulty: Medium

Category: Effective Language Use

Getting to the Answer: Read the sentence for context clues. Decide on the answer choice that makes the sentence's meaning precise and clear. "Conjunction" is the only word that relates to two things occurring at the same time to create a single outcome, which is the intended meaning of the sentence. Choice (B) is correct.

7.   A   Difficulty: Hard

Category: Development

Getting to the Answer: Assess the central idea of the introductory sentence in the paragraph, and determine which additional fact noted in the answer choices would have the greatest benefit to the reader. The introductory sentence states that Varèse worked in New York until he secured his first success. Describing the critical reaction to the next event mentioned would help strengthen the idea that the Philadelphia performance was a successful event in Varèse's career. Choice (A) is the correct answer.

8.   A   Difficulty: Hard

Category: Usage

Getting to the Answer: Consider what kind of situation the author is presenting here, and decide which tense of the verb "has" creates a grammatically correct sentence that reflects this meaning. Keep in mind the time of the events in the sentence. The sentence imagines a situation in which Varèse had been able to use the Internet, an unrealistic action. The double "had had" is correct; it describes past-tense actions that might have occurred in the past but didn't. Choice (A) is correct.

9.   D   Difficulty: Easy

Category: Usage

Getting to the Answer: Read the entire sentence to figure out who is the owner of the burned compositions. Then select the proper personal pronoun for this antecedent. Choice (D) is the correct singular possessive pronoun because the burned compositions belonged to Varèse, one person, and not a group of artists.

10.   B   Difficulty: Medium

Category: Quantitative

Getting to the Answer: Study the information in the graphic to determine which answer choice most accurately finishes the sentence. Choice (B) is correct because it accurately reflects information included in the graphic.

11.   C   Difficulty: Medium

Category: Development

Getting to the Answer: After reading the final paragraph, examine each answer choice to determine which best summarizes the paragraph's overall message. Choice (C) is correct. It is the one sentence that sets up the idea that Varèse's challenging work has been an inspiration to many later artists, an idea supported by the rest of the paragraph.

12.   B   Difficulty: Medium

Category: Quantitative

Getting to the Answer: The table gives specific information about various bridges. Interpret the information to choose the correct answer choice. Choice (B) accurately reflects the information in the table since the Tower Bridge was not built until 1894.

13.   B   Difficulty: Medium

Category: Effective Language Use

Getting to the Answer: Watch out for answer choices that may have incorrect transition words or be incorrect in usage or in punctuation. Choice (B) joins the sentences concisely and correctly by using the conjunction "and" to connect the two complete ideas.

14.   D   Difficulty: Medium

Category: Organization

Getting to the Answer: Study the relationship between the two parts of the sentence to determine which transition word would work logically. Substitute each transition word in the sentence to see which fits best. Only "however" (a contrast transition) in choice (D) creates a correct and logical relationship between the two parts of the sentence because it discusses the difficulties that were encountered in building the bridge.

15. B **Difficulty:** Easy

Category: Effective Language Use

Getting to the Answer: The context of the sentence suggests which word would have the correct connotation. Substitute each word choice in the sentence to see how it fits with the context. Only choice (B) correctly fits the context of the sentence, which suggests that the bridge was something that people very much wanted; "longed" embodies this notion.

16. C **Difficulty:** Easy

Category: Effective Language Use

Getting to the Answer: Watch out for answer choices like A, which are redundant. Be as direct and simple as possible. Additional adjectives do not add more meaning to this content. Choice (C) is the most concise and effective way of stating the information in the passage and is therefore correct.

17. D **Difficulty:** Easy

Category: Usage

Getting to the Answer: Reread the sentence to identify the antecedent for the underlined pronoun and determine if the two agree. The antecedent in this sentence is "Roebling," which calls for a singular masculine possessive pronoun. Choice (D) is correct.

18. D **Difficulty:** Medium

Category: Effective Language Use

Getting to the Answer: Consider the connotations of each word. Substitute each word choice back into the sentence to see how well it fits the context. Choice (D) fits with the context of the sentence, which suggests that such accidents do not happen often. While "special" in A and "exceptional" in choice B can indicate uniqueness, they are too positive. Choice (D) is correct.

19. C **Difficulty:** Medium

Category: Sentence Formation

Getting to the Answer: Look at the other verb in the sentence to see if the verbs are parallel in structure. Choice (C) is the correct form of the verb that is parallel to "succumbed," which appears later in the sentence.

20. D **Difficulty:** Hard

Category: Development

Getting to the Answer: To find the central idea of a paragraph, identify important details and summarize them. Then, find the choice that is the closest to your summary. Do not choose a detail rather than a central idea. The paragraph primarily discusses the hardships faced by workers building the bridge. Choice (D) most accurately summarizes the central idea of the paragraph.

21. B **Difficulty:** Medium

Category: Sentence Formation

Getting to the Answer: Two complete thoughts should be two separate sentences. Be careful of inappropriate transition words. Choice (B) divides the two thoughts into two complete sentences by adding a period and capitalizing the first word of the second sentence and is therefore correct.

22. C **Difficulty:** Hard

Category: Development

Getting to the Answer: To find the correct answer, look for the sentence that does not exclude any necessary details from the underlined portion. Choice (C) correctly maintains the author's inclusion of various details about when the bridge was completed and the significance of Emily's ride.

23. A   Difficulty: Easy

Category: Usage

Getting to the Answer: Review each answer choice against the subject of the sentence to determine which verb creates a grammatically correct agreement. The subject of the sentence, "the artist," is singular, and thus the verb must also be singular. Choice (A) is correct, as it is the only singular verb. All other answer choices agree with a plural subject.

24. D   Difficulty: Medium

Category: Development

Getting to the Answer: After reading the entire passage, review the sentences presented here and determine which answer choice best captures the overarching idea of the passage rather than focusing on details or incorrect information. Unlike the other answer choices that focus on incorrect details, choice (D) is correct as it accurately sums up the central idea of the entire passage.

25. D   Difficulty: Easy

Category: Punctuation

Getting to the Answer: Read the sentence with each answer choice taking the place of the underlined word and assess which is the correct possessive version of the noun in order to create a grammatically correct and logical sentence. Because the "first mural" belongs to one world, the possessive version of the singular world in choice (D) is correct.

26. C   Difficulty: Medium

Category: Effective Language Use

Getting to the Answer: Reread the sentence for context clues to understand its intention. Then, determine which answer choice creates a logical sentence that matches that intention. "Depicted," or represented in an artistic manner, is the only word that correctly fits the intention of the sentence. Choice (C) is correct.

27. D   Difficulty: Medium

Category: Effective Language Use

Getting to the Answer: Read the paragraph to understand the purpose of the sentence and its context for sense; then replace the underlined portion of the sentence with the answer choice that creates a logical and grammatically correct sentence without redundancies. Choice (D) is correct because it eliminates the redundant word "ancient" (as it is used many times throughout the paragraph and "classical" also refers to a similar time period) while remaining grammatically and logically correct.

28. B   Difficulty: Medium

Category: Sentence Formation

Getting to the Answer: Modifiers must be placed precisely in order to make logical sense and create a grammatically correct sentence. Review the sentence to understand its meaning and then examine how the various placements of the modifier "nearly" affect the meaning of the sentence. Select the answer choice that creates a logical sentence. Choice (B) is correct as it places the modifier in a location that means many of the buildings contained murals.

29. B   Difficulty: Medium

Category: Punctuation

Getting to the Answer: Review the punctuation used in each answer choice to assess how each affects the meaning and structure of the entire sentence. Because the text after the word "town" is not a list or an independent clause and does not contain nonessential words or information, it does not need any within-sentence punctuation. Choice (B) is correct.

30. C   Difficulty: Medium

Category: Effective Language Use

Getting to the Answer: Imagine that there is a blank in the sentence instead of the word in question. Read the sentence with each word in the answer choices to assess how the definitions affect the sentence's meaning. "Deteriorate" is the only answer choice that directly relates to a problematic physical decomposition of the paint's properties; therefore, choice (C) is correct.

31. D   Difficulty: Hard

Category: Organization

Getting to the Answer: Read the paragraph to make sense of the content and carefully determine how the information should flow in order to create a logical argument. Sentence 4 discusses how egg is used instead of beeswax to create tempera paint. This should follow immediately after the sentences that discuss using beeswax to create encaustic paint (sentences 1 and 2); therefore, choice (D) is correct.

32. B   Difficulty: Medium

Category: Shifts in Construction

Getting to the Answer: Review the sentence to determine the established tense; then, determine which answer choice follows this tense and creates a grammatically correct sentence. Choice (B) is correct, as the sentence is written in the past tense, established by the phrase "were once used" earlier in the sentence.

33. D   Difficulty: Medium

Category: Development

Getting to the Answer: Reread the final paragraph to understand the central idea. Then, assess which details are supported by examples and which are not. Finally, determine which additional details noted in the answer choices will have the greatest benefit to the reader. The paragraph offers an example of murals being used to spread political and social messages, but no specific example is offered to support the claim that murals helped educate the illiterate. Therefore, choice (D) is correct.

34. B   Difficulty: Medium

Category: Sentence Formation

Getting to the Answer: Read the sentence and determine whether it is grammatically complete. To form a grammatically complete sentence, you

must have an independent clause prior to a colon. As written, the text that comes before the colon is not grammatically complete because it lacks an independent clause with a subject and predicate. Choice (B) correctly adds a verb to the clause before the comma. It also correctly uses the past tense to match with the tense of "hadn't" in the first sentence of the passage.

35. B   Difficulty: Medium

Category: Effective Language Use

Getting to the Answer: Read the sentences surrounding the word to look for context clues. Watch out for near synonyms that are not quite correct. The word "issues" is not precise and does a poor job of conveying the meaning of the sentence. A better word, such as (B), "adversity," more precisely conveys hardship, difficulties, or painful situations.

36. C   Difficulty: Medium

Category: Punctuation

Getting to the Answer: Determine whether a clause is independent or dependent to decide between a comma and a semicolon. The clause is dependent, as it contains only a noun ("an idea") and a relative clause to modify it. A semicolon is used to separate two independent clauses, so it cannot be used here. A comma is the appropriate punctuation mark to separate the dependent clause from the independent clause in the sentence. Choice (C) is the correct answer.

37. A   Difficulty: Medium

Category: Punctuation

Getting to the Answer: Figure out the role of the underlined phrase in the sentence to find the correct punctuation. "Like lift and drag on wings" is a parenthetical element provided as an example. The sentence is correctly punctuated as written because it uses dashes to set off the parenthetical element. The correct answer is choice (A).

38. B   Difficulty: Hard

Category: Development

Getting to the Answer: Read the paragraph and summarize the main idea to predict an answer. Then look for an answer that matches your prediction. Choice (B) correctly establishes that Kranz stood out as a leader in a time of crisis.

39. A   Difficulty: Easy

Category: Shifts in Construction

Getting to the Answer: Read the paragraph to establish the correct verb tense for the sentence. Other verbs in the paragraph, such as "were" and "fueled," are past tense and indicate that another past tense verb is needed for this sentence. Choice (A) is correct because it uses the past tense "was" and logically transitions into the explanation about Kranz's vest making him easy to spot.

40. A   Difficulty: Hard

Category: Development

Getting to the Answer: Quickly summarize the main idea of the paragraph. Eliminate choices that may be accurate but do not support this primary focus. Choice (A) clearly supports the main focus of the paragraph by drawing attention to Kranz's role as a leader in Mission Control.

41. C   Difficulty: Easy

Category: Usage

Getting to the Answer: Be careful with homophones. Figure out the part of speech and what the target word refers to if it is a pronoun. "Their" is a possessive pronoun indicating ownership. "There" is a pronoun that replaces a place name. "They're" is a contraction that is short for "they are." Choice (C), "there," is the correct choice.

42. A   Difficulty: Hard

Category: Effective Language Use

Getting to the Answer: When faced with unfamiliar words, eliminate clearly incorrect answers first. The paragraph indicates that Kranz did not intend for the vest to be stylish. Kranz wore the vest as a military type of symbol, but the correct answer will need to be in contrast to that idea. Choice (A) is the correct answer. The word "sartorial" means "having to do with clothing."

43. D   Difficulty: Medium

Category: Usage

Getting to the Answer: Think about the commonly confused pair between/among. Consider which preposition is usually used to reference two distinct objects. Choice (D) appropriately selects the word "between" because the objects "meetings" and "calculations" are two distinct items. "Among" is used for more than two distinct items.

44. C   Difficulty: Medium

Category: Usage

Getting to the Answer: Read the target sentence and the sentence before it. Figure out whom or what the pronoun refers to and make sure it matches the antecedent in number. The plural antecedent is found in the previous sentence ("Kranz and the NASA staff") and is clearly plural. Choice (C) correctly uses a plural pronoun to refer to a plural antecedent.

45. B   Difficulty: Medium

Category: Sentence Formation

Getting to the Answer: Compare the two parts of the sentence. Is the second part a subordinate or coordinate clause? "Since" is a conjunction used between subordinating ideas. These two clauses are coordinating and require a coordinating conjunction meaning "in addition to." Choice (B) is correct.

46. D   Difficulty: Medium

Category: Effective Language Use

Getting to the Answer: Analyze how the underlined word is used in the sentence. Test each answer choice to see if it improves the overall clarity of the text. The opening sentences of the passage are about how the cold weather makes starting cars difficult. When used as a verb, "credit" means to acknowledge (someone or something). Choice (D), "blame," means to hold responsible, and is correct.

47. D   Difficulty: Hard

Category: Organization

Getting to the Answer: Review how the content of sentence 3 is related to the entire paragraph. Recall that transitions help the reader understand logical relationships between ideas. What words in sentence 3 signal a transition? Sentence 4 explains what happens when the number of electrons increases. Because sentence 3 further develops the explanation of what happens when the number of electrons decreases, the transition "likewise" is a clue that it should follow sentence 4. Choice (D) is correct.

48. A   Difficulty: Hard

Category: Development

Getting to the Answer: Identify the key details in the paragraph. Then, summarize them to find the central idea. All of the sentences in this paragraph describe how a battery is constructed and works. Choice (A) is correct.

49. D   Difficulty: Easy

Category: Punctuation

Getting to the Answer: Determine if the items listed need to be treated as a series. Since there are only two items, no commas are needed. Choice (D) is correct.

50. C   Difficulty: Easy

Category: Usage

Getting to the Answer: Determine the tense and the number of the subject. Then, predict the verb form that matches. Since "lead oxide" is singular and the paragraph is written in present tense, choice (C) is correct.

51. C   Difficulty: Medium

Category: Effective Language Use

Getting to the Answer: Establish how the underlined word is used in the sentence; consider the connotations and denotations of the answer choices. Remember that the correct term should reflect the scientific subject matter. "Boundary" is a term meaning a limitation. "Circuit," a noun, is the scientific term that means circumference or course. Choice (C) is correct.

52. B   Difficulty: Hard

Category: Development

Getting to the Answer: Closely examine the topic sentence and the supporting details; identify the central idea of the paragraph. Choice (B) is the only option that adds supporting information about how a current flows through a battery charger.

53. D   Difficulty: Medium

Category: Effective Language Use

Getting to the Answer: Look at how the word is used in the sentence and analyze its grammatical function. Use context clues to determine which choice is correct. "Practicality" is an adverb meaning in a practical manner and doesn't make sense here. "Probability" is a noun meaning likelihood, which is more appropriate. Choice (D) is correct.

54. A   Difficulty: Medium

Category: Usage

Getting to the Answer: Look for the antecedent of a pronoun to see if the pronoun agrees. The antecedent of "its" is "a battery," which is singular. The contraction "it's" is short for *it is* and is inappropriate here. Choice (A) is correct.

55. A   Difficulty: Hard

Category: Quantitative

Getting to the Answer: Study the graph carefully and consider how its data points connect to the content of the passage. The overall graph trend suggests that battery performance peaks at moderate temperatures, suffers slightly at higher temperatures, and declines greatly at lower ones. Since cold temperatures adversely affect the battery performance of an electric car, choice (A) is correct.

56. C   Difficulty: Medium

Category: Sentence Formation

Getting to the Answer: Check to see whether there are two independent clauses within this sentence. Two independent clauses without punctuation indicate a run-on sentence. As written, this is a run-on sentence. Choice (C) is the correct answer because it separates the two complete but related thoughts with a semicolon.

57. A   Difficulty: Medium

Category: Development

Getting to the Answer: Eliminate answers that might contain details related to the central idea but do not properly express the central idea. This paragraph is mostly about the characteristics of people who are successful entrepreneurs. Choice (A) is the correct answer because it introduces the main idea by summarizing the traits people must have to achieve success as a business owner.

58. B   Difficulty: Hard

Category: Effective Language Use

Getting to the Answer: Eliminate answers such as D that mean nearly the same thing as "grab" but do not clarify the meaning of the sentence. In this context, "derive" best clarifies the meaning of the sentence, which explains how entrepreneurs get ideas for their businesses. Choice (B) is the correct answer.

59. C   Difficulty: Easy

Category: Usage

Getting to the Answer: Read the rest of the paragraph and pay attention to the verb tense used. The verbs in the rest of this paragraph are in past tense. "Graduated" is the past tense of the verb "to graduate"; therefore, (C) is the correct answer.

60. C   Difficulty: Medium

Category: Punctuation

Getting to the Answer: Examine the structure of the whole sentence. Consider whether the punctuation is correct or even necessary. The subject of this sentence is "he," and it is followed by a compound predicate containing the verbs "built" and "founded." When a compound predicate contains only two items, a comma should not separate either verb from the subject. No punctuation is necessary, so (C) is the correct answer.

61. A   Difficulty: Medium

Category: Effective Language Use

Getting to the Answer: Replace the underlined word with each answer choice. Consider which word makes the most sense in context and conveys the clearest meaning. The sentence discusses how Vital began her own business. In this context, "launch" conveys the most precise meaning because it connotes the start of a major endeavor. Choice (A) is the correct answer because no change is needed.

62. D   Difficulty: Easy

Category: Punctuation

Getting to the Answer: This sentence contains a list of items in a series. Think about the rules of punctuation for items in a series. Items in a series should be separated by commas, with a comma following each word except the last item in the series. The word "and" is not an item in the series and, therefore, should not be followed by a comma. Therefore, (D) is the correct answer.

63. D   Difficulty: Easy

Category: Punctuation

Getting to the Answer: Identify the main elements of this sentence, such as the subject, predicate, and any restrictive or nonrestrictive clauses. Remember that a nonrestrictive clause should be set off with a comma. The clause "always seeking a new challenge" is nonrestrictive and should be set off from the rest of the sentence with a comma. Choice (D) is the correct answer.

64. C   Difficulty: Hard

Category: Development

Getting to the Answer: Identify the central idea of the paragraph. Read each answer choice and consider which sentence could be added to the paragraph to provide support for the central idea you identified. This paragraph is mostly about Chris Roth, an entrepreneur who now has several companies. (C) is the correct answer because it provides specific details about one of the companies Roth owns.

65. B   Difficulty: Easy

Category: Usage

Getting to the Answer: Read the entire sentence. Identify the subject and determine whether it is plural or singular. Determine the correct verb tense for the sentence. The subject of this sentence is plural (Gomez, Vital, and Roth), so the verb must be plural, as well. (B) is the correct answer because "agree" is the plural present tense of the verb "to agree."

66. B   Difficulty: Easy

Category: Usage

Getting to the Answer: Read the entire sentence and identify the antecedent for the underlined pronoun. The correct answer will be the pronoun that is in agreement with the antecedent. In this sentence, the antecedent is "entrepreneurs" which requires a third-person plural pronoun. Therefore, choice (B) is the correct answer.

Math

CHAPTER TEN

SAT Math Test Overview

The SAT Math Test

The SAT Math Test is broken down into a calculator section and a no-calculator section. Questions across the sections consist of multiple-choice, student-produced response (Grid-in), and more comprehensive multi-part question sets.

	Calculator Section	No-Calculator Section	Total
Duration (minutes)	55	25	80
Multiple-choice	30	15	45
Grid-in	8	5	13
Total Questions	38	20	58

The SAT Math Test is divided into four content areas: Heart of Algebra, Problem Solving and Data Analysis, Passport to Advanced Math, and Additional Topics in Math.

SAT Math Test Content Area Distribution	
Heart of Algebra (19 questions)	Analyzing and fluently solving equations and systems of equations; creating expressions, equations, and inequalities to represent relationships between quantities and to solve problems; rearranging and interpreting formulas
Problem Solving and Data Analysis (17 questions)	Creating and analyzing relationships using ratios, proportions, percentages, and units; describing relationships shown graphically; summarizing qualitative and quantitative data
Passport to Advanced Math (16 questions)	Rewriting expressions using their structure; creating, analyzing, and fluently solving quadratic and higher-order equations; purposefully manipulating polynomials to solve problems
Additional Topics in Math (6 questions)	Making area and volume calculations in context; investigating lines, angles, triangles, and circles using theorems; and working with trigonometric functions

A few math questions might look like something you'd expect to see on a science or history test. These "crossover" questions are designed to test your ability to use math in real-world scenarios. There are a total of 18 "crossover" questions that will contribute to subscores that span multiple tests. Nine of the questions will contribute to the Analysis in Science subscore, and nine will contribute to the Analysis in History/Social Studies subscore.

CHAPTER ELEVEN

Heart of Algebra

PRACTICE QUESTIONS

The following test-like questions provide an opportunity to practice Heart of Algebra questions. The calculator icon means you are permitted to use a calculator to solve a question. It does not mean that you *should* use it, however.

1.
$$rx + sy = 3$$
$$4x + 6y = 10$$

In the system of equations above, r and s are constants. If the system has infinitely many solutions, what is the value of $\frac{r}{s}$?

A) $-\frac{3}{2}$

B) $-\frac{2}{3}$

C) $\frac{3}{10}$

D) $\frac{2}{3}$

2. A printing press running around the clock can print 54,000 black and white pages per day. Based on this information, what could the function $f(x) = 2,250x$ represent?

A) The number of pages the press can print in x days

B) The number of pages the press can print in x hours

C) The number of days it takes the press to print x pages

D) The number of hours it takes the press to print x pages

3. At a recent charity event, attendees were given colored slips of paper (as many as they wanted) corresponding to certain monetary denominations. Attendees could give donations using any combination of the slips of paper. The blue slip was worth 3 dollars more than a red slip, and a red slip was worth 3 dollars more than a green slip. If 6 green slips were worth m dollars, then which of the following represents the value, in dollars, of 12 blue slips and 6 red slips?

A) $3m + 90$

B) $90m + 3$

C) $45m + 6$

D) $60 + 3m$

4.

Laptop Depreciation

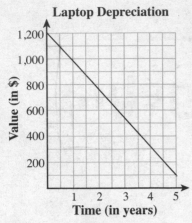

The figure above shows the straight-line depreciation of a laptop computer over the first five years of its use. According to the figure, what is the average rate of change in dollars per year of the value of the computer over the five-year period?

A) −1,100

B) −220

C) −100

D) 100

5.

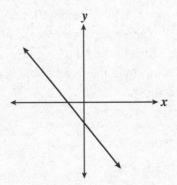

The graph above could represent which of the following equations?

A) $-6x - 4y = 5$

B) $-6x - 4y = -5$

C) $-6x + 4y = 5$

D) $-6x + 4y = -5$

6. A store "breaks even" when its sales equal its expenses. Jon has just opened a new surfboard store at the beach. He buys each surfboard wholesale for $80 and has fixed monthly expenses of $3,600. He sells each surfboard for $120. How many surfboards does Jon need to sell in a month to break even?

A) 18

B) 30

C) 45

D) 90

7.

State	Minimum Wage per Hour
Idaho	$7.25
Montana	$7.90
Oregon	$9.10
Washington	$9.32

The table above shows the 2014 minimum wages for several states that share a border. Assuming an average workweek of between 35 and 40 hours, which inequality represents how much more a worker who earns minimum wage can earn per week in Oregon than in Idaho?

A) $x \geq 1.85$

B) $7.25 \leq x \leq 9.10$

C) $64.75 \leq x \leq 74$

D) $253.75 \leq x \leq 364$

8.
$$\frac{4(d+3)-9}{8} = \frac{10-(2-d)}{6}$$

In the equation above, what is the value of d?

A) $\frac{23}{16}$

B) $\frac{23}{8}$

C) $\frac{25}{8}$

D) $\frac{25}{4}$

9.

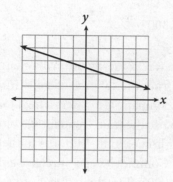

If the equation of the line shown in the graph above is written in the form $y = mx + b$, which of the following is true?

A) $m < 0$ and $b < 0$

B) $m < 0$ and $b > 0$

C) $m > 0$ and $b < 0$

D) $m > 0$ and $b > 0$

10.

x	−9	0	3	9
y	11	8	7	?

If the values in the table represent a linear relationship, what is the missing value?

A) 5

B) 6

C) 11

D) 13

11.

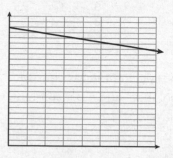

Which of the following scenarios could be supported by the graph shown?

A) As the algae content in a lake increases, the number of fish decreases.

B) As the algae content in a lake decreases, the number of fish decreases.

C) As the algae content in a lake increases, the number of fish increases.

D) As the algae content in a lake increases, the number of fish remains constant.

12. The chief financial officer of a shoe company calculates that the cost C of producing p pairs of a certain shoe is $C = 17p + 1,890$. The marketing department wants to sell the shoe for $35 per pair. The shoe company will make a profit only if the total revenue from selling p pairs is greater than the total cost of producing p pairs. Which of the following inequalities gives the number of pairs of shoes p that the company needs to sell in order to make a profit?

A) $p < 54$

B) $p > 54$

C) $p < 105$

D) $p > 105$

13.
$$\frac{3}{4}x - \frac{1}{2}y = 12$$
$$kx - 2y = 22$$

If the system of linear equations above has no solution, and k is a constant, what is the value of k?

A) $-\frac{4}{3}$

B) $-\frac{3}{4}$

C) 3

D) 4

14.
$$\frac{3(n-2)+5}{4} = \frac{11-(7-n)}{6}$$

In the equation shown, what is the value of n?

A) $-\frac{1}{11}$

B) $\frac{5}{11}$

C) 1

D) $\frac{11}{7}$

15.
$$-2x + 5y = 1$$
$$7x - 10y = -11$$

If (x, y) is a solution to the system of equations above, what is the sum of x and y?

A) $-\frac{137}{30}$

B) -4

C) $-\frac{10}{3}$

D) -3

16. Nadim is hosting a party and is hiring a catering company to make and serve the food. The caterer charges a flat fee for serving the food plus a per person rate for the meals. If the equation used to calculate the total cost of Nadim's party is $y = 11x + 300$, then which of the following most likely represents the number of people attending the party?

A) x

B) y

C) 11

D) 300

17. A railway company normally charges $35 round trip from the suburbs of a city into downtown. The company also offers a deal for commuters who use the train frequently to commute from their homes in the suburbs to their jobs in the city. Commuters can purchase a discount card for $900, after which they only have to pay $12.50 per round trip. How many round trips, t, must a commuter make in order for the discount card to be a better deal?

A) $t < 40$

B) $t > 40$

C) $t < 72$

D) $t > 72$

18. Which of the following systems of inequalities has no solution?

A) $\begin{cases} y \ge x \\ y \le 2x \end{cases}$

B) $\begin{cases} y \ge x \\ y \le -x \end{cases}$

C) $\begin{cases} y \ge x+1 \\ y \le x-1 \end{cases}$

D) $\begin{cases} y \ge -x+1 \\ y \le x-1 \end{cases}$

19. The graph of which of the following linear equations has an undefined slope?

    A) $x = 3$

    B) $y = 0$

    C) $x = -y$

    D) $x - y = 0$

20. In the legal field, "reciprocity" means that an attorney can take and pass a bar exam in one state, and be allowed to practice law in a different state that permits such reciprocity. Each state bar association decides with which other states it will allow reciprocity. For example, Pennsylvania allows reciprocity with the District of Columbia. It costs $25 less than 3 times as much to take the bar in Pennsylvania than in D.C. If both bar exams together cost $775, how much less expensive is it to take the bar exam in D.C. than in Pennsylvania?

    A) $200

    B) $275

    C) $375

    D) $575

21. If $\frac{2}{5}(5x) + 2(x-1) = 4(x+1) - 2$, what is the value of x?

    A) $x = -2$

    B) $x = 2$

    C) There is no value of x for which the equation is true.

    D) There are infinitely many values of x for which the equation is true.

22.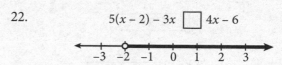

    $5(x-2) - 3x \; \square \; 4x - 6$

    Which symbol correctly completes the inequality whose solution is shown above?

    A) $<$

    B) $>$

    C) $\leq$

    D) $\geq$

23. A landscaper buys a new commercial-grade lawn mower that costs $2,800. Based on past experience, he expects it to last about 8 years, and then he can sell it for scrap metal with a salvage value of about $240. Assuming the value of the lawn mower depreciates at a constant rate, which equation could be used to find its approximate value after x years, given that $x < 8$?

    A) $y = -8x + 2,560$

    B) $y = -240x + 2,800$

    C) $y = -320x + 2,800$

    D) $y = 240x - 2,560$

24.

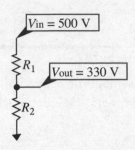

$V_{in} = 500$ V

R_1 $V_{out} = 330$ V

R_2

A voltage divider is a simple circuit that converts a large voltage into a smaller one. The figure above shows a voltage divider that consists of two resistors that together have a total resistance of 294 ohms. To produce the desired voltage of 330 volts, R_2 must be 6 ohms less than twice R_1. Solving which of the following systems of equations gives the individual resistances for R_1 and R_2?

A) $\begin{cases} R_2 = 2R_1 - 6 \\ R_1 + R_2 = 294 \end{cases}$

B) $\begin{cases} R_1 = 2R_2 + 6 \\ R_1 + R_2 = 294 \end{cases}$

C) $\begin{cases} R_2 = 2R_1 - 6 \\ R_1 + R_2 = \dfrac{294}{330} \end{cases}$

D) $\begin{cases} R_1 = 2R_2 + 6 \\ R_1 + R_2 = 330(294) \end{cases}$

25.

$$Hx + 2y = -8$$
$$Kx - 5y = -13$$

If the solution to the system of equations shown above is $(2, -1)$, what is the value of $\dfrac{K}{H}$?

A) -3

B) $-\dfrac{1}{3}$

C) $\dfrac{1}{3}$

D) 3

26. If $0 < \dfrac{d}{2} + 1 \le \dfrac{8}{5}$, which of the following is not a possible value of d?

A) -2

B) $-\dfrac{6}{5}$

C) 0

D) $\dfrac{6}{5}$

27. Damien is throwing darts. He has a total of 6 darts to throw. He gets 5 points for each dart that lands in a blue ring and 10 points for each dart that lands in a red ring. If x of his darts land in a blue ring and the rest land in a red ring, which expression represents his total score?

A) $10x$

B) $10x + 5$

C) $5x + 30$

D) $60 - 5x$

28.

$$\frac{1}{3}x + \frac{1}{2}y = 5$$
$$kx - 4y = 16$$

If the system of linear equations shown above has no solution, and k is a constant, what is the value of k?

A) $-\dfrac{8}{3}$

B) -2

C) $\dfrac{1}{3}$

D) 3

29.

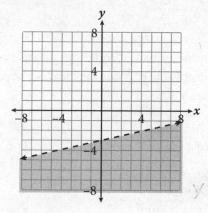

The solution to which inequality is represented in the graph above?

A) $\frac{1}{4}x - y > 3$

B) $\frac{1}{4}x - y < 3$

C) $\frac{1}{4}x + y > -3$

D) $\frac{1}{4}x + y < -3$

30.

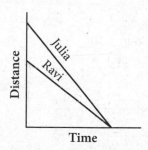

Julia and Ravi are meeting at a museum. The figure above represents the drives from their homes to the museum. Based on the figure, which of the following statements is true?

A) Julia drove to the museum at a faster speed than Ravi.

B) Julia and Ravi drove to the museum at about the same speed.

C) It took Ravi longer to arrive at the museum because his home is farther away.

D) It took Julia longer to arrive at the museum because her home is farther away.

31.
$$\frac{1}{3}x + \frac{2}{3}y = -8$$
$$ax + 6y = 15$$

If the system of linear equations above has no solution, and a is a constant, what is the value of a?

A) $-\frac{1}{3}$

B) $\frac{1}{3}$

C) $\frac{3}{2}$

D) 3

32. Some cars are more fuel-efficient than others. Which graph could represent the fuel efficiency of an efficient car, e, and a less efficient car, i?

A)
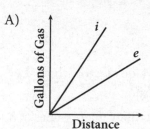

B)
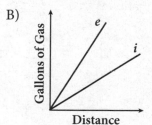

C)
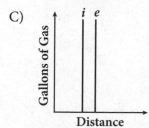

D)
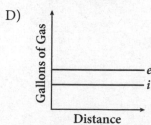

33. A taxi in the city charges $3.00 for the first $\frac{1}{4}$ mile, plus $0.25 for each additional $\frac{1}{8}$ mile. Eric plans to spend no more than $20 on a taxi ride around the city. Which inequality represents the number of miles, m, that Eric could travel without exceeding his limit?

   A) $2.5 + 2m \leq 20$

   B) $3 + 0.25m \leq 20$

   C) $3 + 2m \leq 20$

   D) $12 + 2m \leq 20$

34. $$\frac{1}{4}(10h) - \frac{3}{2}(h+1) = -\frac{2}{3}\left(\frac{9}{2}h\right) + 6$$

   What is the value of h in the equation above?

   A) $\frac{9}{8}$

   B) $\frac{15}{8}$

   C) There is no value of h for which the equation is true.

   D) There are infinitely many values of h for which the equation is true.

35. $$y - 3x = 12$$
   $$9x = 3y + k$$

   In the system of equations given above, for what value of k does the system have at least one solution?

   A) -36

   B) -32

   C) -30

   D) -12

36. In Delray Beach, Florida, you can take a luxury golf cart ride around downtown. The driver charges $4 for the first $\frac{1}{4}$ mile, plus $1.50 for each additional $\frac{1}{2}$ mile. Which inequality represents the number of miles, m, that you could ride and pay no more than $10?

   A) $3.25 + 1.5m \leq 10$

   B) $3.25 + 3m \leq 10$

   C) $4 + 1.5m \leq 10$

   D) $4 + 3m \leq 10$

37.

Legislation Impact on Population

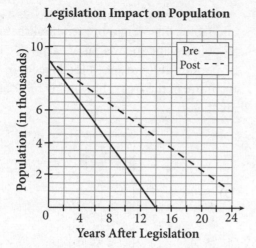

The federal government in the United States has the authority to protect species whose populations have reached dangerously low levels. The graph above represents the expected population of a certain endangered species before and after a proposed law aimed at protecting the animal is passed. Based on the graph, which of the following statements is true?

A) The proposed law is expected to accelerate the decline in population.

B) The proposed law is expected to stop and reverse the decline in population.

C) The proposed law is expected to have no effect on the decline in population.

D) The proposed law is expected to slow, but not stop or reverse, the decline in population.

38. The Bathypelagic Zone (The Midnight Zone) is the layer of the Earth's oceans that is greater than 1,000 meters and less than 4,000 meters below the ocean surface. Which of the following inequalities describes all possible depths, x, in meters, below the ocean surface that are in the Bathypelagic Zone?

A) $|x - 2,500| < 1,500$

B) $|x + 2,500| < 1,500$

C) $|x - 1,500| < 2,500$

D) $|x + 1,500| < 2,500$

39. What was the initial amount of gasoline in a fuel trailer, in gallons, if there are now x gallons, y gallons were pumped into a storage tank, and then 50 gallons were added to the trailer?

A) $x + y + 50$

B) $x + y - 50$

C) $y - x + 50$

D) $x - y - 50$

40. What was the initial amount of fuel in an airplane's tank, in gallons, if there are now x gallons, y gallons were used for the last flight, and 18,000 gallons were added when the plane was refueled?

A) $y + x - 18,000$

B) $y + x + 18,000$

C) $x - y - 18,000$

D) $y - x + 18,000$

41. If $7e = -2f + 11$ and $3f = 4e - 2$, then what is the value of $3e + 5f$?

42. For what value of y does the graph of $\frac{3}{2}y - 2x = 18$ cross the y-axis?

43. A truck is carrying 410 pounds of bookcases and tables. The weight of each bookcase is 25 pounds, and the weight of each table is 37 pounds. If there are 14 total pieces of furniture in the truck, how many bookcases are there?

44. $$0.55x - 1.04 = 0.35x + 0.16$$

    In the equation above, what is the value of x?

45. A company is buying two warehouses near their production plants in two states, New York and Georgia. As is always the case in the real estate market, the geographic location plays a major role in the price of the property. Consequently, the warehouse in New York costs $30,000 less than four times the Georgia warehouse. Together, the two warehouses cost the company $445,000. How many more thousand dollars does the New York property cost than the Georgia property?

$N = 4G - 30$

46. If $Ax + By = C$ is the standard form of the line that passes through the points $(-4, 1)$ and $(3, -2)$, where A is an integer greater than 1, what is the value of B?

47. Mike is considering two different companies to rent a lowboy trailer in order to haul a steam roller across the state. One company charges a flat rental fee of $105 and $0.25 per mile. The other company charges a rental fee of $70 and $0.30 per mile. For what number of miles is the cost of the two rentals equal?

48.
$$x + 3y \leq 18$$
$$2x - 3y \leq 9$$

If (a, b) is a point in the solution region for the system of inequalities shown above and $a = 6$, what is the minimum possible value for b?

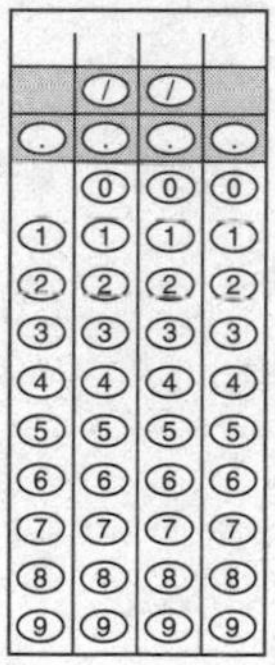

49.
$$\frac{3}{5}x - \frac{1}{2}y = 3$$
$$kx - 10y = 17$$

If the system of linear equations above has no solution, and k is a constant, what is the value of k?

50. If the slope of a line is $-\frac{7}{4}$ and a point on the line is $(4, 7)$, what is the y-intercept of the line?

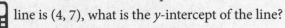

ANSWERS AND EXPLANATIONS

CHAPTER 11

1. D   Difficulty: Medium

Category: Systems of Equations

Getting to the Answer: A system of two equations has infinitely many solutions when the two equations actually represent the same line. In other words, their slopes are equal and their y-intercepts are equal. This means writing the equations in slope-intercept form should lead you to the correct answer.

First Equation
$$rx + sy = 3$$
$$sy = -rx + 3$$
$$y = \boxed{-\frac{r}{s}}x + \frac{3}{s}$$

Second Equation
$$4x + 6y = 10$$
$$6y = -4x + 10$$
$$y = \boxed{-\frac{2}{3}}x + \frac{5}{3}$$

The slope of the first equation is $-\frac{r}{s}$, and the slope of the second equation is $-\frac{2}{3}$. For there to be infinitely many solutions to the system, the slopes must be the same, therefore $-\frac{r}{s} = -\frac{2}{3}$. Notice that the question asks for the value of $\frac{r}{s}$, so all you need to do now is multiply both sides by -1 to get $\frac{r}{s} = \frac{2}{3}$. The answer is choice (D).

2. B   Difficulty: Medium

Category: Linear Equations

Getting to the Answer: There is not a lot of information to go on here, so start by determining the relationship between the number given in the question, 54,000, and the number in the equation, 2,250.

Because $54{,}000 \div 2{,}250 = 24$ and there are 24 hours in a day, 2,250 is the number of pages the press can print in 1 hour. If the press can print 2,250 in 1 hour, then it can print 2,250 times x in x hours. This means the function $f(x) = 2{,}250x$ represents the number of pages the press can print in x hours, which means choice (B) is correct.

3. A   Difficulty: Medium

Category: Linear Equations

Getting to the Answer: If 6 green slips are worth m dollars, then each green slip is worth $\frac{m}{6}$ dollars. If a red slip is worth 3 dollars more than a green slip, then each red slip is worth $\frac{m}{6} + 3$ dollars. If each blue slip is worth 3 dollars more than a red slip, then each blue slip is worth $\frac{m}{6} + 6$ dollars. Therefore, 12 blue slips and 6 red slips are worth $12\left(\frac{m}{6} + 6\right) + 6\left(\frac{m}{6} + 3\right)$ dollars, which simplifies to $2m + 72 + m + 18 = 3m + 90$. This matches (A).

4. B   Difficulty: Medium

Category: Linear Equations

Getting to the Answer: To find the average rate of change over the 5-year period, find the slope between the starting point (0, 1,200) and the ending point (5,100).

$$m = \frac{y_2 - y_1}{x_2 - x_1} = \frac{100 - 1{,}200}{5 - 0} = \frac{-1{,}100}{5} = -220$$

Choice (B) is correct. (The average rate of change is negative because the laptop decreases in value over time.)

Note: Because the question involves *straight-line* depreciation, you could have used any two points on the graph to find the slope. As a general rule, however, you should use the endpoints of the given time interval.

5. A Difficulty: Medium

Category: Linear Equations

Getting to the Answer: The line is decreasing, so the slope (m) is negative. The line crosses the y-axis below 0, so the y-intercept (b) is also negative. Put each answer choice in slope-intercept form, one at a time, and examine the signs of m and b. Begin with (A):

$$-6x - 4y = 5$$
$$-4y = 6x + 5$$
$$y = \frac{6x}{-4} + \frac{5}{-4}$$
$$y = -\frac{3}{2}x - \frac{5}{4}$$

You don't need to check any of the other equations. Choice (A) has a negative slope and a negative y-intercept, so it is the correct equation.

6. D Difficulty: Medium

Category: Linear Equations

Getting to the Answer: Let x be the number of surfboards Jon sells in a month. Write a linear equation that represents the scenario and then solve for x. Sales must equal expenses for the store to break even. Jon's sales are equal to the selling price ($120) times the number of surfboards he sells (x), so write $120x$ on one side of the equal sign. His monthly expenses are his fixed expenses ($3,600) plus the amount he paid for each surfboard ($80) times the number of surfboards (x), so write $3,600 + 80x$ on the other side of the equal sign. Then, solve for x.

$$120x = 3,600 + 80x$$
$$40x = 3,600$$
$$x = 90$$

Therefore, choice (D) is correct.

7. C Difficulty: Medium

Category: Inequalities

Getting to the Answer: Based on the data in the table, a worker would earn $9.10 − $7.25 = $1.85 more for one hour of work in Oregon than in Idaho. If he worked 35 hours per week, he would earn 35(1.85) = $64.75 more. If he worked 40 hours per week, he would earn 40(1.85) = $74 more. So, the worker would earn somewhere between $64.75 and $74 more per week, which can be expressed as the compound inequality $64.75 \le x \le 74$. This matches choice (C).

8. B Difficulty: Medium

Category: Linear Equations

Getting to the Answer: Choose the best strategy to answer the question. You could start by cross-multiplying to get rid of the denominators, but simplifying the numerators first will make the calculations easier.

$$\frac{4(d+3)-9}{8} = \frac{10-(2-d)}{6}$$
$$\frac{4d+12-9}{8} = \frac{10-2+d}{6}$$
$$\frac{4d+3}{8} = \frac{8+d}{6}$$
$$6(4d+3) = 8(8+d)$$
$$24d+18 = 64+8d$$
$$16d = 46$$
$$d = \frac{46}{16} = \frac{23}{8}$$

Choice (B) is correct.

9. B Difficulty: Medium

Category: Linear Equations

Getting to the Answer: When a linear equation is written in the form $y = mx + b$, the variable m represents the slope of the line and b represents the y-intercept of the line. Quickly scan the answer choices—they include inequalities, so you'll need to translate them into something that makes more sense to you. Use the fact that "< 0" means *negative* and "> 0" means *positive*. Now, look at the graph—the line is decreasing (going down from left to right), so the slope is negative ($m < 0$). This means you can eliminate C and D. Finally, look at the y-intercept—it is above the x-axis and is therefore positive ($b > 0$), which means choice (B) is correct.

10. A   Difficulty: Medium

Category: Linear Equations

Getting to the Answer: The rate of change (or slope) of a linear relationship is constant, so find the rate and apply it to the missing value. Choose any two points (preferably ones with the nicest numbers) from the table and substitute them into the slope formula. Using the points (0, 8) and (3, 7), the slope is $\frac{7-8}{3-0}=\frac{-1}{3}$. This means that for every 3 units the x-value increases, the y-value decreases by 1, so to get from $x = 3$ to $x = 9$, decrease the y-value by 1, two times: $7 - 1 - 1 = 5$, making choice (A) correct.

11. A   Difficulty: Medium

Category: Linear Equations

Getting to the Answer: Regardless of the scenario presented or the missing axis labels on the graph, the slope of the line tells you the answer. The line is decreasing from left to right, so it has a negative slope. This means there is an inverse relationship between the amount of algae and the number of fish. In other words, as one increases, the other must decrease, so choice (A) must be correct.

12. D   Difficulty: Medium

Category: Inequalities

Getting to the Answer: You could graph the cost function ($y = 17p + 1,890$) and the revenue function ($y = 35x$) and try to determine where the revenue function is greater (higher on the graph). However, the numbers are quite large and this may prove to be very time-consuming. Instead, create and solve an inequality comparing revenue and cost. If the revenue from a single pair of shoes is $35, then the total revenue from p pairs is $35p$. If revenue must be greater than cost, then the inequality should be $35p > 17p + 1,890$. Now, solve for p using inverse operations:

$$35p > 17p + 1,890$$
$$18p > 1,890$$
$$p > 105$$

This matches (D).

13. C   Difficulty: Hard

Category: Systems of Linear Equations

Getting to the Answer: Graphically, a system of linear equations that has no solution indicates two parallel lines or, in other words, two lines that have the same slope. So, write each of the equations in slope-intercept form ($y = mx + b$) and set their slopes (m) equal to each other to solve for k. Before finding the slopes, multiply the top equation by 4 to make it easier to manipulate.

$$4\left(\frac{3}{4}x - \frac{1}{2}y = 12\right) \rightarrow 3x - 2y = 48 \rightarrow y = \frac{3}{2}x - 24$$

$$kx - 2y = 22 \rightarrow -2y = -kx + 22 \rightarrow y = \frac{k}{2}x - 11$$

The slope of the first line is $\frac{3}{2}$, and the slope of the second line is $\frac{k}{2}$. Set them equal and solve for k.

$$\frac{3}{2} = \frac{k}{2}$$
$$2(3) = 2(k)$$
$$6 = 2k$$
$$3 = k$$

Choice (C) is correct.

14. D   Difficulty: Medium

Category: Linear Equations

Getting to the Answer: You could start by cross-multiplying, but there are so many terms and parentheses that you are likely to forget to distribute a factor. Instead, simplify the numerators first. Don't forget to distribute the negative to both terms inside the parentheses on the right-hand side of the equation. Don't try to do steps in your head—writing each step down will keep you organized.

$$\frac{3(n-2)+5}{4} = \frac{11-(7-n)}{6}$$
$$\frac{3n-6+5}{4} = \frac{11-7+n}{6}$$
$$\frac{3n-1}{4} = \frac{4+n}{6}$$
$$6(3n-1) = 4(4+n)$$
$$18n-6 = 16+4n$$
$$14n = 22$$
$$n = \frac{22}{14} = \frac{11}{7}$$

Choice (D) is correct.

15. B   Difficulty: Medium

Category: Systems of Linear Equations

Getting to the Answer: Because none of the variable terms has a coefficient of 1, solve the system of equations using elimination (combining the equations). Before you choose an answer, check that you answered the right question (the sum of x and y). Multiply the top equation by 2 to eliminate the terms that have y's in them.

$$2\big[-2x+5y=1\big] \to -4x+10y=2$$
$$7x-10y=-11 \to \underline{7x-10y=-11}$$
$$3x=-9$$
$$x=-3$$

Now, substitute the result into either of the original equations and simplify to find y:

$$-2x+5y=1$$
$$-2(-3)+5y=1$$
$$6+5y=1$$
$$5y=-5$$
$$y=-1$$

The question asks for the *sum*, so add x and y to get $-3+(-1)=-4$, which is choice (B).

16. A   Difficulty: Medium

Category: Linear Equations

Getting to the Answer: In this scenario, the total cost is the dependent variable and is calculated by multiplying the per person rate by the number of people attending and then adding the flat serving fee. So the total cost is represented by y. Because the flat serving fee and the per person rate are likely to be fixed amounts (determined by the catering company), they should be represented by numbers in the equations, 300 and 11, respectively. The total cost depends on the number of people attending, so the number of people is the independent variable and is most likely represented by x. Therefore, choice (A) is correct.

17. B   Difficulty: Medium

Category: Inequalities

Getting to the Answer: The question states that t represents the number of round trips. The cost of one round trip without the discount card is $35 per trip, or $35t$. If a commuter purchases the discount card, round trips would equal the cost of the card plus $12.50 per trip, or $900 + 12.5t$. Combine these into an inequality, remembering which way the inequality symbol should be oriented. You want the cost with the discount card to be less than (<) the cost without the card, so the inequality should be $900 + 12.5t < 35t$. Now, solve for t:

$$900 + 12.5t < 35t$$
$$900 < 22.5t$$
$$40 < t$$

Turn the inequality around to find that $t > 40$, which means a commuter must make more than 40 trips for the discount card to be a better deal, which is choice (B).

18. C   Difficulty: Medium

Category: Inequalities

Getting to the Answer: You don't need to use algebra to answer this question, and you also don't need to graph each system. Instead, think about how the graphs would look. The only time a system of linear inequalities has no solution is when it consists of two parallel lines shaded in opposite directions. All the inequalities are written in slope-intercept form, so look for parallel lines (two lines that have the same slope but different y-intercepts). The slopes in A are different ($m = 1$ and $m = 2$), so eliminate this choice. The same is true for B ($m = 1$ and $m = -1$) and D ($m = -1$ and $m = 1$). This means choice (C) must be correct ($m = 1$ and $m = 1$, $b = 1$ and $b = -1$). The graph of the system is shown here:

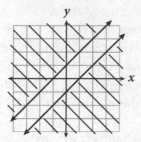

Because the shading never overlaps, the system has no solution.

19.   A   Difficulty: Medium

Category: Linear Equations

Getting to the Answer: A line with an undefined slope is a vertical line (a horizontal line has a slope of 0 because it is flat), so look for an equation that represents a vertical line. Start with the first equation. If $x = 3$ is the only thing you have to go on, choose a few points with an x-coordinate of 3, such as (3, 0), (3, 1), and (3, 2). Plot these points and draw a line through them to see that the graph is a vertical line and therefore has an undefined slope. There is no need to check the other equations. Choice (A) is correct.

20.   C   Difficulty: Medium

Category: Systems of Linear Equations

Getting to the Answer: Use the Kaplan Method for Translating English into Math. Write a system of equations with $p =$ the cost, in dollars, of the Pennsylvania bar exam and $d =$ the cost, in dollars, of the D.C. bar exam. The Pennsylvania bar exam (p) costs $25 less ($-25$) than 3 times as much ($3d$) as the D.C. bar exam, or $p = 3d - 25$. Together, both bar exams cost $775, so $d + p = 775$. The system is:

$$\begin{cases} p = 3d - 25 \\ d + p = 775 \end{cases}$$

The top equation is already solved for p, so substitute $3d - 25$ into the second equation for p, and solve for d:

$$d + (3d - 25) = 775$$
$$4d = 800$$
$$d = 200$$

Be careful—that's not the answer. The D.C. bar exam costs $200, which means the Pennsylvania bar exam costs $775 - $200 = $575. This means the D.C. bar exam is $575 - $200 = $375 less expensive than the Pennsylvania bar exam. Choice (C) is correct.

21.   C   Difficulty: Medium

Category: Linear Equations

Getting to the Answer: Use the distributive property to simplify each of the terms that contains parentheses. Then use inverse operations to solve for x.

$$\frac{2}{5}(5x) + 2(x - 1) = 4(x + 1) - 2$$
$$2x + 2x - 2 = 4x + 4 - 2$$
$$4x - 2 = 4x + 2$$
$$-2 \neq 2$$

All of the variable terms cancel out, and the resulting numerical statement is false (because negative 2 does not equal positive 2), so there is no solution to the equation. Put another way, there is no value of x for which the equation is true, choice (C).

22.   A   Difficulty: Medium

Category: Inequalities

Getting to the Answer: Apply logic to this question first, and then algebra. The dot at the beginning of the shaded portion is an open dot, so -2 is not included in the solution set of the inequality. This means you can eliminate choices C and D because those symbols *would* include the endpoint. Don't immediately choose choice B just because the arrow is pointing to the right, which typically indicates *greater than*. When dealing with an inequality, if you multiply or divide by a negative number, you must flip the symbol, so the answer is not necessarily what you might think. Because you were able to eliminate two of the choices, the quickest approach is to pick one of the remaining symbols, plug it in, and see if it works. If it does, choose that answer. If it doesn't, then it must be the other symbol. Try choice (A):

$$5(x-2)-3x < 4x-6$$
$$5x-10-3x < 4x-6$$
$$2x-10 < 4x-6$$
$$-2x < 4$$
$$x > -2$$

The resulting inequality, $x > -2$, means all the values on the number line greater than (or to the right of) -2, so the initial inequality symbol must have been $<$. Choice (A) is correct.

23. C   Difficulty: Medium

Category: Linear Equations

Getting to the Answer: Write your own equation using the initial cost and the rate of change in the value of the lawn mower. Remember—when something changes at a constant rate, it can be represented by a linear equation. When a linear equation in the form $y = mx + b$ is used to model a real-world scenario, m represents the constant rate of change, and b represents the starting amount. Here, the starting amount is easy—it's the purchase price, $2,800. To find the rate of change, think of the initial cost as the value at 0 years, or the point (0, 2,800), and the salvage amount as the value at 8 years, or the point (8, 240). Substitute these points into the slope formula:

$$m = \frac{y_2 - y_1}{x_2 - x_1} = \frac{240 - 2,800}{8 - 0} = \frac{-2,560}{8} = -320$$

The correct equation is $y = -320x + 2,800$. This matches choice (C).

24. A   Difficulty: Medium

Category: Systems of Linear Equations

Getting to the Answer: Take a quick peek at the answers just to see what variables are being used,

but don't study the equations. Instead, write your own system using the same variables as given in the answer choices. One of the equations in the system needs to represent the sum of the two resistors $(R_1 + R_2)$, which is equal to 294. This means you can eliminate C and D. The second equation needs to satisfy the condition that R_2 is 6 less than twice R_1, or $R_2 = 2R_1 - 6$. This means choice (A) is correct.

25. D   Difficulty: Medium

Category: Systems of Linear Equations

Getting to the Answer: Typically, solving a system of equations means finding the values of x and y that satisfy both equations simultaneously. Because the solution to the system satisfies both equations, you can substitute 2 and -1 for x and y respectively, and then solve for H and K. Before selecting your answer, check that you found what the question was asking for (the value of $\frac{K}{H}$).

$$Hx + 2y = -8$$
$$H(2) + 2(-1) = -8$$
$$2H - 2 = -8$$
$$2H = -6$$
$$H = -3$$

$$Kx - 5y = -13$$
$$K(2) - 5(-1) = -13$$
$$2K + 5 = -13$$
$$2K = -18$$
$$K = -9$$

So, $\frac{K}{H} = \frac{-9}{-3} = 3$, choice (D).

26. A   Difficulty: Medium

Category: Inequalities

Getting to the Answer: You don't need to separate this compound inequality into pieces. Just remember, whatever you do to one piece, you must do to all three pieces. The fractions in this question make it look more complicated than it really is, so start by clearing them. To do this, multiply everything by the least common denominator, 10.

$$0 < \frac{d}{2} + 1 \leq \frac{8}{5}$$

$$10(0) < 10\left(\frac{d}{2}+1\right) \leq \left(\frac{8}{5}\right)10$$

$$0 < 5d + 10 \leq 16$$

$$-10 < 5d \leq 6$$

$$-2 < d \leq \frac{6}{5}$$

Now, read the inequality symbols carefully. The value of d is between -2 and $\frac{6}{5}$, not including -2 because of the $<$ symbol, so choice (A) is the correct answer. Don't let choice C fool you—you can't have a 0 *denominator* in a rational expression, but in this expression, the variable is in the numerator, so it *can* equal 0.

27. D   Difficulty: Medium

Category: Linear Equations

Getting to the Answer: Write the expression in words first: points per blue ring (5) times number of darts in blue ring (x), plus points per red ring (10) times number of darts in red ring ($6 - x$). Now, translate the words into numbers, variables, and operations: $5x + 10(6 - x)$. This is not one of the answer choices, so simplify the expression by distributing the 10 and then combining like terms: $5x + 10(6 - x) = 5x + 60 - 10x = 60 - 5x$. This matches choice (D).

28. A   Difficulty: Medium

Category: Systems of Linear Equations

Getting to the Answer: Graphically, a system of linear equations that has no solution indicates two parallel lines, or in other words, two lines that have the same slope. So, write each of the equations in slope-intercept form ($y = mx + b$) and set their slopes (m) equal to each other to solve for k. Before finding the slopes, multiply the top equation by 6 to make it easier to manipulate.

$$6\left(\frac{1}{3}x + \frac{1}{2}y = 5\right) \rightarrow 2x + 3y = 30 \rightarrow y = -\frac{2}{3}x + 10$$

$$kx - 4y = 16 \rightarrow -4y = -kx + 16 \rightarrow y = \frac{k}{4}x - 4$$

The slope of the first line is $-\frac{2}{3}$, and the slope of the second line is $\frac{k}{4}$. Set them equal and solve for k:

$$-\frac{2}{3} = \frac{k}{4}$$

$$-8 = 3k$$

$$-\frac{8}{3} = k$$

Choice (A) is correct.

29. A   Difficulty: Medium

Category: Inequalities

Getting to the Answer: Don't answer this question too quickly. The shading is below the line, but that does not necessarily mean that the symbol in the equation will be the less than symbol ($<$). Start by writing the equation of the dashed line shown in the graph in slope-intercept form. Then use the shading to determine the correct inequality symbol. The slope of the line shown in the graph is $\frac{1}{4}$ and the y-intercept is -3, so the equation of the dashed line is $y = \frac{1}{4}x - 3$. The graph is shaded below the boundary line, so use the $<$ symbol. When written in slope-intercept form, the inequality is $y < \frac{1}{4}x - 3$. The inequalities in the answer choices are given in standard form ($Ax + By = C$), so rewrite your answer in this form. Don't forget to reverse the inequality symbol if you multiply or divide by a negative number.

$$y < \frac{1}{4}x - 3$$

$$-\frac{1}{4}x + y < -3$$

$$\frac{1}{4}x - y > 3$$

Choice (A) is correct.

30. B   Difficulty: Medium

Category: Inequalities

Getting to the Answer: The question states that t represents the number of round trips. The cost of one round trip without the discount card is $35 per trip, or $35t$. If a commuter purchases the discount card, round trips would equal the cost of the card plus $12.50 per trip, or $900 + 12.5t$. Combine these into an inequality, remembering which way the inequality symbol should be oriented. You want the cost with the discount card to be less than ($<$) the cost without the card, so the inequality should be $900 + 12.5t < 35t$. Now, solve for t:

$$900 + 12.5t < 35t$$
$$900 < 22.5t$$
$$40 < t$$

Turn the inequality around to find that $t > 40$, which means a commuter must make more than 40 trips for the discount card to be a better deal, which is choice (B).

31. D   Difficulty: Hard

Category: Systems of Linear Equations

Getting to the Answer: Graphically, a system of linear equations that has no solution indicates two parallel lines, or in other words, two lines that have the same slope. So, write each of the equations in slope-intercept form ($y = mx + b$) and set their slopes (m) equal to each other to solve for a. Before finding the slopes, multiply the top equation by 3 to make it easier to manipulate.

$$3\left(\frac{1}{3}x + \frac{2}{3}y = -8\right) \rightarrow$$
$$x + 2y = -24 \rightarrow y = -\frac{1}{2}x - 12$$
$$ax + 6y = 15 \rightarrow 6y = -ax + 15 \rightarrow y = -\frac{a}{6}x + \frac{15}{6}$$

The slope of the first line is $-\frac{1}{2}$ and the slope of the second line is $-\frac{a}{6}$.

$$-\frac{1}{2} = -\frac{a}{6}$$
$$-6(1) = -a(2)$$
$$-6 = -2a$$
$$3 = a$$

Choice (D) is correct.

32. A   Difficulty: Hard

Category: Linear Equations

Getting to the Answer: Try to describe the scenario in words first: If a car is more efficient, it can travel a greater distance on less gas. A less efficient car will use more gas to travel the same distance. In other words, the change in gas compared to the change in distance is greater for a less efficient car. Graphically, this means the slope is steeper for the less efficient car.

Look for the graph where the line representing the less efficient car (i) has a steeper slope (more gas per distance) than the line representing the efficient car (e), which is the graph in (A). Note that choices C and D don't represent gas mileage at all—in choice C, the cars aren't traveling anywhere because the distance isn't changing; in D, no gas is being used even though the distance is changing. Choice (A) is correct.

33. A   Difficulty: Hard

Category: Inequalities

Getting to the Answer: Pay careful attention to units, particularly when a question involves rates. The taxi charges $3.00 for the first $\frac{1}{4}$ mile, which is a flat fee, so write 3. The additional charge is $0.25 per $\frac{1}{8}$ mile, or 0.25 times 8 = $2.00 per mile. The number of miles after the first $\frac{1}{4}$ mile is $m - \frac{1}{4}$, so the cost of the trip, not including the first $\frac{1}{4}$ mile, is $2\left(m - \frac{1}{4}\right)$. This means the cost of the whole trip is $3 + 2\left(m - \frac{1}{4}\right)$. The clue "no more than $20" means that much or less, so use the symbol $\leq$. The inequality is $3 + 2\left(m - \frac{1}{4}\right) \leq 20$, which simplifies to $2.5 + 2m \leq 20$, choice (A).

34. B   Difficulty: Hard

Category: Linear Equations

Getting to the Answer: Do not automatically assume that an equation has *no solution* or *infinite solutions* just because those choices are given as possible answers. This question can be simplified quite a bit by clearing the fractions first. To do this, multiply both sides of the equation by the least common denominator, 12. Then solve for h using inverse operations.

$$\frac{1}{4}(10h) - \frac{3}{2}(h+1) = -\frac{2}{3}\left(\frac{9}{2}h\right) + 6$$

$$12\left[\frac{1}{4}(10h)\right] - 12\left[\frac{3}{2}(h+1)\right] = 12\left[-\frac{2}{3}\left(\frac{9}{2}h\right)\right] + 12[6]$$

$$3(10h) - 18(h+1) = -4(9h) + 72$$

$$30h - 18h - 18 = -36h + 72$$

$$12h - 18 = -36h + 72$$

$$48h = 90$$

$$h = \frac{90}{48} = \frac{15}{8}$$

Choice (B) is correct.

35. A   Difficulty: Hard

Category: Systems of Equations

Getting to the Answer: This is a system of two *linear* equations, so its solution is the intersection of those two lines. If you convert the equations to slope-intercept form, you get $y = 3x + 12$ and $y = 3x - \frac{k}{3}$, which reveals that these two lines have the same slope. This means that they are either parallel lines or the same line. Parallel lines never intersect, so the system will have a solution only if the two lines are the same line. This means both the slope and the y-intercept must be the same. It follows that $-\frac{k}{3} = 12$. Multiply both sides of this equation by -3 to find that $k = -36$, which is choice (A).

36. B   Difficulty: Hard

Category: Inequalities

Getting to the Answer: Before you write the inequality, you need to find the per-mile rate for the remaining miles. The driver charges $4.00 for the first $\frac{1}{4}$ mile, which is a flat fee, so write 4. The additional charge is $1.50 per $\frac{1}{2}$ mile, or 1.50 times $2 = $3.00 per mile. The number of miles after the first $\frac{1}{4}$ mile is $m - \frac{1}{4}$, so the cost of the trip, not including

the first $\frac{1}{4}$ mile, is $3\left(m - \frac{1}{4}\right)$. This means the cost of the whole trip is $4 + 3\left(m - \frac{1}{4}\right)$. The clue "no more than $10" means that much or less, so use the symbol $\leq$. The inequality is $4 + 3\left(m - \frac{1}{4}\right) \leq 10$, which simplifies to $3.25 + 3m \leq 10$. This matches choice (B).

37. D   Difficulty: Hard

Category: Linear Equations

Getting to the Answer: Compare the differences in the two lines to the statements in the answer choices. The y-intercept of both lines is the same. The key difference between the lines is their slopes. The solid line (pre-law) has a steeper slope, while the dashed line has a more gradual slope, so you can eliminate choice C. The slope of each line is negative (falling from left to right), so even after the proposed law is implemented, the population is still expected to decline, which means you can eliminate B. Because the dashed line's slope is more gradual, the decline in the population is slowing down (decelerating, not accelerating), so you can eliminate choice A. This means choice (D) is correct.

38. A   Difficulty: Hard

Category: Inequalities

Getting to the Answer: First, write an inequality that represents the scenario: "greater than 1,000 meters and less than 4,000 meters" is the same as "between 1,000 and 4,000." Thus, the possible depths below the ocean surface that are in the Bathypelagic Zone are given by the inequality $1,000 < x < 4,000$. Now, you need to find an absolute value inequality that is equivalent to this inequality.

The inequality $1,000 < x < 4,000$ describes the interval (1,000, 4,000). To describe an interval using an absolute value inequality, think in terms of how far the endpoints of the interval are from the midpoint of the interval. The midpoint of (1,000, 4,000) is $\frac{1,000 + 4,000}{2} = 2,500$. The interval (1,000, 4,000) consists of all points that are within 1,500 of this midpoint (because $2,500 - 1,000$ is 1,500 and $4,000 - 2,500$ is 1,500). That is, $(1,000, 4,000)$ consists of all values of x whose distances from 2,500 on a number line are less than 1,500. The distance between x and 2,500 on the number line is given by $|x - 2,500|$. Therefore, the possible values of x can be described by $|x - 2,500| < 1,500$, which is choice (A).

39. B   Difficulty: Hard

Category: Linear Equations

Getting to the Answer: Call the initial amount A. After you've written your equation, solve for A.

Amount now $(x) =$ Initial amount (A) minus y, plus 50

$$x = A - y + 50$$
$$x + y - 50 = A$$

The initial amount was $x + y - 50$ gallons, choice (B). Note that you could also use Picking Numbers to answer this question.

40. A   Difficulty: Hard

Category: Linear Equations

Getting to the Answer: Write an equation in words first, and then translate from English into math. Then, rearrange your equation to find what you're interested in, which is the initial amount. Call the initial amount of fuel A. After you've written your equation, solve for A:

Amount now (x) equals initial amount (A) minus fuel used on last flight (y) plus amount added (18,000).

$$x = A - y + 18,000$$
$$x + y - 18,000 = A$$

This is the same as $y + x - 18,000$. Thus, choice (A) is correct.

You could also Pick Numbers to answer this question.

41. 9   Difficulty: Medium

Category: Systems of Equations

Getting to the Answer: When you're asked for an unusual quantity that results from solving a system

of equations, rather than just the value of one or both of the variables, there will often be a shortcut you can use. For example, you may be able to simply add or subtract the two equations. To keep things organized, write the equations in the same form (put the variables in the same order). A quick examination of the coefficients reveals that adding the two equations will yield exactly what you're asked to find:

$$\begin{aligned} 7e = -2f + 11 &\rightarrow 7e + 2f = 11 \\ 3f = 4e - 2 &\rightarrow \underline{-4e + 3f = -2} \\ 3e + 5f &= 9 \end{aligned}$$

The sum of the two equations tells you that $3e + 5f$ is 9.

42. 12   Difficulty: Medium

Category: Linear Equations

Getting to the Answer: The place where the line crosses the y-axis is the y-intercept, or b when the equation is written in slope-intercept form $(y = mx + b)$, so rewrite the equation in this form. To make the numbers easier to work with, clear the fraction by multiplying each term by 2.

$$\frac{3}{2}y - 2x = 18$$
$$2 \times \left[\frac{3}{2}y - 2x\right] = 2 \times 18$$
$$3y - 4x = 36$$
$$3y = 4x + 36$$
$$y = \frac{4}{3}x + 12$$

The y-intercept is 12.

Because the y-intercept of a graph is always of the form $(0, y)$, you could also substitute 0 for x in the original equation and solve for y.

43. 9   Difficulty: Medium

Category: Systems of Equations

Getting to the Answer: Recognizing that a question like this requires a system of equations is the key to getting started. Assemble two equations using variables that make sense to help you stay organized. The two "pieces" of information given in this question are the *number* of each type of furniture and the *weight* of those items. Let b and t represent the number of bookcases and tables in the truck. The total number of items in the truck is 14, so one equation is $b + t = 14$. Bookcases weigh 25 pounds each, the tables weigh 37 pounds each, and the total weight is 410 pounds, so the second equation is $25b + 37t = 410$. Write the system vertically so you can easily combine the two equations:

$$b + t = 14$$
$$25b + 37t = 410$$

The question only asks for the number of bookcases in the truck, so solve the system by combining the equations in such a way that the t terms cancel (because you want to keep the b). There is a $37t$ in the second equation, so multiply the first equation by -37 (to create a $-37t$ term that will cancel), and then add the equations:

$$-37(b + t = 14) \rightarrow \quad -37b - 37t = -518$$
$$25b + 37t = 410 \rightarrow \quad \underline{25b + 37t = 410}$$
$$-12b = -108$$
$$\frac{-12b}{-12} = \frac{-108}{-12}$$
$$b = 9$$

There are 9 bookcases in the truck.

44. 6   Difficulty: Medium

Category: Linear Equations

Getting to the Answer: Decimals can be messy, especially without a calculator, so clear the decimals by multiplying each term by 100—this moves the decimal two places to the left, resulting in an equation with only integer values.

$$0.55x - 1.04 = 0.35x + 0.16$$
$$100(0.55x - 1.04) = 100(0.35x + 0.16)$$
$$55x - 104 = 35x + 16$$
$$20x = 120$$
$$x = 6$$

45. 255   Difficulty: Medium

Category: Systems of Linear Equations

Getting to the Answer: Translate English into math to write the two equations: The New York property costs 30 thousand dollars less than four times the cost of the Georgia property, so $N = 4G - 30$; together, the two properties cost 445 thousand dollars, so $N + G = 445$.

The system of equations is:

$$\begin{cases} N = 4G - 30 \\ N + G = 445 \end{cases}$$

The top equation is already solved for N, so substitute $4G - 30$ into the second equation for N and solve for G:

$$4G - 30 + G = 445$$
$$5G - 30 = 445$$
$$5G = 475$$
$$G = 95$$

The Georgia property costs 95 thousand dollars, so the New York property costs $4(95) - 30 = 350$ thousand dollars. This means the New York property costs $350 - 95 = 255$ thousand more dollars than the Georgia property.

46. 7   Difficulty: Hard

Category: Linear Equations

Getting to the Answer: To write the equation of a line, you need two things: the slope and the y-intercept. Start by finding these, substituting them into slope-intercept form of a line ($y = mx + b$), and then manipulate the equation so that it is written in standard form. Use the given points, $(-4, 1)$ and $(3, -2)$, and the slope formula to find m:

$$m = \frac{y_2 - y_1}{x_2 - x_1} = \frac{-2 - 1}{3 - (-4)} = -\frac{3}{7}$$

Next, find the y-intercept, b, using the slope and one of the points:

$$y = -\frac{3}{7}x + b$$

$$1 = -\frac{3}{7}(-4) + b$$

$$1 = \frac{12}{7} + b$$

$$-\frac{5}{7} = b$$

Write the equation in slope-intercept form:

$$y = -\frac{3}{7}x - \frac{5}{7}.$$

Now, rewrite the equation in the form $Ax + By = C$, making sure that A is a positive integer (a whole number greater than 0):

$$y = -\frac{3}{7}x - \frac{5}{7}$$

$$\frac{3}{7}x + y = -\frac{5}{7}$$

$$7\left(\frac{3}{7}x + y = -\frac{5}{7}\right)7$$

$$3x + 7y = -5$$

The question asks for the value of B (the coefficient of y), so the correct answer is 7.

47. 700   Difficulty: Medium

Category: Systems of Equations

Getting to the Answer: Let $m =$ the number of miles. The total cost for the first company can be expressed as $\$105 + 0.25m$, and the total cost for the second company can be expressed as $\$70 + 0.30m$. Set these two expressions equal and solve for m:

$$105 + 0.25m = 70 + 0.30m$$

$$105 = 70 + 0.05m$$

$$35 = 0.05m$$

$$700 = m$$

At 700 miles, the cost of the two rentals are equal.

48. 1   Difficulty: Medium

Category: Inequalities

Getting to the Answer: This question is extremely difficult to answer unless you draw a sketch. It doesn't have to be perfect—you just need to get an idea of where the solution region is. Don't forget to flip the inequality symbol when you graph the second equation.

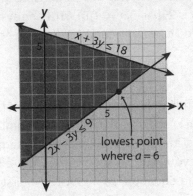

If (a, b) is a solution to the system, then a is the x-coordinate of any point in the darkest shaded region and b is the corresponding y-coordinate. When $a = 6$, the minimum possible value for b lies on the lower boundary line, $2x - 3y \leq 9$. It looks like the y-coordinate is 1, but to be sure, substitute $x = 6$ into the equation and solve for y. You can use $=$ in the equation, instead of the inequality symbol, because you are finding a point on the boundary line.

$$2x - 3y = 9$$

$$2(6) - 3y = 9$$

$$12 - 3y = 9$$

$$-3y = -3$$

$$y = 1$$

49. 12 **Difficulty:** Hard

Category: Systems of Equations

Getting to the Answer: Think about this question graphically: A system of equations has no solution if the graphs don't intersect. Here, both equations are linear, so the graphs must be parallel lines if they don't intersect. Algebraically, parallel lines have the same slope, so write each equation in slope-intercept form ($y = mx + b$) and set their slopes (m) equal to each other to solve for k. To make the numbers in the top equation easier to work with, multiply both sides by the least common denominator, 10:

Top equation:

$$10\left(\frac{3}{5}x - \frac{1}{2}y\right) = 10(3)$$
$$6x - 5y = 30$$
$$-5y = -6x + 30$$
$$y = \boxed{\frac{6}{5}}x - 6$$

Bottom equation:

$$kx - 10y = 17$$
$$-10y = -kx + 17$$
$$y = \boxed{\frac{k}{10}}x - \frac{17}{10}$$

Now, set the slopes equal and cross-multiply to solve for k:

$$\frac{6}{5} = \frac{k}{10}$$
$$60 = 5k$$
$$k = 12$$

50. 14 **Difficulty:** Hard

Category: Linear Equations

Getting to the Answer: When you know the slope and one point on a line, you can use $y = mx + b$ to write the equation. The slope is given as $-\frac{7}{4}$, so substitute this for m. The point is given as (4, 7), so $x = 4$ and $y = 7$. Now, find b:

$$y = mx + b$$
$$7 = -\frac{7}{4}(4) + b$$
$$7 = -7 + b$$
$$14 = b$$

The y-intercept of the line is 14.

You could also very carefully graph the line using the given point and the slope. Start at (4, 7) and move toward the y-axis by rising 7 and running *to the left* 4 (because the slope is negative). You should land at the point (0, 14).

CHAPTER TWELVE

Problem Solving and Data Analysis

PRACTICE QUESTIONS

The following test-like questions provide an opportunity to practice Problem Solving and Data Analysis questions. The calculator icon means you are permitted to use a calculator to solve a question. It does not mean that you *should* use it, however.

1.

The blue whale is the largest creature in the world and has been found in every ocean in the world. A marine biologist surveyed the blue whale population in Monterey Bay, off the coast of California, every three years between 1995 and 2010. The figure above shows her results. If w is the number of blue whales present in Monterey Bay and t is the number of years since the study began in 1995, which of the following equations best represents the blue whale population of Monterey Bay?

A) $w = 100 + 2t$

B) $w = 100 + \dfrac{t^2}{4}$

C) $w = 100 \times 2^t$

D) $w = 100 \times 2^{\frac{t}{4}}$

2. Most people save money before going on vacation. Suppose Etienne saved $800 to spend during vacation, 20 percent of which he uses to pay for gas. If he budgets 25 percent of the remaining money for food, allots $300 for the hotel, and spends the rest of the money on entertainment, what percentage of the original $800 did he spend on entertainment?

A) 14.5

B) 17.5

C) 22.5

D) 28.5

3. In a class of 25 students, 76% are currently passing with a grade of 70% or higher. If two students are selected at random from this class, what is the probability that neither student is passing with a grade of 70% or higher?

A) 0.05

B) 0.06

C) 0.24

D) 0.58

4. In extreme climates, temperatures can vary as much as 20° Celsius in a single day. How many degrees Fahrenheit can these climates vary if the relation between Fahrenheit degrees and Celsius degrees is given by the equation $F = \dfrac{9}{5}C + 32$?

   A) 20°F

   B) 36°F

   C) 62°F

   D) 68°F

5.

	For	Against	Undecided	Total
1L	32	16	10	58
2L	24	12	28	64
3L	17	25	13	55
Total	73	53	51	177

A survey is conducted regarding a proposed change in the attendance policy at a law school. The table above categorizes the results of the survey by year of the student (1L, 2L, or 3L) and whether they are for, against, or undecided about the new policy. What fraction of all 1Ls and 2Ls are against the new policy?

   A) $\dfrac{14}{61}$

   B) $\dfrac{24}{61}$

   C) $\dfrac{28}{53}$

   D) $\dfrac{28}{177}$

6. An airline company purchased two new airplanes. One can travel at speeds of up to 600 miles per hour and the other at speeds of up to 720 miles per hour. How many more miles can the faster airplane travel in 12 seconds than the slower airplane?

   A) $\dfrac{1}{30}$

   B) $\dfrac{2}{5}$

   C) 2

   D) 30

7. Marion is a city planner. The city she works for recently purchased new property on which it plans to build administrative offices. Marion has been given the task of sizing the lots for new buildings, using the following guidelines:

   - The square footage of each lot should be greater than or equal to 3,000 square feet, but less than or equal to 15,000 square feet.

   - Each lot size should be at least 30% greater in area than the size before it.

   - To simplify tax assessment calculations, the square footage of each lot must be a multiple of 1,000 square feet.

   Which list of lot sizes meets the city guidelines and includes as many lots as possible?

   A) 3,000; 5,000; 10,000; 15,000

   B) 3,000; 4,500; 6,000; 7,500; 10,000; 15,000

   C) 3,000; 4,000; 6,000; 8,000; 11,000; 15,000

   D) 3,000; 3,900; 5,100; 6,600; 8,600; 11,200; 14,600

8.

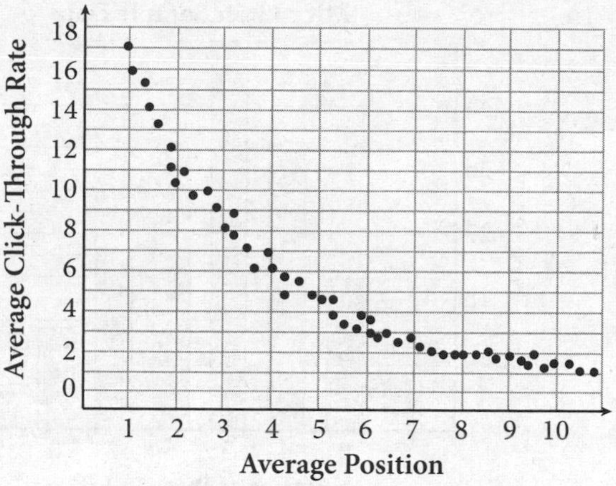

Average Position

The figure above represents a click-through rate curve, which shows the relationship between a search result position in a list of Internet search results and the number of people who clicked on advertisements on that result's page. Which of the following regression types would be the best model for this data?

A)   A linear function

B)   A quadratic function

C)   A polynomial function

D)   An exponential function

9.   According to a hospital's records, the mean age of 17 new mothers who gave birth at the hospital in June was 26 years. When the final new mother who gave birth at that hospital on June 30 was added to the data, the mean age increased to 27 years. What was the age of the final new mother?

A)   27

B)   36

C)   44

D)   47

10. The Great Pyramid of Giza, built in the 26th century BC just outside of Cairo, Egypt, had an original height of 480 feet, 8 inches, before some of the stones in which it was encased fell away. Inside the pyramid is a 53.75-foot passage, called the Dead End Shaft, which archeologists have yet to discover the purpose of. Suppose a museum is building a scale model of the pyramid for patrons to explore. Because of the museum's ceiling height, they can only make the pyramid 71 feet, 6 inches tall. About how many feet long should the museum's Dead End Shaft be?

A)   8

B)   12

C)   30

D)   96

11. The percent increase from 5 to 12 is equal to the percent increase from 12 to what number?

A)   16.8

B)   19.0

C)   26.6

D)   28.8

12.

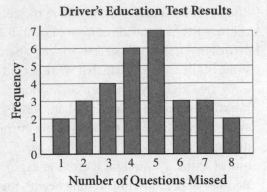

Driver's Education Test Results

Mr. Juno took his driver's education class to the Department of Motor Vehicles to take their driver's license test. The number of questions missed by each student in the class is recorded in the bar graph above. Which of the following statements is true?

A) More than half of the students missed 5 or more questions.

B) The mean number of questions missed was between 4 and 5.

C) More students missed 3 questions than any other number of questions.

D) Thirty-six students from Mr. Juno's class took the driver's license test that day.

13.

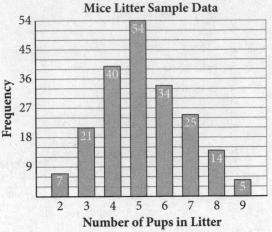

Mice Litter Sample Data

The white-footed mouse, named for its darker body fur and white feet, is primarily found on the east coast of the United States, living in warm, dry forests and brushland. A scientist in Virginia studied a sample of 200 white-footed mice to see how many offspring they had per birth. The results of the study are recorded in the figure above. Based on the data, given a population of 35,000 female white-footed mice living in Virginia, how many would you expect to have a litter of seven or more pups?

A) 3,325

B) 4,375

C) 7,700

D) 15,400

14. According to the American Association of University Women, the mean age of men who have a college degree at their first marriage is 29.9 years. The mean age of women with a college degree at their first marriage is 28.4 years. Which of the following must be true about the combined mean age m of all people with college degrees at their first marriage?

A) $m = 29.15$

B) $m > 29.15$

C) $m < 29.15$

D) $28.4 < m < 29.9$

15. An architect is designing a new stadium-seating movie theater. The theater company has given the architect the following guidelines for designing the rows:

- The length of each row must be at least 20 feet long, but no longer than 90 feet.

- Each row should be at least 20% longer than the row in front of it.

- Each row length must be evenly divisible by the width needed for each seat, 2.5 feet.

 Which list of row lengths meets the theater company's guidelines and includes as many row lengths as possible?

A) 24, 30, 36, 45, 54, 66, 81

B) 20, 32.5, 45, 57.5, 72.5, 85

C) 20, 30, 40, 50, 60, 70, 80, 90

D) 25, 30, 37.5, 45, 55, 67.5, 82.5

16. A microbiologist placed a bacteria sample containing approximately 2,000 microbes in a petri dish. For the first 7 days, the number of microbes in the dish tripled every 24 hours. If n represents the number of microbes after h hours, then which of the following equations is the best model for the data during the 7-day period?

A) $n = 2,000(3)^{\frac{h}{24}}$

B) $n = 2,000(3)^{24h}$

C) $n = \frac{h}{24} \times 2,000$

D) $n = 24h \times 2,000$

17. The United States Senate has two voting members for each of the 50 states. The 113th Congress had a 4:1 male-to-female ratio in the Senate. Forty-five of the male senators were Republican. Only 20 percent of the female senators were Republican. How many senators in the 113th Congress were Republican?

A) 20

B) 49

C) 55

D) 65

18.

From	Distance to LHR
DCA	3,718
MIA	4,470

 Two airplanes departed from different airports at 5:30 AM, both traveling nonstop to London Heathrow Airport (LHR). The distances the planes traveled are recorded in the table. The Washington, D.C. (DCA) flight flew through moderate cloud cover and as a result only averaged 338 mph. The flight from Miami (MIA) had good weather conditions for the first two-thirds of the trip and averaged 596 mph, but then encountered some turbulence and only averaged 447 mph for the last part of the trip. Which plane arrived first and how long was it at the London airport before the other plane arrived?

A) MIA; 2 hours, 40 minutes

B) MIA; 3 hours, 30 minutes

C) DCA; 1 hour, 20 minutes

D) DCA; 3 hours, 40 minutes

19. Each month, the Bureau of Labor Statistics conducts a survey called the Current Population Survey (CPS) to measure unemployment in the United States. Across the country, about 60,000 households are included in the survey sample. These households are grouped by geographic region. A summary of the January 2014 survey results for male respondents in one geographic region is shown in the table below.

Age Group	Employed	Unemployed	Not in the Labor Force	Total
16 to 19	8	5	10	23
20 to 24	26	7	23	56
25 to 34	142	11	28	157
35 to 44	144	8	32	164
45 to 54	66	6	26	98
Over 54	65	7	36	152
Total	451	44	155	650

If one unemployed man from this sample is chosen at random for a follow-up survey, what is the probability that he will be between the ages of 45 and 54 ?

A)   6.0%

B)   13.6%

C)   15.1%

D)   44.9%

20. Crude oil is sold by the barrel, which refers to both the physical container and a unit of measure, abbreviated as bbl. One barrel holds 42 gallons and, consequently, 1 bbl = 42 gallons. An oil company is filling an order for 2,500 barrels. The machine the company uses to fill the barrels pumps at a rate of 37.5 gallons per minute. If the oil company has 8 machines working simultaneously, how long will it take to fill all the barrels in the order?

A)   5 hours and 50 minutes

B)   12 hours and 45 minutes

C)   28 hours and 30 minutes

D)   46 hours and 40 minutes

21. A company reimburses employees for a portion of their gas costs for commuting to and from work based on mileage. Based on the following data, what is the rate in dollars per gallon that the company uses to reimburse employees?

- The company has 126 employees who commute.
- The average employee traveled 12,250 miles to and from work over the course of the year.
- The average gas mileage reported by all employees was 22.5 miles per gallon.
- The company paid out a total of $96,040.00 in gas reimbursements.

A) $0.44

B) $0.71

C) $1.40

D) $1.60

22.

Clinical Trial: Headache Side Effect 900-Participant Study

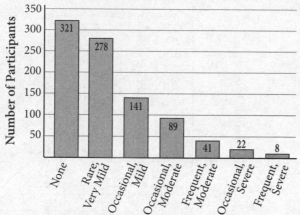

Frequency and Severity of Headaches

When a drug company wants to introduce a new drug, it must subject the drug to rigorous testing. The final stage of this testing is human clinical trials, in which progressively larger groups of volunteers are given the drug and carefully monitored. One aspect of this monitoring is keeping track of the frequency and severity of side effects. The figure above shows the results for the side effect of headaches for a certain drug. According to the trial guidelines, all moderate and severe headaches are considered to be adverse reactions. Which of the following best describes the data?

A) The data is symmetric with over 50% of participants having adverse reactions.

B) The data is skewed to the right with over 50% of participants having adverse reactions.

C) The data is skewed to the right with over 75% of participants failing to have adverse reactions.

D) The data is skewed to the right with approximately 50% of participants having no reaction at all.

23. In a 2010 poll, surveyors asked registered voters in four different New York voting districts whether they would consider voting to ban fracking in the state. Hydraulic fracturing, or "fracking," is a mining process that involves splitting rocks underground to remove natural gas. According to ecologists, environmental damage can occur as a result of fracking, including contamination of water. The results of the 2010 survey are shown in the following table.

	In Favor of Ban	Against Ban	No Opinion	Total
District A	23,247	17,106	3,509	43,862
District B	13,024	12,760	2,117	27,901
District C	43,228	49,125	5,891	98,244
District D	30,563	29,771	3,205	63,539
Total	110,062	108,762	14,722	233,546

A random follow-up survey was administered to 500 of the respondents in District C. They were asked if they planned to vote in the next election. The follow-up survey results were: 218 said they planned to vote, 174 said they did not plan to vote, and 108 said they were unsure. Based on the data from both the initial survey and the follow-up survey, which of the following is most likely an accurate statement?

A) Approximately 19,000 people in District C who support a ban on fracking can be expected to vote in the next election.

B) Approximately 21,000 people in District C who support a ban on fracking can be expected to vote in the next election.

C) Approximately 43,000 people in District C who support a ban on fracking can be expected to vote in the next election.

D) Approximately 48,000 people in District C who support a ban on fracking can be expected to vote in the next election.

24. In the United States, the maintenance and construction of airports, transit systems, and major roads is largely funded through a federal excise tax on gasoline. Based on the 2011 statistics given below, how much did the average household pay per year in federal gasoline taxes?

- The federal gasoline tax rate was 18.4 cents per gallon.

- The average motor vehicle was driven approximately 11,340 miles per year.

- The national average fuel economy for noncommercial vehicles was 21.4 miles per gallon.

- The average American household owned 1.75 vehicles.

A) $55.73

B) $68.91

C) $97.52

D) $170.63

25.

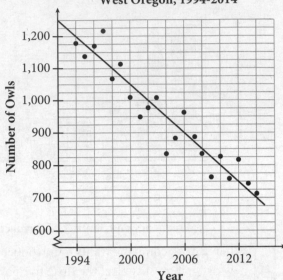

**Northern Spotted Owls
West Oregon, 1994-2014**

The United States Fish and Wildlife Service classifies animals whose populations are at low levels as either threatened or endangered. Endangered species are animals that are currently on the brink of extinction, whereas threatened species have a high probability of being on the brink in the near future. Since 1990, the Northern Spotted Owl has been listed as threatened. The figure above shows the populations of the Northern Spotted Owl in a certain region in Oregon from 1994 to 2014. Based on the line of best fit shown in the figure, which of the following values most accurately reflects the average change per year in the number of Northern Spotted Owls?

A) −25

B) −0.04

C) 0.04

D) 25

26. Red tide is a form of harmful algae that releases toxins as it breaks down in the environment. A marine biologist is testing a new spray, composed of clay and water, hoping to kill the red tide that almost completely covers a beach in southern Florida. He applies the spray to a representative sample of 200 square feet of the beach. By the end of the week, 184 square feet of the beach are free of the red tide. Based on these results, and assuming the same general conditions, how many square feet of the 10,000-square-foot beach would still be covered by red tide if the spray had been used on the entire area?

A)   800

B)   920

C)   8,000

D)   9,200

27. According to the *Project on Student Debt* prepared by The Institute for College Access and Success, 7 out of 10 students graduating in 2012 from a four-year college in the United States had student loan debt. The average amount borrowed per student was $29,400, which is up from $18,750 in 2004. If student debt experiences the same total percent increase over the next eight years, approximately how much will a college student graduating in 2020 owe, assuming she takes out student loans to pay for her education?

A) $40,100

B) $44,300

C) $46,100

D) $48,200

28.

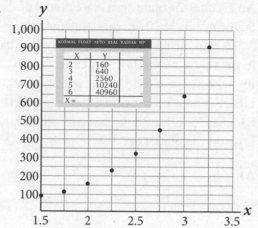

If an exponential function is used to model the data shown in the figure, and it is written in the form $f(x) = f(0)(1 + r)^x$, what would be the value of r?

A)   2

B)   3

C)   4

D)   5

29. Kudzu is a vine-like plant that grows indigenously in Asia. It was brought over to the United States in the early 20th century to help combat soil erosion. As can often happen when foreign species are introduced into a non-native habitat, kudzu growth exploded and it became invasive. In one area of Virginia, kudzu covered approximately 3,200 acres of a farmer's cropland, so he tried a new herbicide. After two weeks of use, 2,800 acres of the farmer's cropland were free of the kudzu. Based on these results, and assuming the same general conditions, how many of the 30,000 acres of kudzu-infested cropland in that region would still be covered if all the farmers in the entire region had used the herbicide?

A)   3,750

B)   4,000

C)   26,000

D)   26,250

30. An architect is building a scale model of the Statue of Liberty. The real statue measures 305 feet, 6 inches from the bottom of the base to the tip of the torch. The architect plans to make her model 26 inches tall. If Lady Liberty's nose on the actual statue is 4 feet, 6 inches long, how long in inches should the nose on the model be?

A) $\frac{1}{26}$

B) $\frac{26}{141}$

C) $\frac{18}{47}$

D) $\frac{13}{27}$

31. An object's weight is dependent upon the gravitational force being exerted upon the object. This is why objects in space are weightless. If 1 pound on Earth is equal to 0.377 pounds on Mars and 2.364 pounds on Jupiter, how many more pounds does an object weighing 1.5 tons on Earth weigh on Jupiter than on Mars?

A) 1,131

B) 4,092

C) 5,961

D) 7,092

32. The figure shows the age distribution of homebuyers and the percent of the market each age range makes up in a particular geographic region.

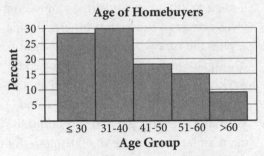

A new real estate agent is deciding which age group she should market toward in order to get the most clients. Which of the following measures of the data would be best for her to use when making this decision?

A) Mean

B) Mode

C) Range

D) Median

33.

Quarterly Profits

	Branch A	Branch B	Branch C	Branch D
Q1	4.1	7.4	8.0	5.4
Q2	3.6	5.2	3.7	6.2
Q3	5.0	4.5	4.9	4.8
Q4	4.9	6.3	5.9	5.6
$\bar{x}$	4.4	5.85	5.625	5.5
s	0.67	1.27	1.82	0.58

A company affected by a downturn in the economy decides to close one of its four branches. The table shows each branch's quarterly profits in millions of dollars for 2014, along with the mean ($\bar{x}$) and the standard deviation (s) of the data. The accounting department recommends that the company's Board of Directors close either the store with the lowest average quarterly profits or the store that performs the least consistently. According to the data in the table, which branches will the accounting department recommend for closure to the board?

A) Branches A or C

B) Branches A or D

C) Branches B or C

D) Branches B or D

34.

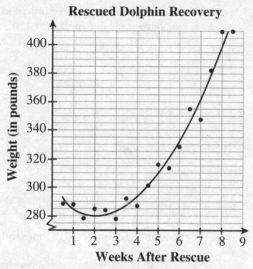

Rescued Dolphin Recovery

Following the catastrophic oil spill in the Gulf of Mexico in April of 2010, more than 900 bottlenose dolphins were found dead or stranded in the oil spill area. The figure above shows the weight of a rescued dolphin during its recovery. Based on the quadratic model fit to the data shown, which of the following is the closest to the average rate of change in the dolphin's weight between week 2 and week 8 of its recovery in pounds per week?

A) 4

B) 16

C) 20

D) 40

35.

Annual Expenditures per Student as a Percentage of Country's GDP

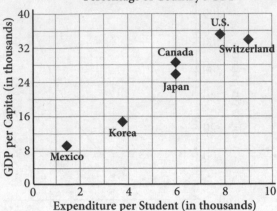

Adapted from the Organization for Economic Cooperation and Development (OECD), 2003.

A student looked at the graph above and determined based on the data that spending more money per student causes the gross domestic product (GDP) to increase. Which of the following statements is true?

A) The student is correct; the data shows that increased spending on students causes an increase in the GDP.

B) The student is incorrect; the data shows that having a higher GDP causes an increase in the amount of money a country spends on students.

C) The student is incorrect; there is no correlation and, therefore, no causation between GDP and expenditures on students.

D) The student is incorrect; the two variables are correlated, but changes in one do not necessarily cause changes in the other.

36.

Bowling Scores			
	Ian	**Mae**	**Jin**
Game 1	160	110	120
Game 2	135	160	180
Game 3	185	140	105
Game 4	135	130	160
Game 5	185	110	135
Mean Score	160	130	140
Standard Deviation	22	19	27

Ian, Mae, and Jin bowled five games during a bowling tournament. The table above shows their scores. According to the data, which of the following conclusions is correct?

A) Ian bowled the most consistently because the mean of his scores is the highest.

B) Mae bowled the least consistently because the standard deviation of her scores is the lowest.

C) Mae bowled the most consistently because the standard deviation of her scores is the lowest.

D) Jin bowled the most consistently because the standard deviation of his scores is the highest.

37. A bakery sells three sizes of muffins—mini, regular, and jumbo. The baker plans daily muffin counts based on the size of his pans and how they fit in the oven, which results in the following ratios: mini to regular equals 5 to 2, and regular to jumbo equals 5 to 4. When the bakery caters events, it usually offers only the regular size, but it recently decided to offer a mix of mini and jumbo instead of regular. If the baker wants to keep the sizes in the same ratio as his daily counts, what ratio of mini to jumbo should he use?

A) 1:1

B) 4:2

C) 5:2

D) 25:8

38. The Federal Reserve controls certain interest rates in the United States. Investors often try to speculate as to whether the Federal Reserve will raise or lower rates and by how much. Suppose a company conducts extensive interviews with financial analysts, and as a result, predicts that "the Fed" will increase rates by an average of 0.25 percentage points every six months for the foreseeable future. Which type of equation could be used to model the predicted interest rates over the next several years, assuming no other significant changes?

A) A linear equation

B) A quadratic equation

C) A polynomial equation

D) An exponential equation

39.

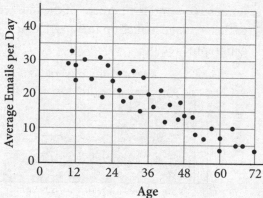

Emails per Day by Age

Which of the following equations best represents the trend of the data shown in the figure above?

A) $y = -2.4x + 30$

B) $y = -1.2x + 40$

C) $y = -0.8x + 40$

D) $y = -0.4x + 36$

40. An online movie subscription service charges a dollars for the first month of membership and b dollars per month after that. If a customer has paid $108.60 so far for the service, which of the following expressions represents the number of months he has subscribed to the service?

A) $\dfrac{108.60}{a+b}$

B) $\dfrac{108.60-a}{b}$

C) $\dfrac{108.60-a-b}{b}$

D) $\dfrac{108.60-a+b}{b}$

41. The figure shows the age distribution of homebuyers and the percent of the market each age range makes up in a particular geographic region.

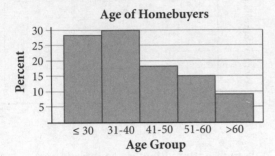

Age of Homebuyers

Based on the information in the figure, which of the following statements is true?

A) The shape of the data is skewed to the right, so the mean age of homebuyers is greater than the median.

B) The shape of the data is skewed to the left, so the median age of homebuyers is greater than the mean.

C) The shape of the data is fairly symmetric, so the mean age of homebuyers is approximately equal to the median.

D) The data has no clear shape, so it is impossible to make a reliable statement comparing the mean and the median.

42. When a certain kitchen appliance store decides to sell a floor model, it marks the retail price of the model down 25% and puts a "Floor Model Sale" sign on it. Every 30 days after that, the price is marked down an additional 10% until it is sold. The store decides to sell a floor model refrigerator on January 15th. If the retail price of the refrigerator was $1,500 and it is sold on April 2nd of the same year, what is the final selling price, not including tax?

A) $820.13

B) $825.00

C) $911.25

D) $1,012.50

43.

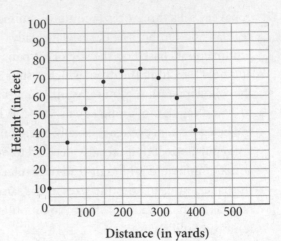

The figure above shows the trajectory of a cannonball shot into the air. Approximately how many feet farther did the cannonball travel horizontally than vertically upward? (1 yard = 3 feet)

A) 335

B) 425

C) 1,035

D) 1,390

44. A certain real estate agent uses what he calls a *step-strategy* to sell houses. He puts a house on the market at a higher-than-expected selling price and if it hasn't sold in two weeks, he drops the price by 5%. If it still hasn't sold in another 2 weeks, he drops the price by another 5%. After that, he continues to drop the price by 3% every two weeks until it reaches a cut-off amount assigned by the homeowner, or the house sells, whichever comes first. If a house is originally listed at $200,000 and the home-owner sets a cut-off amount of $166,000, what is the final selling price given that the house sells after being on the market for 9 weeks?

A) $162,901.25

B) $164,737.48

C) $166,000.00

D) $169,832.45

45.

U.S. Foreign Trade, 2014

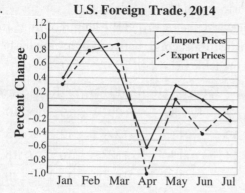

The figure above shows the net change, as a percentage, for U.S. import and export prices from January to July 2014 as reported by the Bureau of Labor Statistics. For example, U.S. import prices declined 0.2 percent in July while export prices remained unchanged for that month. Based on this information, which of the following statements is true for the time period shown in the figure?

A) On average, export prices increased more than import prices.

B) Import prices showed an increase more often than export prices.

C) Import prices showed the greatest change between two consecutive months.

D) From January to July, import prices showed a greater overall decrease than export prices.

46. Every weekend for 48 hours, a law firm backs up all client files by scanning and uploading them to a secure remote server. On average, the size of each client file is 2.5 gigabytes. The law firm's computer can upload the scans at a rate of 5.25 megabytes per second. What is the maximum number of client files the law firm can back up each weekend? (1 gigabyte = 1,000 megabytes)

A) 362

B) 363

C) 476

D) 477

47.

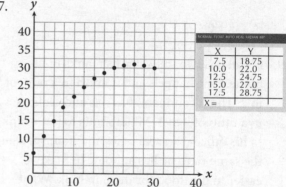

The maximum value of the data shown in the scatterplot above occurs at $x = 25$. If the data is modeled using a quadratic regression and the correlation coefficient is 1.0 (the fit is exact), then what is the y-value when $x = 35$?

A) 10

B) 15

C) 22

D) 27

48. Ethanol is an alcohol commonly added to gasoline to reduce the use of fossil fuels. A commonly used ratio of ethanol to gasoline is 1:4. Another less common and more experimental additive is methanol, with a typical ratio of methanol to gasoline being 1:9. A fuel producer wants to see what happens to cost and fuel efficiency when a combination of ethanol and methanol is used. In order to keep the ratio of gasoline to total additive the same, what ratio of ethanol to methanol should the company use?

A) 1:1

B) 4:9

C) 9:4

D) 36:9

49. Mikal has two saltwater fish tanks in his home. One has eels and lionfish in a ratio of 5 to 2. The second tank has eels and seahorses in a ratio of 2 to 3. Mikal wants to put a tank in his office with seahorses and lionfish, using the same ratio he has at home to make it easier to buy food for them in bulk. What ratio of lionfish to seahorses should he use?

A) 2:3

B) 5:2

C) 7:8

D) 4:15

50. Mario watched a thunderstorm from his backyard. He recorded the length of time, to the nearest second, between lightning flashes in the table below.

Time Between Lightning Flashes (in seconds)				
7	8	8	9	10
10	11	12	12	13
14	15	15	16	16
17	17	18	19	30

The outlier measurement of 30 seconds is an error. Of the mean, median, and range for the values listed, which will change the most if the 30-second measurement is removed from the data?

A) Mean

B) Median

C) Range

D) They will all change by the same amount.

51. Medically speaking, remission is a period in which the symptoms of a disease or condition subside or, for some diseases, a period during which the condition stops spreading or worsening. In a certain drug trial in which a drug designed to treat cancer was tested, exactly 48% of patients experienced remission while taking the drug. What is the fewest number of patients who could have participated in this trial?

52. A county employee is collecting water samples from all the houses in a subdivision where trace amounts of lead were found in the water. There are 45 houses in the subdivision. If he starts the first house at 9:00 AM and starts the sixth house at 10:00 AM, how many minutes will it take the employee to collect samples from all the houses in the subdivision, assuming it takes the same amount of time at each house?

53. A college math professor informs her students that rather than curving final grades, she will replace each student's lowest test score with the next to lowest test score, and then re-average the test grades. If Leeza has test scores of 86, 92, 81, 64, and 83, by how many points does her final test average change based on the professor's policy?

54. A bank offers a long-term savings account with a 1.0% annual interest rate. At the end of each year, the interest is rounded down to the nearest cent and added to the principal. If the initial deposit was $1,500, how much interest has the account earned at the end of 5 years?

Questions 55 and 56 refer to the following information.

The Great Depression began in 1929 and lasted until 1939. It was a period of extreme poverty, marked by low prices and high unemployment. The main catalytic event to the Great Depression was the Wall Street Crash (stock market crash). The Dow, which measures the health of the stock market, started Black Thursday (October 24, 1929) at approximately 306 points.

55. The stock market had been in steady decline since its record high the month before. If the market had declined by 19.5% between its record high and opening on Black Thursday, what was the approximate value of the Dow at its record high? Round your answer to the nearest whole point.

56. By the end of business on Black Thursday, the Dow had dropped by 2%. Over the course of Friday and the half-day Saturday session, there was no significant change. Unfortunately, the market lost 13% on Black Monday, followed by another 12% on Black Tuesday. What was the total percent decrease from opening on Black Thursday to closing on Black Tuesday? Round your answer to the nearest whole percent and ignore the percent sign when entering your answer.

Questions 57 and 58 refer to the following information.

Bridget is starting a tutoring business to help adults get their GEDs. She already has five clients and decides they can share a single textbook, which will be kept at her office, and that she also needs one notebook and four pencils for each of them. She records her supply budget, which includes tax, in the table shown.

Supply	Total Number Needed	Cost Each
Textbook	1	$24.99
Notebooks	5	$3.78
Pencils	20	$0.55

57. The textbook makes up what percent of Bridget's total supply budget? Round to the nearest tenth of a percent and ignore the percent sign when entering your answer.

58. Bridget's business does very well, and she needs more supplies. She always orders them according to the table above, for five clients at a time. At the beginning of this year, she orders the supplies for the whole year, which cost $988.02. Halfway through the year, she decides to take inventory of the supplies. She has used $713.57 worth of the supplies. How many pencils should be left, assuming the supplies were used at the rate for which she originally planned?

59. On a map, the scale is the ratio of the distance shown on the map to the actual distance. A geography teacher has a map on her wall with a scale of 1 inch:100 miles. She uses the school's copier to shrink the large wall map down to the size of a piece of paper to hand out to each of her students. To do this, she makes the map $\frac{1}{4}$ of its original size. Suppose on the students' maps, the distance between two cities is 2.5 inches. How many actual miles apart are those cities?

60.

Regional Manager Job Performance

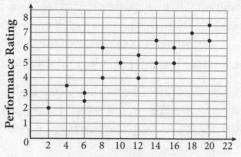

A company conducted a study comparing the overall job performance of its regional managers with the length of time each one spent in the company's management-training program. The scatterplot above shows the results of the study. What is the length of the time spent in training, in months, of the manager represented by the data point that is the greatest distance from the line of best fit (not shown)?

61. Jordan is beginning a marathon training program. During his first day of training, he wears a pedometer to get an idea of how far he can currently run. At the end of the run, the pedometer indicates that he took 24,288 steps.

    Jordan knows from experience that his average stride (step) is 2.5 feet. How many miles did he run on his first day of training? (1 mile = 5,280 feet)

62. A student news reporter chose 500 students at random from each of two schools and asked each student how many video games he or she has. The results are shown in the table below.

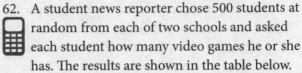

Student Video Game Survey		
Number of Video Games	Jefferson School	Midtown High School
0	100	130
1	120	120
2	90	100
3	130	90
4	60	60

What is the median number of video games for all the students surveyed?

63.

Fuel Efficiency Ratings

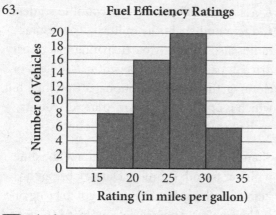

 The histogram above shows the number of vehicles that a car rental agency currently has available to rent, categorized by fuel efficiency ratings. If a customer randomly selects one of the available cars, what is the probability that he will get a car that has a fuel efficiency rating of at least 25 miles per gallon? Enter your answer as a decimal number.

64. The following table shows the number of houses in a development. The table categorizes the houses by type (single-family or townhouse) and by the number of bedrooms.

Development Houses

	2 Br	3 Br	4 Br	Total
Single-Family	5	19	34	58
Townhouse	24	42	30	96
Total	29	61	64	154

The homeowner's association partners with a local daycare center. The HOA has agreed to allow the daycare center to advertise in the development using flyers. In general, families with children typically reside in single-family homes or townhouses that have 3 or more bedrooms. The daycare center has a limited budget and plans to concentrate its marketing efforts on only those homes and townhouses.

In addition to sending out flyers, the daycare center decides to send out invitations for a free day of daycare, but determines that it would be too expensive to do this for all of the family residences in the development. Instead, it decides to market this benefit only to the two categories in the table with the most dwellings. If a dwelling that already received a flyer is chosen at random to receive the second stage of the marketing, what is the probability that the dwelling belongs to one of these two groups? Enter your answer as a decimal.

Questions 65 and 66 refer to the following information.

Three cars all arrive at the same destination at 4:00 PM. The first car traveled 144 miles mostly by highway. The second car traveled 85 miles mainly on rural two-lane roads. The third car traveled 25 miles primarily on busy city streets.

65. The first car traveled at an average speed of 64 miles per hour. The second car started its drive at 2:18 PM. How many minutes had the first car already been traveling before the second car started its drive?

66. The third car encountered heavy traffic for the first 60% of its trip and only averaged 15 miles per hour. Then traffic stopped due to an accident, and the car did not move for 20 minutes. After the accident was cleared, the car averaged 30 miles per hour for the remainder of the trip. At what time in the afternoon did the third car start its trip? Use only digits for your answer. (For example, enter 1:25 PM as 125.)

67. A restaurant offers a 20% discount to students and to members of the military. The restaurant is also currently participating in a charity drive. If patrons donate a gently used item of clothing, they get an additional 5% off their bill, which is applied before any other discounts, such as student or military discounts.

Sharon is a member of the military. She dines with her friend, Damien. Damien brings an item of clothing, but Sharon forgot to bring one. If Sharon's meal before discounts is $16.25 and Damien's is $12.80 before discounts, how much did the discounts save them altogether?

68.

Years at Company	Female	Male
$y < 1$	38	30
$1 \leq y \leq 3$	15	19
$y > 3$	54	48

 A company conducts a survey among its employees and categorizes the results based on gender and longevity (the number of years the employee has been working for the company). The Director of Human Resources wants to conduct a small follow-up focus group meeting with a few employees to discuss the overall survey results. If the HR Director randomly chooses four employees that participated in the initial survey, what is the probability that all of them will have been with the company for longer than 3 years? Enter your answer as a fraction.

69. Seven integers are ordered from least to greatest. If the only mode is 7, and the median is 9, what is the least possible range for the seven numbers?

Questions 70 and 71 refer to the following information.

Chemical Makeup of One Mole of Chloroform

Element	Number of Moles	Mass per Mole (grams)
Carbon	1	12.011
Hydrogen	1	1.008
Chlorine	3	35.453

A chemical solvent is a substance that dissolves another to form a solution. For example, water is a solvent for sugar. Unfortunately, many chemical solvents are hazardous to the environment. One eco-friendly chemical solvent is chloroform, also known as trichloromethane ($CHCl_3$). The table above shows the chemical makeup of one mole of chloroform.

70. Carbon makes up what percent of the mass of one mole of chloroform? Round your answer to the nearest whole percent and ignore the percent sign when entering your answer.

71. If a chemist starts with 1,000 grams of chloroform and uses 522.5 grams, how many moles of chlorine are left?

Questions 72 and 73 refer to the following information.

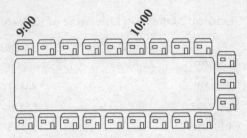

Daniel works for a pest control company and is spraying all the lawns in a neighborhood. The figure above shows the layout of the neighborhood and the times that Daniel started spraying the lawns at two of the houses. Each lawn in the neighborhood is approximately 0.2 acres in size and takes the same amount of time to spray.

72. How many minutes will it take Daniel to spray all of the lawns in the neighborhood?

73. Daniel uses a mobile spray rig that holds 20 gallons of liquid. It takes 1 gallon to spray 2,500 square feet of lawn. How many times, including the first time, will Daniel need to fill the spray rig, assuming he fills it to the very top each time?
(1 acre = 43,560 square feet)

74.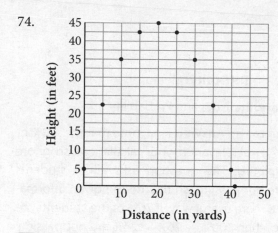

Distance (in yards)

 The figure above represents the trajectory of a t-shirt shot from a t-shirt cannon from one end of a football field toward the other. The quadratic function $h(d) = -\frac{1}{10}(d-20)^2 + 45$ can be used to model the data. Based on the model, approximately how many feet farther did the t-shirt travel horizontally than it did vertically upward, assuming that no one caught the t-shirt and that it did not roll once it hit the ground? Round your answer to the nearest whole foot.

75. Rory left home and drove straight to the airport at an average speed of 45 miles per hour. He returned home along the same route, but traffic slowed him down and he only averaged 30 miles per hour on the return trip. If his total travel time was 2 hours and 30 minutes, how far is it, in miles, from Rory's house to the airport?

K 289

ANSWERS AND EXPLANATIONS

CHAPTER 12

1.   D   Difficulty: Medium

Category: Scatterplots

Getting to the Answer: Use the shape of the data to predict the type of equation that might be used as a model. Then, use specific values from the graph to choose the correct equation. According to the graph, the population of the whales grew slowly at first and then more quickly. This means that an exponential model is probably the best fit, so you can eliminate A (linear) and B (quadratic). The remaining equations are both exponential, so choose a data point and see which equation is the closest fit. Be careful—the vertical axis represents *hundreds* of whales, and the question states that t represents the number of years since the study began, so $t = 0$ for 1995, $t = 3$ for 1998, and so on. If you use the data for 1995, which is the point (0, 100), the results are the same for both equations, so choose a different point. Using the data for 2007, $t = 2007 - 1995 = 12$, and the number of whales was 800. Substitute these values into C and D to see which one is true. Choice C is not true because $800 \neq 100 \times 2^{12}$. Choice (D) is correct because:

$$800 = 100 \times 2^{\frac{12}{4}} = 100 \times 2^3 = 100 \times 8$$

2.   C   Difficulty: Medium

Category: Rates, Ratios, Proportions, and Percentages

Getting to the Answer: Etienne starts with $800. He spends 20% of $800, or 0.2($800) = $160, on gas. He has $800 − $160 = $640 left over. He budgets 25% of $640, or 0.25($640) = $160, for food and allots $300 for the hotel. He spends all the remaining money on entertainment, which is $640 − $160 − $300 = $180. Divide this amount by the original amount to find the percent he spent on entertainment: $\frac{180}{800} = 0.225 = 22.5\%$, choice (C).

3.   A   Difficulty: Medium

Category: Statistics and Probability

Getting to the Answer: First, note that the "70% or higher" is not relevant to your calculations, so ignore it completely. The question asks about students who are *not* passing, so rewrite the given information in a more useful way: If 76% of the students are passing, then 100% − 76% = 24% are not passing. This means 0.24(25) = 6 out of the 25 students are currently not passing. Thus, the probability of randomly selecting two students who are not passing is:

$$\frac{6}{25} \times \frac{5}{24} = \frac{30}{600} = 0.05$$

Choice (A) is correct.

4.   B   Difficulty: Medium

Category: Rates, Ratios, Proportions, and Percentages

Getting to the Answer: The question says temperatures can vary by 20°C during a single day. This is not the same as saying the temperature itself is 20°, so you can't just convert the temperature to Fahrenheit. You aren't given exact numbers, just a range, so you'll need to pick some convenient numbers to work with. You might know (or can tell from the formula) that 0°C is equal to 32°F. So pick 0°C and 20°C. Convert each of these to Fahrenheit and then find the difference:

$$F = \frac{9}{5}(C) + 32$$

$$F_{at\,0} = \frac{9}{5}(0) + 32$$

$$= 0 + 32$$

$$= 32$$

$$F_{at\,20} = \frac{9}{5}(20) + 32$$

$$= 36 + 32$$

$$= 68$$

0°C = 32°F and 20°C = 68°F, which means a change in temperature of 20°C is equivalent to a change of $68° − 32° = 36°F$, which means that choice (B) is correct.

You could also recognize from the formula that Fahrenheit measurements are exactly $\frac{9}{5}$ of Celsius measurements, so you could multiply 20 by $\frac{9}{5}$ to arrive at 36 as well.

5.   A   Difficulty: Medium

Category: Statistics and Probability

Getting to the Answer: When working with two-way tables, always read the question carefully, identifying which pieces of information you need. Here, you need to focus on the "Against" column and the "1L" and "2L" rows. To stay organized, it may help to circle these pieces of information in the table. There are 58 1Ls and 64 2Ls in the survey sample, for a total of $58 + 64 = 122$ 1Ls and 2Ls. There are 16 1Ls and 12 2Ls against the policy, for a total of $16 + 12 = 28$. This means that 28 out of the 122 1Ls and 2Ls are against the new policy. Written as a fraction, this is $\frac{28}{122}$, which reduces to $\frac{14}{61}$, choice (A).

6.   B   Difficulty: Medium

Category: Rates, Ratios, Proportions, and Percentages

Getting to the Answer: Let the units in this question guide you to the solution. The speeds of the airplanes are given in miles per hour, but the question asks about the number of miles each airplane can travel in 12 seconds, so convert miles per hour to miles per second and multiply by 12 seconds.

Slower airplane:

$$\frac{600 \text{ mi}}{\text{hr}} \times \frac{1 \text{ hr}}{60 \text{ min}} \times \frac{1 \text{ min}}{60 \text{ sec}} \times 12 \text{ sec} = 2 \text{ mi}$$

Faster airplane:

$$\frac{720 \text{ mi}}{\text{hr}} \times \frac{1 \text{ hr}}{60 \text{ min}} \times \frac{1 \text{ min}}{60 \text{ sec}} \times 12 \text{ sec} = 2.4 \text{ mi}$$

The faster plane can travel $2.4 − 2 = 0.4$ miles farther, which is the same as $\frac{2}{5}$ miles, choice (B).

7.   C   Difficulty: Medium

Category: Rates, Ratios, Proportions, and Percentages

Getting to the Answer: Start with the smallest possible lot size, 3,000 square feet. The next lot must be at least 30% larger, so multiply by 1.3 to get 3,900 square feet. Then, round up to the next thousand (which is not necessarily the nearest thousand) to meet the tax assessment requirement. You must always round up because rounding down would make the subsequent lot size less than 30% larger than the one before it. Continue this process until you reach the maximum square footage allowed, 15,000 square feet.

$$3,000 \times 1.3 = 3,900 \rightarrow 4,000$$
$$4,000 \times 1.3 = 5,200 \rightarrow 6,000$$
$$6,000 \times 1.3 = 7,800 \rightarrow 8,000$$
$$8,000 \times 1.3 = 10,400 \rightarrow 11,000$$
$$11,000 \times 1.3 = 14,300 \rightarrow 15,000$$

Choice (C) is correct.

8.   D   Difficulty: Medium

Category: Scatterplots

Getting to the Answer: You aren't given much information to go on except the shape of the graph, so you'll need to think about what the shape means. Remember, linear functions increase at a constant rate, exponential functions increase at either an increasing or decreasing rate, gradually at first and then more quickly or vice versa, and quadratics and polynomials reverse direction one or more times. The graph begins by decreasing extremely quickly, but then it almost (but not quite) levels off. Therefore, it can't be linear, and because it doesn't change direction, an exponential function, choice (D), would be the best model for the data.

9.   C   Difficulty: Medium

Category: Statistics and Probability

Getting to the Answer: Use the definition of mean and the sum of the ages. Let s = the sum of the ages of the original 17 new mothers.

$$\text{mean} = \frac{\text{sum of ages}}{\text{number of mothers}}$$
$$26 = \frac{s}{17}$$
$$s = 442$$

Now, let a be the age of the final new mother and use the formula again. Don't forget that now there are 18 new mothers.

$$27 = \frac{442 + a}{18}$$
$$486 = 442 + a$$
$$a = 44$$

This matches choice (C).

10.   A   Difficulty: Medium

Category: Rates, Ratios, Proportions, and Percentages

Getting to the Answer: Pay careful attention to the units. You need to convert all of the dimensions to inches and then set up and solve a proportion. There are 12 inches in one foot, so the real pyramid's height was $(480 \times 12) + 8 = 5{,}760 + 8 = 5{,}768$ inches; the length of the passage in the real pyramid was $53.75 \times 12 = 645$ inches; the museum's pyramid height will be 71 feet, 6 inches, or 858 inches; and the length of the museum's passage is unknown. Set up a proportion and solve for the unknown. Use words first to help you keep the measurements in the right places:

$$\frac{\text{real passage length}}{\text{real height}} = \frac{\text{museum passage length}}{\text{museum height}}$$
$$\frac{645}{5{,}768} = \frac{x}{858}$$
$$553{,}410 = 5{,}768x$$
$$95.94 = x$$

The museum should make the length of its passage about 96 inches, or $96 \div 12 = 8$ feet, choice (A).

11.   D   Difficulty: Medium

Category: Rates, Ratios, Proportions, and Percentages

Getting to the Answer: Even though this question uses the word *percent*, you are never asked to find the actual percent itself. Set this question up as a proportion to get the answer more quickly. Remember, percent change equals amount of change divided by the original amount.

$$\frac{12 - 5}{5} = \frac{x - 12}{12}$$
$$\frac{7}{5} = \frac{x - 12}{12}$$
$$12(7) = 5(x - 12)$$
$$84 = 5x - 60$$
$$144 = 5x$$
$$28.8 = x$$

Choice (D) is correct.

12.   B   Difficulty: Medium

Category: Statistics and Probability

Getting to the Answer: Always read the axis labels carefully when a question involves a chart or graph. *Frequency*, which is plotted along the vertical axis, tells you how many students missed the number of questions indicated under each bar. Evaluate each statement as quickly as you can.

Choice A: Add the bar heights (frequencies) that represent students that missed 5 or more questions: $7 + 3 + 3 + 2 = 15$. Then, find the total number of students represented, which is the number that missed fewer than 5 questions plus the 15 you just found: $2 + 3 + 4 + 6 = 15$, for a total of 30 students. The statement is not true because 15 is exactly half (not more than half) of 30.

Choice (B): This calculation will take a bit of time so skip it for now.

Choice C: The tallest bar tells you which number of questions was missed most often, which was 5 questions, not 3 questions, so this statement is not true.

Choice D: The number of students from Mr. Juno's class who took the test that day is the sum of the heights of the bars, which you already know is 30, not 36.

This means (B) must be correct. Mark it and move on to the next question. In case you're curious, find the mean by multiplying each number of questions missed by the corresponding frequency, adding all the products, and dividing by the total number of students, which you already know is 30:

$$\text{mean} = \frac{2+6+12+24+35+18+21+16}{30}$$

$$= \frac{134}{30} = 4.4\overline{6}$$

The mean is indeed between 4 and 5.

13. C   Difficulty: Medium

Category: Statistics and Probability

Getting to the Answer: Read the question, identifying parts of the graphic you need—the question asks about litters of 7 or more pups, so you'll only use the heights of the bars for 7, 8, and 9 pups. Start by finding the percent of the mice in the study that had a litter of 7 or more pups. Of the 200 mice in the sample, $25 + 14 + 5 = 44$ had a litter of 7 or more pups. This is $\frac{44}{200} = \frac{22}{100} = 22\%$ of the mice in the study. Given the same general conditions (such as living in the same geographic region), you would expect approximately the same results, so multiply the number of female mice in the whole population by the percent you found: $35,000 \times 0.22 = 7,700$, choice (C).

14. D   Difficulty: Medium

Category: Statistics and Probability

Getting to the Answer: Because the mean ages are different and you do not know how many men or women have college degrees and get married, you need to reason logically to arrive at the correct answer. The mean age of the women is lower than that of the men, so the combined mean cannot be

greater than or equal to that of the men. Similarly, the mean age of the men is greater than that of the women, so the combined mean cannot be less than or equal to the mean age of the women. In other words, the combined mean age must fall somewhere between the two means, making choice (D) correct.

15. D   Difficulty: Medium

Category: Rates, Ratios, Proportions, and Percentages

Getting to the Answer: Start with the smallest possible row length, 20 feet. The next length must be at least 20% larger, so multiply by 1.2 to get 24 feet. But 24 is not the next row length because each row length must be evenly divisible by the width of each seat, 2.5. The next highest number that is evenly divisible by 2.5 is 25, so 25 is the next row length. You must always use the next highest number up because rounding down would make the subsequent length less than 20% longer than the row in front of it. Now multiply 25 by 1.2 to get 30 feet. This number is evenly divisible by 2.5, so it is the third row length. Continue this process until you reach the maximum length allowed, 90 feet:

$$20 \times 1.2 = 24 \rightarrow 25$$
$$25 \times 1.2 = 30 \rightarrow 30$$
$$30 \times 1.2 = 36 \rightarrow 37.5$$
$$37.5 \times 1.2 = 45 \rightarrow 45$$
$$45 \times 1.2 = 54 \rightarrow 55$$
$$55 \times 1.2 = 66 \rightarrow 67.5$$
$$67.5 \times 1.2 = 81 \rightarrow 82.5$$
$$82.5 \times 1.2 = 99 \rightarrow \text{Too long}$$

The possible row lengths are 25, 30, 37.5, 45, 55, 67.5, and 82.5, which means choice (D) is correct.

16. A   Difficulty: Medium

Category: Scatterplots

Getting to the Answer: When the dependent variable in a relationship increases by a scale factor, like doubling, tripling, etc., there is an exponential relationship between the variables which can be written in the form $y = a(b)^x$, where a is the initial amount, b is the scale factor, and x is time. The question states that the number of microbes tripled every 24 hours, so the relationship is exponential. This means you can eliminate C and D right away. Choices (A) and B are written in the form $y = a(b)^x$, with the initial amount equal to 2,000 and the scale factor equal to 3, so you can't eliminate either one at first glance. To choose between them, try an easy number for h (like 24) in each equation to see which one matches the information given in the question. In the first equation, $n = 2,000(3)^{\frac{24}{24}} = 2,000 \times (3)^1 = 6,000$, which is 2,000 tripled, so choice (A) is correct.

17. B   Difficulty: Medium

Category: Rates, Ratios, Proportions, and Percentages

Getting to the Answer: Break the question into short steps. *Step 1*: Find the number of female senators. *Step 2*: Use that number to find the number of female Republican senators. *Step 3*: Find the total number of Republican senators.

Each of the 50 states gets 2 voting members in the Senate, so there are $50 \times 2 = 100$ senators. The ratio of males to females in the 113th Congress was 4:1, so 4 parts male plus 1 part female equals a total of 100 senators. Write this as $4x + x = 100$, where x represents one part and therefore the number of females. Next, simplify and solve the equation to find that $x = 20$ female senators. To find the number of female senators that were Republican, multiply 20% (or 0.20) times 20 to get 4. Finally, add to get 45 male plus 4 female $= 49$ Republican senators in the 113th Congress, choice (B).

18. A   Difficulty: Medium

Category: Rates, Ratios, Proportions, and Percents

Getting to the Answer: Questions that involve distance, rate, and time can almost always be solved using the formula Distance $=$ rate $\times$ time. Break the question into short steps (first part of trip, second part of trip). Start with the plane from DCA. Use the

speed, or rate, of the plane, 338 mph, and its distance from London, 3,718 miles, to determine when it arrived. You don't know the time, so call it t.

$$\text{Distance} = \text{rate} \times \text{time}$$
$$3,718 = 338t$$
$$11 = t$$

It took the DCA flight 11 hours. Now determine how long it took the plane from MIA. You'll need to find the distance for each part of the trip—the question only tells you the total distance. Then, use the formula to find how long the plane flew at 596 mph and how long it flew at 447 mph.

First part of trip:

$$\frac{2}{3} \times 4,470 = 2,980 \text{ mi}$$
$$2,980 = 596t$$
$$5 = t$$

Second part of trip:

$$\frac{1}{3} \times 4,470 = 1,490 \text{ mi}$$
$$1,490 = 447t$$
$$3.\overline{3} = t$$

This means it took the MIA flight 5 hours $+$ 3 hours, 20 minutes $=$ 8 hours, 20 minutes. So, the plane from MIA arrived first. It arrived 11 hours $-$ 8 hours, 20 minutes $=$ 2 hours, 40 minutes before the plane from DCA, making choice (A) correct.

19. B   Difficulty: Medium

Category: Statistics and Probability

Getting to the Answer: The follow-up survey targets only those respondents who said they were unemployed, so focus on that column in the table. There were 6 respondents out of 44 unemployed males who were between the ages of 45 and 54, so the probability is $\frac{6}{44} = 0.1\overline{36}$, or about 13.6%, choice (B).

20. A   Difficulty: Medium

Category: Rates, Ratios, Proportions, and Percentages

Getting to the Answer: Let the units in this question guide you to the answer. You can do one conversion at a time, or all of them at once. Just be sure to line up the units so they'll cancel correctly. The company uses 8 machines, each of which pumps at a rate of 37.5 gallons per minute, so the rate is actually $8 \times 37.5 = 300$ gallons per minute. Find the total number of gallons needed, and then use the rate to find the time.

$$2{,}500 \; \cancel{bbl} \times \frac{42 \; \cancel{gal}}{1 \; \cancel{bbl}} \times \frac{1 \; min}{300 \; \cancel{gal}} = 350 \; min$$

The answers are given in hours and minutes, so change 350 minutes to $350 \div 60 = 5.833$ hours, which is 5 hours and 50 minutes, choice (A).

21. C   Difficulty: Medium

Category: Rates, Ratios, Proportions, and Percentages

Getting to the Answer: This is another question where the units can help you find the answer. Use the number of employees to find the total number of miles driven to find the total number of gallons of gas used. Then you can write an equation, with r equal to the reimbursement rate, and set it equal to the amount of total reimbursements paid.

$$126 \; \cancel{employees} \times \frac{12{,}250 \; mi}{\cancel{employee}} = 1{,}543{,}500 \; mi$$

$$1{,}543{,}500 \; \cancel{mi} \times \frac{1 \; gal \; of \; gas}{22.5 \; \cancel{miles}} = 68{,}600 \; gal$$

$$68{,}600r = \$96{,}040.00$$

$$r = \$1.40$$

The reimbursement rate was $1.40 per gallon, which is choice (C).

22. C   Difficulty: Medium

Category: Statistics and Probability

Getting to the Answer: Examine the shape of the data and familiarize yourself with the title and the axis labels on the graph. Data is *symmetric* if it is fairly evenly spread out, and it is *skewed* if it has a long tail on either side. Notice that the data is skewed to the right, so you can immediately eliminate choice A. Choices B, (C), and D all describe the data as skewed to the right, so you'll need to examine those statements more closely. For choice B, "adverse reactions" include the last four bars, which represent $89 + 41 + 22 + 8 = 160$ participants total,

which is not even close to 50% of 900, so eliminate choice B. Note that you don't need to add all the bar heights to find that there were 900 participants— the title of the graph tells you that. Now look at choice (C)—"failed to have adverse reactions" means "None" or "Mild" (the first three bars), which represent $900 - 160 = 740$ of the 900 participants. 75% of $900 = 675$, and 740 is more than 675, so choice (C) is correct. For choice D, the "None" column contains 320 participants, which does not equal approximately 50% of 900, so it too is incorrect.

23. A   Difficulty: Medium

Category: Statistics and Probability

Getting to the Answer: Scan the answer choices quickly to narrow down the amount of information in the table that you need to analyze. Each choice makes a statement about people from District C who support a ban on fracking and can be expected to vote in the next election. To extrapolate from the follow-up survey sample, multiply the fraction of people from the follow-up survey who plan to vote in the upcoming election $\left(\frac{218}{500}\right)$ by the number of people in District C who support a ban on fracking (43,228) to get 18,847.408, or approximately 19,000 people. Choice (A) is correct.

24. D   Difficulty: Medium

Category: Rates, Ratios, Proportions, and Percentages

Getting to the Answer: This is another question where the units can help you find the answer. Use the number of vehicles owned to find the total number of miles driven to find the total number of gallons of gas used to find the total tax paid. Phew!

$$1.75 \; \cancel{vehicles} \times \frac{11{,}340 \; miles}{\cancel{vehicle}} = 19{,}845 \; miles$$

$$19{,}845 \; \cancel{miles} \times \frac{1 \; gallon \; of \; gas}{21.4 \; \cancel{miles}} = 927.336 \; gallons$$

$$927.336 \; \cancel{gallons} \times \frac{\$0.184}{\cancel{gallon}} = \$170.63$$

Choice (D) is correct.

25. A   Difficulty: Medium

Category: Scatterplots

Getting to the Answer: Examine the graph, paying careful attention to units and labels. Here, the years increase by 2 for each grid-line and the number of owls by 25. The average change per year is the same as the slope of the line of best fit. Find the slope of the line of best fit using the slope formula, $m = \dfrac{y_2 - y_1}{x_2 - x_1}$, and any two points that lie on (or very close to) the line. Using the two endpoints of the data, (1994, 1,200) and (2014, 700), the average change per year is $\dfrac{700 - 1,200}{2014 - 1994} = \dfrac{-500}{20} = -25$, which is choice (A). Pay careful attention to the sign of the answer—the number of owls is decreasing, so the rate of change is negative.

26. A   Difficulty: Medium

Category: Statistics and Probability

Getting to the Answer: This is a science crossover question. Read the first two sentences quickly—they are simply describing the context of the question. The last two sentences pose the question, so read those more carefully. In the sample, 184 out of 200 square feet were free of red tide after applying the spray. This is $\dfrac{184}{200} = 0.92 = 92\%$ of the area. For the whole beach, $0.92(10,000) = 9,200$ square feet should be free of the red tide. Be careful—this is *not* the answer. The question asks how much of the beach would still be covered by red tide, so subtract to get $10,000 - 9,200 = 800$ square feet, choice (A).

27. C   Difficulty: Medium

Category: Rates, Ratios, Proportions, and Percentages

Getting to the Answer: Find the percent increase by dividing the amount of change by the original amount. Then apply the same percent increase to the amount for 2012. The amount of increase is $29,400 - 18,750 = 10,650$, so the percent increase is $10,650 \div 18,750 = 0.568 = 56.8\%$ over 8 years. If the total percent increase over the next 8 years is the same, the average student who borrowed money will have loans totaling $29,400 \times 1.568 = 46,099.20$, or about \$46,100. Choice (C) is correct.

28. B   Difficulty: Hard

Category: Scatterplots

Getting to the Answer: When an exponential function is written in the form $f(x) = f(0)(1 + r)^x$, the quantity $(1 + r)$ represents the growth rate or the decay rate depending on whether the y-values are increasing or decreasing. The y-values are increasing in this graph, so r represents a growth rate. Because the data is modeled using an exponential function (not a linear function), the rate is not the same as the slope. Look at the y-values in the calculator screenshot—they are quadrupling as the x-values increase by 1. In the equation, this means that $(1 + r) = 4$. Solve this equation to find that $r = 3$, choice (B).

29. A   Difficulty: Medium

Category: Statistics and Probability

Getting to the Answer: This is a science crossover question. Read the first three sentences quickly—they are simply describing the context. The second half of the paragraph poses the question, so read that more carefully. In the sample, 2,800 out of 3,200 acres were free of kudzu after applying the herbicide. This is $\dfrac{2,800}{3,200} = 0.875 = 87.5\%$ of the area. For the whole region, assuming the same general conditions, $0.875(30,000) = 26,250$ acres should be free of the kudzu. Be careful—this is not the answer. The question asks how much of the cropland would *still be covered* by kudzu, so subtract to get $30,000 - 26,250 = 3,750$ acres, choice (A).

30. C   Difficulty: Medium

Category: Rates, Ratios, Proportions, and Percentages

Getting to the Answer: Pay careful attention to the units. You need to convert all of the dimensions to inches, and then set up and solve a proportion. The real statue's height is $305 \times 12 = 3,660 + 6 = 3,666$ inches; the length of the nose on the real statue is $4 \times 12 = 48 + 6 = 54$ inches; the height of the model statue is 26 inches; the length of the nose on the model is unknown.

$$\frac{3,666}{54} = \frac{26}{x}$$

$$3,666x = 26(54)$$

$$3,666x = 1,404$$

$$x = \frac{1,404}{3,666} = \frac{18}{47}$$

Choice (C) is correct.

31. C   Difficulty: Medium

Category: Rates, Ratios, Proportions, and Percents

Getting to the Answer: The factor-label method (cancelling units) is a great strategy for this question. You're starting with tons, so work from that unit, arranging conversions so that units cancel. To keep units straight, use an E for Earth, an M for Mars, and a J for Jupiter.

$$1.5 \; \cancel{T} \times \frac{2,000 \; \cancel{lb \, (E)}}{1 \; \cancel{T}} \times \frac{0.377 \; lb \, (M)}{1 \; \cancel{lb \, (E)}} = 1,131 \; lb \, (M)$$

$$1.5 \; \cancel{T} \times \frac{2,000 \; \cancel{lb \, (E)}}{1 \; \cancel{T}} \times \frac{2.364 \; lb \, (J)}{1 \; \cancel{lb \, (E)}} = 7,092 \; lb \, (J)$$

The object weighs 1,131 pounds on Mars and 7,092 pounds on Jupiter, so it weighs $7,092 - 1,131 = 5,961$ more pounds on Jupiter, choice (C).

32. B   Difficulty: Medium

Category: Statistics and Probability

Getting to the Answer: Think about what the question is asking. The real estate agent wants to figure out which measure of the data (mean, mode, range, or median) is going to be most useful. The *mode* of a data set tells you the data point, or in this case the age range, that occurs most often. If the real estate agent markets to the age range that represents the mode, choice (B), she will be marketing to the largest group of clients possible.

33. A   Difficulty: Medium

Category: Statistics and Probability

Getting to the Answer: The key words in the question are *average* and *consistently*. The average is the mean and the consistency relates to how spread out each branch's profits are. First, find the branch with the lowest mean profit. This is Branch A, so you can eliminate choices C and D. Standard deviation is a measure of spread, so now focus on that row only. Think about what standard deviation tells you. A lower standard deviation indicates that profits are less spread out and therefore more consistent. Likewise, a higher standard deviation indicates that profits are more spread out and therefore less consistent. Notice the opposite nature of this relationship: lower standard deviation = more consistent; higher standard deviation = less consistent. Choice (A) is correct because the standard deviation of Branch C's quarterly profits is the *highest*, which means it performed the *least* consistently.

34. C   Difficulty: Medium

Category: Scatterplots

Getting to the Answer: The average rate of change of a function over a given interval, from a to b, compares the change in the outputs, $f(b) - f(a)$, to the change in the inputs, $b - a$. In other words, it is the slope of the line that connects the endpoints of the interval, so you can use the slope formula. Look at the quadratic model, not the data points, to find that the endpoints of the given interval, week 2 to week 8, are (2, 280) and (8, 400). The average rate of change is $\frac{400 - 280}{8 - 2} = \frac{120}{6} = 20$, so the dolphin's weight increased by about 20 pounds per week, choice (C).

35. D   Difficulty: Medium

Category: Statistics and Probability

Getting to the Answer: The two variables are certainly correlated—as one goes up, the other goes up. A linear regression model would fit the data fairly well, so you can eliminate C. The spending is graphed on the x-axis, so it is the independent variable and therefore does not depend on the GDP, graphed on the y-axis, so you can eliminate B as well. The data does show that as spending on students increases, so does the GDP, but this is simply correlation, not causation. Without additional data, no statements can be made about whether spending more on students is the reason for the increased GDP, so (D) is correct.

36.   C   Difficulty: Medium

Category: Statistics and Probability

Getting to the Answer: The key word in the answer choices is "consistently," which relates to how spread out a player's scores are. Standard deviation, not mean, is a measure of spread, so you can eliminate choice A right away. A lower standard deviation indicates scores that are less spread out and therefore more consistent. Likewise, a higher standard deviation indicates scores that are more spread out and therefore less consistent. Notice the opposite nature of this relationship: lower standard deviation = more consistent; higher standard deviation = less consistent. Choice (C) is correct because the standard deviation of Mae's scores is the lowest, which means she bowled the most consistently.

37.   D   Difficulty: Hard

Category: Rates, Ratios, Proportions, and Percentages

Getting to the Answer: Read the question, organizing important information as you go. You need to find the ratio of mini muffins to jumbo muffins. You're given two ratios: mini to regular and regular to jumbo. Both of the given ratios contain regular muffin size units, but the regular amounts (2 and 5) are not identical. To directly compare them, find a common multiple (10). Multiply each ratio by the factor that will make the number of regular muffins equal to 10.

Mini to regular: (5:2) × (5:5) = 25:10

Regular to jumbo: (5:4) × (2:2) = 10:8

Now that the number of regular muffins is the same in both ratios (10), you can merge the two ratios to compare mini to jumbo directly: 25:10:8. So, the proper ratio of mini muffins to jumbo muffins is 25:8, which is choice (D).

38.   A   Difficulty: Medium

Category: Scatterplots

Getting to the Answer: Determine whether the predicted change in the interest rate is a common difference (linear function) or a common ratio (exponential function), or if it changes direction (quadratic or polynomial function).

The company predicts that every six months, the Federal Reserve will *raise* rates by 0.25 percentage points. Interest rates are already expressed as percentages, so raising the rates by 0.25 percentage points means *adding* a quarter of a percent every six months. It does not mean it will increase *by* 0.25% every six months. The function therefore involves a common difference, so the best model would be a linear function, which is (A).

39.   D   Difficulty: Hard

Category: Scatterplots

Getting to the Answer: A line that "represents the trend of the data" is another way of saying line of best fit. The trend of the data is clearly linear because the path of the dots does not turn around or curve, so draw a line of best fit on the graph. Remember, about half of the points should be above the line and half below.

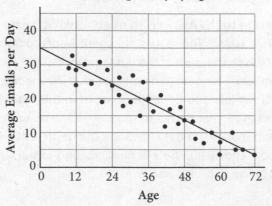

Emails per Day by Age

If you draw your line of best fit all the way to the y-axis, you'll save yourself a step by simply looking at the scatterplot to find the y-intercept. For this graph, it's about 35. This means you can eliminate choices B and C. Next, find the approximate slope using two points that lie on (or very close to) the line. You can use the y-intercept, (0, 35), as one of them to save time and estimate the second, such as (72, 4). Use the slope formula to find the slope:

$$m = \frac{y_2 - y_1}{x_2 - x_1} = \frac{4 - 35}{72 - 0} = \frac{-31}{72} \approx -0.43$$

The equation that has the closest slope and y-intercept is choice (D). (Note that if you choose different points, your line may have a slightly different slope or y-intercept, but the answer choices will be far enough apart that you should be able to determine which is the best fit to the data.)

40. D   Difficulty: Hard

Category: Rates, Ratios, Proportions, and Percentages

Getting to the Answer: The key to answering this question is translating from English into math. Start by assigning a variable to what you're looking for. Let m be the number of months the customer has subscribed to the service. The first month costs a dollars and the remaining months ($m - 1$) are charged at a rate of b dollars per month. So, the total charge for the subscription so far is $a + b(m - 1)$. Set this equal to the amount the customer has paid and solve for m. Note that you're not going to get a nice numerical answer, because the question doesn't give you the actual rates.

$$a + b(m - 1) = 108.60$$
$$a + bm - b = 108.60$$
$$bm = 108.60 - a + b$$
$$m = \frac{108.60 - a + b}{b}$$

The expression for m matches the one in choice (D).

41. A   Difficulty: Hard

Category: Statistics and Probability

Getting to the Answer: Some data sets have a *head*, where many data points are clustered in one area, and one or two *tails*, where the number of data points slowly decreases to 0. Examining the tail will help you describe the shape of the data set. A data set is *skewed* in the direction of its longest tail. The graph in this question has its tail on the right side, so the data is skewed to the right. When data is skewed to the right, the mean is greater than the median because the mean is more sensitive to the higher data values in the tail than is the median, so choice (A) is correct. If you're not sure about the mean/median part, read the rest of the answer choices—none of them describes the data as skewed to the right, so you can eliminate all of them.

42. C   Difficulty: Hard

Category: Rates, Ratios, Proportions, and Percentages

Getting to the Answer: Draw a chart or diagram detailing the various price reductions for each 30 days.

Date	% of Most Recent Price	Resulting Price
Jan. 15	100 − 25% = 75%	$1,500 × 0.75 = $1,125
Feb. 15	100 − 10% = 90%	$1,125 × 0.9 = $1,012.50
Mar. 15	100 − 10% = 90%	$1,012.50 × 0.9 = $911.25

You can stop here because the refrigerator was sold on April 2, which is not 30 days after March 15. The final selling price was $911.25, choice (C).

43. D   Difficulty: Hard

Category: Scatterplots

Getting to the Answer: Make sure you read the axis labels, the question, and the answer choices carefully. The vertical axis is labeled in feet, while the horizontal axis is labeled in yards. The answer choices are given in feet, so you'll need to convert the yards to feet.

The question asks for the difference between the horizontal and vertical distances the cannonball travels. You have a parabola-shaped graph, so sketch in a quadratic model, making sure to extend it past the last point all the way back to the *x*-axis.

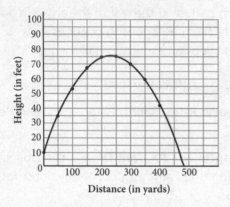

Horizontally the cannonball starts at 0 yards and travels to about 485 yards, or $485 \times 3 = 1{,}455$ feet. Vertical travel is a bit more involved. According to the graph, the cannonball's peak height is about 75 feet, but it started at 10 vertical feet (*not* 0), making the net upward distance traveled 65 feet. Subtract to find the difference, $1{,}455 - 65 = 1{,}390$ feet, which is choice (D).

Note: Don't worry if you didn't draw the model exactly right or if you didn't get the exact same answer. The choices should be far enough apart that you'll still know which one is correct.

44. D   Difficulty: Hard

Category: Rates, Ratios, Proportions, and Percentages

Getting to the Answer: Draw a chart or diagram detailing the various price reductions for each two weeks.

Length of Time on Market	% of Most Recent Price	Resulting Price
List Price	—	$200,000.00
After 2 weeks	100% − 5% = 95%	$190,000.00
After 4 weeks	100% − 5% = 95%	$180,500.00
After 6 weeks	100% − 3% = 97%	$175,085.00
After 8 weeks	100% − 3% = 97%	$169,832.45

You can stop here because the item was sold after 9 weeks and the next price reduction would have been at 10 weeks, so the selling price was $169,832.45, which is choice (D).

45. B   Difficulty: Hard

Category: Statistics and Probability

Getting to the Answer: When a question involves reading data from a graph, it is sometimes better to skip an answer choice if it involves long calculations. Skim the answer choices for this question—A involves finding two averages, each of which is composed of 7 data values. Skip this choice for now. Start with (B). Be careful—you are not looking for places where the line segments are increasing. The *y*-axis already represents the change in prices, so you are simply counting the number of positive values for the imports (5) and for the exports (4). There are more for the imports, so choice (B) is correct and you don't need to check any of the other statements. Move on to the next question.

46. A **Difficulty:** Hard

Category: Rates, Ratios, Proportions, and Percentages

Getting to the Answer: Don't let all the technical words in this question overwhelm you. Solve it step-by-step, examining the units as you go. Notice that some of the numbers in the answer choices are just 1 apart, so think carefully before selecting your answer. *Step 1*: Determine the number of megabytes the computer can upload in 1 weekend (48 hours):

$$\frac{5.25 \text{ megabytes}}{1 \text{ sec}} \times \frac{60 \text{ sec}}{1 \text{ min}} \times \frac{60 \text{ min}}{1 \text{ hr}} \times 48 \text{ hr}$$
$$= 907{,}200 \text{ megabytes}$$

Step 2: Convert this amount to gigabytes (because the information about the scans is given in gigabytes, not megabytes):

$$907{,}200 \text{ megabytes} \times \frac{1 \text{ gigabyte}}{1{,}000 \text{ megabytes}}$$
$$= 907.2 \text{ gigabytes}$$

Step 3: Each client file is about 2.5 gigabytes in size, so divide this number by 2.5 to determine how many client files the computer can upload to the remote server: $907.2 \div 2.5 = 362.88$ files. Remember, you should round this number down to 362, because the question asks for the maximum number the computer can upload, and it cannot complete the 363rd scan in the time allowed. Choice (A) is correct.

47. D **Difficulty:** Hard

Category: Scatterplots

Getting to the Answer: When a regression model has a correlation coefficient of 1.0, it means that the model exactly fits the data. This tells you that you can use what you know about quadratic functions to answer the question.

The graph of a quadratic function is symmetric with respect to its axis of symmetry. The axis of symmetry passes through the *x*-value of the vertex, which also happens to be where the maximum (or minimum) of the function occurs. The question tells you this

value—it's $x = 25$. Because 35 is $35 - 25 = 10$ units to the right of the axis of symmetry, you know that the *y*-value will be the same as the point that is 10 units to the left of the axis of symmetry. This occurs at $x = 25 - 10 = 15$. Read the *y*-value from the graphing calculator screenshot to find the answer, which is 27. Therefore, choice (D) is correct.

48. C **Difficulty:** Hard

Category: Rates, Ratios, Proportions, and Percentages

Getting to the Answer: You're given two ratios: ethanol to gasoline and methanol to gasoline. Your job is to "merge" them so you can directly compare ethanol to methanol. Both of the given ratios contain gasoline, but the gasoline amounts (4 and 9) are not identical. To directly compare them, find a common multiple (36). Multiply each ratio by the factor that will make the number of parts of gasoline equal to 36 in each:

Ethanol to Gasoline: $(1{:}4) \times (9{:}9) = 9{:}36$

Methanol to Gasoline: $(1{:}9) \times (4{:}4) = 4{:}36$

Now that the number of parts of gasoline needed is the same in both ratios, you can merge the two ratios to compare ethanol to methanol directly: 9:36:4. So the proper ratio of ethanol to methanol is 9:4, which is choice (C).

49. D **Difficulty:** Hard

Category: Rates, Ratios, Proportions, and Percentages

Getting to the Answer: You need to find the ratio of lionfish to seahorses. You're given two ratios: eels to lionfish and eels to seahorses.

Both of the given ratios contain eels, but the eel amounts (5 and 2) are not identical. To directly compare them, find a common multiple (10). Multiply each ratio by the factor that will make the number of eels equal to 10:

Eels to Lionfish: $(5{:}2) \times (2{:}2) = 10{:}4$

Eels to Seahorses: $(2{:}3) \times (5{:}5) = 10{:}15$

Now that the number of eels needed is the same in both ratios, you can merge the two ratios to compare lionfish to seahorses directly: 4:10:15. So the proper ratio of lionfish to seahorses is 4:15, which is choice (D).

50. C   Difficulty: Hard

Category: Statistics and Probability

Getting to the Answer: You don't necessarily need to calculate each of the statistics given in the answer choices, but you do need to consider how removing the indicated data value will impact each one. To save some time, start with the statistics that are easier to calculate, such as range and median. The range of a data set is the difference between the largest data value and the smallest data value. With the outlier (30) included, the range is $30 - 7 = 23$; when it is removed, it becomes $19 - 7 = 12$ (reflecting a change of 12).

The question tells you that there are 20 lightning flashes in the sample, so the median is the average of the 10th and the 11th term (13 and 14) prior to removing the outlier, which is 13.5. Once the outlier is removed and 19 terms remain, the new median is the 10th term, 13. Therefore, there is only a slight change of 0.5 when the outlier is removed, so you can eliminate both B and D (because you've just found that the changes in the range and median are not the same).

The mean will also change slightly once the outlier is removed, but there is no need to calculate the change. Because only a single value out of 20 is being removed (and because it is not an outrageously different value than the others), this change will not be as great as the one seen for the range. Choice (C) must therefore be correct.

51. 25   Difficulty: Medium

Category: Rates, Ratios, Proportions, and Percentages

Getting to the Answer: The key to answering this question is reading carefully—the word "exactly" is very important because it tells you that there cannot be a portion of a patient, so you are looking for the smallest whole number of which 48% is also a whole number. Every percent can be written as a number over 100 (because *per cent* means *per hundred*), so start by writing 48% as a fraction and reducing it: $\frac{48}{100} = \frac{12}{25}$. The denominator of this fraction (25) gives the least possible number of patients who could have participated in the trial because it is the first number that will cancel when multiplied by the fraction.

52. 540   Difficulty: Medium

Category: Rates, Ratios, Proportions, and Percentages

Getting to the Answer: Break the questions into steps. First, find how long it took the employee to collect samples from one house, and then use that amount to find how long it should take the employee to collect samples from all of the houses.

The employee *started* the 1st house at 9:00 and the 6th house at 10:00, so it took him 1 hour, or 60 minutes, to collect samples from 5 houses. This gives a unit rate of $60 \div 5 = 12$ minutes per house. Multiply the unit rate by the number of houses in the subdivision (45) to get a total of $12 \times 45 = 540$ minutes to collect samples from all the houses.

53. 3.4   Difficulty: Medium

Category: Statistics and Probability

Getting to the Answer: The test average is the same as the mean of the data. The *mean* is the sum of all the values divided by the number of values. Break the question into short steps to keep your calculations organized. Before gridding in your answer, make sure you answered the right question (how much the final test average changes).

Step 1: Find the original test average:

$$\frac{86 + 92 + 81 + 64 + 83}{5} = \frac{406}{5} = 81.2$$

Step 2: Find the average of the tests after replacing the lowest score (64) with the next to lowest score (81):

$$\frac{86 + 92 + 81 + 81 + 83}{5} = \frac{423}{5} = 84.6$$

Step 3: Subtract the original average from the new average: $84.6 - 81.2 = 3.4$.

54. 76.5   Difficulty: Medium

Category: Rates, Ratios, Proportions, and Percentages

Getting to the Answer: This question is tricky. The interest (after being rounded down) is added to the account at the end of each year. The next year, the new, higher amount is the amount that will earn interest.

Start by multiplying the principal by the interest rate: $1,500 \times 0.01 = 15$. Now, add this amount back to the principal: $1,500 + 15 = 1,515$.

This is the amount that will earn interest in the next year. Repeat this process for 4 more years. Multiply the principal by the interest rate, round the interest down to the nearest cent, and then add it to the principal to use for the next year's calculation.

> *Year two*:
> $1,515 \times 0.01 = 15.15$
> $1,515 + 15.15 = 1,530.15$
> *Year three*:
> $1,530.15 \times 0.01 = 15.3015 \rightarrow 15.30$
> $1,530.15 + 15.30 = 1,545.45$
> *Year four*:
> $1,545.45 \times 0.01 = 15.4545 \rightarrow 15.45$
> $1,545.45 + 15.45 = 1,560.90$
> *Year five*:
> $1,560.90 \times 0.01 = 15.609 \rightarrow 15.60$
> $1,560.90 + 15.60 = 1,576.50$

Over five years, the account earned $1,576.50 - 1,500 = 76.50 in interest. Enter this as 76.5.

Be careful here—you might be tempted to use the exponential function $f(5) = 1,500(1.01)^5$ to arrive at the answer more quickly. However, the question specifically states that the interest is rounded down to the nearest whole cent each year, which changes the answer by just a couple of cents.

55. 380   Difficulty: Medium

Category: Rates, Ratios, Proportions, and Percents

Getting to the Answer: You can use the formula Percent $\times$ whole $=$ part to solve this question, but you will first need to think conceptually about what the question is asking. The question is asking for the Dow value *before* the 19.5% decrease to 306. This means that 306 represents $100 - 19.5 = 80.5\%$ of what the stock market was at its record high. Fill these amounts into the equation and solve for the original whole, the record high Dow value.

$$0.805 \times w = 306$$

$$w = \frac{306}{0.805}$$

$$w = 380.124$$

Rounded to the nearest whole point, the record high was approximately 380 points.

56. 25   Difficulty: Hard

Category: Rates, Ratios, Proportions, and Percents

Getting to the Answer: Percent change is given by the ratio $\frac{\text{amount of change}}{\text{original amount}}$. To find the total percent change, you'll need to work your way through each of the days, and then use the ratio. Jot down the Dow value at the end of each day as you go. Do not round until you reach your final answer. First, calculate the value of the Dow at closing on Black Thursday: It opened at 306 and decreased by 2%, which means the value at the end of the day was $100 - 2 = 98\%$ of the starting amount, or $306 \times 0.98 = 299.88$. Then, it decreased again on Monday by 13% to close at $100 - 13 = 87\%$ of the opening amount, or $299.88 \times 0.87 = 260.8956$. Finally, it decreased on Tuesday by another 12% to end at $100 - 12 = 88\%$ of the starting amount, or $260.8956 \times 0.88 = 229.588$. Now use the percent change formula to calculate the percent decrease from opening on Black Thursday (306) to closing on Black Tuesday (229.588):

$$\text{Percent decrease} = \frac{306 - 229.588}{306} = \frac{76.412}{306} = 0.2497$$

The Dow had a total percent decrease of approximately 25% between opening on Black Thursday and closing on Black Tuesday.

57. 45.5 **Difficulty:** Medium

Category: Rates, Ratios, Proportions, and Percentages

Getting to the Answer: Use the three-part percent formula, $\text{Percent} = \frac{\text{part}}{\text{whole}} \times 100\%$. You'll need to do some preliminary calculations to find the *whole*.

The *part* of the budget represented by the textbook is $24.99. The total cost of all the supplies (or the *whole*) is:

1 textbook ($24.99) + 5 notebooks (5 × $3.78 = $18.90) + 20 pencils (20 × $0.55 = $11.00) = $54.89.

Now use the formula:

$$\text{Percent} = \frac{24.99}{54.89} \times 100\%$$
$$= 0.45527 \times 100\%$$
$$= 45.527\%$$

Before you grid in your answer, make sure you followed the directions—round to the nearest tenth of a percent and ignore the percent sign, which is 45.5.

58. 100 **Difficulty:** Hard

Category: Rates, Ratios, Proportions, and Percentages

Getting to the Answer: This question contains several steps. Be careful—there are lots of calculations that involve decimals, and you shouldn't round until the very end.

Start with the total cost of the year's supplies: $988.02. After taking inventory, Bridget knows she has used $713.57 worth of supplies, which means she should have $988.02 − $713.57 = $274.45 worth of supplies left. From the previous question, you know that 1 textbook, 5 notebooks, and 20 pencils together cost $54.89, which means Bridget has $274.45 ÷ $54.89 = 5 sets of the initial supplies left. Don't grid in this amount, because you're not finished yet! The question asks for the *number of pencils* left. According to the table, each order (set) contains 20 pencils, so there should be 5 × 20 = 100 pencils left.

59. 1000 **Difficulty:** Medium

Category: Rates, Ratios, Proportions, and Percentages

Getting to the Answer: If the student map is $\frac{1}{4}$ the size of the wall map, then 2.5 inches on the student map would be 2.5 × 4 = 10 inches on the wall map. Now set up a proportion to find the actual distance between the cities using the scale of the wall map:

$$\frac{1}{100} = \frac{10}{x}$$
$$x = 1,000$$

The correct answer is 1000.

60. 8 **Difficulty:** Medium

Category: Scatterplots

Getting to the Answer: Draw the line of best fit so that approximately half the data points fall above the line and half fall below it:

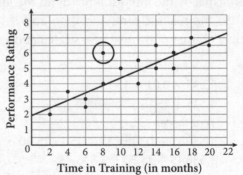

Regional Manager Job Performance

Look for the point that is farthest from the line you drew, which is (8, 6). Because time is plotted along the horizontal axis, this point represents a manager who spent 8 months in the training program.

61. 11.5 **Difficulty:** Medium

Category: Rates, Ratios, Proportions, and Percentages

Getting to the Answer: This question involves a proportion and a unit conversion. You may be tempted to divide the number of steps by the number of feet in Jordan's stride (because the number of steps is already very large), but this isn't correct. To be safe, start by writing a proportion comparing feet and steps.

Let f represent the number of feet Jordan ran. There are 2.5 feet to every 1 of Jordan's steps, and he took 24,288 steps.

$$\frac{2.5 \text{ feet}}{1 \text{ step}} = \frac{f \text{ feet}}{24,288 \text{ steps}}$$
$$f = 2.5(24,288)$$
$$f = 60,720$$

Jordan ran 60,720 feet. Now convert this to miles. There are 5,280 feet in one mile, so divide to get $60,720 \div 5,280 = 11.5$ miles. Don't forget—if the question doesn't tell you to round and the answer will fit in the grid, don't round! Enter the answer as 11.5.

You could also use the factor-label method to answer this question:

$$24,288 \ \text{steps} \times \frac{2.5 \ \text{ft}}{1 \ \text{step}} \times \frac{1 \ \text{mi}}{5,280 \ \text{ft}} = 11.5 \text{ miles}$$

62. 2   Difficulty: Medium

Category: Statistics and Probability

Getting to the Answer: The median of a data set is the middle value when the data are arranged in ascending (or descending) order. If there is an even number of data points, the median is the average of the two middle values. Start by determining how many data points are in the survey (you don't have to add up all the numbers). The question states that the student reporter chose 500 students from each of two schools, which means there are 1,000 data points. This is an even number, so the median is the average of the 500th and 501st data points (the last number in the first half of the data and the first number in the second half of the data). Arrange the data points presented in the table in numerical order (grouped by numbers of video games). There are $100 + 130 = 230$ students with 0 video games. The next $120 + 120 = 240$ students have 1 video game, bringing the total so far to 470. The next $90 + 100 = 190$ students have 2 video games. You don't need to go any further because you can already see that both the 500th and 501st data points must be 2, which makes the median 2.

63. 0.52   Difficulty: Medium

Category: Statistics and Probability

Getting to the Answer: The probability that an event will occur is the number of desired outcomes (number of available cars that have a rating of at least 25 mpg) divided by the number of total possible outcomes (total number of cars). "At least" means that much or greater, so find the number of cars represented by the two bars to the right of 25 in the histogram: $20 + 6 = 26$ cars. Now find the total number of available cars: $8 + 16 + 20 + 6 = 50$. Finally, divide to find the indicated probability: $\frac{26}{50} = 0.52$.

64. .608   Difficulty: Medium

Category: Statistics and Probability

Getting to the Answer: The categories to which the daycare center plans to send an invitation are limited to the 3- and 4-bedroom dwellings (because those are the ones that already received the flyer), so focus on those two columns. The two categories with the most houses are Townhouses/3-bedroom and Single-Family/4-bedroom, with a total of $42 + 34 = 76$ dwellings. There are sixty-one 3-bedroom dwellings and sixty-four 4-bedroom dwellings, so there are $61 + 64 = 125$ total dwellings in the development that have 3 or more bedrooms. So, the probability of randomly selecting one from the two specified groups is $\frac{76}{125} = 0.608$. Grid in .608.

65. 33   Difficulty: Medium

Category: Rates, Ratios, Proportions, and Percentages

Getting to the Answer: Questions that involve distance, rate, and time can almost always be solved using the formula Distance = rate × time. Use the speed, or rate, of the first car (64 mph) and its distance from the destination (144 mi) to determine how long it traveled. You don't know the time, so call it t.

$$\text{Distance} = \text{rate} \times \text{time}$$
$$144 = 64t$$
$$2.25 = t$$

This means it took 2.25 hours for the first car to arrive. You need the number of minutes, so multiply 2.25 by 60 to get $60 \times 2.25 = 135$ minutes. Now determine how long it took the second car. It started its drive at 2:18 PM and arrived at 4:00 PM, so it took 1 hour and 42 minutes, or 102 minutes. This means that the first car had been traveling for $135 - 102 = 33$ minutes before the second car started its drive.

66. 220   Difficulty: Hard

Category: Rates, Ratios, Proportions, and Percentages

Getting to the Answer: To get started, you'll need to find the distance for each part of the third car's trip—the question only tells you the total distance (25 miles). Then, use the formula Distance = rate × time to find how long the car traveled at 15 mph and then how long it traveled at 30 mph.

First part of trip: (60% of the drive)

$$0.6 \times 25 \text{ mi} = 15 \text{ mi}$$
$$15 = 15t$$
$$1 = t$$

So the first part of the trip took 1 hour. Then the car did not move for 20 minutes due to the accident.

Last part of trip: (40% of the drive remained)

$$0.4 \times 25 \text{ mi} = 10 \text{ mi}$$
$$10 = 30t$$
$$\frac{10}{30} = t$$
$$t = \frac{1}{3}$$

So the last part of the trip took one-third of an hour, or 20 minutes. This means it took the third car a total of 1 hour and 40 minutes to arrive at the destination. Because the car arrived at 4:00 PM, it must have left at 2:20 PM. Enter the answer as 220.

67. 3.89   Difficulty: Medium

Category: Rates, Ratios, Proportions, and Percentages

Getting to the Answer: Calculate the discount for each person. Make sure you answer the right question. The question asks about the *savings*, not about

what each person pays, so this time, you *should* multiply by the discount amounts (either 20% or 5%) to save time. Calculate Sharon's military discount first: $\$16.25 \times 0.2 = \$3.25$ saved. Now, Damien's discount for participating in the clothing drive: $\$12.80 \times 0.05 = \$0.64$ saved. Add the two amounts to find that together they saved a total of $\$3.25 + \$0.64 = \$3.89$.

68. $\frac{1}{16}$ Difficulty: Medium

Category: Statistics and Probability

Getting to the Answer: The probability that the same event (the employee has been there longer than 3 years) will occur 4 times can be found by finding the probability that the event will occur once and then multiplying it by itself 4 times. First, find the probability that if an employee is chosen at random, it will be one who has been with the company for longer than 3 years. The total number of employees who participated in the study is $38 + 30 + 15 + 19 + 54 + 48 = 204$. The total number of both females and males who have been with the company longer (greater) than 3 years is $54 + 48 = 102$. Therefore, the probability of choosing one employee who has been with the company longer than 3 years is: $\frac{102}{204} = \frac{1}{2}$. This means the probability that all 4 employees would have been with the company longer than 3 years is $\frac{1}{2} \times \frac{1}{2} \times \frac{1}{2} \times \frac{1}{2} = \frac{1}{16}$. Grid in $\frac{1}{16}$.

69. 3   Difficulty: Hard

Category: Statistics and Probability

Getting to the Answer: When seven terms are arranged in order, the median, or middle term, is the 4th term. You're told that the median is 9, so the 4th term in the list of integers is 9. You're also told that the mode is 7, so either 2 or 3 of the numbers less than 9 are 7s. Start by assuming that all three numbers are 7s. Because you're looking for the *least possible range*, when you list the numbers greater than 9, keep them as small as possible.

7, 7, 7, 9, 9, 10, 10 (The range is $10 - 7 = 3$.)

7, 7, 7, 9, 10, 10, 11 (The range is $11 - 7 = 4$.)

Now suppose there are only two 7s, which means no other number can be repeated because the question states that 7 is the only mode.

7, 7, 8, 9, 10, 11, 12 (The range is 12 − 7 = 5.)

6, 7, 7, 9, 10, 11, 12 (The range is 12 − 6 = 6.)

Based on the possible arrangements, the least possible range is 3.

70. 10   Difficulty: Medium

Category: Rates, Ratios, Proportions, and Percentages

Getting to the Answer: You don't need to know chemistry to answer this question. All the information you need is in the table. Use the formula $\text{Percent} = \frac{\text{part}}{\text{whole}} \times 100\%$. To use the formula, find the part of the mass represented by the carbon; there is 1 mole of carbon, and it has a mass of 12.011 g. Next, find the whole mass of the mole of chloroform: 1 mole carbon (12.011 g) + 1 mole hydrogen (1.008 g) + 3 moles chlorine (3 × 35.453 = 106.359 g) = 12.011 + 1.008 + 106.359 = 119.378. Now use the formula:

$$\text{Percent} = \frac{12.011}{119.378} \times 100\%$$
$$= 0.10053 \times 100\%$$
$$= 10.053\%$$

Before you grid in your answer, make sure you follow the directions—round to the nearest whole percent, which is 10.

71. 12   Difficulty: Hard

Category: Rates, Ratios, Proportions, and Percentages

Getting to the Answer: Think about the units given in the question and how you can use what you know to find what you need. Start with grams of chloroform; the chemist starts with 1,000 and uses 522.5, so there are 1,000 − 522.5 = 477.5 grams left. From the previous question, you know that 1 mole of chloroform has a mass of 119.378 grams, so there are 477.5 ÷ 119.378 = 3.999, or about 4 moles of chloroform left. Be careful—you're not finished yet. The question asks for the number of moles of *chlorine*, not chloroform. According to the table, each mole of chloroform contains 3 moles of chlorine, so there are 4 × 3 = 12 moles of chlorine left.

72. 252   Difficulty: Medium

Category: Rates, Ratios, Proportions, and Percentages

Getting to the Answer: Break the question into steps. First, find how long it took Daniel to spray one lawn, and then use that amount to find how long it took him to spray all the lawns. According to the figure, he started the first house at 9:00 and the sixth house at 10:00, so it took him 1 hour, or 60 minutes, to spray 5 houses. This gives a unit rate of 60 ÷ 5 = 12 minutes per house. Count the houses in the figure—there are 21. Multiply the unit rate by the number of houses to get 12 × 21 = 252 minutes to spray all the lawns.

73. 4   Difficulty: Hard

Category: Rates, Ratios, Proportions, and Percentages

Getting to the Answer: This part of the question contains several steps. Think about the units given in the question and what you need to convert so that you can get to the answer. The total acreage of all the lawns in the neighborhood is 21 × 0.2 = 4.2 acres. This is equivalent to 4.2 × 43,560 = 182,952 square feet. Each gallon of spray covers 2,500 square feet, so divide to find that Daniel needs 182,952 ÷ 2,500 = 73.1808 gallons to spray all the lawns. The spray rig holds 20 gallons, so Daniel will need to fill it 4 times. After he fills it the fourth time and finishes all the lawns, there will be some spray left over.

74. 84   Difficulty: Hard

Category: Scatterplots

Getting to the Answer: The question asks for the difference between the horizontal and upward vertical distance the t-shirt traveled. Horizontally, the t-shirt started at 0 yards and stopped when its height was once again 0 (when it hit the ground). Use your calculator to find the rightmost x-intercept of the graph; the result is 41.21 yards, or 123.63 feet. (Note that you could also set the equation equal to 0 and solve it algebraically, by expanding the equation and then either completing the square or using the quadratic formula, but this would be very time-consuming.) Calculating the upward vertical distance requires more thought. According to the graph (and the equation), the t-shirt's peak height is 45 feet, but it started at 5 vertical feet (not 0), making the net upward distance traveled 40 feet. Subtract to find the difference: $123.63 - 40 = 83.63$ feet, which, rounded to the nearest whole foot, is 84 feet.

75. 45   Difficulty: Hard

Category: Rates, Ratios, Proportions, and Percentages

Getting to the Answer: Make a chart that represents rate, time, and distance and fill in what you know.

	Rate	Time	Distance
To airport	45 mph	t	d
Back to home	30 mph	$2.5 - t$	d

Now use the formula $d = r \times t$ for both parts of the trip: $d = 45t$ and $d = 30(2.5 - t)$. Because both are equal to d, you can set them equal to each other and solve for t:

$$45t = 30(2.5 - t)$$
$$45t = 75 - 30t$$
$$75t = 75$$
$$t = 1$$

Now plug the value of t back in to solve for d:

$$d = 45t$$
$$d = 45(1)$$
$$d = 45$$

Passport to Advanced Math

PRACTICE QUESTIONS

The following test-like questions provide an opportunity to practice Passport to Advanced Math questions. The calculator icon means you are permitted to use a calculator to solve a question. It does not mean that you *should* use it, however.

1. Which of the following expressions is equal to 0 for some value of a?

   A) $3 + |5 - a|$

   B) $3 + |5 + a|$

   C) $|a - 3| - 5$

   D) $|a + 3| + 5$

2. Plutonium 239 (Pu-239) decays at an annual rate of 10 percent. If the initial amount of Pu-239 is 500 grams, which of the following functions, $A(t)$, models the remaining amount of the substance, in grams, t years later?

   A) $A(t) = 500(0.10)^t$

   B) $A(t) = 500(0.90)^t$

   C) $A(t) = 0.90(500)^t$

   D) $A(t) = 0.10(500)^t$

3. Which of the following are solutions to the quadratic equation $(x - 1)^2 = \frac{4}{9}$?

   A) $x = -\frac{5}{3}, x = \frac{5}{3}$

   B) $x = \frac{1}{3}, x = \frac{5}{3}$

   C) $x = \frac{5}{9}, x = \frac{13}{9}$

   D) $x = 1 \pm \sqrt{\frac{2}{3}}$

4. $$\frac{4x}{x - 7} = \frac{5}{35 - 5x}$$

   If the two expressions above are added, which of the following could be the numerator of the sum?

   A) $5 + 20x$

   B) $20 + 5x$

   C) $4x + 5$

   D) $5 - 20x$

5. How many real values of x satisfy the quadratic equation $9x^2 - 12x + 4 = 0$?

A) 0

B) 1

C) 2

D) 4

6.

$$\frac{12x^2 + 23x + 10}{4x + 5}$$

If $ax + b$ represents the simplified form of the expression above, then what is the value of $a + b$?

A) 2

B) 5

C) 6

D) 8

7. $$\sqrt{0.75} \times \sqrt{0.8}$$

Which of the following has the same value as the expression above?

A) $\frac{3}{5}$

B) $\frac{\sqrt{15}}{5}$

C) $\sqrt[4]{0.6}$

D) $\sqrt{1.55}$

8. Which of the following equations could represent a parabola that has a minimum value of -5 and whose axis of symmetry is the line $x = 1$?

A) $y = (x - 5)^2 + 1$

B) $y = (x + 5)^2 + 1$

C) $y = (x - 1)^2 - 5$

D) $y = (x + 1)^2 - 5$

9. A microbiologist is studying the effects of a new antibiotic on a culture of 20,000 bacteria. When the antibiotic is added to the culture, the number of bacteria is reduced by half every hour. What kind of function best models the number of bacteria remaining in the culture after the antibiotic is added?

A) A linear function

B) A quadratic function

C) A polynomial function

D) An exponential function

10. If $\frac{x - y}{y} = \frac{2}{3}$, which of the following must also be true?

A) $\frac{x}{y} = \frac{5}{3}$

B) $x - 1 = \frac{2}{3}$

C) $\frac{x}{y} + 1 = \frac{5}{3}$

D) $\frac{x + y}{y} = -\frac{2}{3}$

11. Which of the following expressions is equivalent to $\left(27x^6y^{12}\right)^{\frac{1}{3}}$?

A) $3x^2y^4$

B) $9x^2y^4$

C) $\frac{27x^6y^{12}}{3}$

D) $(27x^6y^{12})^{-3}$

12.

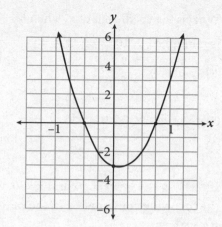

Which of the following could be the factored form of the equation graphed in the figure shown?

A) $y = (2x + 1)(4x - 3)$

B) $y = (x + 2)(x - 3)$

C) $y = \left(x - \dfrac{1}{2}\right)\left(x + \dfrac{3}{4}\right)$

D) $y = \dfrac{1}{2}(x + 1)(x - 3)$

13.

$$\dfrac{1}{\dfrac{1}{x+3} - \dfrac{1}{x+1}}$$

 Which of the following is equivalent to the expression above?

A) $\dfrac{-2}{x^2 + 4x + 3}$

B) $\dfrac{4}{x^2 + 4x + 3}$

C) $\dfrac{x^2 + 4x + 3}{4}$

D) $\dfrac{x^2 + 4x + 3}{-2}$

14. At what value(s) of x do the graphs of $y = -2x + 1$ and $y = 2x^2 + 5x + 4$ intersect?

A) -8 and $\dfrac{1}{2}$

B) -3 and $-\dfrac{1}{2}$

C) -3 and 3

D) $-\dfrac{1}{2}$ and 3

15. Suppose $g(x) = ax^2 + 5$. If $g(1) = 2$, what is the value of a?

A) -6

B) -5

C) -3

D) 6

16.

$$\dfrac{12x^3 y^2 - 9x^2 y}{6x^4 y + 18x^3 y^3}$$

Which of the following is equivalent to the expression above?

A) $\dfrac{4xy - 3}{x + 3y^2}$

B) $\dfrac{3x^2 y - 3xy}{x + 3y^2}$

C) $\dfrac{4xy - 3}{2x^2 + 6xy^2}$

D) $\dfrac{4xy - 9}{2x^2 + 18xy^3}$

17. If the equation of the axis of symmetry of the parabola given by $y = 3x^2 + 12x - 8$ is $x = m$, then what is the value of m?

A) -8

B) -4

C) -2

D) 0

18. If 2 and −3 are both roots of a certain polynomial, then which of the following must be a factor of that polynomial?

    A) $x + 2$

    B) $x - 3$

    C) $x^2 + x - 6$

    D) $x^2 - x - 6$

19. Given the function $g(x) = \frac{2}{3}x + 7$, what domain value corresponds to a range value of 3?

    A) −6

    B) −2

    C) 6

    D) 9

20.

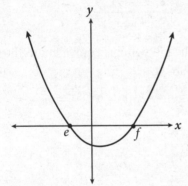

    If e is half as far from the origin as f in the figure above, which of the following could be the factored form of the graph's equation?

    A) $y = \left(x - \frac{1}{2}\right)(x + 1)$

    B) $y = (x - 1)(x + 2)$

    C) $y = (x - 1)(2x + 1)$

    D) $y = \left(x + \frac{1}{2}\right)(2x + 1)$

21. What is the coefficient of x^2 when $6x^2 - \frac{2}{5}x + 1$ is multiplied by $10x + \frac{1}{3}$?

    A) −4

    B) −2

    C) 2

    D) 4

22. If $f(x) = x - 1$, $g(x) = x^3$, and $x \le 0$, which of the following could not be in the range of $f(g(x))$?

    A) −27

    B) −3

    C) −1

    D) 1

23. When $18x^2 + 24x - 10$ is divided by $3x + 5$, there is no remainder. What is the constant in the resulting quotient?

    A) −2

    B) $-\frac{1}{2}$

    C) 0

    D) 2

24.

x	−2	−1	0	1	2	3
g(x)	5	3	1	−1	−3	−5
h(x)	−3	−2	−1	0	1	2

    Several values for the functions $g(x)$ and $h(x)$ are shown in the table. What is the value of $g(h(3))$?

    A) −5

    B) −3

    C) −1

    D) 2

25. Which of the following equations could represent a parabola that has a minimum value of 5 and whose axis of symmetry is the line $x = -3$?

A) $y = (x-3)^2 + 5$

B) $y = (x+3)^2 + 5$

C) $y = (x-5)^2 + 3$

D) $y = (x+5)^2 - 3$

26.
$$\frac{-x^2 - 10x + 24}{2-x}$$

Which of the following is equivalent to the expression above, given that $x \neq 2$?

A) $-x - 12$

B) $x - 12$

C) $12 - x$

D) $x + 12$

27.
$$\begin{cases} x + y = 4 \\ y = x^2 - 2x - 15 \end{cases}$$

If (a, b) and (c, d) represent the solutions to the system of equations above, and $a < c$, then which of the following statements is true?

A) $a > 0$ and $c > 0$

B) $a < 0$ and $c < 0$

C) $a > 0$ and $c < 0$

D) $a < 0$ and $c > 0$

28. If $m = \dfrac{1}{n^{-\frac{1}{4}}}$, where both $m > 0$ and $n > 0$, which of the following gives n in terms of m?

A) $n = m^4$

B) $n = \dfrac{1}{m^4}$

C) $n = \dfrac{1}{\sqrt[4]{m}}$

D) $n = m^{\frac{1}{4}}$

29.

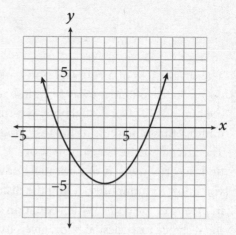

If $f(x) = ax^2 + bx + c$ represents the quadratic function whose graph is shown in the figure above, which of the following statements is not true?

A) $a > 0$

B) $b > 0$

C) $c < 0$

D) All of the statements are true.

30. The x-coordinates of the solutions to a system of equations are -4 and 2. Which of the following could be the system?

A) $\begin{cases} y = 2x - 4 \\ y = (x+4)^2 \end{cases}$

B) $\begin{cases} y = x - 2 \\ y = (x+4)^2 + 2 \end{cases}$

C) $\begin{cases} y = x - 2 \\ y = (x-4)^2 - 16 \end{cases}$

D) $\begin{cases} y = 2x - 4 \\ y = (x+2)^2 - 16 \end{cases}$

31.

$$b = \frac{L}{4\pi d^2}$$

The brightness of a celestial body, like a star, decreases as you move away from it. In contrast, the luminosity of a celestial body is a constant number that represents its intrinsic brightness. The inverse square law, shown above, is used to find the brightness, b, of a celestial body when you know its luminosity, L, and the distance, d, in meters to the body. Which equation shows the distance to a celestial body, given its brightness and luminosity?

A) $d = \frac{1}{2}\sqrt{\frac{L}{\pi b}}$

B) $d = \sqrt{\frac{L}{2\pi b}}$

C) $d = \frac{\sqrt{L}}{2\pi b}$

D) $d = \frac{L}{2\sqrt{\pi b}}$

32.

$$\frac{6x+2}{x+5} - \frac{3x-8}{x+5}$$

Which of the following is equivalent to the expression above?

A) $\frac{3x-6}{x+5}$

B) $\frac{3x+10}{x+5}$

C) $\frac{3x-6}{2x+10}$

D) $\frac{3x+10}{2x+10}$

33. Which of the following is equivalent to the expression $4\sqrt[3]{ab^9}$?

A) $4a^{\frac{1}{3}}b^3$

B) $4a^3b^{\frac{1}{3}}$

C) $4a^3b^{27}$

D) $\frac{4}{a^{\frac{1}{3}}b^3}$

34. Which of the following are roots of the equation $3x^2 - 6x - 5 = 0$?

A) $1 \pm 2\sqrt{6}$

B) $\frac{1 \pm 2\sqrt{2}}{3}$

C) $\frac{3 \pm 2\sqrt{2}}{3}$

D) $\frac{3 \pm 2\sqrt{6}}{3}$

35. Escape velocity is the speed that a traveling object needs to break free of a planet's or moon's gravitational field without additional propulsion (for example, without using fuel). The formula used to calculate escape velocity is $v = \sqrt{\frac{2Gm}{r}}$, where G represents the universal gravitational constant, m is the mass of the body from which the object is escaping, and r is the distance between the object and the body's center of gravity. Which equation represents the value of r in terms of v, G, and m?

A) $r = \frac{2Gm}{v^2}$

B) $r = \frac{4G^2m^2}{v^2}$

C) $r = \sqrt{\frac{2Gm}{v}}$

D) $r = \sqrt{\frac{v}{2Gm}}$

 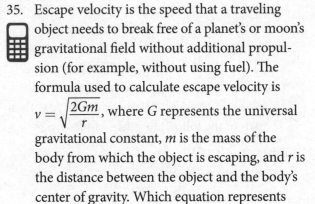

36. If $30x^3 + 45x^2 - 10x$ is divided by $5x$, what is the resulting coefficient of x?

A) 6

B) 9

C) 25

D) 40

37.

	Jan	Feb	Mar	April
Company A	54	146	238	330
Company B	15	30	60	120

Company A and Company B are selling two similar toys. The sales figures for each toy are recorded in the table above. The marketing department at Company A predicts that its monthly sales for this particular toy will continue to be higher than Company B's through the end of the year. Based on the data in the table, and assuming that each company sustains the pattern of growth the data suggests, which company will sell more of this toy in December of that year and how much more?

A) Company A; 182

B) Company A; 978

C) Company B; 29,654

D) Company B; 60,282

38. If $4x^2 + 7x + 1$ is multiplied by $3x + 5$, what is the coefficient of x in the resulting polynomial?

A) 3

B) 12

C) 35

D) 38

39. $$\sqrt{9m^5n^2 - m^4n^2}$$

Which of the following is equivalent to the expression above, given that m and n are positive?

A) $3\sqrt{m}$

B) $3mn$

C) $3n\sqrt{m}$

D) $m^2n\sqrt{9m-1}$

40. $$d(n) = \frac{12}{\sqrt{n^2 - 1}}$$

An engineer wants to minimize the amount that support beams bend when positioned under a horizontal beam that is 12 feet long. She uses the function above, $d(n)$, to represent the distance, in feet, needed between n supports to accomplish this goal. About how much farther apart should consecutive supports be placed when there are 3 supports compared to when there are 4 supports?

A) 1.1 feet

B) 1.6 feet

C) 2.3 feet

D) 3.1 feet

41. Which of the following quadratic equations has no solution?

A) $0 = -3(x+1)(x-8)$

B) $0 = 3(x+1)(x-8)$

C) $0 = -3(x+1)^2 + 8$

D) $0 = 3(x+1)^2 + 8$

42. If $y^2 = b^{-\frac{1}{2}}$, where $y > 0$ and $b > 0$, which of the following gives b in terms of y?

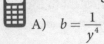

   A) $b = \dfrac{1}{y^4}$

   B) $b = \dfrac{2}{y^2}$

   C) $b = -y$

   D) $b = -y^4$

43. If $f(g(2)) = -1$ and $f(x) = x + 1$, then which of the following could define $g(x)$?

   A) $g(x) = x - 6$

   B) $g(x) = x - 4$

   C) $g(x) = x - 2$

   D) $g(x) = x - 1$

44. Which of the following is a factor of the polynomial $15x^4 + 107x^3 + 193x^2 + 17x - 12$?

   A) $3x - 5$

   B) $3x - 1$

   C) $3x + 1$

   D) $3x + 5$

45. Which of the following expressions is equal to $\dfrac{z^{570} - z^{480}}{2z^{30}}$?

   A) $\dfrac{z^{540} - z^{450}}{2}$

   B) $\dfrac{z^{60}}{2}$

   C) z^{30}

   D) $\dfrac{z^{19} - z^{16}}{2}$

46. An even function is defined as one for which $f(-x) = f(x)$ for all values of x. Which of the following is *not* an even function?

   A) $g(x) = x^2 + 1$

   B) $h(x) = 3x^2 + 2$

   C) $p(x) = 4x^2 - 5$

   D) $q(x) = 4x^2 + 2x - 8$

47.

Which of the following piecewise functions could have been used to generate the graph above?

   A) $g(x) = \begin{cases} -\dfrac{3}{2}x - 4, & \text{if } x < 0 \\ \sqrt{x} - 1, & \text{if } x \geq 0 \end{cases}$

   B) $g(x) = \begin{cases} -\dfrac{3}{2}x - 4, & \text{if } x < 0 \\ \sqrt{x-1}, & \text{if } x \geq 0 \end{cases}$

   C) $g(x) = \begin{cases} -\dfrac{3}{2}x - 4, & \text{if } x < 0 \\ \sqrt{x} + 1, & \text{if } x > 0 \end{cases}$

   D) $g(x) = \begin{cases} -\dfrac{2}{3}x - 4, & \text{if } x < 0 \\ \sqrt{x} + 1, & \text{if } x \geq 0 \end{cases}$

48.
$$\frac{1}{x} + \frac{4}{x} = \frac{1}{72}$$

In order to create safe drinking water, cities and towns use water treatment facilities to remove contaminants from surface water and groundwater. Suppose a town has a treatment plant but decides to build a second, more efficient facility. The new treatment plant can filter the water in the reservoir four times as quickly as the older facility. Working together, the two facilities can filter all the water in the reservoir in 72 hours. The equation above represents the scenario. Which of the following describes what the term $\frac{1}{x}$ represents?

A) The portion of the water the older treatment plant can filter in 1 hour

B) The time it takes the older treatment plant to filter the water in the reservoir

C) The time it takes the older treatment plant to filter $\frac{1}{72}$ of the water in the reservoir

D) The portion of the water the new treatment plant can filter in 4 hours

49. If $x^2 - 4x + 3 = (x - a)^2 + c$, then what is the value of c?

A) -3

B) -1

C) 2

D) 4

50. Which of the following is equivalent to the expression $\left| \dfrac{x^{\frac{1}{2}}}{x^{-2}} \right|^2$?

A) x^2

B) $\left(\dfrac{x^2}{x} \right)^{\frac{1}{2}}$

C) $\left| \dfrac{(x^2)(x^{\frac{1}{3}})}{x^4} \right|^3$

D) $\left(\dfrac{(x^3)(x^4)}{x^{-3}} \right)^{\frac{1}{2}}$

51.

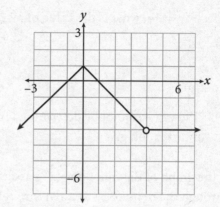

Which of the following piecewise functions could have been used to generate the graph above?

A) $g(x) = \begin{cases} -|x|, & \text{if } x \le 4 \\ -3, & \text{if } x > 4 \end{cases}$

B) $g(x) = \begin{cases} -|x|, & \text{if } x < 4 \\ x - 3, & \text{if } x > 4 \end{cases}$

C) $g(x) = \begin{cases} -|x| + 1, & \text{if } x < 4 \\ -3x, & \text{if } x > 4 \end{cases}$

D) $g(x) = \begin{cases} -|x| + 1, & \text{if } x < 4 \\ -3, & \text{if } x > 4 \end{cases}$

52.

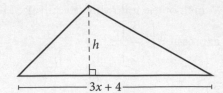

The area of the triangle shown above is given by the expression $3x^2 - 5x - 12$. Which of the following expressions is equivalent to h?

A) $x - 3$

B) $2x - 6$

C) $4x - 6$

D) $4x - 12$

53. If $2x - y = 14$, what is the value of $\dfrac{16^x}{4^y}$?

A) 4^2

B) 4^{14}

C) 14^{14}

D) The value cannot be determined from the information given.

54. If the graph of the function $g(x)$ passes through the point $(8, -3)$, then through which point does the graph of $-g(x - 4) - 6$ pass?

A) $(-12, -9)$

B) $(-12, -3)$

C) $(4, -3)$

D) $(12, -3)$

55. Which of the following is equivalent to $(a + b + 5)(a + b - 5)$?

A) $a^2 + b^2 - 25$

B) $(a + b)^2 - 25$

C) $a^2 + 2ab + b^2 - 25$

D) $(a + b)^2 - 10(a + b) - 25$

56. If $\left(\sqrt{x}\sqrt{y}\right)^4 = 8y^2$, such that x and y are nonzero real numbers, then x could be which of the following?

A) -8

B) $\dfrac{1}{8}$

C) $\sqrt[4]{8}$

D) $\sqrt{8}$

57. The graph of $f(x)$ passes through the point $(5, 1)$. Through which point does the graph of $-f(x + 3) - 2$ pass?

A) $(-2, -1)$

B) $(2, -3)$

C) $(2, 1)$

D) $(8, -3)$

58. What is the value of $3^{90} \times 27^{90} \div \left(\dfrac{1}{9}\right)^{30}$?

A) 9^{60}

B) 9^{120}

C) 9^{150}

D) 9^{210}

59. Given that $f(x) = ax^2 + bx + c$, if $f(0) = -1$, $f(1) = 3$, and $f(2) = 11$, then which of the following is $f(x)$?

A) $-2x^2 + 6x - 1$

B) $-x^2 + 5x - 1$

C) $x^2 + 3x - 1$

D) $2x^2 + 2x - 1$

60. A projectile is any moving object that is thrown near the Earth's surface. The path of the projectile is called the trajectory and can be modeled by a quadratic equation, assuming the only force acting on the motion is gravity (no friction). If a projectile is launched from a platform 8 feet above the ground with an initial velocity of 64 feet per second, then its trajectory can be modeled by the equation $h = -16t^2 + 64t + 8$, where h represents the height of the projectile t seconds after it was launched. Based on this model, what is the maximum height in feet that the projectile will reach?

A) 72

B) 80

C) 92

D) 108

61. Which of the following best describes the solutions to the rational equation
$\dfrac{3}{x-2} - \dfrac{12}{x^2-4} = 1$?

A) No solution

B) Two valid solutions

C) Two extraneous solutions

D) One valid solution and one extraneous solution

62. If $A = 3x^2 - 4x + 1$ and $A + 3B = 6x^2 - x + 10$, then which expression represents B?

A) $x^2 + x + 3$

B) $x^2 + 3x + 9$

C) $3x^2 - 5x + 9$

D) $3x^2 + 3x + 9$

63.

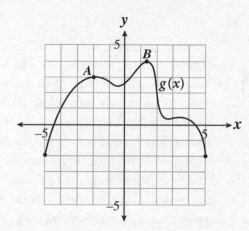

The graph of $g(x)$ is shown in the figure above. If $h(x) = -g(x) + 1$, which of the following statements is true?

A) The range of $h(x)$ is $-3 \le y \le 3$.

B) The minimum value of $h(x)$ is -4.

C) The coordinates of point A on the function $h(x)$ are $(2, 4)$.

D) The graph of $h(x)$ is increasing between $x = -5$ and $x = -2$.

64. $$\sqrt{2} \times \sqrt[4]{2}$$

Which of the following is equivalent to the product given above?

A) $\sqrt[4]{8}$

B) $\sqrt[6]{2}$

C) $\sqrt[8]{2}$

D) $\sqrt[8]{4}$

65. A company determines that the cost of producing n of a certain item can be modeled using the equation $C = 0.02n^2 - 80n + 20{,}000$. Producing how many units, n, would minimize the company's cost for this item?

A) 500

B) 1,000

C) 2,000

D) 4,000

66.

$$b = \frac{L}{4\pi d^2}$$

 The brightness of a celestial body, like a star, decreases as you move away from it. In contrast, the luminosity of a celestial body is a constant number that represents its intrinsic brightness. The inverse square law, shown above, is used to find the brightness, b, of a celestial body when you know its luminosity, L, and the distance, d, in meters to the body. Which equation shows the distance to a celestial body, given its brightness and luminosity?

A) $d = \frac{1}{2}\sqrt{\frac{L}{\pi b}}$

B) $d = \sqrt{\frac{L}{2\pi b}}$

C) $d = \frac{\sqrt{L}}{2\pi b}$

D) $d = \frac{L}{2\sqrt{\pi b}}$

67. Which of the following is equivalent to the expression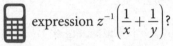

A) $\frac{xy}{z}$

B) $\frac{x + y}{z}$

C) $\frac{1}{xyz}$

D) $\frac{x + y}{xyz}$

68. Given that a, b, and c are all positive integers such that $ac > \frac{b^2}{4}$, how many times does the graph of the equation $y = ax^2 + bx + c$ cross the x-axis?

A) 0

B) 1

C) 2

D) There is not enough information to determine how many times the graph crosses the x-axis.

69. The expression $\frac{6x + 2}{2x - 1}$ is equivalent to which 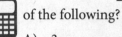 of the following?

A) 3

B) $3x - 1$

C) $3 + \frac{5}{2x - 1}$

D) $3 - \frac{1}{2x - 1}$

70. If the graph of a function $g(x)$ passes through the point $(2, 4)$, and $h(x)$ is defined as $h(x) = -g(x + 4) + 3$, through which point does the graph of $h(x)$ pass?

A) $(-2, -1)$

B) $(-2, 7)$

C) $(6, -1)$

D) $(6, 7)$

71. If the graph of the equation $y = ax^2 + bx + c$ passes through the points $(0, 2)$, $(-6, -7)$, and $(8, -14)$, what is the value of $a + b + c$?

A) -19

B) -2

C) 1.75

D) 2.25

72. Which of the following is NOT a factor of the polynomial $x^4 - 3x^3 - 11x^2 + 3x + 10$?

   A) $x - 5$

   B) $x - 2$

   C) $x - 1$

   D) $x + 1$

73. Given the equation $y = -3(x - 5)^2 + 8$, which of the following statements is not true?

   A) The y-intercept is $(0, 8)$.

   B) The axis of symmetry is $x = 5$.

   C) The vertex is $(5, 8)$.

   D) The parabola opens downward.

74. If $g(x) = 4x - 1$ and $g(h(6)) = -\frac{1}{3}$, then $h(x)$ could be which of the following?

   A) $-\dfrac{x}{18}$

   B) $\dfrac{1}{x}$

   C) $\dfrac{2}{x}$

   D) $2x$

75. What value of x satisfies the equation $\frac{4}{3}\sqrt{2x+5} - 2 = \frac{1}{3}$?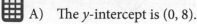

   A) $-\dfrac{31}{8}$

   B) $-\dfrac{31}{32}$

   C) $\dfrac{1}{8}$

   D) $\dfrac{29}{8}$

76. If $y = ax^2 + 18$, where a is a constant, and the graph of y passes through the point $(2, 14)$, what is the y-coordinate of the point on the graph that has an x-coordinate of -2?

77. Laura and Donnie are researching mortgage options for a home purchase. They plan to apply for a 30-year $300,000 loan with a 3.375% annual interest rate, which they will pay off in monthly installments. They can calculate their monthly payment (m) using the formula $m = \dfrac{Pr}{1 - (1 + r)^{-N}}$, where P is the initial principal balance, r is the monthly interest rate expressed as a decimal, and N is the number of monthly payments that will be made over the life of the mortgage. How much will Laura and Donnie pay in mortgage payments over a six-month period? Round your answer to the nearest dollar.

78. Given the function $f(x) = \frac{2}{3}x - 5$, what input value corresponds to an output of 3?

79. What is the remainder when $x^3 + 12$ is divided by $x + 2$?

80.

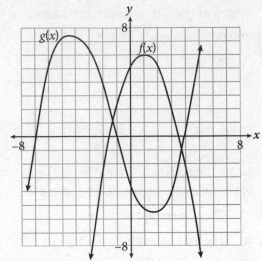

The graph above shows a quadratic function $f(x)$ and a cubic function $g(x)$. Based on the graph, what is the value of $(f - g)(3)$, assuming all integer values?

81. Some doctors base the dosage of a drug to be given to a patient on the patient's body surface area (*BSA*). The most commonly used formula for calculating *BSA* is $BSA = \sqrt{\dfrac{wh}{3{,}600}}$, where w is the patient's weight (in kilograms), h is the patient's height (in centimeters), and *BSA* is measured in square meters. How tall (in centimeters) is a patient who weighs 150 kilograms and has a *BSA* of $2\sqrt{2}\ m^2$?

82. If m and n are positive integers where n is 2 less than three times m, and the product of m and n is 176, what is the smaller of the two integers?

83. If $\dfrac{5x + 8}{2x + 4} - \dfrac{ax + b}{2x + 4} = 1$, then what is the product of ab?

84.

x	p(x)
−2	3
0	−3
2	−5
4	−3
6	3
8	13

The table above shows several points that lie on the graph of quadratic function $p(x)$. Based on the data in the table, what is $p(-4)$?

85. Marcia has two window air-conditioning units, one in each bedroom of her townhouse. Both bedrooms are upstairs and can be closed off from the rest of the townhouse by shutting a door at the top of the stairs. The first AC unit, an older model, can lower the temperature of the 260-square foot guest bedroom by 15 degrees Fahrenheit in 3 hours and 15 minutes. The second, a new energy-efficient model, can lower the temperature of the 300-square foot master bedroom by 15 degrees Fahrenheit in 2.5 hours. If Marcia closes the door at the top of the stairs, opens the bedroom doors, and lets both air conditioners work together to cool the two bedrooms, how many hours should it take to lower the temperature of both rooms by 15 degrees Fahrenheit? Do not round your answer.

86.
$$\frac{3x^{\frac{3}{2}} \times \left(16x^2\right)^3}{8x^{-\frac{1}{2}}}$$

What is the exponent on x when the expression above is written in simplest form?

87. In economics, the law of demand states that as the price of a commodity rises, the demand for that commodity goes down. A company determines that the monthly demand for a certain item that it sells can be modeled by the function $q(p) = -2p + 34$, where q represents the quantity sold in hundreds and p represents the selling price in dollars. It costs $7 to produce this item. How much more per month in profits can the company expect to earn by selling the item at $12 instead of $10? (Profit = sales − costs)

88. The area of a rectangle is equal to the product of its length and width. Suppose a rectangle has an area of $x^4 + 8x^3 + 9x^2 - 6x$, and its shorter side has length $x^2 + 2x$. If $x > 1$, for what value of x will one side of the rectangle be 25 units longer than the other side?

90.
$$\frac{\sqrt{x} \cdot x^{\frac{5}{4}} \cdot x^2}{\sqrt[4]{x^3}}$$

If the expression above is combined into a single power of x with a positive exponent, what is that exponent?

89. If $12 + \dfrac{3\sqrt{x-5}}{2} = 18$, then what is the value of x?

91.
$$\frac{b \times b^{\frac{1}{3}} \times \sqrt[5]{b}}{\sqrt[3]{b^4}}$$

If the expression above is written in the form b^n, what is the value of n?

92. An exponential function is given in the form $f(x) = a \cdot b^x$. If $f(0) = 3$ and $f(1) = 15$, what is the value of $f(-2)$?

93. If $(2^{32})^{(2^{32})} = 2^{(2^x)}$, what is the value of x?

94. After a surface has been cleaned, bacteria begin to regrow. Because bacteria reproduce in all directions, the area covered is usually in the shape of a circle. The diameter of the circle in millimeters can give scientists an idea of how long the bacteria have been growing. For a certain kind of bacteria, the equation $d = 0.015 \times \sqrt{h - 24}$ can be used to find the number of hours, $h \geq 24$, that the bacteria have been growing. If the diameter of a circle of these bacteria is 0.12 millimeters, how many hours have the bacteria been growing?

95. If $y = ax^2 + bx + c$ passes through the points $(-3, 10)$, $(0, 1)$, and $(2, 15)$, what is the value of $a + b + c$?

96. If $\dfrac{x^{a^2 - 4a}}{x^{12}} = x^{20}$ and $a > 0$, then what is the value of a?

97.

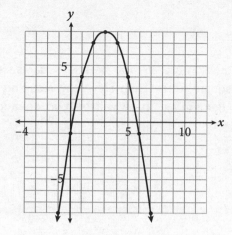

If the equation of the parabola shown in the graph is written in standard quadratic form, $y = ax^2 + bx + c$, and $a = -1$, then what is the value of b?

98. The graph of $f(x) = |x|$ is translated down 5 units, to the left 1 unit, and then reflected over the x-axis. If the resulting graph represents $g(x)$, then what is the value of $g(-2)$?

99. $$\dfrac{\sqrt{x} \cdot x^{\frac{5}{6}} \cdot x}{\sqrt[3]{x}}$$

If x^n is the simplified form of the expression above, what is the value of n?

100. Given that $11x - 2y = -4$ and $x^2 = y + 1$, what is the value of y, assuming $y \geq 0$?

ANSWERS AND EXPLANATIONS

CHAPTER 13

1. C   Difficulty: Medium

Category: Exponents

Getting to the Answer: Think about this question relative to how the absolute value of a number behaves. The expression in choice (C), $|a - 3| - 5$, equals 0 when $|a - 3| = 5$. This statement is true when $a = -2$ and when $a = 8$. None of the other given expressions can equal 0 because the absolute value of any quantity is a nonnegative number, which, when added to either 3 (in choices A and B) or 5 (in choice D) yields a positive number, not 0. Choice (C) is correct.

2. B   Difficulty: Medium

Category: Functions

Getting to the Answer: When an amount (of a substance, population, etc.) increases or decreases (decays) by a common ratio (which is often given as a percent), the appropriate function is an exponential function. Exponential growth and decay can be modeled by a function that takes the form $A(t) = ab^t$, where a is the starting amount, b is the growth or decay rate, and t is time (usually in years). For example, if $b = 1.05$, then the amount *increases* by 5% each year; if $b = 0.95$, then the amount *decreases* by 5% each year. In this scenario, the initial amount is given as 500 grams, so you can immediately eliminate choices C and D. Because the amount of the substance decreases (decays) by 10 percent each year, the decay rate (b) is $100\% - 10\% = 90\%$, or written as a decimal, 0.90. The function is $A(t) = 500(0.90)^t$, which is choice (B).

3. B   Difficulty: Medium

Category: Quadratics

Getting to the Answer: Taking the square root is the inverse operation of squaring, and both sides of

the equation are already perfect squares, so take their square roots. Then solve the resulting equations. Remember, there will be two equations to solve.

$$(x - 1)^2 = \frac{4}{9}$$

$$\sqrt{(x - 1)^2} = \sqrt{\frac{4}{9}}$$

$$x - 1 = \pm\frac{\sqrt{4}}{\sqrt{9}}$$

$$x = 1 \pm \frac{2}{3}$$

Now, simplify each equation: $x = 1 + \frac{2}{3} = \frac{3}{3} + \frac{2}{3} = \frac{5}{3}$ and $x = 1 - \frac{2}{3} = \frac{3}{3} - \frac{2}{3} = \frac{1}{3}$. Choice (B) is correct.

4. D   Difficulty: Medium

Category: Exponents

Getting to the Answer: To add two rational expressions, the denominators must be the same, so you need to find the common denominator, rewrite both expressions using that denominator, and then add the numerators. Start with the more complex denominator: $35 - 5x$ is the same as $5(7 - x)$, which almost looks like the other denominator ($x - 7$). To make it look just right, factor out a -5 instead of a 5. The common denominator is $-5(x - 7)$. This means you need to multiply the first term by $\frac{-5}{-5}$ (which is the same as multiplying by 1). You don't need to multiply the second term by anything.

$$\frac{4x}{x - 7} + \frac{5}{35 - 5x}$$

$$= \frac{-5}{-5}\left(\frac{4x}{x - 7}\right) + \frac{5}{35 - 5x}$$

$$= \frac{-20x}{-5x + 35} + \frac{5}{35 - 5x}$$

$$= \frac{-20x}{35 - 5x} + \frac{5}{35 - 5x}$$

$$= \frac{-20x + 5}{35 - 5x}$$

The numerator (top) of the sum is $-20x + 5$, which is the same as $5 - 20x$, so choice (D) is correct.

5. B   Difficulty: Medium

Category: Quadratics

Getting to the Answer: A quadratic equation can have zero, one, or two real solutions. There are several ways to determine exactly how many. You could graph the equation and see how many times it crosses the x-axis; you could calculate the discriminant (the value under the square root in the quadratic formula); or you could try to factor the equation. Use whichever method gets you to the answer the quickest. Notice that the first and last terms in the equation are perfect squares—this is a hint that it could be a perfect square trinomial, which it is. The factored form of the equation is $(3x - 2)(3x - 2)$. Both factors are the same, so there is only one real value, $x = \frac{2}{3}$, that satisfies the equation, so choice (B) is correct.

6. B   Difficulty: Medium

Category: Exponents

Getting to the Answer: A fraction is the same as division, so you can use polynomial long division to simplify the expression.

$$\require{enclose}\begin{array}{r} 3x+2 \\ 4x+5 \enclose{longdiv}{12x^2 + 23x + 10} \\ \underline{-\left(12x^2 + 15x\right)} \\ 8x + 10 \\ \underline{-(8x + 10)} \\ 0 \end{array}$$

The simplified expression is $3x + 2$, so $a + b = 3 + 2 = 5$, which is choice (B). As an alternate method, you could factor the numerator of the expression, and cancel common factors. Use the denominator as a hint as to what one of the factors of the numerator might be.

$$\frac{12x^2 + 23x + 10}{4x + 5} = \frac{(4x+5)(3x+2)}{(4x+5)} = 3x + 2$$

Use whichever method gets you to the correct answer in the shortest amount of time.

7. B   Difficulty: Medium

Category: Exponents

Getting to the Answer: Chances are that the test makers do not expect you to multiply decimals and then take a square root. Rather, the decimals are likely to have fairly common fraction equivalents that will multiply together nicely. Start with that:

$$\sqrt{0.75} \times \sqrt{0.8} = \sqrt{\frac{3}{4}} \times \sqrt{\frac{4}{5}} = \sqrt{\frac{3}{\cancel{4}} \times \frac{\cancel{4}}{5}} = \sqrt{\frac{3}{5}} = \frac{\sqrt{3}}{\sqrt{5}}$$

Don't forget—you're not allowed to leave a radical in the denominator of a fraction, so you need to rationalize the denominator. To do this, multiply the top and bottom of the fraction by the radical in the bottom. The result is $\frac{\sqrt{3}}{\sqrt{5}} \times \frac{\sqrt{5}}{\sqrt{5}} = \frac{\sqrt{15}}{5}$, which matches choice (B).

8. C   Difficulty: Medium

Category: Quadratics

Getting to the Answer: Imagine the graph of a parabola. The minimum value is the y-coordinate of its vertex, and the axis of symmetry also passes through the vertex. Use these properties to identify the vertex, and then use it to write the equation of the parabola in vertex form, $y = a(x - h)^2 + k$, where (h, k) is the vertex. If the minimum of the parabola is -5, then the vertex of the parabola looks like $(x, -5)$. The axis of symmetry, $x = 1$, tells you the x-coordinate—it's 1. That means (h, k) is $(1, -5)$, and the equation of the parabola looks like $y = a(x - 1)^2 - 5$. The value of a in each of the answer choices is 1, so choice (C) is correct.

9. D   Difficulty: Medium

Category: Functions

Getting to the Answer: Determine whether the change in the number of bacteria is a common difference (linear function) or a common ratio (exponential function) or if the number of bacteria changes direction (quadratic or polynomial function). The question tells you that the number of bacteria is reduced by half every hour after the antibiotic is applied. The microbiologist started with 20,000, so after one hour, there are 10,000 left, or $20{,}000 \times \frac{1}{2}$. After 2 hours, there are 5,000 left, or $20{,}000 \times \frac{1}{2} \times \frac{1}{2}$, and so on. The change in the number of bacteria is a common ratio $\left(\frac{1}{2}\right)$, so the best model is an exponential function, choice (D), of the form $y = a\left(\frac{1}{2}\right)^x$. In this scenario, a is 20,000.

10. A   Difficulty: Medium

Category: Exponents

Getting to the Answer: With a question like this, take a peek at the answer choices and then look for ways to rewrite the equation or expression so that it resembles one or more of the answers. Choices (A) and C each have an $\frac{x}{y}$ term, so start by breaking the fraction on the left into two terms:

$$\frac{x - y}{y} = \frac{2}{3}$$

$$\frac{x}{y} - \frac{y}{y} = \frac{2}{3}$$

Because anything over itself, here $\frac{y}{y}$, is equal to 1, the equation can be rewritten as $\frac{x}{y} - 1 = \frac{2}{3}$. Add 1 to both sides to get:

$$\frac{x}{y} - 1 + 1 = \frac{2}{3} + 1$$

$$\frac{x}{y} = \frac{2}{3} + \frac{3}{3}$$

$$\frac{x}{y} = \frac{5}{3}$$

Choice (A) is correct.

11. A   Difficulty: Medium

Category: Exponents

Getting to the Answer: Write 27 as 3^3 and then use exponent rules. Don't forget—when you raise an

exponent to another exponent, you multiply the exponents.

$$\left(27x^6 y^{12}\right)^{\frac{1}{3}}$$
$$= 3^{\left(3 \times \frac{1}{3}\right)} x^{\left(6 \times \frac{1}{3}\right)} y^{\left(12 \times \frac{1}{3}\right)}$$
$$= 3x^2 y^4$$

Choice (A) is correct.

12. A   Difficulty: Medium

Category: Quadratics

Getting to the Answer: Factored form of a quadratic equation reveals the roots, or x-intercepts, of the equation, so start by identifying the x-intercepts on the graph. An x-intercept is an x-value that corresponds to a y-value of 0. Read the axis labels carefully—each grid-line represents $\frac{1}{4}$, so the x-intercepts of the graph, and therefore the roots of the equation, are $x = -\frac{1}{2}$ and $x = \frac{3}{4}$. This means you are looking for factors that when solved result in these values of x. Choice (A) is correct because $2x + 1$ gives you $x = -\frac{1}{2}$ and $4x - 3$ gives you $x = \frac{3}{4}$.

13. D   Difficulty: Medium

Category: Exponents

Getting to the Answer: Use the structure of the expression to rewrite it. Ignore the big "1 over" part initially. Rewrite the entire denominator as a single fraction, and then take the reciprocal (flip it) to get the final answer. To combine the two terms, find the least common denominator, $(x + 3)(x + 1)$, and write each term as a fraction with that denominator. Then, simplify as needed by using FOIL and combining like terms:

$$\frac{1}{x + 3} - \frac{1}{x + 1} = \left(\frac{x + 1}{x + 1}\right)\left(\frac{1}{x + 3}\right) - \left(\frac{x + 3}{x + 3}\right)\left(\frac{1}{x + 1}\right)$$
$$= \frac{(x + 1) - (x + 3)}{(x + 1)(x + 3)}$$
$$= \frac{-2}{x^2 + 4x + 3}$$

But wait! Choice A is not correct. You still need to take the reciprocal of the simplified expression, which yields $\frac{x^2 + 4x + 3}{-2}$, to perform the final "1 over" part of the original expression, making choice (D) the correct answer. Note that a quick examination of the answer choices tells you to look carefully at the "1 over" part of the original fraction (because the expressions are reciprocals of each other).

14. B   Difficulty: Medium

Category: Quadratics

Getting to the Answer: Although this question asks where the graphs intersect, it is not necessary to actually graph them. The point(s) at which the two graphs intersect are the points where the two equations are equal to each other. So, set the equations equal and use algebra to solve for x. Because the question only asks for the x-values, you don't need to substitute the results back into the equations to solve for y.

$$-2x + 1 = 2x^2 + 5x + 4$$
$$-2x = 2x^2 + 5x + 3$$
$$0 = 2x^2 + 7x + 3$$
$$0 = (2x + 1)(x + 3)$$

Now that the equation is factored, use the Zero-Product Property to solve for x:

$$2x + 1 = 0 \quad \text{and} \quad x + 3 = 0$$
$$2x = -1 \qquad\qquad x = -3$$
$$x = -\frac{1}{2}$$

Choice (B) is correct.

15. C   Difficulty: Medium

Category: Functions

Getting to the Answer: Understanding function notation is the key to answering this question. The notation $g(1)$ means plug 1 into the function for each x. The notation $g(1) = 2$ means that when you plug 1 into the function for each x, the result is 2. Thus, here

$2 = a(1)^2 + 5$. Simplifying gives $2 = a + 5$, or $a = -3$. That's choice (C).

16. C   Difficulty: Medium

Category: Exponents

Getting to the Answer: Factor out the GCF of *both* the numerator and the denominator. Then cancel what you can. In this expression, the GCF is $3x^2y$.

$$\frac{12x^3y^2 - 9x^2y}{6x^4y + 18x^3y^3}$$
$$= \frac{3x^2y(4xy - 3)}{3x^2y(2x^2 + 6xy^2)}$$
$$= \frac{4xy - 3}{2x^2 + 6xy^2}$$

This matches choice (C).

17. C   Difficulty: Medium

Category: Quadratics

Getting to the Answer: The axis of symmetry of a parabola always passes through the x-coordinate of the parabola's vertex. The trick for finding the x-coordinate of the vertex is to calculate $\frac{-b}{2a}$ (the quadratic formula without the radical part). In the equation, $a = 3$ and $b = 12$, so the equation of the axis of symmetry is $x = \frac{(12)}{2(3)} = \frac{-12}{6} = -2$. In the question, the equation is $x = m$, so m must be -2, which makes choice (C) correct.

18. C   Difficulty: Medium

Category: Exponents

Getting to the Answer: If 2 and -3 are roots of the polynomial, then $(x - 2)$ and $(x + 3)$ must be factors of the polynomial. The product of the two factors must also be a factor, so FOIL the factors:

$$(x - 2)(x + 3) = x^2 + 3x - 2x - 6$$
$$= x^2 + x - 6$$

Choice (C) is correct.

19. A **Difficulty:** Medium

Category: Functions

Getting to the Answer: The given range value is an output value, so substitute 3 for $g(x)$ and use inverse operations to solve for x, which is the corresponding domain value.

$$g(x) = \frac{2}{3}x + 7$$

$$3 = \frac{2}{3}x + 7$$

$$-4 = \frac{2}{3}x$$

$$-12 = 2x$$

$$-6 = x$$

Choice (A) is correct. Note that you could also graph the function and find the value of x (the domain value) for which the value of y (the range value) is 3. The point on the graph is $(-6, 3)$.

20. C **Difficulty:** Medium

Category: Quadratics

Getting to the Answer: According to the graph, one x-intercept is to the left of the y-axis, and the other is to the right. This tells you that one value of x is positive, while the other is negative, so you can immediately eliminate D (both factors have the same sign). To choose between the remaining equations, find the x-intercepts by setting each factor equal to 0 and solving for x (mentally if possible). In A, the x-intercepts are $\frac{1}{2}$ and -1, but that would mean that e (the negative intercept) is *twice* as far from the origin as f, not *half* as far, so eliminate choice A. In choice B, the x-intercepts are 1 and -2. Again, that would mean that e is twice as far from the origin as f, not half as far, so eliminate choice B. This means choice (C) must be correct. The x-intercepts are 1 and $-\frac{1}{2}$, which fits the criterion that e is half as far from the origin as f.

21. B **Difficulty:** Medium

Category: Exponents

Getting to the Answer: When multiplying polynomials, carefully multiply each term in the first factor by each term in the second factor. This question doesn't ask for the entire product, so check to make sure you answered the right question (the coefficient of x^2).

$$\left(6x^2 - \frac{2}{5}x + 1\right)\left(10x + \frac{1}{3}\right)$$

$$= 6x^2\left(10x + \frac{1}{3}\right) - \frac{2}{5}x\left(10x + \frac{1}{3}\right) + 1\left(10x + \frac{1}{3}\right)$$

$$= 60x^3 \underline{+ 2x^2 - 4x^2} - \frac{2}{15}x + 10x + \frac{1}{3}$$

The coefficient of x^2 is $2 + (-4) = -2$, which is choice (B).

22. D **Difficulty:** Medium

Category: Functions

Getting to the Answer: Sometimes, a question requires thought rather than brute force. Here, you need to understand that when dealing with compositions, the range of the inner function becomes the domain of the outer function, which in turn produces the range of the composition. In the composition $f(g(x))$, the function $g(x) = x^3$ is the inner function. Because the question states that x is either zero or a negative number ($x \le 0$), every value of x, when substituted into this function, will result in zero or a negative number (because a negative number raised to an odd power is always negative). This means that the largest possible range value for $g(x)$ is 0, and consequently that the largest possible domain value for $f(x)$ is also 0. Substituting 0 for x in $f(x)$ results in -1, which is the largest possible range value for the composition. Because $1 > -1$, it is not in the range of $f(g(x))$, so choice (D) is correct.

K

23. A   Difficulty: Medium

Category: Exponents

Getting to the Answer: While you could use long division or factoring to find the quotient and then identify the constant, it is quicker to simply recognize that when a polynomial with a constant is divided by another polynomial with a constant, and there is no remainder, you can simply divide the constants to find the resulting constant of the quotient. Just be careful to use the correct signs. Because $-10 \div 5 = -2$, the constant in the resulting quotient is -2, which is (A).

24. B   Difficulty: Medium

Category: Functions

Getting to the Answer: The notation $g(h(x))$ indicates a composition of two functions, which can be read "g of h of x." It means that the output when x is substituted in $h(x)$ becomes the input for $g(x)$. First, use the top and bottom rows of the table to find that $h(3)$ is 2. This is your new input. Now, use the top and middle rows of the table to find $g(2)$, which is -3, choice (B).

25. B   Difficulty: Medium

Category: Quadratics

Getting to the Answer: When a quadratic equation is written in the form $y = a(x - h)^2 + k$, the minimum value (or the maximum value if $a < 0$) is given by k, and the axis of symmetry is given by the equation $x = h$. The question states that the minimum of the parabola is 5, so look for an equation where k is 5. You can eliminate C and D because k is 3 in C and -3 in D. The question also states that the axis of symmetry is $x = -3$, so h must be -3. Be careful—this is tricky. The equation in A is not correct because the vertex form of a parabola has a negative before the h, so $(x - 3)$ would produce an axis of symmetry at $x = 3$, not -3. This means choice (B) is correct.

You could also graph each equation in your graphing calculator to see which one matches the criteria

given in the question, but this is likely to use up valuable time on Test Day.

26. D   Difficulty: Medium

Category: Exponents

Getting to the Answer: You could use polynomial long division to answer this question, or you could try to factor the numerator and see if any terms cancel. It is very tricky to factor a quadratic equation with a negative coefficient on x^2, so start by factoring -1 out of both the numerator and the denominator. To factor the resulting quadratic in the numerator, you need to find two numbers whose product is -24 and whose sum is 10. The numbers are -2 and $+12$.

$$\frac{-x^2 - 10x + 24}{2 - x} = \frac{\cancel{-1}(x^2 + 10x - 24)}{\cancel{-1}(x - 2)}$$
$$= \frac{\cancel{(x - 2)}(x + 12)}{\cancel{x - 2}}$$
$$= x + 12$$

This matches choice (D).

27. D   Difficulty: Medium

Category: Quadratics

Getting to the Answer: Take a peek at the answer choices—they are really just describing the sign of the x-coordinates of the solutions. This means you don't need to find the exact values of the solutions. Instead, draw a quick sketch of the system (or graph it in your calculator), and translate < 0 as *negative* and > 0 as *positive*.

The top equation is a line and the bottom equation is a parabola. Write the linear equation in slope-intercept form and the quadratic equation in factored form to make them easier to sketch: $x + y = 4 \rightarrow y = -x + 4$ and $y = x^2 - 2x - 15 \rightarrow (x - 5)(x + 3)$. A quick sketch is all you need—don't waste valuable time labeling things. The line has a y-intercept of 4 and a negative slope, and the parabola opens upward and crosses the x-axis at 5 and −3. The sketch looks like:

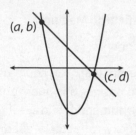

The solutions to the system are the points where the graphs intersect. The question tells you that $a < c$, so (a, b) must be the point on the left and (c, d) is the point on the right. Look at the x-values: a is to the left of the y-axis so it must be negative (or $a < 0$), and c is to the right of the y-axis so it must be positive (or $c > 0$). This means choice (D) is correct.

28. A   Difficulty: Medium

Category: Exponents

Getting to the Answer: When you write an equation in terms of a specific variable, you are simply solving the equation for that variable. To do this, you'll need to use the property that raising a quantity to the one-fourth power is the same as taking its fourth root and that applying a negative exponent to a quantity is the same as writing its reciprocal. Rewrite the equation using these properties, and then solve for n using inverse operations. Note that the inverse of taking a fourth root of a quantity is raising the quantity to the fourth power.

$$m = \frac{1}{n^{-\frac{1}{4}}}$$

$$m = \frac{\sqrt[4]{n}}{1}$$

$$(m)^4 = \left(\sqrt[4]{n}\right)^4$$

$$m^4 = n$$

Choice (A) is correct.

29. B   Difficulty: Medium

Category: Quadratics

Getting to the Answer: Compare each statement to the graph to determine whether it is true, eliminating choices as you go. Remember, you are looking for the statement that is *not* true. The parabola opens upward, so the value of a must be positive, which means you can eliminate choice A because it *is* true (> 0 means positive). The value of b is the tricky one, so skip it for now, and consider C. When written in standard form, the value of c tells you the y-intercept. According to the graph, the y-intercept is below the x-axis and is therefore negative, so $c < 0$ is true. Eliminate choice C. Unfortunately, this means you'll need to consider choice (B). Based on the equation alone, it is not easy to determine whether b is positive or negative, so you'll need to think outside the box. The trick for finding the x-coordinate of the vertex of a parabola is to calculate $\frac{-b}{2a}$ (the quadratic formula without the radical part). In the graph, the x-coordinate of the vertex is 3, so set the formula equal to 3, solve for b, and see what happens.

$$\frac{-b}{2a} = \frac{3}{1}$$

$$-b = 6a$$

$$b = -6a$$

You have already determined that a is positive (because the parabola opens upward), so b must be negative. This means b is less than 0, not greater, making choice (B) correct.

30. D   Difficulty: Medium

Category: Quadratics

Getting to the Answer: The solution to a system of equations is the point(s) where their graphs intersect. You could solve this question algebraically, one system at a time, but this is not time efficient. Instead, graph each pair of equations in your graphing calculator and look for the graphs that intersect at $x = -4$ and $x = 2$. The graphs of the equations in choices A and B don't intersect at all, so you can eliminate them right away. The graphs in choice C intersect, but both points of intersection have a positive x-coordinate. This means choice (D) must be correct. The graph looks like:

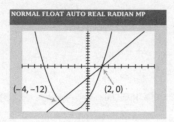

31. A   Difficulty: Medium

Category: Exponents

Getting to the Answer: Focus on the question at the very end—it's just asking you to solve the equation for d. First, cross-multiply to get rid of the denominator. Then, divide both sides of the equation by $4\pi b$ to isolate d^2. Finally, take the square root of both sides to find d.

$$b(4\pi d^2) = L$$
$$\frac{b(4\pi d^2)}{4\pi b} = \frac{L}{4\pi b}$$
$$d^2 = \frac{L}{4\pi b}$$
$$\sqrt{d^2} = \sqrt{\frac{L}{4\pi b}}$$
$$d = \sqrt{\frac{L}{4\pi b}}$$

Unfortunately, this is not one of the answer choices, so you'll need to simplify further. You can take the square root of 4 (it's 2), but be careful—it's in the denominator of the fraction, so it comes out of the square root as $\frac{1}{2}$.

The simplified equation is $d = \frac{1}{2}\sqrt{\frac{L}{\pi b}}$. This matches choice (A).

32. B   Difficulty: Medium

Category: Exponents

Getting to the Answer: The terms in the expression have the same denominator, $x + 5$, so their numerators can be subtracted. Simply combine like terms and keep the denominator the same. Don't forget to distribute the negative to both $3x$ and -8.

$$\frac{6x+2}{x+5} - \frac{3x-8}{x+5} = \frac{6x+2-(3x-8)}{x+5}$$
$$= \frac{6x+2-3x-(-8)}{x+5}$$
$$= \frac{6x-3x+2+8}{x+5}$$
$$= \frac{3x+10}{x+5}$$

Choice (B) is correct.

33. A   Difficulty: Medium

Category: Exponents

Getting to the Answer: Write each factor in the expression in exponential form and use exponent rules to simplify the expression. The number 4 is simply being multiplied by the variables. The power of a under the radical is 1 and the root is 3, so the exponent on a is $\frac{1}{3}$ (remember the saying "power over root"). The power of b is 9 and the root is 3, so the exponent on b is $\frac{9}{3} = 3$ (power over root). This means $4\sqrt[3]{ab^9} = 4 \times a^{\frac{1}{3}}b^{\frac{9}{3}} = 4a^{\frac{1}{3}}b^3$, which matches choice (A).

34. D   Difficulty: Medium

Category: Quadratics

Getting to the Answer: The roots of an equation are the same as its solutions. Take a peek at the answer choices—they contain radicals, which tells you that the equation can't be factored. Instead, either complete the square or solve the equation using the quadratic formula, whichever you are most comfortable with. The equation is already written in the form $y = ax^2 + bx + c$ and the coefficients are fairly small, so using the quadratic formula is probably the quickest method. Jot down the values that you'll need: $a = 3$, $b = -6$, and $c = -5$. Then, substitute these values into the quadratic formula and simplify:

$$x = \frac{-b \pm \sqrt{b^2 - 4ac}}{2a}$$

$$= \frac{-(-6) \pm \sqrt{(-6)^2 - 4(3)(-5)}}{2(3)}$$

$$= \frac{6 \pm \sqrt{36 + 60}}{6}$$

$$= \frac{6 \pm \sqrt{96}}{6}$$

This is not one of the answer choices, so simplify the radical. To do this, look for a perfect square that divides into 96 and take its square root. Then, if possible, cancel any factors that are common to the numerator and the denominator.

$$x = \frac{6 \pm \sqrt{16 \times 6}}{6}$$

$$= \frac{6 \pm 4\sqrt{6}}{6}$$

$$= \frac{\cancel{2}(3 \pm 2\sqrt{6})}{\cancel{2}(3)}$$

$$= \frac{3 \pm 2\sqrt{6}}{3}$$

Choice (D) is correct. Be careful—you can't simplify the answer any further because you cannot divide the square root of 6 by 3.

35. A   Difficulty: Medium

Category: Exponents

Getting to the Answer: Don't spend too much time reading the scientific explanation of the equation. Solve for r using inverse operations. First, square both sides of the equation to remove the radical. Then, multiply both sides by r to get

the r out of the denominator. Finally, divide both sides by v^2.

$$v = \sqrt{\frac{2Gm}{r}}$$

$$v^2 = \frac{2Gm}{r}$$

$$v^2 r = 2Gm$$

$$r = \frac{2Gm}{v^2}$$

This matches choice (A).

36. B   Difficulty: Medium

Category: Exponents

Getting to the Answer: Look closely at the dividend and the divisor. The divisor, $5x$, can be divided into each term in the dividend evenly, which means you don't need to use polynomial long division. Just divide each term by $5x$ and leave the signs the same. You could divide each term mentally, but it may be safer to write each term over $5x$, and then use rules of exponents to simplify.

$$\frac{30x^3}{5x} + \frac{45x^2}{5x} - \frac{10x}{5x} = 6x^2 + 9x - 2$$

The question asks for the coefficient of x, so the correct answer is 9, which is choice (B).

37. C   Difficulty: Medium

Category: Functions

Getting to the Answer: Look for a pattern for the sales of each company. Then apply that pattern to see which one will sell more in the last month of the year. Writing a function that represents each pattern will also help, but you have to be careful that you evaluate the function at the correct input value. Company A's sales can be represented by a linear function because each month the company sells 92 more of the toy than the month before, which is a constant difference. The sales can be represented by the function $f(t) = 92t + 54$, where t is the number of months *after January*. December is 11 months (not 12) after January, so during the last month of the year Company A should sell $f(11) = 92(11) + 54 = 1{,}066$ of the toy. Company B's sales can be represented by an exponential function because the sales are doubling each month, which is a constant ratio (2 for doubling). The function is $g(t) = 15(2)^t$, where t is again the number of months *after January*. In December, Company B should sell $g(11) = 15(2)^{11} = 30{,}720$. This means that in December, Company B should sell $30{,}720 - 1{,}066 = 29{,}654$ more of the toy than Company A. Choice (C) is correct.

38. D   Difficulty: Medium

Category: Exponents

Getting to the Answer: When multiplying polynomials, carefully multiply each term in the first factor by each term in the second factor. This question doesn't ask for the entire product, so check to make sure you answered the right question (the coefficient of x). After performing the initial multiplication, look for the x terms and add their coefficients. To save time, you do not need to simplify the other terms in the expression.

$$\left(4x^2 + 7x + 1\right)(3x + 5)$$
$$= 4x^2(3x + 5) + 7x(3x + 5) + 1(3x + 5)$$
$$= 12x^3 + 20x^2 + 21x^2 + \underline{35x + 3x} + 5$$

The coefficient of x is $35 + 3 = 38$, which is choice (D).

39. D   Difficulty: Medium

Category: Exponents

Getting to the Answer: The GCF of the terms under the radical is $m^4 n^2$. Factor this out and see if you can take the square root of anything:

$$\sqrt{9m^5 n^2 - m^4 n^2} = \sqrt{m^4 n^2 (9m - 1)}$$
$$= m^2 n \sqrt{9m - 1}$$

The result matches choice (D).

40. A   Difficulty: Medium

Category: Functions

Getting to the Answer: Although the given function looks somewhat complicated, this question is fairly straightforward. You need to find the distance between supports when there are 3 of them (by finding $d(3)$), find the distance between supports when there are 4 of them (by finding $d(4)$), and subtract the results.

$$d(3) = \frac{12}{\sqrt{3^2 - 1}}$$
$$= \frac{12}{\sqrt{8}} \approx 4.24$$

$$d(4) = \frac{12}{\sqrt{4^2 - 1}}$$
$$= \frac{12}{\sqrt{15}} \approx 3.10$$

The difference is $4.24 - 3.10 = 1.14$, or about 1.1 feet. Choice (A) is correct.

41. D   Difficulty: Medium

Category: Quadratics

Getting to the Answer: The graph of every quadratic equation is a parabola, which may or may not cross the x-axis, depending on where its vertex is and which way it opens. When an equation has no solution, its graph does not cross the x-axis, so try to envision the graph of each of the answer choices (or you could graph each one in your graphing calculator, but this will probably take longer). Don't forget—if the equation is written in vertex form, $y = a(x - h)^2 + k$, then the vertex is (h, k) and the value of a tells you which way the parabola opens. When a quadratic equation is written in factored form, the factors tell you the x-intercepts, which means choices A and B (which are factored) must cross the x-axis, so eliminate them. Now, imagine the graph of the equation in choice C: The vertex is $(-1, 8)$ and a is negative, so the parabola opens downward and consequently must cross the x-axis. This means choice (D) must be correct. The vertex is also (−1, 8), but *a* is positive, so the graph opens up and does not cross the *x*-axis.

42. A   Difficulty: Hard

Category: Exponents

Getting to the Answer: When a number (or a variable) is raised to a negative exponent, rewrite it as the reciprocal of the number with a positive exponent. You can also write fractional exponents as radicals to make using an inverse operation more recognizable.

To write *b* in terms of *y*, you need to solve for *b*. To do this, you need to eliminate the fractional exponent, which also happens to be negative:

$$y^2 = b^{-\frac{1}{2}} = \frac{1}{b^{\frac{1}{2}}} = \frac{1}{\sqrt{b}}$$

To eliminate the radical (the square root), square both sides of the equation.

$$\left(y^2\right)^2 = \left(\frac{1}{\sqrt{b}}\right)^2$$
$$y^4 = \frac{1}{b}$$

Cross-multiply to get the *b* out of the denominator, and then divide both sides by y^4:

$$by^4 = 1$$
$$b = \frac{1}{y^4}$$

This matches choice (A).

43. B   Difficulty: Medium

Category: Functions

Getting to the Answer: Understanding the language of functions will make questions that seem complicated much more doable. When you know the output of a function (or in this question, a composition of two functions), you can work backward to find the input. Because *g(x)* is the inside function for this composition, its output becomes the input for *f(x)*. Unfortunately, you don't have any information about *g* yet. You do know, however, that *f* of some number, *g(2)*, is −1, so set *f(x)* equal to −1 and solve for *x*:

$$-1 = x + 1$$
$$-2 = x$$

You now know that *f*(−2) = −1. In the equation for the composition, *g*(2) represents *x*, so you also know that *g*(2) must be −2. Your only option now is to use brute force to determine which equation for *g*, when evaluated at 2, results in −2.

Choice A: *g*(2) = 2 − 6 = −4 (not −2), so eliminate.

Choice (B): *g*(2) = 2 − 4 = −2

You don't need to go any further; choice (B) is correct.

You could check your answer by working forward, starting with *g*(2):

$$g(2) = 2 - 4 = -2$$
$$f(g(2)) = f(-2) = -2 + 1 = -1$$

44. C   Difficulty: Hard

Category: Exponents

Getting to the Answer: Factors of polynomials must divide evenly into the polynomial, which means there is no remainder. This is a *long* polynomial, so think *long* division. In polynomial long division, the only time there is no remainder is when the *constant* in the factor divides evenly into the *constant* in the polynomial. This means you can eliminate choices A and D (because 5 does not divide evenly into 12). To decide between choices B and (C), use long division. Start with choice (C) because it has all positive values, which means faster calculations and fewer potential mistakes:

$$3x + 1 \overline{\smash{\big)}\ 15x^4 + 107x^3 + 193x^2 + 17x - 12}$$

with quotient $5x^3 + 34x^2 + 53x - 3$

$$\underline{-(15x^4 + 5x^3)}$$
$$102x^3 + 193x^2 + 17x - 12$$
$$\underline{-(102x^3 + 34x^2)}$$
$$159x^2 + 17x - 12$$
$$\underline{-(159x^2 + 53x)}$$
$$-36x - 12$$
$$\underline{-(-36x - 12)}$$
$$0$$

Good news! You don't have to check choice B because $3x + 1$ is indeed a factor of the polynomial, making choice (C) correct.

45. A   Difficulty: Medium

Category: Exponents

Getting to the Answer: You can't simplify the expression as it's written, so break it into two fractions first. You can then subtract the exponents of the z terms in each fraction. Once finished, combine the two new fractions back into one. The work for these steps is shown here.

$$\frac{z^{570} - z^{480}}{2z^{30}} = \frac{z^{570}}{2z^{30}} - \frac{z^{480}}{2z^{30}}$$
$$= \frac{z^{570-30}}{2} - \frac{z^{480-30}}{2}$$
$$= \frac{z^{540}}{2} - \frac{z^{450}}{2}$$
$$= \frac{z^{540} - z^{450}}{2}$$

Choice (A) is the correct answer.

46. D   Difficulty: Hard

Category: Functions

Getting to the Answer: You could use brute force here and plug x and $-x$ into each function and see which one gives a different result. Or, you could think more concretely: Suppose $x = 2$; then $-x = -2$. Try each of these in the answer choices:

A: $g(2) = 2^2 + 1 = 4 + 1 = 5$ and $g(-2) = (-2)^2 + 1 = 4 + 1 = 5$. These are the same, so eliminate A.

B: $h(2) = 3(2)^2 + 2 = 12 + 2 = 14$ and $g(-2) = 3(-2)^2 + 2 = 12 + 2 = 14$. These are the same, so eliminate B.

C: $p(2) = 4(2)^2 - 5 = 16 - 5 = 11$ and $p(-2) = 4(-2)^2 - 5 = 16 - 5 = 11$. These are the same, so eliminate C.

(D): $q(2) = 4(2)^2 + 2(2) - 8 = 16 + 4 - 8 = 12$ and $q(-2) = 4(-2)^2 + 2(-2) - 8 = 16 - 4 - 8 = 4$. These are NOT the same, so (D) is not an even function.

On a more conceptual level, even functions consist of only even powers of the variable. Constant terms are considered even powers of the variable because they can be written as ax^0, and 0 is an even number. The only function among the answer choices that contains an odd power of x is choice (D). The middle term, $2x$, is 2 times x raised to the first power, and is therefore not an even function.

47. A   Difficulty: Hard

Category: Functions

Getting to the Answer: Graphing piecewise functions can be tricky. Try describing the graph in words first and then find the matching function. Use words like "to the left of" (which translates as *less than*) and "to the right of" (which translates as *greater than*).

First, notice that both pieces of the graph either start or stop at 0, but one has a closed dot and the other has an open dot. This means you can eliminate C right away because the inequality symbol in both equations would lead to open dots on the graph. To choose among the remaining answers, think about parent functions and transformations. To the left of $x = 0$, the graph is a line with a slope of $-\frac{3}{2}$ and a y-intercept of -4, so you can eliminate D because the slope of the line is incorrect. Now, look to the right of $x = 0$—the graph is a square root function that has been moved down 1 unit, so its equation is $y = \sqrt{x} - 1$. This means choice (A) is correct. (The square root portion of C would have been moved to the left 1 unit rather than down 1.)

48. A   Difficulty: Hard

Category: Exponents

Getting to the Answer: Think of the rate given in the question in terms of the constant term you see on the right-hand side of the equation. Working together, the two treatment plants can filter the water in 72 hours. This is equivalent to saying that they can filter $\frac{1}{72}$ of the water in 1 hour. If $\frac{1}{72}$ is the portion of the water the two treatment plants can filter *together*, then each term on the left side of the equation represents the portion that each plant can filter *individually* in 1 hour. Because the new facility is 4 times as fast as the older facility, $\frac{4}{x}$ represents the portion of the water the new plant can filter in 1 hour, and $\frac{1}{x}$ represents the portion of the water the older plant can filter in 1 hour. This matches choice (A).

49. B   Difficulty: Hard

Category: Quadratics

Getting to the Answer: You have two options here: You could complete the square on the left side of the equation and then compare the result to the right side, or you could expand the right side of the equation and set the coefficients of the x terms equal, and then set the constants equal. The second method is shown here.

The coefficient of x in the original equation on the left is -4, so $-2a = -4$, or $a = 2$. The constant on the left is 3, so $2^2 + c = 3$, which gives $c = -1$. That's choice (B).

50. D   Difficulty: Hard

Category: Exponents

Getting to the Answer: For this question, use the following rules of exponents: When you raise a power to a power, you multiply the exponents, and when you divide with exponents, you subtract them. Distribute the 2 outside the parentheses to the exponent in the numerator and in the denominator:

$$\left(\frac{x^{\frac{1}{2}}}{x^{-2}}\right)^2 = \frac{x^{\frac{1}{2}\times 2}}{x^{-2\times 2}} = \frac{x^1}{x^{-4}}$$

Now, subtract the exponents:

$$\frac{x}{x^{-4}} = x^{1-(-4)} = x^{1+4} = x^5$$

Unfortunately, x^5 is not one of the answer choices, so look for an answer choice that is also equivalent to x^5. You can eliminate A right away, and the exponents in B look too small, so start with C, which simplifies to $\frac{x^7}{x^{12}} = \frac{1}{x^5}$ and is therefore not correct. Choice (D) is correct because:

$$\left(\frac{\left(x^3\right)\left(x^4\right)}{x^{-3}}\right)^{\frac{1}{2}} = \left(\frac{x^7}{x^{-3}}\right)^{\frac{1}{2}}$$
$$= \left(x^{7-(-3)}\right)^{\frac{1}{2}}$$
$$= \left(x^{10}\right)^{\frac{1}{2}}$$
$$= x^5$$

51. D   Difficulty: Hard

Category: Functions

Getting to the Answer: Graphing piecewise functions can be tricky. Try describing the graph in words first, and then find the matching function. Use words such as "to the left of" (which translates as *less than*) and "to the right of" (which translates as *greater than*).

First, notice that there is a hole in the graph at $x = 4$. This means you can eliminate A right away because the inequality symbol in the top piece would include the endpoint at 4. To choose between the remaining answers, think about parent functions and transformations. To the left of $x = 4$, the graph is an absolute value function that has been reflected vertically across the x-axis and then shifted up one unit. This means either choice C or (D) must be correct. Now look to the right of $x = 4$: The graph is a horizontal line, which means a line that has a slope of 0. The slope of the line in choice C is negative 3, so it can't be correct. This means choice (D) is correct. (The equation of a horizontal line always looks like $y = b$, or in this case, $g(x) = -3$.)

52. B   Difficulty: Hard

Category: Exponents

Getting to the Answer: The area of a triangle is given by the formula $A = \frac{1}{2}bh$. When you know the area and either of the dimensions, multiply both sides of the formula by 2 (to get rid of the fraction) and then divide by the known dimension to find the other one. First, plug in what you do know. $A = \frac{1}{2}bh$, $A = 3x^2 - 5x - 12$, and $b = 3x + 4$. Thus, $3x^2 - 5x - 12 = \frac{1}{2}(3x + 4)h$. Multiply both sides by 2 and use polynomial long division to solve for h.

$$
\begin{array}{r}
2x - 6 \\
3x + 4 \overline{)6x^2 - 10x - 24} \\
\underline{-(6x^2 + 8x)} \\
-18x - 24 \\
\underline{-(18x - 24)} \\
0
\end{array}
$$

The correct answer is choice (B). Note that you could have stopped as soon as you determined the first term in the quotient ($2x$) because the only answer choice that starts with $2x$ is choice (B).

53. B   Difficulty: Hard

Category: Exponents

Getting to the Answer: Whenever a question gives you one expression (or equation) and asks for another unusual one (rather than the value of one or both of the variables), look for any possible relationship between the two. Also look for relationships between the numbers in the expressions so you can simplify if possible. Here, start by manipulating the expression $\frac{16^x}{4^y}$ so that the numerator and denominator have the same base. This will allow you to combine the exponents. Because 16 is a multiple of 4 (specifically 4×4), you can rewrite 16 as 4^2. Now, simplify the expression using rules of exponents (when you divide powers of the same base, subtract the exponents):

$$\frac{16^x}{4^y} = \frac{\left(4^2\right)^x}{4^y} = \frac{4^{2x}}{4^y} = 4^{2x-y}$$

Now look carefully—the expression in the exponent is the same as the left-hand side of the equation given in the question. You are told that $2x - y = 14$, which means you can replace the new exponent ($2x - y$) with 14, making 4^{14}, or choice (B), the correct answer.

54. D   Difficulty: Hard

Category: Functions

Getting to the Answer: Transformations that are grouped with the x in a function shift the graph horizontally and therefore affect the x-coordinates of points on the graph. Transformations that are not grouped with the x shift the graph vertically and therefore affect the y-coordinates of points on the graph. Remember, horizontal shifts are always backward of what they look like.

Perform each transformation on the coordinates of the point, one at a time, following the same order of operations that you use when simplifying arithmetic expressions. Start with $(x - 4)$. This shifts the graph right 4 units, so add 4 to the x-coordinate of the given point: $(8, -3) \rightarrow (8 + 4, -3) = (12, -3)$. Next, apply the negative in front of g, which is not grouped with the x, so it makes the y-coordinate the opposite of what it was: $(12, -3) \rightarrow (12, 3)$. Finally, the -6 is not grouped with x, so subtract 6 from the y-coordinate: $(12, 3) \rightarrow (12, 3 - 6) = (12, -3)$. Therefore, choice (D) is correct. You could also plot the point on a coordinate plane, perform the transformations (right 4, reflect vertically over the x-axis, and then down 6), and find the resulting point.

55. B   Difficulty: Hard

Category: Quadratics

Getting to the Answer: You don't need to multiply out the trinomial times the trinomial if you recognize that there is a special product here, specifically $(x + y)(x - y)$, which, when multiplied together, produces a difference of squares, $x^2 - y^2$. Group the $a + b$ in each factor, and see where that takes you.

$$(a + b + 5)(a + b - 5) = [(a + b) + 5][(a + b) - 5]$$
$$= (a + b)^2 - 5^2$$
$$= (a + b)^2 - 25$$

This matches choice (B).

56. D   Difficulty: Hard

Category: Exponents

Getting to the Answer: This question looks impossible to solve because there are two variables and only one equation. This is usually a tipoff that one of the variables will disappear once the equation is simplified a bit. Here, part of the given expression is written in radical notation and part is written using exponents, so begin by rewriting everything using exponents. To do this, recall that $\sqrt{x}$ can be written

as $x^{\frac{1}{2}}$. After rewriting the radical numbers, you can simplify using rules of exponents.

$$\left(\sqrt{x}\sqrt{y}\right)^4 = 8y^2$$
$$\left(x^{\frac{1}{2}}y^{\frac{1}{2}}\right)^4 = 8y^2$$
$$x^{\left(\frac{1}{2} \times 4\right)} y^{\left(\frac{1}{2} \times 4\right)} = 8y^2$$
$$x^2 y^2 = 8y^2$$
$$x^2 = 8$$
$$x = \pm\sqrt{8}$$

The positive solution matches choice (D).

57. B   Difficulty: Hard

Category: Functions

Getting to the Answer: Transformations that are grouped with the x in a function shift the graph horizontally and, therefore, affect the x-coordinates of points on the graph. Transformations that are not grouped with the x shift the graph vertically and, therefore, affect the y-coordinates of points on the graph. Remember, horizontal shifts are always backward of what they look like. Start with $(x + 3)$. This shifts the graph left 3, so subtract 3 from the x-coordinate of the given point: $(5, 1) \rightarrow (5 - 3, 1) = (2, 1)$. Next, apply the negative in front of f, which is not grouped with the x, so it makes the y-coordinate negative: $(2, 1) \rightarrow (2, -1)$. Finally, -2 is not grouped with x, so subtract 2 from the y-coordinate: $(2, -1 - 2) \rightarrow (2, -3)$, which is choice (B).

58. D   Difficulty: Hard

Category: Exponents

Getting to the Answer: The numbers in some questions are simply too large to use a calculator (you get an "overflow" error message). Instead, you'll have to rely on rules of exponents. Notice that all of the base numbers have 3 as a factor, so rewrite everything in terms of 3. This will allow you to use the rules of exponents. Because 27 is the cube of 3, you can rewrite 27^{90} as a power of 3.

$$27^{90} = \left(3^3\right)^{90}$$
$$= 3^{3\times90}$$
$$= 3^{270}$$

Now the product should read: $3^{90} \times 3^{270}$, which is equal to $3^{90+270} = 3^{360}$. Repeat this process for the quantity that is being divided:

$$\left(\frac{1}{9}\right)^{30} = \left(\frac{1}{3^2}\right)^{30} = \left(3^{-2}\right)^{30} = 3^{-60}$$

Finally, use rules of exponents one more time to simplify the new expression:

$$\frac{3^{360}}{3^{-60}} = 3^{360+60} = 3^{420}$$

All the answer choices are given as powers of 9, so rewrite your answer as a power of 9:

$$3^{420} = 3^{2\times210} = \left(3^2\right)^{210} = 9^{210}$$

Choice (D) is correct.

59. D   Difficulty: Hard

Category: Functions

Getting to the Answer: To answer a question like this, you need to be willing to plug in values and see where that leads without knowing exactly how to proceed. Each of the given function values provides a bit of information, which you'll have to piece together at some point.

Because $f(0) = -1$, $a(0)^2 + b(0) + c = -1$, which simplifies to $c = -1$. Plug this into the next value you calculate.

Because $f(1) = 3$, $a(1)^2 + b(1) + (-1) = 3$, which simplifies to $a + b = 4$.

Finally, because $f(2) = 11$, $a(2)^2 + b(2) + (-1) = 11$, which simplifies to $4a + 2b = 12$.

You now have a system of equations: $a + b = 4$ and $4a + 2b = 12$. Multiplying the first equation by -2 and adding the result to the second equation gives $(-2a - 2b = -8) + (4a + 2b = 12)$, which simplifies to $2a + 0b = 4$, or $a = 2$. This is actually enough information to answer the question as only one of the choices has a leading coefficient of 2. Choice (D) is correct.

If you want to confirm your choice, you could plug 2 in for a in the equation $a + b = 4$ to get $b = 2$, which also matches choice (D).

60. A   Difficulty: Hard

Category: Quadratics

Getting to the Answer: The quadratic equation is given in standard form, so use the method of completing the square to rewrite the equation in vertex form. Then, read the value of k to find the maximum height of the projectile.

$$h = -16t^2 + 64t + 8$$
$$= -16\left(t^2 - 4t + \underline{\quad}\right) + 8 - \underline{\quad}$$
$$= -16\left(t^2 - 4t + 4\right) + 8 - (-16\times4)$$
$$= -16(t-2)^2 + 8 - (-64)$$
$$= -16(t-2)^2 + 72$$

The vertex is (2, 72), so the maximum height is 72 feet, choice (A).

61. D   Difficulty: Hard

Category: Exponents

Getting to the Answer: Factor the denominator in the second term to find that the common denominator for all three terms is $(x - 2)(x + 2)$. Multiply each term in the equation by the common denominator (in factored form or the original form, whichever is more convenient) to clear the fractions. Then solve the resulting equation for x:

$$(x+2)\left(x^2-4\right)\left(\frac{3}{x-2}\right)-\left(x^2-4\right)\left(\frac{12}{x^2-4}\right)=1\left(x^2-4\right)$$

$$3(x+2)-12=x^2-4$$

$$3x+6-12=x^2-4$$

$$3x-6=x^2-4$$

$$0=x^2-3x+2$$

$$0=(x-1)(x-2)$$

Set each factor equal to 0 to find that the potential solutions are $x=1$ and $x=2$. But wait, these are only *potential* solutions because the original equation was a rational equation. When x is 2, the denominators in both terms on the left side are equal to 0, so 2 is an extraneous solution, which means choice (D) is correct.

62. A   Difficulty: Hard

Category: Exponents

Getting to the Answer: Although you could try each answer choice to see which is correct, this strategy will waste valuable time. Instead, set the equation up as if you are solving for a single variable, B. Substitute the expression given for A into the equation given for $A+3B$, and then solve for B:

$$\boxed{A}+3B=6x^2-x+10$$

$$\boxed{3x^2-4x+1}+3B=6x^2-x+10$$

$$3B=6x^2-x+10-\left(3x^2-4x+1\right)$$

$$3B=6x^2-x+10-3x^2+4x-1$$

$$3B=3x^2+3x+9$$

$$B=\frac{3x^2+3x+9}{3}$$

$$B=x^2+x+3$$

This expression matches choice (A).

63. A   Difficulty: Hard

Category: Functions

Getting to the Answer: Based on the equation, the graph of $h(x)=-g(x)+1$ is a vertical reflection of $g(x)$, over the x-axis, that is then shifted up 1 unit. The graph looks like the dashed line in the following graph:

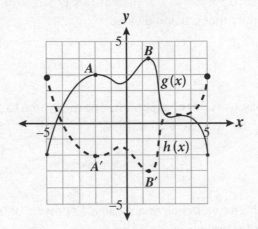

Now, compare the dashed line to each of the answer choices: The range of $h(x)$ is the set of y-values from lowest to highest (based on the dashed line). The lowest point occurs at point B' and has a y-value of -3; the highest value occurs at both ends of the graph and is 3, so the range is $-3\le y\le 3$. This means choice (A) is correct and you can move on to the next question. Don't waste valuable time checking the other answer choices unless you are not sure about the range. (Choice B: The minimum value of $h(x)$ is -3, not -4. Choice C: The coordinates of point A on $h(x)$ are $(-2,-2)$, not $(2,4)$. Choice D: the graph of $h(x)$ is decreasing, not increasing, between $x=-5$ and $x=-2$.)

64. A   Difficulty: Hard

Category: Exponents

Getting to the Answer: It is not possible to add, subtract, multiply, or divide radicals that represent roots of different degrees (such as a square root and a cube root) when they are written in radical form. Instead, you must write the radicals using fraction exponents and then use rules of exponents to combine the terms.

Write each radical using a fraction exponent, and then use the rule $a^x \times a^y = a^{x+y}$ to answer the question.

$$\sqrt{2} \times \sqrt[4]{2} = 2^{\frac{1}{2}} \times 2^{\frac{1}{4}}$$
$$= 2^{\frac{1}{2}+\frac{1}{4}}$$
$$= 2^{\frac{2}{4}+\frac{1}{4}}$$
$$= 2^{\frac{3}{4}}$$

The answers are written as radicals, so convert back to radicals using the saying "power over root." The result is $\sqrt[4]{2^3} = \sqrt[4]{8}$, which is choice (A).

65. C   Difficulty: Hard

Category: Quadratics

Getting to the Answer: Whenever a question involves a quadratic equation and *maximizing* or *minimizing* something, you need to find the vertex (or at least one coordinate of the vertex). Here, n is the independent variable (the x-coordinate if written as ordered pairs), and you're looking for n, so use the equation $x = -\frac{b}{2a}$ (the quadratic formula without the radical part) to find that the minimum occurs at $n = \frac{-(-80)}{2(0.02)} = \frac{80}{0.04} = 2{,}000$. That's choice (C).

66. A   Difficulty: Medium

Category: Exponents

Getting to the Answer: Focus on the question at the very end—it's just asking you to solve the equation for d. First, cross-multiply to get rid of the denominator. Then, divide both sides of the

equation by $4\pi b$ to isolate d^2. Finally, take the square root of both sides to find d.

$$b(4\pi d^2) = L$$
$$\frac{b(4\pi d^2)}{4\pi b} = \frac{L}{4\pi b}$$
$$d^2 = \frac{L}{4\pi b}$$
$$\sqrt{d^2} = \sqrt{\frac{L}{4\pi b}}$$
$$d = \sqrt{\frac{L}{4\pi b}}$$

Unfortunately, this is not one of the answer choices, so you'll need to simplify further. You can take the square root of 4 (it's 2), but be careful—it's in the denominator of the fraction, so it comes out of the square root as $\frac{1}{2}$.

The simplified equation is $d = \frac{1}{2}\sqrt{\frac{L}{\pi b}}$. This matches choice (A).

67. D   Difficulty: Hard

Category: Exponents

Getting to the Answer: Take a peek at the answer choices. Notice that in every one, the xs and ys are combined in some way in the numerator or denominator (or both). Also recall that a quantity raised to a negative power indicates the reciprocal of that quantity. Simplify the expression using the steps below:

$$z^{-1}\left(\frac{1}{x}+\frac{1}{y}\right) = \frac{1}{z}\left[\frac{y}{y}\left(\frac{1}{x}\right)+\frac{x}{x}\left(\frac{1}{y}\right)\right]$$
$$= \frac{1}{z}\left(\frac{y+x}{xy}\right)$$
$$= \frac{x+y}{xyz}$$

This matches choice (D).

68. A **Difficulty:** Hard

Category: Quadratics

Getting to the Answer: The quantity under the radical in the quadratic formula ($b^2 - 4ac$) is called the discriminant because it tells you what kind of solutions to expect. If $b^2 - 4ac = 0$, then the equation has exactly one unique real solution and the graph just touches the x-axis at that value. If $b^2 - 4ac > 0$, then the equation has two real solutions and the graph crosses the x-axis twice. If $b^2 - 4ac < 0$, then the equation has two imaginary solutions (because the square root of a negative number is imaginary) and does not cross the x-axis at all. Now, take a look at the criteria given in the question: $ac > \dfrac{b^2}{4}$.

Notice that there is an ac, a b^2, and a 4, so try to manipulate the inequality to make it look like the discriminant:

$$ac > \frac{b^2}{4}$$
$$\frac{ac}{1} > \frac{b^2}{4}$$
$$4ac > b^2$$
$$0 > b^2 - 4ac$$
$$b^2 - 4ac < 0$$

This means the solutions are imaginary and the graph does not cross the x-axis at all; therefore, choice (A) is correct.

69. C **Difficulty:** Hard

Category: Exponents

Getting to the Answer: This question is actually more difficult than it appears at first. To find the equivalent expression, you need to divide $6x + 2$ by $2x - 1$ because the expression is already as simplified as it can get in its current form (nothing to add, subtract, multiply, or even factor out and cancel). Be careful here—you cannot cancel out the xs in the numerator and denominator because they are each part of a quantity that includes

addition and/or subtraction, so use polynomial long division instead.

$$2x-1\overline{)6x+2} \\ \underline{-(6x-3)} \\ 5$$

Remember, when you have a remainder, place it over the divisor (which, in a fraction, is the denominator). Therefore, the correct answer is $3 + \dfrac{5}{2x - 1}$, which is choice (C).

70. A **Difficulty:** Hard

Category: Functions

Getting to the Answer: Transformations that are grouped with the x in a function shift the graph horizontally and therefore affect the x-coordinates of points on the graph. Transformations that are not grouped with the x shift the graph vertically and therefore affect the y-coordinates of points on the graph. Remember, horizontal shifts are always the opposite of what they look like. When working with multiple transformations, follow the same order of operations as always—parentheses first, then multiply and divide, then add and subtract.

Start with the parentheses: $(x + 4)$. This shifts the graph left 4 units, so subtract 4 from the x-coordinate of the given point: $(2, 4) \rightarrow (2 - 4, 4) = (-2, 4)$. Next, apply the negative in front of g because it represents multiplication. The negative is not grouped with the x, so multiply the y-coordinate by -1 to get $(-2, 4) \rightarrow (-2, -4)$. Finally, the $+3$ is not grouped with x, so add 3 to the y-coordinate: $(-2, -4) \rightarrow (-2, -4 + 3) = (-2, -1)$. Choice (A) is correct.

You could also plot the point on a coordinate plane, perform the transformations (left 4, reflect vertically over the x-axis, and then up 3), to find the new point. The result will be the same.

71. C   Difficulty: Hard

Category: Quadratics

Getting to the Answer: Writing quadratic equations can be tricky and time-consuming. If you know the roots, you can use factors to write the equation. If you don't know the roots, you need to create a system of equations to find the coefficients of the variable terms. You don't know the roots of this equation, so start with the point that has the nicest values (0, 2) and substitute them into the equation, $y = ax^2 + bx + c$, to get $2 = a(0)^2 + b(0) + c$, or $2 = c$. Now your equation looks like $y = ax^2 + bx + 2$. Next, use the other two points to create a system of two equations in two variables.

$(-6, -7) \rightarrow -7 = a(-6)^2 + b(-6) + 2 \rightarrow -9 = 36a - 6b$

$(8, -14) \rightarrow -14 = a(8)^2 + b(8) + 2 \rightarrow -16 = 64a + 8b$

You now have a system of equations to solve. If you multiply the top equation by 4 and the bottom equation by 3, and then add the equations, the b terms will eliminate each other.

$$
\begin{aligned}
4[-9 = 36a - 6b] &\rightarrow -36 = 144a - 24b \\
3[-16 = 64a + 8b] &\rightarrow \underline{-48 = 192a + 24b} \\
&\quad\;\; -84 = 336a \\
&\quad -0.25 = a
\end{aligned}
$$

Now, find b by substituting $a = -0.25$ into either of the original equations. Using the top equation, you get:

$$-9 = 36(-0.25) - 6b$$
$$-9 = -9 - 6b$$
$$0 = 6b$$
$$0 = b$$

The value of $a + b + c$ is $(-0.25) + 0 + 2 = 1.75$, choice (C).

72. B   Difficulty: Hard

Category: Exponents

Getting to the Answer: There are several ways to answer this question. You could use polynomial long division to divide the polynomial by each of the choices to determine which one does *not* give a remainder of 0, or you could use synthetic division if you're familiar with that process. However, the fastest route is to recall that a factor of a polynomial tells you a root of the polynomial, and if you plug that root into the polynomial, the result is 0. The answer choices translate, in order, to roots of 5, 2, 1, and −1. Plug each of these into the polynomial and use your calculator to simplify. Note that you can stop as soon as you find a non-zero remainder, but all the calculations are presented below.

$$(5)^4 - 3(5)^3 - 11(5)^2 + 3(5) + 10 = 0$$
$$(2)^4 - 3(2)^3 - 11(2)^2 + 3(2) + 10 = -36$$
$$(1)^4 - 3(1)^3 - 11(1)^2 + 3(1) + 10 = 0$$
$$(-1)^4 - 3(-1)^3 - 11(-1)^2 + 3(-1) + 10 = 0$$

Based on the calculations, 2 is not a root of the polynomial, so $x - 2$ is not a factor, making choice (B) the correct answer.

73. A   Difficulty: Hard

Category: Quadratics

Getting to the Answer: To answer this question, you need to recall nearly everything you've learned about quadratic graphs. The equation is given in vertex form ($y = a(x - h)^2 + k$), which reveals the vertex (h, k), the direction in which the parabola opens (upward when $a > 0$ and downward when $a < 0$), the axis of symmetry ($x = h$), and the minimum/maximum value of the function (k).

Start by comparing each answer choice to the equation, $y = -3(x - 5)^2 + 8$. The only choice that you cannot immediately compare is choice (A), because vertex form does not readily reveal the y-intercept, so start with choice B. Don't forget, you are looking for the statement that is not true. *Choice B*: The axis of symmetry is given by $x = h$, and h is 5, so this statement is true and therefore not correct. *Choice C*: The vertex is given by (h, k), so the vertex is indeed (5, 8) and this choice is not correct. *Choice D*: The value of a

is −3, which indicates that the parabola opens downward, so this choice is also incorrect. That means choice (A) must be the correct answer. To confirm, you could substitute 0 for x in the equation to find the y-intercept.

$$y = -3(x-5)^2 + 8$$
$$= -3(0-5)^2 + 8$$
$$= -3(-5)^2 + 8$$
$$= -3(25) + 8$$
$$= -75 + 8$$
$$= -67$$

The y-intercept is $(0, -67)$, not $(0, 8)$, so the statement is not true and therefore the correct answer.

74. B   Difficulty: Hard

Category: Functions

Getting to the Answer: You need to work backwards to answer this question. Using the definition of $g(x)$, the statement $g(h(6)) = -\frac{1}{3}$ tells you that $4(h(6)) - 1 = -\frac{1}{3}$. Solve this equation for $h(6)$:

$$4(h(6)) - 1 = -\frac{1}{3} \qquad \text{Add 1 to both sides.}$$
$$4(h(6)) = \frac{2}{3} \qquad \text{Multiply both sides by } \frac{1}{4}.$$
$$h(6) = \frac{2}{12} = \frac{1}{6}$$

Now try each answer choice until you find one for which $h(6) = \frac{1}{6}$.

Choice (B): If $h(x) = \frac{1}{x}$, then $h(6) = \frac{1}{6}$. Choice (B) is correct.

75. B   Difficulty: Hard

Category: Exponents

Getting to the Answer: The equation and the answers are too complicated to efficiently Backsolve, so straightforward algebra is the best

approach to answer this question. You need to isolate the square root, then square both sides of the equation, then solve for the variable. There are a LOT of steps, so take them one at a time.

$$\frac{4}{3}\sqrt{2x+5} - 2 = \frac{1}{3}$$
$$\frac{4}{3}\sqrt{2x+5} = \frac{1}{3} + 2$$
$$\frac{4}{3}\sqrt{2x+5} = \frac{7}{3}$$
$$\frac{3}{4} \cdot \left(\frac{4}{3}\sqrt{2x+5}\right) = \frac{3}{4} \cdot \left(\frac{7}{3}\right)$$
$$\sqrt{2x+5} = \frac{7}{4}$$
$$\left(\sqrt{2x+5}\right)^2 = \left(\frac{7}{4}\right)^2$$
$$2x + 5 = \frac{49}{16}$$
$$2x = \frac{49}{16} - \frac{80}{16}$$
$$2x = -\frac{31}{16}$$
$$x = -\frac{31}{16} \cdot \frac{1}{2} = -\frac{31}{32}$$

This makes choice (B) correct.

76. 14   Difficulty: Medium

Category: Quadratics

Getting to the Answer: You could plug the given point into the equation, solve for a, and then plug −2 into the new equation, but this will take a bit of time (you'll find that $a = -1$).

A quicker way to the correct answer is to recognize that the given equation graphs as a parabola that is shifted vertically (regardless of whether the graph opens up or down). This means the vertex is still on the y-axis and the point on the graph that has an x-coordinate of −2 will have the same y-coordinate as the point on the graph that has an x-coordinate of 2 (due to symmetry). Thus, the correct answer is 14.

77. 7958   Difficulty: Medium

Category: Exponents

Getting to the Answer: The nice thing about this question is that some of the steps have been done for you: You already know your variables and are given an equation that relates them. All you need to do is plug in the appropriate values. You're told that $P = 300,000$, $r = \dfrac{0.03375}{12} = 0.0028125$ (because r is the monthly interest rate, not the annual rate), and $N = 12 \times 30 = 360$. Plug these values into the formula $m = \dfrac{Pr}{1-(1+r)^{-N}}$, and then solve for m as shown below.

$$m = \frac{300000 \times 0.0028125}{1-(1+0.0028125)^{-360}}$$

$$m = \frac{843.75}{1-(1.0028125)^{-360}}$$

$$m = \frac{843.75}{0.6362}$$

$$m = 1,326.2886$$

Don't stop yet and don't round yet! The question asks for the amount paid for the mortgage after six months, so multiply 1,326.2886 by 6 to get 7,957.7318. Round to 7958, and you're done!

Note that if you rounded 1,326.29 to 1,326, your answer would be off. Avoid rounding until you have your final answer!

78. 12   Difficulty: Medium

Category: Functions

Getting to the Answer: For any function $f(x)$, the x is the input value, and the output is the result after plugging in the input and simplifying. The question tells you that the *output* is 3 (not the input), so set the equation equal to 3 and solve for x.

$$3 = \frac{2}{3}x - 5$$

$$8 = \frac{2}{3}x$$

$$3 \times 8 = \not{3} \times \frac{2}{\not{3}}x$$

$$24 = 2x$$

$$12 = x$$

79. 4   Difficulty: Medium

Category: Exponents

Getting to the Answer: To find a remainder, you must use polynomial long division (or synthetic division if you happen to know that nifty technique). Don't forget to set up the dividend with 0 place-holders for all missing terms.

$$
\begin{array}{r}
x^2 - 2x + 4 \\
x+2 \overline{)\ x^3 + 0x^2 + 0x + 12} \\
\underline{-(x^3 + 2x^2)} \\
-2x^2 + 0x \\
\underline{-(-2x^2 - 4x)} \\
4x + 12 \\
\underline{-(4x + 8)} \\
4
\end{array}
$$

The remainder is the number left over at the bottom, which is 4.

80. 6   Difficulty: Medium

Category: Functions

Getting to the Answer: The notation $(f - g)(3)$ means $f(3) - g(3)$. You don't know the equations of the functions, so you'll need to read the values from the graph. Graphically, $f(3)$ means the y-value at $x = 3$ on the graph of f, which is 2. Likewise, $g(3)$ means the y-value at $x = 3$ on the graph of g, which is -4. The difference, $f - g$, is $2 - (-4) = 6$.

81. 192   Difficulty: Medium

Category: Exponents

Getting to the Answer: Before you start substituting values, quickly check that the units given match the units required to use the equation—they do, so proceed. The patient's weight (w) is 150 and the patient's BSA is $2\sqrt{2}$, so the equation becomes $2\sqrt{2} = \sqrt{\dfrac{150h}{3,600}}$. The only variable left in the equation is h, and you are trying to find the patient's height, so you're ready to solve the equation. To do this, square both sides of the equation and then continue using inverse operations. Be careful when you square the left side—you must square both the 2 and the root 2.

$$2\sqrt{2} = \sqrt{\frac{150h}{3,600}}$$

$$\left(2\sqrt{2}\right)^2 = \left(\sqrt{\frac{150h}{3,600}}\right)^2$$

$$2^2\left(\sqrt{2}\right)^2 = \frac{150h}{3,600}$$

$$4(2) = \frac{150h}{3,600}$$

$$28,800 = 150h$$

$$192 = h$$

82. 8   Difficulty: Medium

Category: Quadratics

Getting to the Answer: Start by translating from English into math. You have two statements to translate, so chances are you'll be solving a system of equations. Before you select your answer, make sure you found what the question is asking for (the smaller of the two integers). Translate "n is 2 less than three times m" as $n = 3m - 2$. Translate "the product of m and n is 176" as $mn = 176$. Use substitution to solve the equations simultaneously:

$$n = 3m - 2$$
$$mn = 176$$
$$m(3m - 2) = 176$$
$$3m^2 - 2m - 176 = 0$$
$$(3m + 22)(m - 8) = 0$$

Setting each factor equal to 0 and solving results in $m = -\dfrac{22}{3}$ and $m = 8$. The question states that m and n are positive integers, so $m = 8$. This means $n = 3(8) - 2 = 22$. The smaller of the two integers is 8.

83. 12   Difficulty: Medium

Category: Exponents

Getting to the Answer: You can think logically to answer this question. If the difference of the two expressions is 1, then the final numerator must be equal to the final denominator (so they cancel out). Both denominators are already $2x + 4$, so the final numerator, once the two original numerators are subtracted, must also be $2x + 4$. Thus, the difference of $5x$ and ax must be $2x$, which means a must equal 3. Likewise, the difference of 8 and b must be 4, so b must be 4. The question asks for the product of a and b, so the correct answer is $3(4) = 12$.

Note that you could also combine the two terms on the left side of the equal sign and then cross-multiply to solve the equation. If you opt for this strategy, be sure to distribute the negative sign to both terms in the second numerator.

84. 13   Difficulty: Medium

Category: Quadratics

Getting to the Answer: The question states that the function is quadratic, so use what you know about the graphs of parabolas to answer the question. Notice that the x-values in the table increase by two each time. To find $p(-4)$, you just need to imagine adding one extra row to the top of the table. Now, think about symmetry—you can see from the points in the table that $(2, -5)$ is the vertex of the parabola. The points $(0, -3)$ and $(4, -3)$ are equidistant from the vertex, as are the points $(-2, 3)$ and $(6, 3)$. This means the point whose x-value is -4 should have the same y-value as the last point in the table $(8, 13)$. So, $f(-4) = 13$.

85. 2.8   Difficulty: Hard

Category: Exponents

Getting to the Answer: This is a *work* question, so you'll need to use the formula $W = rt$ or some manipulation of this formula, such as $r = \dfrac{W}{t}$ or $t = \dfrac{W}{r}$. The first unit can cool 260 square feet in 3 hours and 15 minutes, or 3.25 hours. The second unit can cool 300 square feet in 2.5 hours. The question asks how long it would take for both units to cool $260 + 300 = 560$ square feet. Set up a rational expression comparing the square feet (the amount of work) and the corresponding time for each unit and set it equal to the combined square feet and the combined time, which you don't know, so call it h for hours:

Find the unit rates first to make the numbers easier to work with. Then, cross multiply and solve for h:

The question tells you not to round, so enter 2.8 and you're done.

without the coefficients and simplify using the rules of exponents.

$$\frac{3x^{\frac{3}{2}} \cdot \left(16x^2\right)^3}{8x^{-\frac{1}{2}}} \rightarrow \frac{x^{\frac{3}{2}} \cdot \left(x^2\right)^3}{x^{-\frac{1}{2}}}$$

$$= x^{\frac{3}{2} - \left(-\frac{1}{2}\right)} \cdot x^{2 \times 3}$$

$$= x^{\frac{3}{2} + \frac{1}{2}} \cdot x^6$$

$$= x^2 \cdot x^6$$

$$= x^8$$

The exponent on x is 8.

87. 800   Difficulty: Hard

Domain: Functions

Getting to the Answer: Think about this question logically and in terms of function notation. Find the quantity that the company can expect to sell at each price using the demand function. Don't forget that the quantity is given in hundreds. Then, find the total sales, the total costs, and the total profits using multiplication.

Price	$12	$10
Quantity	$q(12) = -2(12) + 34$	$q(10) = -2(10) + 34$
	$= -24 + 34$	$= -20 + 34$
	$= 10$	$= 14$
In hundreds	$10(100) = 1{,}000$	$14(100) = 1{,}400$
Sales	$1{,}000(12) = \$12{,}000$	$1{,}400(10) = \$14{,}000$
Costs	$1{,}000(7) = \$7{,}000$	$1{,}400(7) = \$9{,}800$
Profits	$\$5{,}000$	$\$4{,}200$

The company will earn $\$5{,}000 - \$4{,}200 = \$800$ more per month.

88. 7   Difficulty: Hard

Category: Exponents

Getting to the Answer: The area of a rectangle is found by multiplying its length times its width. If you know the area and one dimension, you can divide to find the missing dimension. Start by dividing $x^4 + 8x^3 + 9x^2 - 6x$ by $x^2 + 2x$ using polynomial long division:

$$
\begin{array}{r}
x^2 + 6x - 3 \\
x^2 + 2x\overline{\smash{\big)}\ x^4 + 8x^3 + 9x^2 - 6x} \\
\underline{-(x^4 + 2x^3)} \\
6x^3 + 9x^2 - 6x \\
\underline{-(6x^3 + 12x^2)} \\
-3x^2 - 6x \\
\underline{-(-3x^2 - 6x)} \\
0
\end{array}
$$

Be careful; the question asks for something less conventional. To determine when the dimensions are 25 units apart, add 25 to the smaller dimension and set that expression equal to the other dimension. Then solve for x.

$$x^2 + 2x + 25 = x^2 + 6x - 3$$
$$-4x = -28$$
$$x = 7$$

The dimensions are 25 units apart when x is 7.

89. 21   Difficulty: Hard

Category: Exponents

Getting to the Answer: Solve this radical equation the same way you would solve any other equation: isolate the variable using inverse operations.

$$12 + \frac{3\sqrt{x-5}}{2} = 18 \qquad \text{Subtract 12.}$$
$$\frac{3\sqrt{x-5}}{2} = 6 \qquad \text{Multiply by 2.}$$
$$3\sqrt{x-5} = 12 \qquad \text{Divide by 3.}$$
$$\sqrt{x-5} = 4 \qquad \text{Square both sides.}$$
$$x - 5 = 16 \qquad \text{Add 5.}$$
$$x = 21$$

The correct answer is 21. This is a Grid-in question, so if you have time it wouldn't hurt to check your answer by plugging 21 back into the original equation.

90. 3   Difficulty: Hard

Category: Exponents

Getting to the Answer: You need to use rules of exponents to simplify the expression. Before you can do that, you must rewrite the radicals as fraction exponents. Use the phrase "power over root" to help you convert the radicals:

$$\sqrt{x} = \sqrt[\text{root}\rightarrow 2]{x^{1\leftarrow\text{power}}} = x^{\frac{1}{2}} \text{ and } \sqrt[\text{root}\rightarrow 4]{x^{3\leftarrow\text{power}}} = x^{\frac{3}{4}}.$$

Then use rules of exponents to simplify the expression. Add the exponents of the factors that are being multiplied and subtract the exponent of the factor that is being divided:

$$\frac{\sqrt{x} \cdot x^{\frac{5}{4}} \cdot x^2}{\sqrt[4]{x^3}} = \frac{x^{\frac{1}{2}} \cdot x^{\frac{5}{4}} \cdot x^{\frac{2}{1}}}{x^{\frac{3}{4}}}$$
$$= x^{\frac{1}{2} + \frac{5}{4} + \frac{2}{1} - \frac{3}{4}} = x^{\frac{2}{4} + \frac{5}{4} + \frac{8}{4} - \frac{3}{4}} = x^{\frac{12}{4}} = x^3$$

The exponent of the simplified expression is 3.

91. 1/5 or 0.2   Difficulty: Hard

Category: Exponents

Getting to the Answer: Rewrite the radicals using fractional exponents so you can use rules of exponents to combine them. Then, add the exponents of the factors that are being multiplied and subtract the exponent of the factor that is being divided. Make sure your fraction is completely simplified:

$$\frac{b \times b^{\frac{1}{3}} \times \sqrt[5]{b}}{\sqrt[3]{b^4}} = \frac{b^{\frac{1}{1}} \times b^{\frac{1}{3}} \times b^{\frac{1}{5}}}{b^{\frac{4}{3}}}$$
$$= b^{\frac{1}{1} + \frac{1}{3} + \frac{1}{5} - \frac{4}{3}} = b^{\frac{15}{15} + \frac{5}{15} + \frac{3}{15} - \frac{20}{15}}$$
$$= b^{\frac{3}{15}} = b^{\frac{1}{5}}$$

The question states that n is the power of b, so the correct answer is 1/5 or 0.2.

92. 3/25 or .12   Difficulty: Hard

Category: Functions

Getting to the Answer: When a question involving a function provides one or more ordered pairs, substitute them into the function to see what information you can glean. Start with $x = 0$ because doing so often results in the elimination of a variable.

$$f(x) = a \cdot b^x$$
$$f(0) = a \cdot b^0$$
$$3 = a \cdot b^0$$
$$3 = a \cdot 1$$
$$3 = a$$

Now you know the value of a, so the equation looks like $f(x) = 3 \cdot b^x$. Substitute the second pair of values into the new equation:

$$f(x) = 3 \cdot b^x$$
$$f(1) = 3 \cdot b^1$$
$$15 = 3 \cdot b^1$$
$$15 = 3b$$
$$5 = b$$

The exponential function is $f(x) = 3 \cdot 5^x$. The final step is to find the value being asked for, $f(-2)$. Substitute -2 for x and simplify:

$$f(-2) = 3 \cdot 5^{-2} = \frac{3}{5^2} = \frac{3}{25}$$

Grid this in as 3/25 or 0.12.

93. 37   Difficulty: Hard

Category: Exponents

Getting to the Answer: Although this question is in the calculator portion of the test, you get an overflow error if you try to use your calculator. This is because the numbers are simply too large. You'll need to rely on the rules of exponents to answer this question. When a power is raised to a power, multiply the exponents. You want to be able to add the exponents later, so the bases need to be the same, and you'll need to recognize that 32 is the same as 2 raised to the 5th power.

$$\left(2^{32}\right)^{\left(2^{32}\right)}$$
$$= 2^{\left(32 \times 2^{32}\right)}$$
$$= 2^{\left(2^5 \times 2^{32}\right)}$$

Now that the two bases in the exponent are the same, you can add their exponents.

$$= 2^{\left(2^{5+32}\right)}$$
$$= 2^{\left(2^{37}\right)}$$

Therefore, $x = 37$.

94. 88   Difficulty: Hard

Category: Exponents

Getting to the Answer: When you're asked to solve an equation that has two variables, the question usually gives you the value of one of the variables. Read carefully to see which variable is given and which one you're solving for. You are given the diameter (0.12), so substitute this value for d in the equation and then solve for the other variable, h. Before dealing with the radical, divide both sides of the equation by 0.015.

$$0.12 = 0.015 \times \sqrt{h - 24}$$
$$8 = \sqrt{h - 24}$$
$$8^2 = \left(\sqrt{h - 24}\right)^2$$
$$64 = h - 24$$
$$88 = h$$

95. 6   Difficulty: Hard

Category: Quadratics

Getting to the Answer: The highest power of x in the equation is 2, so the function is quadratic. Writing quadratic equations can be tricky and time-consuming. If you know the roots, you can use factors to write the equation. If you don't know the roots, you need to create a system of equations to find the coefficients of the variable terms. You don't know the roots of this equation, so start with the point that has the easiest values to work with, $(0, 1)$, and substitute them into the equation $y = ax^2 + bx + c$.

$$1 = a(0)^2 + b(0) + c$$
$$1 = c$$

Now your equation looks like $y = ax^2 + bx + 1$. Next, use the other two points to create a system of two equations in two variables.

$$(-3,10) \to 10 = a(-3)^2 + b(-3) + 1 \to 9 = 9a - 3b$$
$$(2,15) \to 15 = a(2)^2 + b(2) + 1 \to 14 = 4a + 2b$$

You now have a system of equations to solve. None of the variables has a coefficient of 1, so use elimination to solve the system. If you multiply the top equation by 2 and the bottom equation by 3, the b terms will eliminate each other.

$$2[9a - 3b = 9] \to 18a - 6b = 18$$
$$3[4a + 2b = 14] \to \underline{12a + 6b = 42}$$
$$30a = 60$$
$$a = 2$$

Now, find b by substituting $a = 2$ into either of the original equations. Using the top equation, you get:

$$9(2) - 3b = 9$$
$$18 - 3b = 9$$
$$-3b = -9$$
$$b = 3$$

The value of $a + b + c$ is $2 + 3 + 1 = 6$.

96. 8   Difficulty: Hard

Category: Exponents

Getting to the Answer: When you are given a complicated-looking exponential expression, look for ways to rewrite it in a simpler form. Remember, when terms with exponents are divided, and the terms have the same base, their exponents can be subtracted. Here, the numerator and denominator of the term on the left share a common base, x, so you can rewrite the expression without the fraction by subtracting the exponents.

$$\frac{x^{a^2 - 4a}}{x^{12}} = x^{20}$$
$$x^{\boxed{a^2 - 4a - 12}} = x^{\boxed{20}}$$

Because the terms on either side of the equation share a common base, x, the exponents must be equivalent, which means $a^2 - 4a - 12 = 20$. This simplifies to $a^2 - 4a - 32 = 0$. Factor the left side to find that $(a - 8)(a + 4) = 0$, which gives $a = 8$ or $a = -4$. The question states that $a > 0$, so $a = 8$.

97. 6   Difficulty: Hard

Category: Quadratics

Getting to the Answer: When you are given the graph of a parabola, try to use what you know about intercepts, the vertex, and the axis of symmetry to answer the question. Here, you could try to use points from the graph to find its equation, but this is not necessary because the question only asks for the value of b. As a shortcut, recall that you can find the vertex of a parabola using the formula $x = -\dfrac{b}{2a}$ (the quadratic formula without the radical part). You are given that $a = -1$. Now look at the graph—the vertex of the parabola is (3, 8), so substitute 3 for x, -1 for a, and solve for b.

$$3 = -\frac{b}{2(-1)}$$
$$3 = -\left(\frac{b}{-2}\right)$$
$$3 = \frac{b}{2}$$
$$3(2) = b$$
$$6 = b$$

As an alternate method, you could plug the value of a and the vertex (from the graph) into vertex form of a quadratic equation and simplify:

$$y = a(x - h)^2 + k$$
$$= -1(x - 3)^2 + 8$$
$$= -1(x^2 - 6x + 9) + 8$$
$$= -x^2 + 6x - 9 + 8$$
$$= -x^2 + 6x - 1$$

The coefficient of x is b, so $b = 6$.

98. 4   Difficulty: Hard

Category: Functions

Getting to the Answer: You'll need to recall the rules of transformations to answer this question. To translate a function down 5 units, subtract 5 from the entire function. To translate the function to the left 1 unit, *add* 1 to the *x* inside the absolute value bars. So far, the transformed function looks like $|x+1|-5$. Finally, to reflect the function over the *x*-axis (which is a vertical reflection), multiply the entire function by -1. So $g(x) = -(|x+1|-5)$. Caution: Don't try to distribute the -1—the absolute value symbols make it too tricky. Instead, wait until you've plugged in the given number.

$$g(x) = -(|x+1|-5)$$
$$g(-2) = -(|-2+1|-5)$$
$$= -(|-1|-5) = -(1-5) = -(-4) = 4$$

The correct answer is 4.

99. 2   Difficulty: Hard

Category: Exponents

Getting to the Answer: Write each factor in the expression in exponential form: $\sqrt{x} = x^{\frac{1}{2}}$ and $\sqrt[3]{x} = x^{\frac{1}{3}}$. Then use the rules of exponents to simplify the expression. Add the exponents of the factors that are being multiplied and subtract the exponent of the factor that is being divided:

$$\frac{\sqrt{x} \cdot x^{\frac{5}{6}} \cdot x}{\sqrt[3]{x}} = \frac{x^{\frac{1}{2}} \cdot x^{\frac{5}{6}} \cdot x^1}{x^{\frac{1}{3}}}$$
$$= x^{\frac{1}{2}+\frac{5}{6}+1-\frac{1}{3}} = x^{\frac{3}{6}+\frac{5}{6}+\frac{6}{6}-\frac{2}{6}}$$
$$= x^{\frac{12}{6}} = x^2$$

Because *n* is the power of *x*, the value of *n* is 2.

100. 35   Difficulty: Hard

Category: Quadratics

Getting to the Answer: Because you're looking for the value of *y*, it would be ideal if you could somehow eliminate the *x* terms from this system of equations. Unfortunately, that would lead to very messy calculations, so your best option is to solve for *x* and see where that takes you.

The second equation is easily solved for *y*, so rewrite that equation in terms of *y* and then substitute the result into the first equation.

$$x^2 = y+1 \rightarrow \boxed{y = x^2 - 1}$$
$$11x - 2\boxed{y} = -4$$
$$11x - 2(x^2 - 1) = -4$$
$$11x - 2x^2 + 2 = -4$$
$$0 = 2x^2 - 11x - 6$$

Factor the resulting equation using the AC Method or trial and error to get $(2x+1)(x-6) = 0$. Set each factor equal to 0 and solve to find that the solutions to this equation are $x = -\frac{1}{2}$ and $x = 6$. Substituting these values into the equation you solved for *y* gives $y = -\frac{3}{4}$ and $y = 35$. Only the latter is greater than or equal to 0, so the correct answer is 35.

CHAPTER FOURTEEN

Additional Topics in Math

PRACTICE QUESTIONS

The following test-like questions provide an opportunity to practice Additional Topics in Math questions. The calculator icon means you are permitted to use a calculator to solve a question. It does not mean that you *should* use it, however.

1. A cannon is fired at a target that is placed at the edge of a cliff, as shown below. The angle of elevation from the cannon to the target is 52°. If the distance between the base of the cliff and the cannon is 200 feet, which expression could be used to approximate the distance between the cannon and the target?

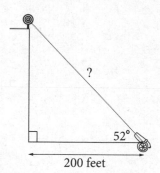

A) 200 sin 52°

B) $\dfrac{200}{\sin 52°}$

C) $\dfrac{200}{\cos 52°}$

D) $\dfrac{200}{\tan 52°}$

2. The longer leg of a right triangle is three times the length of the shorter leg. Given that the length of each leg is a whole number, which of the following could be the length of the hypotenuse?

A) $\sqrt{40}$

B) $\sqrt{47}$

C) $\sqrt{55}$

D) $\sqrt{63}$

3.

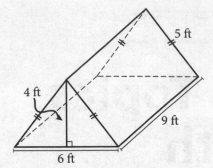

5 ft

4 ft

9 ft

6 ft

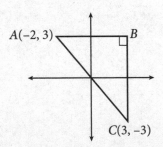

The figure above represents a camping tent that will be sprayed using a waterproofing agent. If it takes 1 ounce of the agent to cover 3 square feet, how many ounces will it take to spray the entire tent, inside and outside, including the tent bottom and its front door flaps?

A)   56

B)   112

C)   168

D)   336

4. Which of the following is NOT equal to i^{25} ?
(Note: $i = \sqrt{-1}$.)

A) i^9

B) i^{17}

C) i^{35}

D) i^{49}

5.

A(−2, 3)

B

C(3, −3)

Which angle has the smallest measure in the figure above?

A)   Angle A

B)   Angle B

C)   Angle C

D)   All three angles have equal measures.

6. Crude oil is being transferred from a full rectangular storage container with dimensions 4 meters by 9 meters by 10 meters into a cylindrical transportation container that has a diameter of 6 meters. What is the minimum possible length for a transportation container that will hold all of the oil?

A) 40π

B) $\dfrac{40}{\pi}$

C) 60π

D) $\dfrac{120}{\pi}$

7. Rupert has a collection of Blu-ray discs he wants to store in a cubical box with edges of length 10 inches. If each Blu-ray has dimensions of 5 inches by 5 inches by $\dfrac{1}{4}$ inch, what is the maximum number of discs that can fit into the box?

A)   60

B)   80

C)   120

D)   160

8.

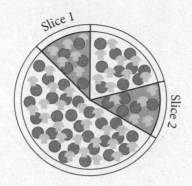

Four cuts are made from the center of a perfectly circular pizza to form Slice 1 and Slice 2. The arc lengths of the crusts of both slices are congruent. Which of the following statements regarding the two slices is true?

A) The two slices may or may not be congruent, depending on the length of each side of each slice.

B) The two slices may or may not be congruent, depending on the angle created by the cuts that were made.

C) The two slices cannot be congruent because the side lengths of each slice cannot be the same length.

D) The two slices must be congruent because the arc lengths are congruent and the side lengths of each slice are congruent.

9.

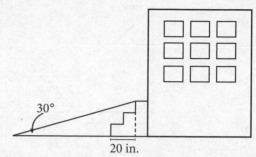

Note: Figure not drawn to scale.

 A company designs removable handicapped-access ramps as temporary measures for buildings to become compliant with the Americans with Disabilities Act (ADA). The particular ramp shown in the figure must be placed at a 30° angle, eight feet from the bottom step. About how long, in inches, is the ramp? (There are 12 inches in 1 foot.)

A) 67

B) 116

C) 128

D) 134

10. One of the three most expensive cheeses in the world is a Swedish cheese made from moose milk, which sells for about $500 a pound. Suppose a moose cheesemaker produces his cheese in rectangular blocks, each with a volume of 576 cubic inches. Customers or restaurants can buy this cheese in increments of $\frac{1}{8}$ blocks. One day, a customer buys $\frac{1}{8}$ of a block and a restaurant buys $\frac{1}{2}$ of a block. If the height of a cheese block is always 8 inches and the width is always 6 inches, what is the difference, in inches, in the lengths of the two purchases?

A) 4.5

B) 6

C) 7.6

D) 12

11.

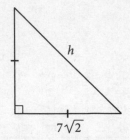

7√2

What is the value of *h* in the figure above?

A)   3.5

B)   7

C)   12.5

D)   14

12. If $a + bi$ represents the complex number that results from multiplying $3 + 2i$ times $5 - i$, what is the value of a ?

A)   2

B)   13

C)   15

D)   17

13. If the vertices of a right triangle have coordinates $(-6, 4)$, $(1, 4)$, and $(1, -2)$, what is the length of the hypotenuse of the triangle?

A) 7

B) 8

C) $\sqrt{85}$

D) $5\sqrt{17}$

14.

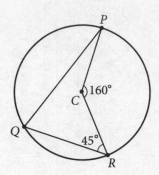

 What is the measure of $\angle QPC$ in the figure above?

A)   25°

B)   30°

C)   35°

D)   40°

15.

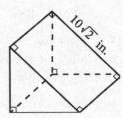

A solid wood cube is cut perfectly in half diagonally from corner to corner, as shown above, to be used as chocks, which are wedges placed behind wheels of vehicles to prevent them from rolling. What is the volume in cubic inches of one of these chocks?

A)   10

B)   100

C)   500

D)   1,000

16. Which system of equations has no solution?

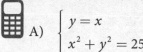

A) $\begin{cases} y = x \\ x^2 + y^2 = 25 \end{cases}$

B) $\begin{cases} y = x + 6 \\ x^2 + y^2 = 9 \end{cases}$

C) $\begin{cases} y = x - 4 \\ x^2 + y^2 = 16 \end{cases}$

D) $\begin{cases} y = x + 8 \\ x^2 + y^2 = 100 \end{cases}$

17. Triangle *BED* is similar to triangle *COT*. Triangle *COT* has side lengths of 8, 15, and 17. Which of the following could be the side lengths of triangle *BED* ?

A) 3, 4, 5

B) 5, 12, 13

C) 10, 17, 19

D) 24, 45, 51

18.

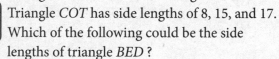

Note: Figures not drawn to scale.

What is the area, in square units, of the triangle that is not similar to the other three?

A) 120

B) 270

C) 288

D) 384

19. The Washington Monument in Washington, D.C., is the world's tallest obelisk-shaped building. The tall part of the monument is a rectangular prism-like shape that is wider at the bottom than it is at the top. At the very top of the monument, there is a regular pyramid with a square base that is 34.5 feet wide. If the volume of the pyramid top is 21,821.25 cubic feet, what is its height in feet?

A) 6.1

B) 18.3

C) 55.0

D) 210

20. The value of cos 40° is the same as which of the following?

A) sin 50°

B) sin(−40°)

C) cos(−50°)

D) cos 140°

21.

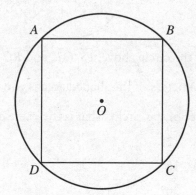

Square *ABCD* is inscribed in the circle with center *O*. If the area of the square is 64, what is the area of the circle?

A) 8π

B) 16π

C) 24π

D) 32π

22.

At 2:15, the short hand of an analog clock lines up exactly with the 11-minute tick mark, and the long hand lines up with the 15-minute tick mark. What central angle do the hands form at 2:15 ?

A) 18°

B) 20°

C) 24°

D) 28°

23.

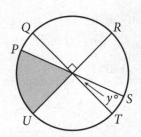

In the circle above, $\overline{PS}$, $\overline{QT}$, and $\overline{RU}$ are diameters. If the shaded area is equal to $\frac{1}{5}$ the area of the circle, what is the value of y ?

A) 12°

B) 18°

C) 30°

D) 72°

24. Which of the following expressions is equivalent to $(6 + 5i)^3$? (Note: $i = \sqrt{-1}$.)

A) $11 + 60i$

B) $216 - 125i$

C) $-234 + 415i$

D) $-3,479 + 1,320i$

25.

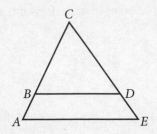

Note: Figure not drawn to scale.

In the figure above, $\overline{BD} \parallel \overline{AE}$ and $\overline{AB} = 6$. If $\overline{BC}$ is twice $\overline{AB}$, and $\overline{CD}$ is 4 less than $\overline{AC}$, then what is the length of $\overline{DE}$?

A) 6

B) 6.6

C) 7

D) 7.5

26.

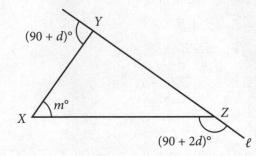

In the figure above, side YZ of $\triangle XYZ$ is on line l. What is m in terms of d ?

A) $\frac{1}{3}d$

B) d

C) $3d$

D) $180 - d$

27.

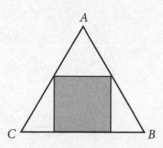

In the figure above, the shaded region is a square of area 3, and $\triangle ABC$ is equilateral. What is the perimeter of $\triangle ABC$?

A) $9\sqrt{3}$

B) $2+\sqrt{3}$

C) $3+6\sqrt{3}$

D) $6+3\sqrt{3}$

28.

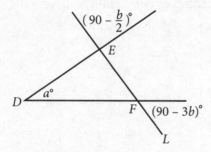

In the figure above, $\overline{EF}$ of $\triangle DEF$ is on line L. What is a in terms of b ?

A) $3b$

B) $\dfrac{3b}{2}$

C) $\dfrac{7b}{2}$

D) $180 - b$

29.

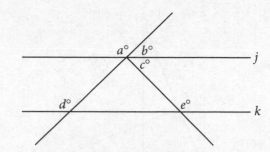

Note: Figure not drawn to scale.

In the figure above, if lines j and k are parallel, which of the following statements must be true?

A) $a = e$

B) $b = c$

C) $d = 180 - c$

D) $b + d - c = e$

30.

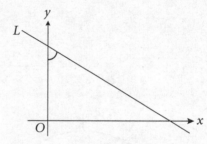

Note: Figure not drawn to scale.

The equation of line L shown above is

$y = -\dfrac{5}{12}x + 15$. Given that angle A is the

acute angle formed by the intersection of line L and the y-axis (marked on the triangle), which expression could be used to find the measure of angle A ?

A) $\cos A = \dfrac{5}{12}$

B) $\tan A = \dfrac{12}{5}$

C) $\sin A = \dfrac{5}{12}$

D) $\sin A = \dfrac{12}{5}$

31.

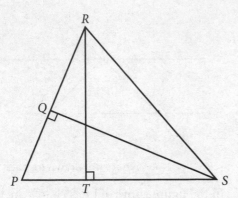

In $\triangle PRS$ above, $\overline{RT}$ is the altitude to side $\overline{PS}$, and $\overline{QS}$ is the altitude to side $\overline{PR}$. If $\overline{RT} = 7$, $\overline{PR} = 8$, and $\overline{QS} = 9$, what is the length of $\overline{PS}$?

A) $6\frac{2}{9}$

B) $7\frac{7}{8}$

C) $10\frac{2}{7}$

D) $13\frac{4}{9}$

32.

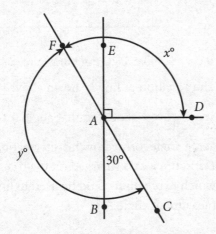

In the figure above, $\overline{EB}$, $\overline{AD}$, and $\overline{CF}$ intersect at point A; and $\overline{EB}$ is perpendicular to $\overline{AD}$.

What is the value of $\dfrac{x + y}{2}$?

A) 75

B) 120

C) 135

D) 150

33.

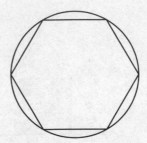

Holly is designing a kaleidoscope for a friend's birthday gift. To the body of the kaleidoscope, she plans to arrange six identical rectangular mirrors in the shape of a hexagon inside a right cylindrical casing that is open on both ends. A cross section of the interior is shown above. If the casing is 30.5 centimeters in length and has a surface area of 61π centimeters^2, what is the distance, in centimeters, between the centers of two parallel mirrors?

A) $\sqrt{2}$

B) $\dfrac{\sqrt{3}}{2}$

C) $\sqrt{3}$

D) 2

34.

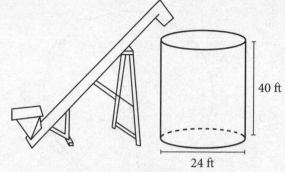

Note: Figure not drawn to scale.

 A soybean distributor is filling the cylindrical grain bin shown above with dry soybeans using an auger conveyor. The conveyor can move 5,500 dry bushels of soybeans per hour. About how long will it take to fill 75% of the grain bin given that 1 dry bushel is equal to 1.24 cubic feet?

A)   2 hours

B)   2 hours, 40 minutes

C)   3 hours, 15 minutes

D)   4 hours

35.

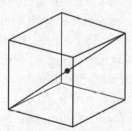

Each edge of the cube shown above measures $2\sqrt{6}$ centimeters. What is the distance, in centimeters, from a vertex of this cube to its center?

A) $\sqrt{6}$

B) $3\sqrt{2}$

C) $2\sqrt{6}$

D) $6\sqrt{2}$

36. A basic megaphone is a truncated cone; that is, a cone with its apex (pointed end) removed. Suppose the openings (ends) of a megaphone have diameters of 2 inches and 10 inches. If the original cone from which the megaphone was created had a height of 20 inches, what is the volume, in cubed inches, inside the megaphone?

A) 150π

B) $165\frac{1}{3}\pi$

C) 496π

D) $661\frac{1}{3}\pi$

37. It is given that $\sin A = k$, where A is an angle measured in radians and $\pi < A < \frac{3\pi}{2}$. If $\sin B = k$, which of the following could be the value of B ?

A) $A - \pi$

B) $\pi + A$

C) $2\pi - A$

D) $3\pi - A$

38.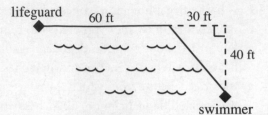

lifeguard

60 ft   30 ft

40 ft

swimmer

As shown in the figure above, a lifeguard sees a struggling swimmer who is 40 feet from the beach. The lifeguard runs 60 feet along the edge of the water at a speed of 12 feet per second. He pauses for 1 second to locate the swimmer again, and then dives into the water and swims along a diagonal path to the swimmer at a speed of 5 feet per second. How many seconds go by between the time the lifeguard sees the struggling swimmer and the time he reaches the swimmer?

A) 16

B) 22

C) 50

D) 56

39.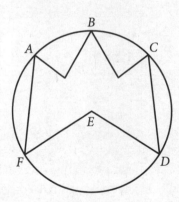

Shunyo is designing a pin for her college's academic honor society; her basic template is shown above. If the sector whose central angle is ∠FED is one-third of the entire circle, what is the sum of the measures of ∠A, ∠B, and ∠C?

A) 60°

B) 120°

C) 180°

D) It cannot be determined from the given information.

40.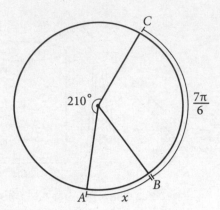

If the length of the radius of the circle shown above is 2, what is the value of x?

A) $\dfrac{\pi}{6}$

B) $\dfrac{\pi}{2}$

C) $\dfrac{7\pi}{12}$

D) $\dfrac{7\pi}{3}$

41. The roof of a certain bell tower is in the shape of a square pyramid with a length and width of 20 feet and a slant height of 18 feet. The roof needs new shingles, which are 72 square inches in size. The shingles must overlap so that water doesn't leak between the seams. What is the minimum number of shingles needed to cover the roof, assuming 20% extra to account for the overlap?

A)   432

B)   518

C)   1,440

D)   1,728

42.

Note: Figure not drawn to scale.

The semicircle above has a radius of r inches, and chord $\overline{YZ}$ is parallel to diameter $\overline{WX}$. If the length of $\overline{YZ}$ is 25% shorter than the length of $\overline{WX}$, what is the greatest distance between $\overline{YZ}$ and $\overline{WX}$ in terms of r?

A) $\frac{1}{4}\pi r$

B) $\frac{3}{4}\pi r$

C) $\frac{\sqrt{2}}{4}r$

D) $\frac{\sqrt{7}}{4}r$

43. When New York City built its 34th Street subway station, which has multiple underground levels, it built an elevator that runs along a diagonal track approximately 170 feet long to connect the upper and lower levels. The angle formed between the elevator track and the bottom level is just under 30 degrees. What is the approximate vertical distance in feet between the upper and lower levels of the subway station?

A) 85

B) 98

C) 120

D) 147

44.

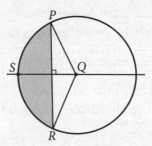

If the measure of $\angle PQR$ in the figure above is 120°, and the radius of the circle is 4 units, what is the area in square units of the shaded portion of the circle?

A) $\frac{4\pi}{3} - 8\sqrt{3}$

B) $\frac{5\pi}{3} - 4\sqrt{3}$

C) $\frac{8\pi}{3} - 4\sqrt{3}$

D) $\frac{16\pi}{3} - 4\sqrt{3}$

45. A hexagonal wooden #2 pencil measures 190 millimeters in length (pencil only, no eraser or metal eraser connector; unsharpened). Normally a pencil is drilled through from one hexagonal face to the other, and this cavity is filled with graphite. A recent equipment malfunction led to pencils being drilled only halfway through, resulting in 50% less graphite than usual. If the graphite component has a diameter of 2 millimeters and the pencil's hexagonal faces have diagonals of 8 millimeters, what fraction of one of the defective pencils is graphite?

A) $\frac{\pi\sqrt{3}}{18}$

B) $\frac{\pi\sqrt{3}}{36}$

C) $\frac{\pi\sqrt{3}}{72}$

D) $\frac{\pi\sqrt{3}}{144}$

46. A medical test tube is made up of a cylinder with a half-sphere on the bottom. The volume in square inches of the tube is $\frac{19}{12}\pi$. The diameter of the cylinder (and the half-sphere) is 1 inch. How tall in inches is the test tube?

A) 4.75

B) 5

C) 6

D) 6.5

47.

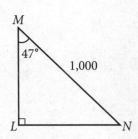

If MN in the triangle above is equal to 1,000, and $\cos 47° \approx \frac{341}{500}$, what is the approximate length of side LN?

A)   86

B)   318

C)   731

D)   917

48.

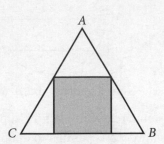

In the figure above, the shaded region is a square with an area of 12 square units, inscribed inside equilateral triangle ABC. What is the perimeter of triangle ABC?

A) $18\sqrt{3}$

B) $4+\sqrt{3}$

C) $4+6\sqrt{3}$

D) $12+6\sqrt{3}$

49.
$$x^2 + y^2 - 4x - 8y = 16$$

The equation of circle O in the xy-coordinate plane is given above. What is the length of the radius of circle O?

A)   4

B)   6

C)   16

D)   36

50. If a right cone is three times as wide at its base as it is tall, and the volume of the cone is 384π cubic inches, what is the diameter in inches of the base of the cone?

A)   8

B)   12

C)   16

D)   24

51. Which of the following shows $\left(3+\sqrt{-16}\right)$ $\left(-3-\sqrt{-25}\right)$ written in the form $a + bi$?

    (Note: $i = \sqrt{-1}$.)

    A) $-29 - 27i$

    B) $-29 - 3i$

    C) $11 - 27i$

    D) $11 - 3i$

52. Which of the following is an equation of a circle in the xy-coordinate plane with center $(1, 0)$ and a radius with endpoint $\left(2, \dfrac{5}{2}\right)$?

    A) $(x + 1)^2 + y^2 = \dfrac{13}{2}$

    B) $(x - 1)^2 + y^2 = \dfrac{13}{2}$

    C) $(x + 1)^2 + y^2 = \dfrac{29}{4}$

    D) $(x - 1)^2 + y^2 = \dfrac{29}{4}$

53.

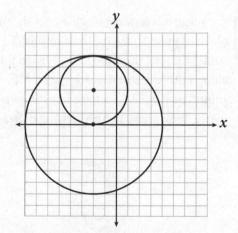

    If the area of the smaller circle shown above is 144π square units, then what is the equation of the larger circle?

    A) $(x + 2)^2 + y^2 = 36$

    B) $(x + 2)^2 + (y - 3)^2 = 9$

    C) $(x + 8)^2 + (y - 12)^2 = 144$

    D) $(x + 8)^2 + y^2 = 576$

54. A rectangular block with a volume of 250 cubic inches was sliced into two cubes of equal volume. How much greater, in square inches, is the combined surface area of the two cubes than the original surface area of the rectangular block?

    A) 2

    B) 25

    C) 50

    D) 125

55. Which of the following is equivalent to the complex number $\dfrac{1}{5 - 4i} + (3 + i)$?

    (Note: $i = \sqrt{-1}$.)

    A) $\dfrac{20 - 7i}{5 - 4i}$

    B) $\dfrac{20 + 7i}{5 - 4i}$

    C) $\dfrac{12 - 7i}{5 - 4i}$

    D) $\dfrac{12 + 7i}{5 - 4i}$

56. The absolute value of a complex number $a + bi$ is defined as $\sqrt{a^2 + b^2}$. What is $|15 + 8i|$?

    (Note: $i = \sqrt{-1}$.)

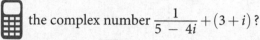

57.

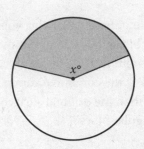

In the figure above, the ratio of the shaded area to the unshaded area is 5 to 7. What is the value of x ?

58.

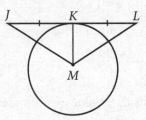

In the figure above, $\overline{JL}$ is tangent to circle M at point K. If the area of the circle is 36π, and $JL = 16$, what is the length of $\overline{LM}$?

59. If the expression $\dfrac{\sqrt{-27}}{\sqrt{12}}$ is simplified and written in the form bi, what is the value of b ? (Note: $i = \sqrt{-1}$.)

60.

56 ft

42 ft

Note: Figure not drawn to scale.

A college has a sidewalk that cuts through a block of greenspace on the campus. To ensure student safety, the college decides to put lights along both sides of the sidewalk. If the lights should be placed 5 feet apart, as shown in the figure, how many lights does the college need?

61. The length, width, and height of a rectangular prism are in the ratio 4:2:1 (in that order). If the volume of the prism is 216 cubic inches, how many inches wide is the prism?

63.

When the top of a pyramid (or a cone) is cut off, the remaining bottom part is called a frustum. Suppose the top third (based on the height) of the square pyramid shown above is cut off and discarded. What will be the volume, in cubic meters, of the remaining frustum?

62. Steve and Autumn are skiing at a local mountain resort. Steve wants to maneuver through a mogul field at the start of a certain trail; Autumn opts to take an easier trail and meet Steve on his trail just after the mogul field ends and ski to the bottom with him. If Steve drops 375 feet in elevation after skiing through the 1,000-foot mogul field, and the two skiers will drop another 1,125 feet in elevation by the time they reach the bottom of the trail, how many feet long is the full trail Steve took?

64. What is the measure in degrees of the smallest angle of a triangle that has sides of length 1.5, $\frac{3\sqrt{3}}{2}$, and 3 ?

65. The opening of a perfectly circular sewer tunnel has a circumference of 8π. The tunnel has a volume of $2{,}048\pi$ cubic feet. How many feet long is the tunnel?

66. What is the diameter of the circle given by the equation $x^2 + y^2 + 10x - 4y = 20$?

67. If the product of $\left(3 + \sqrt{-16}\right)\left(1 - \sqrt{-36}\right)$ is written as a complex number in the form $a + bi$, what is the value of a ? (Note: $\sqrt{-1} = i$.)

68.

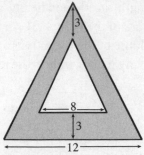

Note: Figure not drawn to scale.

In the figure above, the area of the shaded region is 52 square units. What is the height of the larger triangle?

69. In a right triangle, one angle measures $x°$, where $\cos x° = \dfrac{5}{12}$. What is the value of $\sin(90° - x°)$ for this triangle?

70.

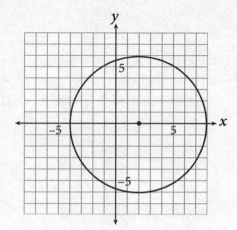

If the equation of the circle shown above is written in the form $x^2 + y^2 + ax + by = c$, what is the value of $a + b + c$?

71.

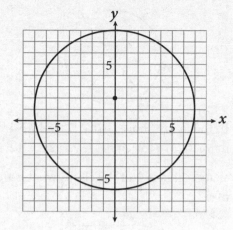

If the equation of the circle shown above is written in the form $x^2 + y^2 + ax + by = c$, what is the value of $a + b + c$?

72.

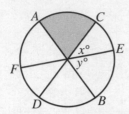

In the figure above, $\overline{AB}$, $\overline{CD}$, and $\overline{EF}$ are diameters of the circle. If $y = 2x - 12$, and the shaded area is $\frac{1}{5}$ of the circle, what is the value of x?

73.

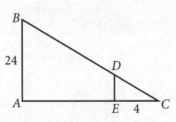

In the figure above, $\overline{DE} \| \overline{AB}$ and $\overline{DE} \perp \overline{AC}$. If $AE = 28$, what is the length of BD?

74.

$$\frac{5 - 5i}{5 + 4i}$$

If the expression above is rewritten in the form $a + bi$, where a and b are real numbers, what is the value of a? (Note: $i = \sqrt{-1}$.)

75. In triangle PQR, the measure of $\angle Q$ is $90°$, $QR = 6$, and $PR = 10$. Triangle TUV is similar to triangle PQR, where vertices T, U, and V correspond to vertices P, Q, and R, respectively, and each side of triangle TUV is $\frac{1}{2}$ the length of the corresponding side of triangle PQR. What is the value of $\sin V$?

ANSWERS AND EXPLANATIONS

CHAPTER 14

1. C **Difficulty:** Medium

Category: Trigonometry

Getting to the Answer: Use SOHCAHTOA. When you're presented with a trigonometry question, your first step should be to identify the sides and/or angles you're given and the side you're trying to find. Then figure out which trig function gives you a relationship between the side you know and the side you want to know. The distance between the base of the cliff and the cannon (which you know) is adjacent to the given angle. The distance between the cannon and the target (which you're looking for) is the hypotenuse. The trig function that gives a relationship between the adjacent side and the hypotenuse is cosine (adjacent over hypotenuse).

$$\cos 52° = \frac{200}{\text{hyp}}$$
$$\text{hyp} \times \cos 52° = 200$$
$$\text{hyp} = \frac{200}{\cos 52°}$$

Because the hypotenuse represents the distance between the cannon and the target, the correct answer is choice (C).

2. A **Difficulty:** Medium

Category: Geometry

Getting to the Answer: Start by translating from English into math. Because one leg of the triangle is three times as long as the other, let x and $3x$ represent the lengths. Use the Pythagorean theorem to find the hypotenuse.

$$a^2 + b^2 = c^2$$
$$x^2 + (3x)^2 = c^2$$
$$x^2 + 9x^2 = c^2$$
$$10x^2 = c^2$$
$$\sqrt{10x^2} = c$$

Although you can't find a numerical value for c, you do know that the number under the radical must be a multiple of 10, so choice (A) is correct.

3. B **Difficulty:** Medium

Category: Geometry

Getting to the Answer: In a question like this, you're looking for surface area (not volume) because you would spray the faces of the tent (not the space inside the tent). If you check the formula page, you'll notice that there are no surface area formulas for 3-D shapes. This means you need to decompose the figure into 2-D shapes. Pay careful attention to the dimensions of each shape.

The bottom of the tent is a rectangle: $A = lw = (9)(6) = 54$; the two sides of the tent are also rectangles, but one of the dimensions is different from that of the bottom: $2A = 2(lw) = 2(9)(5) = 90$; the front and back of the tent are triangles:

$$2A_{\text{triangle}} = 2\left(\frac{1}{2}bh\right) = bh = (6)(4) = 24$$

Thus, the total surface area of the tent is $54 + 90 + 24 = 168$ square feet. You're not done: both the inside and outside of the tent need to be sprayed, so double the surface area to get 336 square feet. And finally, 1 ounce can cover 3 square feet, so divide 336 by 3 to arrive at the final answer, 112 ounces of the waterproofing agent, which is choice (B).

4. C   Difficulty: Medium

Category: Imaginary Numbers

Getting to the Answer: Recall that powers of i repeat in a cycle of 4; the cycle is i, -1, $-i$, and 1. The remainder when the exponent is divided by 4 gives the location in the cycle; $25 \div 4 = 6$ R 1, so i^{25} has the same value as i^1, which is i. Raising i to any power that results in a remainder of 1 when the exponent is divided by 4 will also equal i. Checking each of the answer choices reveals that $35 \div 4 = 8$ R 3, so i^{35} is equivalent to $i^3 = -i$, not i. Thus, choice (C) is correct.

5. C   Difficulty: Medium

Category: Geometry

Getting to the Answer: In a triangle, the angle across from the shortest side will have the smallest measure. Use the coordinate grid to figure out which side is the shortest. Point B has the same x-coordinate as C and the same y-coordinate as A, so its coordinates are (3, 3). The length of AB is 5 and the length of BC is 6, so AB is the shortest side. This means the angle opposite it, which is C, has the smallest measure, making choice (C) correct.

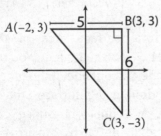

6. B   Difficulty: Medium

Category: Geometry

Getting to the Answer: Think about this question logically before you start writing things down—after it's transferred, the volume of the oil in the cylindrical container will be the same volume as the rectangular container, so you need to set the two volumes equal and solve for h. The volume of the rectangular container is $4 \times 9 \times 10$, or 360 cubic meters. The volume of a cylinder equals the area of its base times its height, or $\pi r^2 h$. Because the diameter is 6 meters, the radius, r, is half that, or 3 meters. Now we're ready to set up an equation and solve for h (which is the height of the cylinder or, in this case, the length of the transportation container):

Volume of oil = Volume of rectangular container

$$\pi(3)^2 h = 360$$
$$9\pi h = 360$$
$$h = \frac{360}{9\pi} = \frac{40}{\pi}$$

Choice (B) is correct.

7. D   Difficulty: Medium

Category: Geometry

Getting to the Answer: There are two ways to approach this question—but only because both shapes (the storage box and the discs) are rectangular prisms and the dimensions match up nicely (two rows of two discs will exactly fill one layer in the box with no extra space left over). One strategy is to find the volume of the storage box and divide by the volume of each disc. Another strategy is to find how many discs Rupert can fit in length, then in width, then in height, and multiply. The second approach must be used when the shapes are different and when the dimensions don't match up just right.

Strategy 1: The volume of a rectangular prism (or a cube) is given by the formula $V = l \times w \times h$, so the volume of the storage box is $10 \times 10 \times 10 = 1,000$ cubic units. The volume of each disc is $5 \times 5 \times \frac{1}{4} = 6.25$. The number of discs that can fit in the box is $1,000 \div 6.25 = 160$ discs, which is choice (D).

Strategy 2: The box has dimensions of 10 inches by 10 inches by 10 inches. Because each disc is 5 inches in length, he can fit $10 \div 5 = 2$ rows of discs along the length of the box. Each disc is 5 inches in width, so he can fit $10 \div 5 = 2$ rows of discs along the width of the box. Finally, each disc is $\frac{1}{4}$ inch tall, so he can fit $10 \div \frac{1}{4} = 10 \times 4 = 40$ rows of discs along the depth of the box. Multiply to find that Rupert can fit $2 \times 2 \times 40 = 160$ Blu-ray discs in the box.

8. D   **Difficulty:** Medium

Category: Geometry

Getting to the Answer: Because each cut is made from the center, each side of Slice 1 and Slice 2 is a radius of the circle, and all radii of a circle are congruent. Therefore, both pairs of corresponding sides are congruent. The arc lengths (edges of the crust) are also congruent, which means the central angle that subtends these arcs must be congruent. Now think SAS—the two slices must be congruent, making choice (D) correct.

9. D   **Difficulty:** Medium

Category: Geometry

Getting to the Answer: Two of the angles in the triangle have degree measures 30 and 90, which means the third angle must measure 60 degrees. This means you are dealing with a special right triangle and can use the 30-60-90 shortcut. In a 30-60-90 triangle, the sides are always in the ratio $x:x\sqrt{3}:2x$ (short leg : long leg : hypotenuse). The only length you know is the long leg—the side represented by the ground and the width of the bottom two steps. The ramp is to be placed 8 feet, or 96 inches, from the bottom step, and the steps themselves account for an additional 20 inches, which means this leg of the triangle is 116 inches long. Use the ratio to determine that you need to divide by $\sqrt{3}$ to find the length of the shorter leg, and then multiply the result by 2 to find the length of the hypotenuse, which represents the ramp.

$$116 \div \sqrt{3} = 66.97$$
$$66.97 \times 2 = 133.95$$

The result is about 134 inches, which matches choice (D).

10. A   **Difficulty:** Medium

Category: Geometry

Getting to the Answer: The cheese block purchases have the same height and width, so the block must be cut according to length. Find the original length of the entire block using the formula for volume of a rectangular solid, $V = lwh$, and then solve for length.

$$V = lwh$$
$$576 = (l)(6)(8)$$
$$12 = l$$

Don't stop here—the question asks for the difference in the two lengths. The customer bought $\frac{1}{8}$ block, which is equal to $(12)\left(\frac{1}{8}\right) = 1.5$ inches. The restaurant bought $\frac{1}{2}$ block, which is equal to $(12)\left(\frac{1}{2}\right) = 6$ inches. The difference in the lengths is $6 - 1.5 = 4.5$ inches, which is choice (A).

11. D   **Difficulty:** Medium

Category: Geometry

Getting to the Answer: Because one angle of the triangle measures $90°$ and the two legs are congruent (notice the tick marks), this is a 45-45-90 triangle. The side lengths of a 45-45-90 triangle are in the ratio $x:x:x\sqrt{2}$, where x represents the length of a leg and $x\sqrt{2}$ represents the length of the hypotenuse. (Don't forget—the formula page provides this information.) Don't be too hasty in choosing your answer—it's not 7. Set up an equation using the ratio and the length of the side ($7\sqrt{2}$) to find h:

$$h = x\sqrt{2}$$
$$= 7\sqrt{2} \times \sqrt{2}$$
$$= 7\sqrt{4}$$
$$= 7(2)$$
$$= 14$$

The length of the hypotenuse is 14, so choice (D) is correct.

12. D   Difficulty: Medium

Category: Imaginary Numbers

Getting to the Answer: Multiply the two complex numbers just as you would two binomials (using FOIL). Then, combine like terms and use the definition $i^2 = -1$ to simplify the result.

$$(3+2i)(5-i) = 3(5-i) + 2i(5-i)$$
$$= 15 - 3i + 10i - 2i^2$$
$$= 15 + 7i - 2(-1)$$
$$= 15 + 7i + 2$$
$$= 17 + 7i$$

The question asks for a in $a + bi$, so the correct answer is 17, choice (D).

13. C   Difficulty: Medium

Category: Geometry

Getting to the Answer: Whenever you're given coordinates in a geometry question, start by drawing a quick sketch. You won't have graph paper, so draw carefully and label the coordinates of the points.

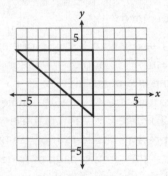

After drawing a sketch, you can see that the triangle is a right triangle. Subtract the coordinates to find the lengths of the legs and use the Pythagorean theorem to find the length of the hypotenuse. To find the length of the horizontal leg, subtract the x-coordinates: $1 - (-6) = 7$. To find the length of the vertical leg, subtract the y-coordinates: $4 - (-2) = 6$. The leg lengths are 6 and 7. Substitute these values

into the Pythagorean theorem to find the length of the hypotenuse:

$$a^2 + b^2 = c^2$$
$$6^2 + 7^2 = c^2$$
$$36 + 49 = c^2$$
$$85 = c^2$$
$$\sqrt{85} = \sqrt{c^2}$$
$$\sqrt{85} = c$$

Choice (C) is correct.

14. C   Difficulty: Medium

Category: Geometry

Getting to the Answer: Angle QPC is one angle of a quadrilateral, so you can subtract the measures of the other three angles from 360° to answer the question. However, you're only given one of those angles, so you'll have to use properties of circles to find the other two. Angle PQR is an inscribed angle that intercepts the same arc $(\overset{\frown}{PR})$ as the 160° central angle, which means the measure of $\angle PQR$ is half that, or 80°. The obtuse angle in the quadrilateral at the center completes a full circle with the 160° central angle, so its measure is $360° - 160° = 200°$. Now you have all the angles you need:

$$m\angle QPR = 360° - (200 + 45 + 80)°$$
$$= 360° - 325°$$
$$= 35°$$

This means choice (C) is correct.

15. C   Difficulty: Medium

Category: Geometry

Getting to the Answer: A wedge shape is an unfamiliar solid, so you shouldn't try to calculate the volume directly. You are told that the solid is half of a cube. Now imagine the other half lying on top of the solid, forming a complete cube.

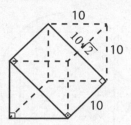

The question tells you that the hypotenuse is $10\sqrt{2}$. Notice that this diagonal with length $10\sqrt{2}$ and two of the cube's edges form an isosceles right triangle, or in other words, a 45-45-90 degree triangle. In a 45-45-90 triangle, the hypotenuse is $\sqrt{2}$ times the length of a leg, so the legs have length 10. Thus, the volume of the whole cube is $10 \times 10 \times 10 = 1,000$, and the volume of the chock is half that, or 500 cubic inches, which is choice (C).

16. B   Difficulty: Medium

Category: Geometry

Getting to the Answer: You would not be expected to algebraically solve four systems of equations on Test Day for one question—there simply isn't enough time. This means there must be another way to answer this question. Think graphing!

Take a peek at the answer choices—each one contains a line that is already written in slope-intercept form and a circle that has its center at the origin. Drawing a quick sketch will get you to the answer much quicker than trying to solve the systems algebraically. If the line and the circle don't intersect, then the system has no solution.

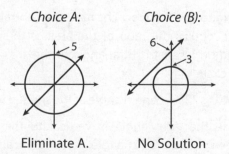

There is no need to go any further; choice (B) is correct because the graphs do not intersect.

17. D   Difficulty: Medium

Category: Geometry

Getting to the Answer: Corresponding sides of similar triangles are proportional. This is the same as saying the larger triangle is a scaled-up version of the smaller triangle. So, you're looking for the same ratio of sides (8:15:17), multiplied by a scale factor. This means choice (D) is correct because each side length of *COT* has been scaled up by a factor of 3.

18. D   Difficulty: Medium

Category: Geometry

Getting to the Answer: All four triangles are right triangles, so you can't immediately eliminate any of the choices. Because they are all right triangles, try simplifying the side lengths of the smallest one to look for a Pythagorean triplet. Then see if you can identify scaled-up versions of that one. The second triangle is the smallest with side lengths of 10, 24, and 26. If you divide each of these lengths by 2, you get the common Pythagorean triplet 5, 12, 13. Notice that if you triple these numbers, you get the first triangle; likewise, if you quadruple the numbers, you get the third triangle. The last triangle with side lengths of 24, 32, and 40 is *not* a scaled-up version of a 5, 12, 13 triangle, so it is the one that is not similar. Now, find its area. Remember the area of a triangle is $A = \frac{1}{2}bh$, and in right triangles, the base and height are the leg lengths.

$$A = \frac{1}{2}(24)(32)$$
$$A = \frac{1}{2}(768)$$
$$A = 384$$

This means choice (D) is correct.

19. C   Difficulty: Medium

Category: Geometry

Getting to the Answer: The volume of a pyramid is given by $V = \frac{1}{3}lwh$. Here, the base is a square, so both the length and the width are equal to 34.5 feet. You're looking for the height of the pyramid, so substitute all the other values into the formula and solve for h:

$$V = \frac{1}{3}lwh$$

$$21{,}821.25 = \frac{1}{3}(34.5)(34.5)h$$

$$65{,}463.75 = 1{,}190.25h$$

$$55 = h$$

Therefore, the height of the pyramid top is 55 feet, which matches choice (C).

20. A   Difficulty: Medium

Category: Trigonometry

Getting to the Answer: The measure of 40° does not appear on the unit circle, which should give you a clue that there must be a property or relationship on which you can rely to help you answer the question. Complementary angles have a special relationship relative to trig values: The cosine of an acute angle is equal to the sine of the angle's complement and vice versa. Because only one of the answers can be correct, look for the simplest relationship (complementary angles): 50° is complementary to 40°, so cos 40° = sin 50°, which means choice (A) is correct.

21. D   Difficulty: Hard

Category: Geometry

Getting to the Answer: Whenever you see a circle, you know you'll need the radius. No radius is shown on this diagram, so look for a place where you can

add one that will also be part of the square. Draw $\overline{AC}$ into the figure.

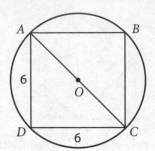

Notice that $\overline{AC}$ is both the diagonal of the square and the diameter of the circle. Because the area of the square is 64, each of its sides must be 8. $\triangle ADC$ is a 45-45-90 right triangle, so its sides are in the ratio $x : x : x\sqrt{2}$ and $\overline{AC} = 8\sqrt{2}$. The radius of the circle is half that, or $4\sqrt{2}$. Now find the area of the circle:

$$A = \pi r^2 = \pi\left(4\sqrt{2}\right)^2 = \pi\left(4^2(\sqrt{2})^2\right) = \pi(16 \times 2) = 32\pi.$$

22. C   Difficulty: Medium

Category: Geometry

Getting to the Answer: An analog clock has 12 hours marked off, each of which has 5 tick marks representing minutes, for a total of $12 \times 5 = 60$ tick marks. There are 360° in a circle, so the degree measure between each pair of tick marks is $360 \div 60 = 6°$. At 2:15, the hands of the clock are 4 tick marks apart $(15 - 11)$, so the angle between them is $4 \times 6 = 24°$, which is choice (C).

23. B   Difficulty: Hard

Category: Geometry

Getting to the Answer: The ratio of a central angle to 360° equals the ratio of the area of the sector marked off by that central angle to the area of the entire circle.

$$\frac{1}{5} \times 360° = 72° = \text{central angle of the shaded region.}$$

Because the right angle is vertical to the angle between $y°$ and the 72° angle, that angle is also 90°, so $72° + 90° + y = 180°$ and $y = 18$. Choice (B) is correct.

24. C   Difficulty: Medium

Category: Imaginary Numbers

Getting to the Answer: You will not be expected to raise a complex number like the one in this question to the third power by hand. That's a clue that you should be able to use your calculator. The definition of i has been programmed into all graphing calculators, so you can perform basic operations on complex numbers using the calculator (in the Calculator Section of the test). Enter the expression as follows: $(6 + 5i)^3$. On the TI83/84 calculators, you can find i on the button with the decimal point. After entering the expression and pressing Enter, the calculator should return $-234 + 415i$, which is choice (C).

You could, however, expand the number by hand, by writing it as $(6 + 5i)(6 + 5i)(6 + 5i)$ and carefully multiplying it all out.

25. C   Difficulty: Hard

Category: Geometry

Getting to the Answer: There are two triangles in this figure, $\triangle ACE$ and $\triangle BCD$. Because $\overline{BD}$ is parallel to $\overline{AE}$, $\angle A$ and $\angle B$ must be congruent (they are corresponding angles), and $\angle D$ and $\angle E$ must be congruent (they are also corresponding angles). $\angle C$ is shared by both triangles and is equal to itself by the reflexive property. This means the side lengths of the two triangles are different, but the angles are the same, so the triangles are similar by AAA. Side lengths of similar triangles are in proportion to one another.

You know the two triangles are similar, so set up a proportion using their side lengths. You'll need to translate from English into math as you go: $\overline{AB} = 6$ and $\overline{BC}$ is twice that, or 12. This means $AC = 6 + 12 = 18$. $\overline{CD}$ is 4 less than $\overline{AC}$ or $18 - 4 = 14$. Now you know

three side lengths, so you can set up and solve a proportion:

$$\frac{\overline{BC}}{\overline{AC}} = \frac{\overline{DC}}{\overline{EC}}$$

$$\frac{12}{18} = \frac{14}{\overline{EC}}$$

$$12\overline{EC} = 252$$

$$\overline{EC} = 21$$

This is the length of $\overline{EC}$, but the question asks for the length of $\overline{DE}$, which is $21 - 14 = 7$. Choice (C) is correct.

26. C   Difficulty: Hard

Category: Geometry

Getting to the Answer: $\angle XYZ$ is supplementary to the angle that measures $(90 + d)°$ and therefore has a measure of $180° - (90 + d)°$, or $(90 - d)°$. Likewise, $\angle XYZ$ is supplementary to the angle that measures $(90 + 2d)°$ and therefore has a measure of $180° - (90 + 2d)°$, or $(90 - 2d)°$. To find m in terms of d, set the sum of triangle XYZ's angles equal to $180°$ and solve for m:

$$m° + (90 - d)° + (90 - 2d)° = 180°$$
$$m + 180 - 3d = 180$$
$$m - 3d = 0$$
$$m = 3d$$

27. D   Difficulty: Hard

Category: Geometry

Getting to the Answer: Start with what you know about the shaded square. Because its area is 3, each side must be $\sqrt{3}$.

The two vertical sides of the square each form a leg of a 30-60-90 right triangle, making the short legs each 1. You now have the length of the base of the large equilateral triangle: $1 + \sqrt{3} + 1 = 2 + \sqrt{3}$. Therefore, each side of the large equilateral triangle has length $2 + \sqrt{3}$. The perimeter is the sum of all three sides, so multiply by 3 to get $6 + 3\sqrt{3}$, which is choice (D).

28. C   Difficulty: Hard

Category: Geometry

Getting to the Answer: The two most useful geometry properties you can memorize are that the interior angles of a triangle and supplementary angles both sum to 180°.

Remember, vertical angles formed by intersecting lines are congruent. This means the angle with the measure $90 - \dfrac{b}{2}$ is congruent to the interior angle of the triangle vertical to it. Likewise, the angle with the measure $90 - 3b$ is vertical to the other interior angle of the triangle. To find a in terms of b, set the sum of triangle *DEF*'s angles equal to 180° and solve for *a*:

$$a + \left(90 - \frac{b}{2}\right) + (90 - 3b) = 180$$

$$a - \frac{b}{2} - 3b = 0$$

$$a = 3b + \frac{b}{2}$$

$$a = \frac{6b}{2} + \frac{b}{2}$$

$$a = \frac{7b}{2}$$

This matches choice (C).

29. D   Difficulty: Medium

Category: Geometry

Getting to the Answer: The left transversal forms angles *a*, *b*, and *d*. From the figure you know *a* and *d* are corresponding (and therefore equal) angles. Together, angles *a* and *b* form a straight line, so they are supplementary; because *a* and *d* are equal, *b* and *d* are also supplementary. The other transversal forms *c* and *e*, which are supplementary. Consider angles *a*, *b*, and *d* as belonging to Group 1 and angles *c* and *e* as belonging to Group 2. None of the angles in Group 1 are necessarily equal, supplementary, or in any way related to any of the angles in Group 2 because they are formed by different transversals. For this reason, choices A, B, and C are incorrect, as they all try to relate angles from two different groups. That leaves choice (D), which is correct.

If you're not fully confident that choice (D) is correct, remember that *b* and *d* are supplementary, as are *c* and *e*. Therefore, $b + d = e + c = 180$. Rearrange the equation to yield $b + d - c = e$.

30. B   Difficulty: Hard

Category: Trigonometry

Getting to the Answer: The answer choices are all trig expressions, so use SOHCAHTOA and your equation solving skills. To find an angle in a triangle using trig, you need to know the measure of another angle and a side length, or two side lengths. It doesn't appear that you have any of these here. However, you do know the slope of the line $\left(-\dfrac{5}{12}\right)$, which you can use to sketch in a triangle that contains angle *A*. Your sketch might look like the following:

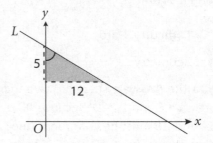

Note: Figure not drawn to scale.

You now know the lengths of the sides that are opposite and adjacent to angle *A*. This means you can use tangent (opposite over adjacent) to represent the measure of the angle. The side opposite the angle has length 12 and the side adjacent to the angle has length 5 (don't worry about whether 5 is positive or negative—you are using the length of the side, which is always positive), so choice (B) is correct.

31. C   Difficulty: Hard

Category: Geometry

Getting to the Answer: Always start complex questions by labeling the figure with all the information given in the question stem. This question tests your understanding of similar triangles. To review, similar triangles have the same angles and proportional sides. This figure contains a whopping five triangles, so it's important to carefully track the information. Start with $\triangle PRT$ because it has the most information. $\overline{RT}$ is the longer leg of a right triangle and is equal to 7; $\overline{PR}$ is the hypotenuse and is equal to 8. Avoid the time trap of using the Pythagorean theorem to find $\overline{PT}$. Instead, move forward with the triangle relationships. The next triangle to target is $\triangle PQS$, where $\overline{QS}$ is the longer leg equal to 9 and $\overline{PS}$ is the hypotenuse. Notice that both $\triangle PRT$ and $\triangle PQS$ are right triangles that share $\angle P$, which means that $\angle PRT$ and $\angle QSP$ are equal. Because the angles are all congruent, you have a pair of similar triangles and can set up a proportion for the sides to find $\overline{PS}$:

$\dfrac{Longer\ leg}{Hypotenuse} = \dfrac{\overline{RT}}{\overline{PR}} = \dfrac{\overline{QS}}{\overline{PS}}$, so $\dfrac{7}{8} = \dfrac{9}{\overline{PS}}$. $\overline{PS} \times 7 = 8 \times 9$,

so $\overline{PS} = \dfrac{72}{7} = 10\frac{2}{7}$. Choice (C) is correct.

32. D   Difficulty: Hard

Category: Geometry

Getting to the Answer: Because $\overline{CF}$ is a straight line, $\angle FAB$ and $\angle BAC$ add up to 180°. This means $y = 180$. $\angle FAE$ and $\angle BAC$ are vertical angles, so $\angle FAE$ is also 30°, which translates to $x = 90 + 30 = 120$. Therefore, $\dfrac{x+y}{2} = \dfrac{120+180}{2} = 150$. Choice (D) is the correct answer.

33. C   Difficulty: Hard

Category: Geometry

Getting to the Answer: Imagine cutting open the cylindrical casing and flattening it out; you'd get a rectangle. Its area is 61π cm^2 and its length is the height of the cylinder, which is 30.5 cm. Dividing the area by the length gives a width of 2π cm, which is also the circumference of the circular cross section of the kaleidoscope. Divide 2π by π to get the diameter, which is 2 cm. Add three diameters to the figure as shown to create six equilateral triangles, and then draw in the distance you're asked to find. The distance between the centers of two parallel mirrors bisects the equilateral triangles, creating 30-60-90

triangles; a close-up of one of these is also shown in the following figure.

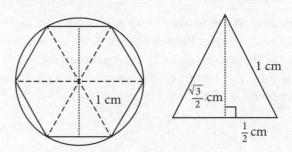

Using the ratio $x : x\sqrt{3} : 2x$, you'll find that the longer leg (which is half the distance you need) is $\dfrac{\sqrt{3}}{2}$. Doubling this quantity yields $\sqrt{3}$, which matches choice (C).

34. A   Difficulty: Hard

Category: Geometry

Getting to the Answer: Break this question into short steps. Step 1: Find the volume of the grain bin. Step 2: Find 75% of this volume. Step 3: Convert cubic feet to bushels. Step 4: Use the given rate, 5,500 bushels per hour.

Step 1: $V = \pi r^2 h$

If the diameter is 24, then the radius is 12.

$V = \pi (12^2)(40)$

$V = 5,760\pi$

$V = 18,095.57$

Step 2: $75\% = 0.75$

$18,095.57 \times 0.75 = 13,571.68$ cubic ft

Step 3: 1 bushel $= 1.24$ ft^3

$13,571.68\ \cancel{\text{ft}^3} \times \dfrac{1\ \text{bu}}{1.24\ \cancel{\text{ft}^3}} = \dfrac{13,571.68}{1.24} \approx 10,944.9$ bu

Step 4:

$10,944.9\ \cancel{\text{bu}} \times \dfrac{1\ \text{hr}}{5,500\ \cancel{\text{bu}}} = \dfrac{10,944.9}{5,500}$ hr ≈ 1.99 hr

Therefore, it should take about 2 hours to fill 75% of the grain bin, choice (A).

35. B   Difficulty: Hard

Category: Geometry

Getting to the Answer: Add additional lines to the figure to uncover hidden shapes. A diagonal drawn across the bottom face of the cube reveals a 45-45-90 triangle. The length of the diagonal (which is the hypotenuse of the triangle) is $2\sqrt{6} \times \sqrt{2} = 2\sqrt{12}$ cm.

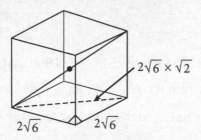

Do you see another right triangle you can use along with the Pythagorean theorem?

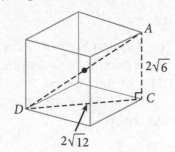

$$AC^2 + CD^2 = AD^2$$
$$\left(2\sqrt{6}\right)^2 + \left(2\sqrt{12}\right)^2 = AD^2$$
$$24 + 48 = AD^2$$
$$AD = \sqrt{72} = 6\sqrt{2}$$

The length of the diagonal from vertex to vertex is $6\sqrt{2}$, but you only need half that distance, so divide by 2 to yield $3\sqrt{2}$, the distance from a vertex to the center of the cube. Choice (B) is your match.

36. B   Difficulty: Hard

Category: Geometry

Getting to the Answer: The original cone has a height of 20 in. and a diameter of 10 in. (therefore, the radius is 5 in.), so its volume is $\frac{1}{3}\pi \times 5^2 \times 20 = \frac{500}{3}\pi$ in.² You can use a proportion to solve for the height of

the small cone that was truncated using the radii of both cones and height of the original cone: $\frac{x}{20} = \frac{1}{5} \rightarrow x = 4$ in. Therefore, the volume of the small cone is $\frac{1}{3}\pi \times 1^2 \times 4 = \frac{4}{3}\pi$ in.² Subtract this from the volume of the original cone to find the volume inside the megaphone: $\frac{500}{3}\pi - \frac{4}{3}\pi = \frac{496}{3}\pi$ in.³ This becomes $165\frac{1}{3}\pi$ in.³, which is choice (B).

37. D   Difficulty: Hard

Category: Trigonometry

Getting to the Answer: If an angle with measure A such that $\pi < A < \frac{3\pi}{2}$ is drawn on a unit circle, its terminal side will fall in Quadrant III, and $\sin A = k$ will be a negative value (because sine represents the y-value of the point that intersects the unit circle). If $\sin B = k$ also (and k is negative), then the terminal side of B must land in either of Quadrants III or IV (because sine is negative in those quadrants). Choose an easy radian measure (in Quadrant III) for angle A, such as $\frac{5\pi}{4}$. Try each answer choice to see which one results in an angle that lies in the third or fourth quadrant:

Choice A: $\frac{5\pi}{4} - \pi = \frac{5\pi}{4} - \frac{4\pi}{4} = \frac{\pi}{4}$, which is in Quadrant I, so eliminate choice A.

Choice B: $\pi + \frac{5\pi}{4} = \frac{4\pi}{4} + \frac{5\pi}{4} = \frac{9\pi}{4}$, which is in Quadrant I (because it is the same as $\frac{\pi}{4}$ rotated one full circle), so eliminate choice B.

Choice C: $2\pi - \frac{5\pi}{4} = \frac{8\pi}{4} - \frac{5\pi}{4} = \frac{3\pi}{4}$, which is in Quadrant II, so eliminate choice C.

Choice (D): $3\pi - \frac{5\pi}{4} = \frac{12\pi}{4} - \frac{5\pi}{4} = \frac{7\pi}{4}$, which is in Quadrant IV, so choice (D) is correct.

38. A   Difficulty: Hard

Category: Geometry

Getting to the Answer: In this question, information is given in both the diagram and the text. You need to relate the text to the diagram, one piece of information at a time, to calculate how long the lifeguard ran along the beach and how long he swam. Before you find the swim time, you need to know how *far* he swam. Whenever you see a right triangle symbol in a diagram, you should think Pythagorean theorem or, in this question, special right triangles. All multiples of 3-4-5 triangles are right triangles, so the length of the lifeguard's swim is the hypotenuse of a 30-40-50 triangle, or 50 feet. Add this number to the diagram. Now calculate the times using the distances and the speeds given. Don't forget the 1 second that the lifeguard paused.

$$\text{Run time} = 60 \ \cancel{ft} \times \frac{1 \sec}{12 \ \cancel{ft}} = \frac{60}{12} = 5 \sec$$

Pause time = 1 second

$$\text{Swim time} = 50 \ \cancel{ft} \times \frac{1 \sec}{5 \ \cancel{ft}} = \frac{50}{5} = 10 \sec$$

Total time = 5 + 1 + 10 = 16 seconds, choice (A).

39. C   Difficulty: Hard

Category: Geometry

Getting to the Answer: Draw additional lines in the figure to glean more information. Knowing the angle marked $\angle E$ is a central angle means $\overline{FE}$ and $\overline{ED}$ are radii that subtend $\overset{\frown}{FD}$. $\overline{AF}$ and $\overline{CD}$ are chords that share points F and D, respectively, with the radii, so you should be thinking inscribed angles. The following figure extends the partial chords in the pin template to reveal three inscribed angles.

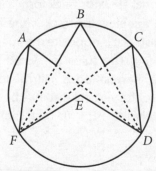

$\angle FED$ is one-third of the circle, which is $\frac{1}{3} \times 360° = 120°$. When a central angle and inscribed angle subtend the same arc ($\overset{\frown}{FD}$ here), the inscribed angle is half the central angle, making each of the inscribed angles 60°. Multiply this by 3 to get 180°, the sum of the three inscribed angles. Choice (C) is correct.

40. B   Difficulty: Hard

Category: Geometry

Getting to the Answer: Together, arcs AB, BC, and CA make up the entire circumference of the circle, which is $2\pi r = 2\pi(2) = 4\pi$. Use the central angle given (210°) to find the length of arc CA, and then subtract the sum of BC and CA from 4π to find the value of x.

Use the relationship between the central angle and the whole circle to find the length of arc CA:

$$\frac{\text{central angle}}{\text{whole circle}} = \frac{\text{arc length}}{\text{circumference}}.$$

$$\frac{210°}{360°} = \frac{CA}{4\pi}$$

$$\frac{7}{12} = \frac{CA}{4\pi}$$

$$28\pi = 12(CA)$$

$$\frac{7\pi}{3} = CA$$

Now, subtract the two arc lengths from the circumference of the circle to find the value of x:

$$x = 4\pi - \frac{7\pi}{6} - \frac{7\pi}{3}$$

$$= \frac{24\pi}{6} - \frac{7\pi}{6} - \frac{14\pi}{6}$$

$$= \frac{3\pi}{6} = \frac{\pi}{2}$$

The correct answer is choice (B).

41. D **Difficulty:** Hard

Category: Geometry

Getting to the Answer: Don't let this real-world scenario fool you. You aren't being asked to calculate the surface area or the volume of the pyramid. You only need to calculate the area of the four triangular faces, which is where the shingles will go. Drawing a sketch will help you visualize this and keep the dimensions straight.

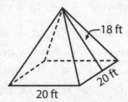

Use the formula for area of a triangle, $A = \frac{1}{2}bh$. The base of each triangular face is 20 feet and the height is the slant height of the pyramid, 18 feet, so the area of one side of the roof is $\frac{1}{2}(20)(18) = 180$. There are four sides, so the total area to be covered is $4(180) = 720$ square feet. Be careful—this is the area in square *feet* and the shingle size is given in square inches. Convert the square feet to square inches by multiplying 720 by 144 (12 inches × 12 inches). Then, divide the result by 72 to see how many shingles are needed: $720 \times 144 = 103,680 \div 72 = 1,440$. Finally, add 20% to this amount to account for the overlap in the shingles: $1,440 \times 1.2 = 1,728$ shingles, which is choice (D).

42. D **Difficulty:** Hard

Category: Geometry

Getting to the Answer: Draw additional lines (such as those that create hidden triangles) in the figure to glean more information.

Draw in a radius from the center of the circle (on the diameter of the semicircle) to $\overline{YZ}$ and a line that represents the greatest distance between $\overline{YZ}$ and $\overline{WX}$ to form a right triangle.

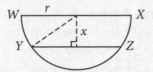

Because YZ is 25% less than WX, $YZ = \frac{3}{4}\overline{WX}$. In addition, $\frac{1}{2}\overline{WX} = r$; therefore, $\frac{1}{2}\overline{YZ} = \frac{3}{4}r$. Plug the known quantities into the Pythagorean theorem and solve for x:

$$\left(\frac{3}{4}r\right)^2 + x^2 = r^2$$

$$\frac{9}{16}r^2 + x^2 = r^2$$

$$x^2 = \frac{7}{16}r^2$$

$$x = \pm\frac{\sqrt{7}}{4}r$$

Choice (D) is the correct answer.

43. A **Difficulty:** Hard

Category: Geometry

Getting to the Answer: Organize information as you read the question. Here, you'll definitely want to draw and label a sketch.

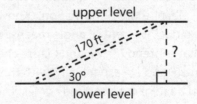

The lower level, the vertical distance between levels, and the diagonal elevator track form a 30-60-90 triangle, where the elevator track is the hypotenuse. The vertical distance is opposite the 30° angle so it is the shortest leg. The rules for 30-60-90 triangles state that the shortest leg is half the length of the hypotenuse, so the vertical distance between levels is approximately $170 \div 2 = 85$ feet, choice (A).

44. D   **Difficulty:** Hard

Category: Geometry

Getting to the Answer: Don't answer this question too quickly—the shaded portion is *not* the same as the sector because the triangular part at the center is not shaded. However, you'll need to find the area of the sector and then *subtract* the area of the triangle. To find the area of the sector, you'll need the area of the whole circle: $A = \pi r^2 = \pi(4)^2 = 16\pi$. Now use the formula:

$$\frac{\text{area of sector}}{\text{area of circle}} = \frac{\text{central angle}}{360°}$$

$$\frac{A_{\text{sector}}}{16\pi} = \frac{120}{360}$$

$$A_{\text{sector}} = \frac{120 \times 16\pi}{360}$$

$$A_{\text{sector}} = \frac{16\pi}{3}$$

Time-saving tip: You could actually determine the answer right now—it's (D). The first term in each expression has a π in it, which means it must represent the area of the sector. The second term does not, so it must represent the area of the triangle. Choice (D) is the only one that correctly gives the area of the sector.

In case you really want to know . . . To find the area of the triangle, notice that triangle *PQR* is formed by two radii and a chord. The height of the triangle represents the shorter leg of each of the smaller triangles inside *PQR*. The small triangles are congruent, and because $\angle PQR$ has a measure of 120°, each of the small triangles is a 30-60-90 triangle. The radius of the circle, which is the hypotenuse of each small triangle, is 4, so the shorter leg (the height) is half that (2), and the longer leg (half the base of *PQR*) is $2\sqrt{3}$, making the base of *PQR* equal to $4\sqrt{3}$. The area of triangle *PQR* is $\frac{1}{2}\left(4\sqrt{3}\right)\left(2\right) = 4\sqrt{3}$. Choice (D) is correct.

45. D   **Difficulty:** Hard

Category: Geometry

Getting to the Answer: You're told that the hexagonal face's diagonal is 8 mm. Drawing in three diagonals will split the hexagon into six congruent equilateral triangles. Drop in a height to form a 30-60-90 triangle that you can use to find the triangle height, which is $2\sqrt{3}$ cm.

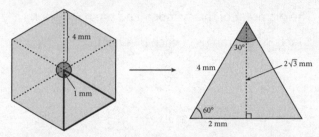

Each triangle has an area of $\frac{1}{2} \times 4 \times 2\sqrt{3} = 4\sqrt{3}$ mm²; therefore, the entire hexagonal face is $6 \times 4\sqrt{3} = 24\sqrt{3}$ mm². Multiply this value by the length of the pencil, 190 mm, to get the total volume of the pencil: $24\sqrt{3} \times 190 = 4{,}560\sqrt{3}$ mm³.

To find the graphite volume, treat the graphite core as a cylinder. You're told the diameter of the graphite is 2 mm, so the radius is 1 mm. The area of the cylinder top is $\pi r^2 = \pi$ mm². Because the defective pencils were only filled with graphite halfway, you should take half of 190 mm to get 95 mm for the height in your volume calculation, making the graphite volume 95π mm³. The graphite fraction is easily found with a ratio comparing graphite volume to total pencil volume: $\frac{95\pi}{4560\sqrt{3}} = \frac{\pi}{48\sqrt{3}} = \frac{\pi\sqrt{3}}{144}$. Choice (D) is correct.

46. D   Difficulty: Hard

Category: Geometry

Getting to the Answer: Try setting this question up in words first, and then translate from English into math: the volume of the test tube is equal to the volume of the cylinder plus the volume of the half-sphere. Use the formulas from the formula page to write an equation. Then, solve for the height.

The diameter of the cylinder (and the half-sphere) is 1 inch, so the radius of each is $\frac{1}{2}$ inch.

$$V_{tube} = V_{cylinder} + \frac{1}{2}V_{sphere}$$

$$\frac{19}{12}\pi = \pi r^2 h + \frac{1}{2}\left(\frac{4}{3}\pi r^3\right)$$

$$\frac{19}{12}\pi = \pi \left(\frac{1}{2}\right)^2 h + \frac{2}{3}\pi\left(\frac{1}{2}\right)^3$$

$$\frac{19}{12}\pi = \frac{1}{4}\pi h + \frac{2}{3}\left(\frac{1}{8}\pi\right)$$

$$\frac{19}{12}\pi - \frac{1}{12}\pi = \frac{1}{4}\pi h$$

$$\frac{3}{2}\pi = \frac{1}{4}\pi h$$

$$6 = h$$

Finally, add 6 to the height created by the half sphere (its radius) to get $6 + 0.5 = 6.5$ inches, which matches choice (D).

47. C   Difficulty: Hard

Category: Trigonometry

Getting to the Answer: Start by adjusting the given trig ratio to match the given side length, 1,000. The cosine of an angle is defined as $\cos x = \frac{adj}{hyp}$. According to the figure, the hypotenuse has length 1,000 (which is 500×2), so scale the trig ratio up by a factor of 2. This tells you that the adjacent side ($\overline{ML}$) has length $341 \times 2 = 682$. Now you know two sides of the right triangle and can use the Pythagorean theorem to find the missing side:

$$682^2 + b^2 = 1{,}000^2$$

$$b^2 = 1{,}000{,}000 - 465{,}124$$

$$b^2 = 534{,}876$$

$$b \approx 731.35$$

The length of side *LN* is approximately 731, which is choice (C).

48. D   Difficulty: Hard

Category: Geometry

Getting to the Answer: Start with what you know about the shaded square. Because its area is 12, each side must be $\sqrt{12} = 2\sqrt{3}$. Jot this down because you'll need it later.

Triangle *ABC* is an equilateral triangle, so each of its interior angles measures 60 degrees. This means that the two vertical sides of the square each represent the longer leg of a 30-60-90 triangle (the small white triangles on the sides). This leg has a length of $2\sqrt{3}$, making the short legs 2 each. You now have the length of the base of the large equilateral triangle: $2 + 2\sqrt{3} + 2 = 4 + 2\sqrt{3}$. Therefore, each side of the large equilateral triangle has length $4 + 2\sqrt{3}$. The perimeter is the sum of all three sides, so multiply by 3 to get $12 + 6\sqrt{3}$, making choice (D) correct.

49. B   Difficulty: Hard

Category: Geometry

Getting to the Answer: To find the radius of a circle that is given in standard form, rewrite the equation in the form $(x - h)^2 + (y - k)^2 = r^2$ by completing the square for the *x* terms and the *y* terms. Once you have accomplished this, the radius is *r* (so take the square root of the number on the right-hand side) and the center is (h, k). To complete the square for each variable, start by grouping the *x*s and *y*s together. Then, take the coefficient of the *x* term (4) and divide it by 2, square it, and add it to the two terms with *x* variables. Repeat the process for the *y*s. Don't forget to add these same amounts to the other side of the equation as well to keep it balanced. This should create the squares of two binomials, which will look like the required form:

$$x^2 + y^2 - 4x - 8y = 16$$

$$x^2 - 4x + y^2 - 8y = 16$$

$$(x^2 - 4x + 4) + (y^2 - 8y + 16) = 16 + 4 + 16$$

$$(x - 2)^2 + (y - 4)^2 = 36$$

From the equation, you know that r^2 is 36, which means the radius, *r*, is 6. Choice (B) is correct.

50. D   Difficulty: Hard

Category: Geometry

Getting to the Answer: If needed, don't forget to check the formulas provided for you at the beginning of each math section. The volume of a right cone is given by $V = \frac{1}{3}\pi r^2 h$. Here, you only know the value of one of the variables, *V*, so you'll need to use the information in the question to somehow write *r* and *h* in terms of just one variable. If the cone is three times as wide at the base as it is tall, then call the diameter 3*x* and the height of the cone one-third of that, or *x*. The volume formula calls for the radius, which is half the diameter, or $\frac{3x}{2}$. Substitute these values into the formula and solve for *x*:

$$V = \frac{1}{3}\pi r^2 h$$

$$384\pi = \frac{1}{3}\pi\left(\frac{3}{2}x\right)^2 x$$

$$384 = \left(\frac{1}{3}\right)\left(\frac{9}{4}x^2\right)x$$

$$384 = \frac{3}{4}x^3$$

$$512 = x^3$$

$$\sqrt[3]{512} = x$$

$$8 = x$$

The question asks for the diameter of the base, which is $3x = 3(8) = 24$, choice (D).

51. C   Difficulty: Hard

Category: Imaginary Numbers

Getting to the Answer: Each of the factors in this product has two terms, so they behave like binomials. This means you can use FOIL to find the product, but you must simplify the two radicals first using the definition of *i*. Write each of the numbers under the radicals as a product of −1 and the number, take the square roots, and then FOIL the resulting expressions.

$$\left(3 + \sqrt{-16}\right)\left(-3 + \sqrt{-25}\right)$$

$$= \left(3 + \sqrt{-1 \times 16}\right)\left(-3 - \sqrt{-1 \times 25}\right)$$

$$= (3 + 4i)(-3 - 5i)$$

$$= -9 - 15i - 12i - 20i^2$$

$$= -9 - 27i - 20(-1)$$

$$= 11 - 27i$$

This matches choice (C).

52. D   Difficulty: Hard

Category: Geometry

Getting to the Answer: When the equation of a circle is written in the form $(x - h)^2 + (y - k)^2 = r^2$, the center of the circle is (*h*, *k*), and the radius of the circle is *r*. The question gives the center of the circle, (1, 0); therefore, the left side of the equation is $(x - 1)^2 + (y - 0)^2$, which simplifies to $(x - 1)^2 + y^2$. This means that you can eliminate A and C because the left side of the equation is incorrect.

The length of the radius is equal to the distance between the center of the circle, (1, 0) and the endpoint of the radius $\left(2, \frac{5}{2}\right)$. Use the Distance formula to determine this length. Because the circle equation contains r^2, (not *r*), you can save a step (and time) by calculating the square of the distance (d^2), which in turn gives you r^2:

$$d = \sqrt{\left(x_2 - x_1\right)^2 + \left(y_2 - y_1\right)^2}$$

$$d^2 = \left(x_2 - x_1\right)^2 + \left(y_2 - y_1\right)^2$$

$$= \left(2 - 1\right)^2 + \left(\frac{5}{2} - 0\right)^2$$

$$= 1 + \frac{25}{4}$$

$$= \frac{4}{4} + \frac{25}{4}$$

$$d^2 = \frac{29}{4}$$

The correct equation for this circle is $\left(x - 1\right)^2 + y^2 = \frac{29}{4}$, which matches the equation in choice (D).

53. D   Difficulty: Hard

Category: Geometry

Getting to the Answer: To find the equation of a circle, you need the radius and the *x*- and *y*-coordinates of the center point. Then, you can use the standard equation: $(x - h)^2 + (y - k)^2 = r^2$, where (h, k) is the center of the circle and r is the length of the radius.

Be careful—choice B is a trap! Sometimes finding the center and the radius from a graph is not as straightforward as you may think. This graph has no number labels on it, so you'll need to use the information given in the question about the smaller circle to determine the value of each grid-line:

$$A = \pi r^2$$

$$144\pi = \pi r^2$$

$$144 = r^2$$

$$\pm 12 = r$$

The radius can't be negative, so it must be 12. There are only 3 grid-lines between the center of the smaller circle and its edge, so each grid-line must be equal to 4 units. This means the center of the larger circle is $(-8, 0)$ and its radius is $6 \times 4 = 24$. Therefore,

the equation must be $(x - (-8))^2 + (y - 0)^2 = 24^2$, or written in simplified form, $(x + 8)^2 + y^2 = 576$, making choice (D) the correct answer.

54. C   Difficulty: Hard

Category: Geometry

Getting to the Answer: When the rectangular solid was cut into two identical cubes, two new faces were formed: one on each cube along the line of the cut. Therefore, the difference between the original surface area and the combined surface area of the resulting cubes is equal to the surface area of the two new faces. To find the area of each of these faces, you need to find the length of an edge of the cube.

Because the rectangular block was divided into two equal cubes, the volume of each of these cubes is equal to $\frac{1}{2}$ the volume of the original solid, or 250 cubic inches $\div 2 = 125$ cubic inches. So, an edge of one of these cubes has a length equal to the cube root of 125, which is 5. Therefore, the area of one face of the cube equals 5×5, or 25. So, two of these faces have a total area of 2×25, or 50 square inches, which is choice (C).

55. A   Difficulty: Hard

Category: Imaginary Numbers

Getting to the Answer: The denominator in each of the answer choices is the same as the denominator in the expression in the question. This means you're not trying to rationalize the expression, but rather simply adding the two terms. Fractions with complex numbers are no different from any other fraction. You must find a common denominator before adding them. Find a common denominator by multiplying the second term by $5 - 4i$. As always, you're given that $i = \sqrt{-1}$, but a more useful fact is that $i^2 = -1$, so be sure to make this substitution as you work. Once you've found the common denominator, you can simply add like terms.

$$\frac{1}{5-4i} + (3+i) = \frac{1}{5-4i} + \frac{3+i}{1}$$

$$= \frac{1}{5-4i} + \frac{3+i}{1}\left(\frac{5-4i}{5-4i}\right)$$

$$= \frac{1}{5-4i} + \frac{15-12i+5i-4i^2}{5-4i}$$

$$= \frac{1}{5-4i} + \frac{15-7i-4(-1)}{5-4i}$$

$$= \frac{1+15-7i+4}{5-4i}$$

$$= \frac{20-7i}{5-4i}$$

This matches choice (A).

56. 17 Difficulty: Medium

Category: Imaginary Numbers

Getting to the Answer: Don't let this "new" definition intimidate you. All you're asked to do is to find the square root of the sum of a^2 and b^2. You don't even have to involve the i at all.

$$|15+8i| = \sqrt{15^2 + 8^2}$$

$$= \sqrt{225+64}$$

$$= \sqrt{289}$$

$$= 17$$

There is nothing else to do—the answer is 17.

57. 150 Difficulty: Medium

Category: Geometry

Getting to the Answer: In this question, you're given a part-to-part ratio (shaded:unshaded) that you need to convert into a part-to-whole ratio (shaded:whole circle). Remember that the ratio between the interior angle of a sector and 360° is the same as the ratio between the area of that sector and the area of the whole circle.

Because the ratio of the shaded area to the unshaded area is 5:7, the ratio of the shaded area to the entire circle is 5:(5 + 7) = 5:12. This ratio is the same as the ratio of the interior angle of the shaded sector to 360°, or x:360. Set up a proportion using these ratios:

$$\frac{5}{12} = \frac{x}{360}$$

$$360(5) = 12x$$

$$1,800 = 12x$$

$$150 = x$$

The correct answer is 150.

58. 10 Difficulty: Medium

Category: Geometry

Getting to the Answer: The key to this question is that the radius of a circle is perpendicular to a tangent line—a line that touches a curve at a point without crossing over—at that point. Once you draw the crucial right angle in, just proceed step-by-step until you have enough information to apply the Pythagorean theorem or (if you've been studying your Kaplan tips) your knowledge of Pythagorean triplets.

$$A = \pi r^2$$

$$36\pi = \pi r^2$$

$$36 = r^2$$

$$6 = r$$

So, $KM = 6$. You also know that $JL = 16$, and the tick marks on the figure indicate congruence, so KL equals half that, or 8.

With $KM = 6$ and $KL = 8$, apply the Pythagorean theorem:

$$c^2 = a^2 + b^2$$

$$c^2 = 36 + 64$$

$$c^2 = 100$$

$$c = 10$$

You may have also noticed that this is a multiple of a 3-4-5 Pythagorean triplet, making it a 6-8-10 triplet, which means 10 is the correct answer.

59. 3/2 or 1.5   Difficulty: Medium

Category: Imaginary Numbers

Getting to the Answer: Use the definition of *i* to simplify the numerator by writing the quantity under the radical as a product of −1 and 27. Look for other perfect squares that can be divided out of both the numerator and the denominator. Then simplify:

$$\frac{\sqrt{-27}}{\sqrt{12}} = \frac{\sqrt{-1 \times 9 \times 3}}{\sqrt{4 \times 3}} = \frac{3i\sqrt{3}}{2\sqrt{3}} = \frac{3}{2}i$$

The question asks for the coefficient of *i*, so the correct answer is 3/2 or 1.5.

60. 28   Difficulty: Medium

Category: Geometry

Getting to the Answer: Use the Pythagorean theorem to find the length of the diagonal shown in the figure.

$$a^2 + b^2 = c^2$$
$$42^2 + 56^2 = c^2$$
$$1{,}764 + 3{,}136 = c^2$$
$$4{,}900 = c^2$$
$$\sqrt{4{,}900} = \sqrt{c^2}$$
$$70 = c$$

The length of the sidewalk is 70 feet. Now, divide by 5 to get $70 \div 5 = 14$, but be careful—this is not the answer. The college plans to put the lights on *both* sides of the sidewalk, so it actually needs $14 \times 2 = 28$ lights.

61. 6   Difficulty: Medium

Category: Geometry

Getting to the Answer: Use the formula for volume of a rectangular solid, $V = lwh$, to write an equation. Because the dimensions are given as the ratio 4:2:1, let the length, width, and height be represented by

$4x$, $2x$, and $1x$. Substitute the expressions into the formula and solve for *x*.

$$216 = (4x)(2x)(1x)$$
$$216 = 8x^3$$
$$27 = x^3$$
$$3 = x$$

The width was represented by $2x$, so multiply to find that the width is $2(3) = 6$ inches.

62. 4000   Difficulty: Hard

Category: Geometry

Getting to the Answer: Draw a figure to represent the situation.

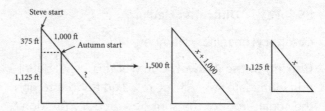

You have two similar triangles, so you can set up a proportion to solve for *x*, the trail footage that Steve and Autumn ski together.

$$\frac{1{,}125}{1{,}500} = \frac{x}{x + 1{,}000}$$
$$1{,}125(x + 1{,}000) = 1{,}500(x)$$
$$1{,}125x + 1{,}125{,}000x = 1{,}500x$$
$$x = 3{,}000$$

Don't stop yet; the question asks for the full length of the trail Steve took. Add 3,000 to 1,000 to get 4,000, his total trail footage.

63. 9984   Difficulty: Hard

Category: Geometry

Getting to the Answer: Don't be too quick to answer a question like this. You can't simply find two-thirds of the volume of the pyramid because the top is considerably smaller than the bottom. Instead, you'll need to find the volume of the whole pyramid and subtract the volume of the top piece that is being discarded.

The figure shows a right triangle inside the pyramid. The bottom leg is given as 18 and the slant height, or hypotenuse of the triangle, is given as 30. You might recognize this as a multiple of the Pythagorean triplet, 3-4-5, which is in this case 18-24-30. This means the height of the original pyramid is 24. You now have enough information to find the volume of the original pyramid.

$$V = \frac{1}{3}lwh$$

$$V = \frac{1}{3}(36)(36)(24)$$

$$V = \frac{1}{3}(31,104)$$

$$V = 10,368$$

To determine the dimensions of the top piece that is cut off, use similar triangles.

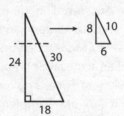

One-third of the original height is $24 \div 3 = 8$, resulting in a 6-8-10 triangle, making the length of the smaller leg 6, which means the length of the whole cutoff pyramid is $6 \times 2 = 12$. Substitute this into the formula for volume again.

$$V = \frac{1}{3}lwh$$

$$V = \frac{1}{3}(12)(12)(8)$$

$$V = \frac{1}{3}(1,152)$$

$$V = 384$$

Thus, the volume of the frustum is $10,368 - 384 = 9,984$ cubic meters.

64. 30   Difficulty: Medium

Category: Geometry

Getting to the Answer: Write the given lengths of the sides as a ratio (shortest to longest), $1.5:\frac{3\sqrt{3}}{2}:3$. Try to manipulate this ratio so that it looks like one you're familiar with. Clear the fraction by doubling each part of the ratio to get $3:3\sqrt{3}:6$. Notice that each part of the ratio is divisible by 3, so divide a 3 out. The result is $1:\sqrt{3}:2$, which should look very familiar by now. The triangle is a 30-60-90 triangle, which means the measure of the smallest angle is 30 degrees.

65. 128   Difficulty: Medium

Category: Geometry

Getting to the Answer: The question tells you that the circumference of the opening (which is a circle) is 8π, so substitute this value in the formula for circumference and solve for r.

$$C = 2\pi r$$

$$8\pi = 2\pi r$$

$$4 = r$$

You now have everything you need to find h, which in this case is the length of the tunnel. Use the formula $V = \pi r^2 h$:

$$2,048\pi = \pi(4)^2(h)$$

$$2,048 = 16h$$

$$128 = h$$

The tunnel is 128 feet long.

66. 14   Difficulty: Hard

Category: Geometry

Getting to the Answer: When the equation of a circle is in the form $(x - h)^2 + (y - k)^2 = r^2$, the r represents the length of the radius. To get the equation into this form, complete the squares. You already have an x^2 and a y^2 in the given equation and the coefficients of x and y are even, so completing the square is fairly straightforward—there are just a lot of steps. Start by grouping the xs and ys together. Then, take the coefficient of the x term and divide it by 2, square it, and add it to the two terms with x variables. Do the same with the y term. Don't forget to add these amounts to the other side of the equation as well. This creates a perfect square of x terms and y terms, so take the square root of each.

$$x^2 + y^2 + 10x - 4y = 20$$
$$x^2 + 10x + y^2 - 4y = 20$$
$$\left(x^2 + 10x + 25\right) + \left(y^2 - 4y + 4\right) = 20 + 25 + 4$$
$$\left(x + 5\right)^2 + \left(y - 2\right)^2 = 49$$

The equation tells you that $r^2 = 49$, which means that the radius is 7 and the diameter is twice that, so 14 is the correct answer.

67. 27   Difficulty: Hard

Category: Imaginary Numbers

Getting to the Answer: Each of the factors in this product has two terms, so they behave like binomials. This means you can use FOIL to find the product. To avoid messy numbers, simplify the two radicals first using the definition of i. Write each of the numbers under the radicals as a product of -1 and the number, take the square roots, and then FOIL the resulting expressions:

$$\left(3 + \sqrt{-16}\right)\left(1 - \sqrt{-36}\right)$$
$$= \left(3 + \sqrt{16 \times (-1)}\right)\left(1 - \sqrt{36 \times (-1)}\right)$$
$$= (3 + 4i)(1 - 6i)$$
$$= 3 - 18i + 4i - 24i^2$$
$$= 3 - 14i - 24(-1)$$
$$= 3 - 14i + 24$$
$$= 27 - 14i$$

The question asks for the value of a (the real part of the expression), so the correct answer is 27.

68. 14   Difficulty: Hard

Category: Geometry

Getting to the Answer: The shaded region is the area of the larger triangle minus the area of the smaller triangle. Set up and solve an equation using the information from the figure. You don't know the height of the smaller triangle, so call it h. You do know the area of the shaded region—it's 52 square units.

Larger triangle: base $= 12$; height $= h + 3 + 3$

Smaller triangle: base $= 8$; height $= h$

Shaded area $=$ large area $-$ small area

The question asks for the height of the *larger* triangle, so the correct answer is $8 + 3 + 3 = 14$.

69. 5/12 or .417   Difficulty: Hard

Category: Trigonometry

Getting to the Answer: This question is quick if you know the complementary angle relationship: $\cos x° = \sin(90° - x°)$. More simply stated, this means that the cosine of an acute angle is equal to the sine of the angle's complement. For example, $\cos 20° = \sin 70°$ because $20°$ and $70°$ are complementary angles. The property works in reverse as well: $\sin 10° = \cos 80°$ because $10°$ and $80°$ are complementary angles. By the relationship given above, because $\cos x° = \dfrac{5}{12}$, $\sin(90° - x°)$ must equal the same thing, so grid in 5/12 or .417.

70. 28   Difficulty: Hard

Category: Geometry

Getting to the Answer: Knowing how to write the equation of a circle will earn you points on Test Day. You'll also need to be able to algebraically expand that equation. Don't forget—when you square a binomial, you should write it as repeated multiplication and use FOIL. First, find the center and the radius of the circle: Because each grid-line represents one unit on the graph, the center is (2, 0) and the radius is 6. Substitute these values into the equation for a circle, $(x - h)^2 + (y - k)^2 = r^2$, and then simplify until the equation looks like the one given in the question:

$$(x - 2)^2 + (y - 0)^2 = 6^2$$
$$(x - 2)(x - 2) + y^2 = 36$$
$$x^2 + y^2 - 4x + 4 = 36$$
$$x^2 + y^2 - 4x = 32$$

The coefficient of x is -4 and $c = 32$. Because there is no y term, $b = 0$. Therefore, $a + b + c = -4 + 0 + 32 = 28$.

71. 46   Difficulty: Hard

Category: Geometry

Getting to the Answer: First, find the center and the radius of the circle: Each grid-line represents one unit on the graph, so the center is (0, 1) and the radius is 7. Substitute these values into the equation for a circle, $(x - h)^2 + (y - k)^2 = r^2$, and then simplify until the equation looks like the one given in the question:

$$\left(x - 0\right)^2 + \left(y - 1\right)^2 = 7^2$$
$$x^2 + (y - 1)(y - 1) = 49$$
$$x^2 + y^2 - 2y + 1 = 49$$
$$x^2 + y^2 - 2y = 48$$

There is no x term, so $a = 0$. The coefficient of y is -2 and $c = 48$, so $a + b + c = 0 + (-2) + 48 = 46$.

72. 40   Difficulty: Hard

Category: Geometry

Getting to the Answer: Because $\overline{AB}$, $\overline{CD}$, and $\overline{EF}$ are diameters, the sum of x, y, and the interior angle of the shaded region is 180 degrees. The question tells you that the shaded region is $\frac{1}{5}$ of the circle, so the interior angle must equal $\frac{1}{5}$ of the degrees in the whole circle, or $\frac{1}{5}$ of 360. Use what you know about y (that it is equal to $2x - 12$) and what you know about the shaded region (that it is $\frac{1}{5}$ of 360 degrees) to write and solve an equation.

$$x + y + \frac{1}{5}(360) = 180$$
$$x + (2x - 12) + 72 = 180$$
$$3x + 60 = 180$$
$$3x = 120$$
$$x = 40$$

73. 35   Difficulty: Hard

Category: Geometry

Getting to the Answer: Start by determining whether there is a relationship between triangles ABC and EDC. The two triangles share a common angle, C. It is given that $\overline{DE} \perp \overline{AC}$, so angle DEC is a right angle. Because $\overline{DE} \parallel \overline{AB}$, $\overline{BA}$ is also perpendicular to $\overline{AC}$, making angle BAC another right angle. Finally, because $\overline{AB}$ and $\overline{DE}$ are parallel lines intersected by a transversal (side BC), angles ABD and EDC are also congruent. This means the two triangles are similar by AAA. Now, start with what you know and find what you can. The length of AE is 28, which means the length of AC is $28 + 4 = 32$. The length of EC is 4, which means that the side lengths of triangle ABC are 8 times the side lengths of triangle EDC. Now use this to find DE: $24 \div 8 = 3$. You might now recognize the Pythagorean triplet 3-4-5, but you could also use the Pythagorean theorem to find that $DC = 5$. Multiply this by 8 to find BC: $5 \times 8 = 40$. Be careful—this isn't the answer. The question asks for the length of BD, which is $40 - 5 = 35$.

74. 5/41   Difficulty: Hard

Category: Imaginary Numbers

Getting to the Answer: Because *i* is defined as the square root of −1, it's not considered proper notation to leave an *i* in the denominator of a fraction. To "rationalize" a denominator containing an imaginary number, multiply both the numerator and denominator by the conjugate of the denominator. (To find the conjugate, simply change the sign of the imaginary part of the number.) The conjugate of $5 + 4i$ is $5 - 4i$. As you work through the calculations, use FOIL and remember that when you multiply *i* by *i*, the result is −1.

$$\frac{5-5i}{5+4i} \times \frac{5-4i}{5-4i}$$

$$= \frac{(5-5i)(5-4i)}{(5+4i)(5-4i)}$$

$$= \frac{25 - 25i - 20i + 20i^2}{25 + 20i - 20i - 16i^2}$$

$$= \frac{25 - 45i + 20(-1)}{25 - 16(-1)}$$

$$= \frac{5 - 45i}{41}$$

$$= \frac{5}{41} - \frac{45}{41}i$$

The question asks for *a*, the real part of the complex number, so the correct answer is 5/41.

75. 4/5 or 0.8   Difficulty: Hard

Category: Trigonometry

Getting to the Answer: When a question involves a trig function and one or more right triangles, drawing a quick sketch is absolutely key to answering the question (unless the complementary angles rule applies, which it doesn't here). After drawing a sketch, use what you know about similar triangles and then use SOHCAHTOA. Be sure to keep the vertices correctly matched from one triangle to the next:

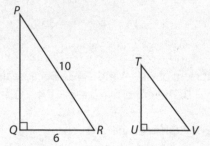

Because the triangles are similar, the corresponding angle measures are equal (angles *P* and *T*, *Q* and *U*, and *R* and *V*). Trig functions are based on angle measures, so $\sin V = \sin R$ (the $\frac{1}{2}$ doesn't come into play at all). To find sin *R*, you need to know the length of the side opposite to angle *R* (which is *PQ*) and the length of the hypotenuse (which is 10). You might recognize that triangle *PQR* is a multiple of a 3-4-5 right triangle (multiplied by a factor of 2), which means side *PQ* has length $4 \times 2 = 8$. (You could also use the Pythagorean theorem to find this length.) Therefore:

$$\sin R = \frac{\text{opp}}{\text{hyp}} = \frac{8}{10} = \frac{4}{5}$$

Because $\sin V = \sin R$, grid in 4/5 or 0.8 as the correct answer.

UNIT FOUR

Essay

CHAPTER FIFTEEN

SAT Essay Test Overview

THE SAT ESSAY TEST (OPTIONAL)

The SAT Essay Test will assess your college and career readiness by testing your abilities to read and analyze a high-quality source document and write a coherent analysis of the source supported with critical reasoning and evidence from the given text.

The SAT Essay Test features an argumentative source text of 650–750 words aimed toward a large audience. Passages will examine ideas, debates, and shifts in the arts and sciences as well as civic, cultural, and political life. Rather than having a simple for/against structure, these passages will be nuanced and will relate views on complex subjects. These passages will also be logical in their structure and reasoning.

It is important to note that prior knowledge is not required.

The SAT Essay Test prompt will ask you to explain how the presented passage's author builds an argument to convince an audience. In writing your essay, you may analyze elements such as the author's use of evidence, reasoning, style, and persuasion; you will not be limited to those elements listed, however.

Rather than writing about whether you agree or disagree with the presented argument, you will write an essay in which you analyze *how* the author makes an argument.

The SAT Essay Test will be broken down into three categories for scoring: Reading, Analysis, and Writing. Each of these elements will be scored on a scale of 1 to 4 by two graders, for a total score of 2 to 8 for each category.

CHAPTER SIXTEEN

SAT Essay

THE KAPLAN METHOD FOR THE SAT ESSAY

The SAT Essay, while optional, presents you with a challenge: to read and understand a high-quality source text and write an essay analyzing the author's argument in 50 minutes. By using the Kaplan Method for the SAT Essay, you will be able to make the most out of those 50 minutes and produce a high-scoring written response to a previously published, sophisticated source.

The Kaplan Method for the SAT Essay consists of four steps:

Step 1: Read the source text, taking notes on how the author uses:

- Evidence to support claims
- Reasoning to develop ideas and to connect claims and evidence
- Stylistic or persuasive elements to add power to the ideas expressed

Step 2: Use the Kaplan Template to create an outline

Step 3: Write your essay

Step 4: Check your essay for mistakes in grammar, spelling, and clarity

Let's take a closer look at each step.

Step 1: Read the Source Text, Taking Notes on How the Author Uses:

- **Evidence to support claims**
- **Reasoning to develop ideas and to connect claims and evidence**
- **Stylistic or persuasive elements to add power to the ideas expressed**

What is the source text?

The source text for the SAT Essay will consist of a passage that is very similar to the passages you'll see in the Reading Test. It will typically be 500–750 words and will deal with topics of general interest in the arts, sciences, and public life. In many cases, the passages will be biased in favor of the author's argument.

While the source text changes from test to test, the directions and essay prompt remain similar. Spend more time reading and understanding the text—the prompt will likely be very similar to other prompts that you've encountered.

What kinds of notes should I take?

The notes you take while reading the source text are similar to those you would take when creating a Passage Map on the SAT Reading Test. However, these notes will focus on how the author connects central ideas and important details.

Your notes should focus on:

- Evidence to support claims (e.g., cited data or statistics, or authoritative sources that support the author's argument)
- Reasoning to develop ideas and make connections (e.g., the author explains his logic for using a specific piece of evidence to support a specific claim)
- Stylistic or persuasive elements to add power to the ideas expressed (e.g., using figurative language, irony, metaphor, and other elements to appeal to emotions)

✔ **Remember**

Focus on *how* the author develops the argument and *why* the author chose the features he or she used. Your task is to analyze the effectiveness of the author's argument.

In addition to taking notes in the margins of the passage, it is also helpful to underline and circle the following:

- Central ideas
- Important details
- Facts and opinions
- Textual evidence (quotations, paraphrases, or both)

Your goal is to identify three features such as juxtaposition, imagery, and symbolism that the author uses to build his or her argument.

✔ **Definition**

Features are the key elements of the essay that you marked in your notes. They could include stylistic techniques (such as irony) or data (such as statistics) used to bolster a claim.

You should spend approximately 10 minutes on Step 1.

Step 2: Use the Kaplan Template to Create an Outline

Why do I need an outline?

Creating an outline before you write your essay is a huge time-saver, which is essential when you have only 50 minutes to complete the SAT Essay. Spending the first part of the allotted time effectively (i.e., reading and taking notes on the source text and creating an outline) will lead to a well-organized, more convincing essay. You'll also find that organizing your thoughts ahead of time will enable you to write much more quickly!

What should I put in my outline?

Kaplan has created an efficient and effective template to outline the SAT Essay. Using the template will prevent you from encountering a writing or thinking block. With the template and the Kaplan Method, you will know what you want to write about the source text and not waste any time.

You should spend approximately 8 minutes on Step 2.

> ✔ *On Test Day*
>
> **You will not be able to bring this template with you to Test Day. Therefore, it is important that you memorize the gist and logical flow of the template well before Test Day so that creating an outline is second nature to you when you sit down to write your essay.**

Step 3: Write Your Essay

After you have read and analyzed the source text, your next goal is to write a cohesive essay that demonstrates your use and command of standard written English. To demonstrate your proficiency, you must:

- Provide your own precise central claim
- Use a variety of sentence structures
- Employ precise word choice
- Maintain a constant and appropriate style and tone

You should spend approximately 30 minutes on Step 3.

> ✔ *Remember*
>
> **Your task is to analyze the author's effectiveness in the use of rhetorical features to develop the argument. Do *not* agree or disagree with the argument.**

Step 4: Check Your Essay for Mistakes in Grammar, Spelling, and Clarity

While a few grammar and spelling mistakes won't drastically harm your SAT Essay score, setting aside some time to proofread can help you catch careless errors that you can easily correct, thereby increasing your Writing score on the SAT Essay.

You should spend the remaining 2 minutes on Step 4.

THE SAT ESSAY PROMPT

As mentioned previously in this chapter, the SAT Essay source text will change from administration to administration, but the prompt will remain largely the same in both format and wording.

Become familiar with the idea behind the prompt and assignment as soon as you can so that on Test Day, you will be able to focus on reading, analyzing, and writing, rather than figuring out what the prompt is asking you to accomplish.

The generic SAT Essay prompt is as follows:

As you read the passage below, consider how [the author] uses

- evidence, such as facts or examples, to support claims.

- reasoning to develop ideas and to connect claims and evidence.

- stylistic or persuasive elements, such as word choice or appeals to emotion, to add power to the ideas expressed.

Source Text Will Appear Here

Write an essay in which you explain how [the author] builds an argument to persuade [his/her] audience that [author's claim]. In your essay, analyze how [the author] uses one or more of the features listed above (or features of your own choice) to strengthen the logic and persuasiveness of [his/her] argument. Be sure that your analysis focuses on the most relevant features of the passage.

Your essay should not explain whether you agree with [the author's] claims, but rather explain how [the author] builds an argument to persuade [his/her] audience.

SAT ESSAY SCORING RUBRIC

There are three different scores for the SAT Essay: Reading, Analysis, and Writing. Each category will be scored on a scale of 1 to 4. The scores you receive will range from 2 to 8, as they will be the scores of two raters.

The raters will use the following rubric to determine each area score.

	1	2	3	4
Reading	• Demonstrates **little or no comprehension** of the source text • Fails to show an understanding of the text's central idea(s), and may include only details without reference to central idea(s) • May contain numerous errors of fact and/or interpretation with regard to the text • Makes little or no use of textual evidence	• Demonstrates **some comprehension** of the source text • Shows an understanding of the text's central idea(s) but not of important details • May contain errors of fact and/or interpretation with regard to the text • Makes limited and/or haphazard use of textual evidence	• Demonstrates **effective comprehension** of the source text • Shows an understanding of the text's central idea(s) and important details • Is free of substantive errors of fact and interpretation with regard to the text • Makes appropriate use of textual evidence	• Demonstrates **thorough comprehension** of the source text • Shows an understanding of the text's central idea(s) and most important details and how they interrelate • Is free of errors of fact or interpretation with regard to the text • Makes skillful use of textual evidence

(continued)

	1	2	3	4
Analysis	• Offers **little or no analysis or ineffective analysis** of the source text and demonstrates **little to no understanding** of the analytical task • Identifies without explanation some aspects of the author's use of evidence, reasoning, and/or stylistic and persuasive elements, and/or feature(s) of the student's own choosing • Numerous aspects of analysis are unwarranted based on the text • Contains little or no support for claim(s) or point(s) made, or support is largely irrelevant • May not focus on features of the text that are relevant to addressing the task • Offers no discernible analysis (e.g., is largely or exclusively summary)	• Offers **limited analysis** of the source text and demonstrates only **partial understanding** of the analytical task • Identifies and attempts to describe the author's use of evidence, reasoning, and/or stylistic and persuasive elements, and/or feature(s) of the student's own choosing, but merely asserts rather than explains their importance • One or more aspects of analysis are unwarranted based on the text • Contains little or no support for claim(s) or point(s) made • May lack a clear focus on those features of the text that are most relevant to addressing the task	• Offers an **effective analysis** of the source text and demonstrates an **understanding** of the analytical task • Competently evaluates the author's use of evidence, reasoning, and/or stylistic and persuasive elements, and/or feature(s) of the student's own choosing • Contains relevant and sufficient support for claim(s) or point(s) made • Focuses primarily on those features of the text that are most relevant to addressing the task	• Offers an **insightful analysis** of the source text and demonstrates a **sophisticated understanding** of the analytical task • Offers a thorough, well-considered evaluation of the author's use of evidence, reasoning, and/or stylistic and persuasive elements, and/or feature(s) of the student's own choosing • Contains relevant, sufficient, and strategically chosen support for claim(s) or point(s) made • Focuses consistently on those features of the text that are most relevant to addressing the task

	1	2	3	4
Writing	• Demonstrates **little or no cohesion** and **inadequate skill** in the use and control of language • May lack a clear central claim or controlling idea • Lacks a recognizable introduction and conclusion; does not have a discernible progression of ideas • Lacks variety in sentence structures; sentence structures may be repetitive; demonstrates general and vague word choice; word choice may be poor or inaccurate; may lack a formal style and objective tone • Shows a weak control of the conventions of standard written English and may contain numerous errors that undermine the quality of writing	• Demonstrates **little or no cohesion** and **limited skill** in the use and control of language • May lack a clear central claim or controlling idea or may deviate from the claim or idea • May include an ineffective introduction and/or conclusion; may demonstrate some progression of ideas within paragraphs but not throughout • Has limited variety in sentence structures; sentence structures may be repetitive; demonstrates general or vague word choice; word choice may be repetitive; may deviate noticeably from a formal style and objective tone • Shows a limited control of the conventions of standard written English and contains errors that detract from the quality of writing and may impede understanding	• Is **mostly cohesive** and demonstrates **effective use and control** of language • Includes a central claim or implicit controlling idea • Includes an effective introduction and conclusion; demonstrates a clear progression of ideas both within paragraphs and throughout the essay • Has variety in sentence structures; demonstrates some precise word choice; maintains a formal style and objective tone • Shows a good control of the conventions of standard written English and is free of significant errors that detract from the quality of writing	• Is **cohesive** and demonstrates a **highly effective use and command** of language • Includes a precise central claim • Includes a skillful introduction and conclusion; demonstrates a deliberate and highly effective progression of ideas both within paragraphs and throughout the essay • Has a wide variety of sentence structures; demonstrates a consistent use of precise word choice; maintains a formal style and objective tone • Shows a strong command of the conventions of standard written English and is free or virtually free of errors

THE KAPLAN TEMPLATE FOR THE SAT ESSAY

To maximize your essay score, organize your notes using Kaplan's SAT Essay Template.

¶1: Introductory paragraph

- Introductory statement
- Paraphrase the author's central idea or claim
- Specifically state the Features the author uses to support the central idea or claim

¶2: First body paragraph

- Introduce Feature 1 and provide a quote or paraphrase of the feature
- Specifically state how Feature 1 provides evidence to support the author's reasoning
- Discuss how Feature 1 reflects the author's thinking and the way the author ties his or her claim and evidence together
- Analyze the effect Feature 1 is likely to have on the audience

¶3: Second body paragraph

- Introduce Feature 2 and provide a quote or paraphrase of the feature
- Specifically state how Feature 2 provides evidence to support the author's reasoning
- Discuss how Feature 2 reflects the author's thinking and the way the author ties his or her claim and evidence together
- Analyze the effect Feature 2 is likely to have on the audience

—Time valve: If you are running out of time, don't write a 3rd body paragraph. Instead, take the time to write a thorough conclusion paragraph and proofread your essay. —

¶4: Third body paragraph

- Introduce Feature 3 and provide a quote or paraphrase of the feature
- Specifically state how Feature 3 provides evidence to support the author's reasoning
- Discuss how Feature 3 reflects the author's thinking and the way the author ties his or her claim and evidence together
- Analyze the effect Feature 3 is likely to have on the audience

¶5: Conclusion paragraph

- Recap author's central idea or claim
- Recap what Features the author used to build his or her argument
- Recap how effective the Features are on the audience

> ✔ *Expert Tip*
>
> **Use the time valve option to your advantage. If you are running out of time, focusing on two strong body paragraphs and a complete conclusion is much better than rushing through a third body paragraph or leaving your essay unfinished.**

THE SAT ESSAY: READING

One of the three scores you'll receive on the SAT Essay is the Reading score. Graded on a scale of 1 to 4 by two different readers for a total score of 2 to 8, the Reading score is based on:

- Your understanding of the source text
- Your comprehension of the source text's central ideas, important details, and their interrelationship
- The accuracy of your interpretation of the source text
- Your use of textual evidence to demonstrate your understanding of the source text

Your ability to achieve a high Reading score depends on how well you accomplish Step 1 of the Kaplan Method for the SAT Essay:

Step 1: Read the source text, taking notes on how the author uses:

- **Evidence to support claims**
- **Reasoning to develop ideas and to connect claims and evidence**
- **Stylistic or persuasive elements to add power to the ideas expressed**

Central Ideas

The **central idea** of a text is the key point the author wants to make. The central idea is also often referred to as the text's theme or thesis. Here are some questions to help you pinpoint a text's central idea:

- What is the author's central idea or claim?
- Why did the author write this passage?
- What is the tone of the passage?
- What is this passage primarily about?

> ✔ *Expert Tip*
>
> **Do not confuse a text's topic and its central idea. The topic is what the author is writing about, such as ecology, politics, or literary criticism. The central idea is the author's opinion about the topic. The topic can usually be summarized in one sentence; the central idea often requires several sentences to describe the author's point of view and why he or she takes that position.**

Important Details

While a source text will inevitably be full of details, the important details are those that support or explain the author's central idea. Authors often use certain structural clues or keywords to highlight important details. The following chart lists common categories of keywords and examples.

Common Categories of Keywords	Examples
List	to begin with, first, secondly, next, then, finally, most important, also, for instance, in fact, for example, another
Chronology	on (date), not long after, now, as, before, after, when
Compare-and-Contrast	however, but, as well as, on the other hand, not only . . . but also, either . . . or, while, although, unless, similarly, yet, neither . . . nor
Cause-and-Effect	because, since, therefore, consequently, as a result, this led to, so that, nevertheless, accordingly, if . . . then, thus

If you're unsure if a detail is important when reading a source text, it probably isn't. Always ask: "Does this detail support or enhance the author's central idea? How?"

THE SAT ESSAY: ANALYSIS

One of the three scores you'll receive on the SAT Essay is the Analysis score. Graded on a scale of 1 to 4 by two different readers for a total score of 2 to 8, the Analysis score is based on:

- Your analysis of the source text and understanding of the analytical task
- Your evaluation of the author's use of evidence, reasoning, and/or stylistic and persuasive elements, and/or features of your own choosing
- Your support for the claims or points you make in your response
- Your focus on features of the text that are most relevant to addressing the task

The SAT Essay prompt dictates that you analyze one or more features the author uses to strengthen the logic and persuasiveness of his or her argument. The Kaplan Template for the SAT Essay detailed above suggests that you pick three features to discuss in your response. Because the source text is different for every administration of the SAT, the three features you pick to analyze will depend on the source text.

Commonly Used Features and Styles

Feature	Definition	Example
Allusion	A literary, historical, religious, or mythological reference	*Eli's weakness for sugary drinks is his Achilles' heel.*
Appeals to authority, emotion, and/ or logic	Rhetorical arguments in which the speaker claims to be an authority or expert in a field, attempts to play upon the emotions, or appeals to the use of reason	*As the eminent scientist Dr. Carl Sagan suggested, though the world is dependent on science and technology, few understand either. Sound reasoning, then, requires that we expose children to both from their earliest cognitive years.*
Claim	The assertion of something as fact	*It is very clear that the pursuit of riches is the driving force in society today; morality has given way to greed.*
Compare/ contrast	A discussion in which two or more things are compared, contrasted, or both	*For years, people have debated the benefits of running for exercise. On one hand, running puts stress on your joints. On the other hand, running can strengthen tissues and tendons if you include moderation, rest, and recovery as part of your approach.*
Diction	The author's word choice, which often reveals an author's attitude and point of view	*It was quite a surprise when the timid Mr. Patel jumped to his feet, pounded the table, and roared his opposition.*
Hyperbole	Overstatement characterized by exaggerated language, usually to make a point or draw attention	*I told my sister that because she made me wait for an eternity to get a table at her favorite restaurant, I was now dying of hunger.*
Irony	A contrast between what is stated and what is really meant, or between what is expected and what actually happens	*As Petros walked into the classroom and glanced at what his teacher had written on the board, he grimaced and muttered, "A pop quiz in my first class— what a great way to start the day."*
Juxtaposition	Placing two things or ideas together to contrast them	*As Charles Dickens wrote in* A Tale of Two Cities, *"It was the best of times, it was the worst of times, it was the age of wisdom, it was the age of foolishness, it was the epoch of belief, it was the epoch of incredulity . . . "*

(continued)

Feature	Definition	Example
Rebuttal/ refutation	An argument technique wherein opposing arguments are anticipated and countered	*To formulate a convincing rebuttal to the claim that technology is detrimental to positive social interaction, I compiled information and statistics that show how technology enhances social communication and expression.*
Rhetorical question	A question that is asked simply for the sake of stylistic effect and is not expected to be answered	*Who would not want to have a great, satisfying job that allows you to do what you love every day? And what is more satisfying than fulfilling one's dreams?*
Symbolism	Use of a person, place, thing, event, or pattern that figuratively represents or "stands for" something else; often the thing or idea represented is more abstract or general than the symbol, which is concrete	*In William Blake's poem "Ah Sunflower," the sunflower refers to humankind and the sun represents life: "Ah Sunflower, weary of time, Who countest the steps of the sun."*

You can choose to analyze any of these features in your SAT Essay response; however, make sure to select features that are easily found within the source text and that the author uses to further his or her argument. If you cannot answer the questions posed in the Kaplan Template for the SAT Essay, pick another feature.

✔ **Expert Tip**

After identifying a feature, illustrate it with a brief quotation from the text or paraphrase. The reader must know exactly which part of the passage contains the feature you're discussing.

THE SAT ESSAY: WRITING

Just as the SAT Writing & Language Test assesses your knowledge of expression of ideas and conformity to the conventions of standard written English grammar, usage, and punctuation by having you revise and edit texts, so too does the SAT Essay Test by having you craft an original response. Therefore, the stronger your mastery of the writing and grammar concepts outlined in Unit 2: Writing & Language, the better able you will be to earn a high Writing score on the SAT Essay.

One of the three scores you'll receive on the SAT Essay is the Writing score. Graded on a scale of 1 to 4 by two different readers for a total score of 2 to 8, the Writing score is based on:

- Your use of a central claim
- Your use of effective organization and progression of ideas

- Your use of varied sentence structures
- Your employment of precise word choice
- Your ability to maintain a consistent and appropriate style and tone
- Your command of the conventions of standard written English

Grammar Tips for the SAT Essay

1. **Avoid Sentence Fragments and Run-On Sentences.** Technically, a sentence fragment has no independent clause. A run-on sentence has two or more independent clauses that are improperly connected.

2. **Use Commas Correctly.** When using the comma, follow these guidelines:

   - Use commas to separate items in a series. If more than two items are listed in a series, they should be separated by commas.

   - Do not place commas before the first element of a series or after the last element.

   - Use commas to separate two or more adjectives before a noun; do not use a comma after the last adjective in the series.

   - Use commas to set off parenthetical clauses and phrases. A parenthetical expression is one that is not necessary to the central idea of the sentence.

   - Use commas after most introductory phrases.

   - Use commas to separate independent clauses (clauses that could stand alone as complete sentences) connected by coordinating conjunctions such as *and*, *but*, *not*, and *yet*.

3. **Use Semicolons Correctly.** Follow these guidelines for correct semicolon usage:

   - A semicolon may be used instead of a coordinating conjunction such as *and*, *or*, or *but* to link two closely related independent clauses.

   - A semicolon may also be used between independent clauses connected by words like *therefore*, *nevertheless*, and *moreover*.

4. **Use Colons Correctly.** When you see a colon, it means "something's coming." Follow these rules for correct colon usage:

   - In formal writing, the colon is used only as a means of signaling that what follows is a list, definition, explanation, or concise summary of what has gone before. The colon usually follows an independent clause, and it will frequently be accompanied by a reinforcing expression like *the following*, *as follows*, or *namely*, or by an explicit demonstrative like *this*.

   - Be careful not to put a colon between a verb and its direct object.

   - Context will occasionally make clear that a second independent clause is closely linked to its predecessor, even without an explicit expression. Here, too, a colon is appropriate, although a period will always be correct too.

5. **Use Apostrophes Correctly.** Follow these guidelines for correct apostrophe usage:

- Use the apostrophe with contracted forms of verbs to indicate that one or more letters have been eliminated in writing. Generally, though, you should try to avoid contractions when writing your SAT Essay response.

- Use the apostrophe to indicate the possessive form of a noun.

- The apostrophe is used to indicate possession only with nouns; in the case of pronouns, there are separate possessives for each person and number, with the exception of the neutral *one*, which forms its possessive by adding an apostrophe and an *s*.

6. **Pay Attention to Subject-Verb Agreement.** Singular subjects and plural subjects take different forms of the verb in the present tense. Usually, the difference lies in the presence or absence of a final *s*, but sometimes the difference is more radical. You can usually trust your ear to give you the correct verb form. However, certain situations may cause difficulty, such as:

- When the subject and verb are separated by a number of words

- When the subject is an indefinite pronoun

- When the subject consists of more than one noun

7. **Use Modifiers Correctly.** In English, the position of a word within a sentence often establishes the word's relationship to other words in the sentence. This is especially true with modifying phrases. Modifiers, like pronouns, are generally connected to the nearest word that agrees with the modifier in person and number. If a modifier is placed too far from the word it modifies (the referent), the meaning may be lost or obscured. Avoid ambiguity by placing modifiers as close as possible to the words they are intended to modify.

8. **Use Pronouns Correctly.** A pronoun is a word that replaces a noun in a sentence. Every time you write a pronoun—*he, him, his, she, her, it, its, they, their, that,* or *which*—be sure there can be absolutely no doubt what its antecedent is. The antecedent is the particular noun a pronoun refers to or stands for. Careless use of pronouns can obscure your intended meaning.

9. **Pay Attention to Parallelism.** Matching constructions must be expressed in parallel form. It is often rhetorically effective to use a particular construction several times in succession in order to provide emphasis. The technique is called parallel construction, and it is effective only when used sparingly. If your sentences are varied, a parallel construction will stand out. If your sentences are already repetitive, a parallel structure will further obscure your meaning.

Style Tips For The SAT Essay

1. **Write succinctly.**

- Do not use several words when one word will do.

- If you have something to say, just say it.

2. **Write assertively.**
   - Avoid overuse of qualifiers.
   - You don't need to overly clarify your statements.
   - Put verbs in the active voice whenever possible.

3. **Write clearly.**
   - Try not to begin sentences with *there is*, *there are*, *it would be*, *it could be*, *it can be*, or *it is*.
   - Avoid vague references, indirect language, and general wordiness. Choose specific, descriptive words.
   - Avoid clichés, which are overused expressions. Always substitute more specific language for a cliché.
   - Limit your use of jargon.
   - Avoid using slang and colloquialisms.

> ✔ *Expert Tip*
>
> **Be sure to save 2 minutes to proofread your essay. This will allow you to correct the simple mistakes anyone can make when writing quickly and improve the clarity of your essay.**

Let's look at examples of how to correct common style issues.

The left column contains the issue. The column in the middle features a sample sentence. The column on the right demonstrates how to improve the sample sentence.

Issue	Incorrect	Correct
Needless qualification	This rather serious breach of etiquette may possibly shake the very foundations of the diplomatic community.	This serious breach of etiquette may shake the foundations of the diplomatic community.
Filling up space	Which idea of the author's is more in line with what I believe? This is a very interesting question. . . .	The author's beliefs are similar to mine.
Needless self-reference	I am of the opinion that air pollution is a more serious problem than the government has led us to believe.	Air pollution is a more serious problem than the government has led us to believe.
Weak openings	There are several reasons why Andre and his brother will not share an apartment.	Andre and his brother will not share an apartment for several reasons.
Vagueness	Chantal is highly educated.	Chantal has a master's degree in business administration.

PRACTICE QUESTIONS

Essay 1

The essay gives you an opportunity to show how effectively you can read and comprehend a passage and write an essay analyzing the passage. In your essay, you should demonstrate that you have read the passage carefully, present a clear and logical analysis, and use language precisely.

Your essay must be written on the lines provided in your answer booklet; except for the planning page of the answer booklet, you will receive no other paper on which to write. You will have enough space if you write on every line, avoid wide margins, and keep your handwriting to a reasonable size. Remember that people who are not familiar with your handwriting will read what you write. Try to write or print so that what you are writing is legible to those readers.

You have 50 minutes to read the passage and write an essay in response to the prompt provided inside this booklet.

1. Do not write your essay in this booklet. Only what you write on the lined pages of your answer booklet will be evaluated.
2. An off-topic essay will not be evaluated.

As you read the passage below, consider how Morris uses

- evidence, such as facts or examples, to support claims.

- reasoning to develop ideas and to connect claims and evidence.

- stylistic or persuasive elements, such as word choice or appeals to emotion, to add power to the ideas expressed.

Adapted from Elisabeth Woodbridge Morris's essay "The Tyranny of Things." In this portion, Morris paints a portrait of American consumerism in 1917 and offers a distinct perspective on the joy of freedom from "things, things, things."

Two fifteen-year-old girls stood eyeing one another on first acquaintance. Finally one little girl said, "Which do you like best, people or things?" The other little girl said, "Things." They were friends at once.

I suppose we all go through a phase when we like things best; and not only like them, but want to possess them under our hand. The passion for accumulation is upon us. We make

"collections," we fill our rooms, our walls, our tables, our desks, with things, things, things.

Many people never pass out of this phase. They never see a flower without wanting to pick it and put it in a vase, they never enjoy a book without wanting to own it, nor a picture without wanting to hang it on their walls. They keep photographs of all their friends and Kodak albums of all the places they visit, they save all their theater programmes and dinner cards, they bring home all their alpenstocks.* Their houses are filled with an undigested mass of things, like the terminal moraine where a

---

* alpenstocks: strong pointed poles used by mountain climbers

glacier dumps at length everything it has picked up during its progress through the lands.

But to some of us a day comes when we begin to grow weary of things. We realize that we do not possess them; they possess us. Our books are a burden to us, our pictures have destroyed every restful wall-space, our china is a care, our photographs drive us mad, our programmes and alpenstocks fill us with loathing. We feel stifled with the sense of things, and our problem becomes, not how much we can accumulate, but how much we can do without. We send our books to the village library, and our pictures to the college settlement. Such things as we cannot give away, and have not the courage to destroy, we stack in the garret, where they lie huddled in dim and dusty heaps, removed from our sight, to be sure, yet still faintly importunate.

Then, as we breathe more freely in the clear space that we have made for ourselves, we grow aware that we must not relax our vigilance, or we shall be once more overwhelmed. . . .

It extends to all our doings. For every event there is a "souvenir." We cannot go to luncheon and meet our friends but we must receive a token to carry away. Even our children cannot have a birthday party, and play games, and eat good things, and be happy. The host must receive gifts from every little guest, and provide in return some little remembrance for each to take home. Truly, on all sides we are beset, and we go lumbering along through life like a ship encrusted with barnacles, which can never cut the waves clean and sure and swift until she has been scraped bare again. And there seems little hope for us this side our last port.

And to think that there was a time when folk had not even that hope! When a man's possessions were burned with him, so that he might, forsooth, have them all about him in the next world! Suffocating thought! To think one could not even then be clear of things, and make at least a fresh start! That must, indeed, have been in the childhood of the race.

Once upon a time, when I was very tired, I chanced to go away to a little house by the sea. . . . There was nothing in the house to demand care, to claim attention, to cumber my consciousness with its insistent, unchanging companionship. There was nothing but a shelter, and outside, the fields and marshes, the shore and the sea. These did not have to be taken down and put up and arranged and dusted and cared for. They were not things at all, they were powers, presences. . . .

If we could but free ourselves once for all, how simple life might become! One of my friends, who, with six young children and only one servant, keeps a spotless house and a soul serene, told me once how she did it. "My dear, once a month I give away every single thing in the house that we do not imperatively need. It sounds wasteful, but I don't believe it really is. . . ."

Write an essay in which you explain how Morris builds an argument to persuade her audience that possessions are oppressive. In your essay, analyze how Morris uses one or more of the features listed in the box that precedes the passage (or features of your own choice) to strengthen the logic and persuasiveness of her argument. Be sure that your analysis focuses on the most relevant features of the passage.

Your essay should not explain whether you agree with Morris's claims, but rather explain how Morris builds an argument to persuade her audience.

_____

_____

_____

_____

_____

_____

_____

_____

_____

_____

_____

_____

_____

_____

_____

_____

_____

_____

_____

_____

_____

_____

_____

_____

_____

_____
_____
_____
_____
_____
_____
_____
_____
_____
_____
_____
_____
_____
_____
_____
_____
_____
_____
_____
_____
_____
_____
_____
_____
_____

Essay 2

The essay gives you an opportunity to show how effectively you can read and comprehend a passage and write an essay analyzing the passage. In your essay, you should demonstrate that you have read the passage carefully, present a clear and logical analysis, and use language precisely.

Your essay must be written on the lines provided in your answer booklet; except for the planning page of the answer booklet, you will receive no other paper on which to write. You will have enough space if you write on every line, avoid wide margins, and keep your handwriting to a reasonable size. Remember that people who are not familiar with your handwriting will read what you write. Try to write or print so that what you are writing is legible to those readers.

You have 50 minutes to read the passage and write an essay in response to the prompt provided inside this booklet.

1. Do not write your essay in this booklet. Only what you write on the lined pages of your answer booklet will be evaluated.

2. An off-topic essay will not be evaluated.

As you read the passage below, consider how William Faulkner uses

- evidence, such as facts or examples, to support claims.

- reasoning to develop ideas and to connect claims and evidence.

- stylistic or persuasive elements, such as word choice or appeals to emotion, to add power to the ideas expressed.

Adapted from William Faulkner's Nobel Prize Acceptance Speech, delivered in Stockholm on December 10, 1950.

I feel that this award was not made to me as a man, but to my work—a life's work in the agony and sweat of the human spirit, not for glory and least of all for profit, but to create out of the materials of the human spirit something which did not exist before. So this award is only mine in trust. It will not be difficult to find a dedication for the money part of it commensurate with the purpose and significance of its origin. But I would like to do the same with the acclaim too, by using this moment as a pinnacle from which I might be listened to by the young men and women already dedicated to the same anguish and travail, among whom is already that one who will some day stand where I am standing.

Our tragedy today is a general and universal physical fear so long sustained by now that we can even bear it. There are no longer problems of the spirit. There is only the question: When will I be blown up? Because of this, the young man or woman writing today has forgotten the problems of the human heart in conflict with itself which alone can make good writing because only that is worth writing about, worth the agony and the sweat.

He must learn them again. He must teach himself that the basest of all things is to be afraid: and, teaching himself that, forget it forever, leaving no room in his workshop for anything but the old verities and truths of the heart, the universal truths lacking which any story is ephemeral and doomed—love and honor and pity and pride and compassion and sacrifice. Until he does so, he labors under a curse. He writes not of love but of . . . defeats in which nobody loses anything of value, of victories without hope and, worst of all, without pity or compassion. His griefs grieve on no universal bones, leaving no scars . . .

Until he learns these things, he will write as though he stood among and watched the end of man. I decline to accept the end of man. It is easy enough to say that man is immortal because he will endure: that when the last ding-dong of doom has clanged and faded from the last worthless rock hanging tideless in the last red and dying evening, that even then there will still be one more sound: that of his puny inexhaustible voice, still talking. I refuse to accept this. I believe that man will not merely endure: he will prevail. He is immortal, not because he alone among creatures has an inexhaustible voice, but because he has a soul, a spirit capable of compassion and sacrifice and endurance. The poet's, the writer's, duty is to write about these things. It is his privilege to help man endure by lifting his heart, by reminding him of the courage and honor and hope and pride and compassion and pity and sacrifice which have been the glory of his past. The poet's voice need not merely be the record of man, it can be one of the props, the pillars to help him endure and prevail.

Write an essay in which you explain how William Faulkner builds an argument to persuade his audience that authors must write from the heart to ensure that mankind prevails. In your essay, analyze how Faulkner uses one or more of the features listed in the box that precedes the passage (or features of your own choice) to strengthen the logic and persuasiveness of his argument. Be sure that your analysis focuses on the most relevant features of the passage.

Your essay should not explain whether you agree with Faulkner's claims, but rather explain how Faulkner builds an argument to persuade his audience.

_____

_____

_____

_____

_____

_____

_____

_____

_____

_____

_____

_____

_____

_____

_____

_____

_____

_____

_____

_____

_____

_____

Essay 3

The essay gives you an opportunity to show how effectively you can read and comprehend a passage and write an essay analyzing the passage. In your essay, you should demonstrate that you have read the passage carefully, present a clear and logical analysis, and use language precisely.

Your essay must be written on the lines provided in your answer booklet; except for the planning page of the answer booklet, you will receive no other paper on which to write. You will have enough space if you write on every line, avoid wide margins, and keep your handwriting to a reasonable size. Remember that people who are not familiar with your handwriting will read what you write. Try to write or print so that what you are writing is legible to those readers.

You have 50 minutes to read the passage and write an essay in response to the prompt provided inside this booklet.

1. Do not write your essay in this booklet. Only what you write on the lined pages of your answer booklet will be evaluated.
2. An off-topic essay will not be evaluated.

As you read the passage below, consider how Robert F. Kennedy uses

- evidence, such as facts or examples, to support claims.

- reasoning to develop ideas and to connect claims and evidence.

- stylistic or persuasive elements, such as word choice or appeals to emotion, to add power to the ideas expressed.

Adapted from Robert F. Kennedy's address to the National Union of South African Students' Day of Affirmation, 6 June 1966.

We stand here in the name of freedom.

At the heart of that Western freedom and democracy is the belief that the individual man, the child of God, is the touchstone of value, and all society, groups, the state, exist for his benefit. Therefore the enlargement of liberty for individual human beings must be the supreme goal and the abiding practice of any Western society.

The first element of this individual liberty is the freedom of speech.

The right to express and communicate ideas, to set oneself apart from the dumb beasts of field and forest; to recall governments to their duties and obligations; above all, the right to affirm one's membership and allegiance to the body politic—to society—to the men with whom we share our land, our heritage and our children's future.

Hand in hand with freedom of speech goes the power to be heard—to share the decisions of government which shape men's lives. Everything that makes life worthwhile—family, work, education, a place to rear one's children and a place to rest one's head—all this rests on decisions of government; all can be swept away by a government which does not heed the demands of its people. Therefore, the essential humanity of men can be protected and preserved only where government must answer—not just to those of a particular religion, or a particular race; but to all its people.

These are the sacred rights of Western society. These are the essential differences between us and Nazi Germany, as they were between Athens and Persia. . . .

For two centuries, my own country has struggled to overcome the self-imposed handicap of prejudice and discrimination based on nationality, social class or race—discrimination profoundly repugnant to the theory and command of our Constitution. Even as my father grew up in Boston, signs told him that "No Irish need apply."

Two generations later President Kennedy became the first Catholic to head the nation; but how many men of ability had, before 1961, been denied the opportunity to contribute to the nation's progress because they were Catholic, or of Irish extraction.

In the last five years, the winds of change have blown as fiercely in the United States as anywhere in the world. But they will not—they cannot—abate.

For there are millions of African Americans untrained for the simplest jobs, and thousands every day denied their full equal rights under the law; and the violence of the disinherited, the insulated, the injured, looms over the streets of Harlem and Watts and South Chicago.

But an African American trains as an astronaut, one of mankind's first explorers into outer space; another is the chief barrister of the United States Government, and dozens sit on the benches of court; and another, Dr. Martin Luther King, is the second man of African descent to win the Nobel Peace Prize for his nonviolent efforts for social justice between the races.

We must recognize the full human equality of all our people before God, before the law, and in the councils of government. We must do this not because it is economically advantageous, although it is; not because the laws of God and man command it, although they do command it; not because people in other lands wish it so. We must do it for the single and fundamental reason that it is the right thing to do.

And this must be our commitment outside our borders as well as within.

It is your job, the task of the young people of this world, to strip the last remnants of that ancient, cruel belief from the civilization of man.

Each nation has different obstacles and different goals, shadowed by the vagaries of history and experience. Yet as I talk to young people around the world I am impressed not by the diversity but by the closeness of their goals, their desires and concerns and hopes for the future. There is discrimination in New York, apartheid in South Africa and serfdom in the mountains of Peru. People stagnate in the streets of India; intellectuals go to jail in Russia; thousands are slaughtered in Indonesia; wealth is lavished on armaments everywhere. These are differing evils. But they are common works of man.

And therefore they call upon common qualities of conscience and of indignation, a shared determination to wipe away the unnecessary sufferings of our fellow human beings at home and particularly around the world.

Write an essay in which you explain how Robert F. Kennedy builds an argument to persuade his audience that the expansion of liberty for all must be the guiding principle of any Western society. In your essay, analyze how Kennedy uses one or more of the features listed in the box that precedes the passage (or features of your own choice) to strengthen the logic and persuasiveness of his argument. Be sure that your analysis focuses on the most relevant features of the passage.

Your essay should not explain whether you agree with Kennedy's claims, but rather explain how Kennedy builds an argument to persuade his audience.

_____

_____

_____

_____

_____

_____

_____

_____

_____

_____

_____

_____

_____

_____

_____

_____

_____

_____

_____

_____

_____

_____

_____

_____

_____

_____

_____

_____

_____

_____

_____

_____

_____

_____

_____

_____

_____

_____

_____

_____

_____

_____

_____

_____

_____

_____

_____

_____

_____

_____

_____

_____

Essay 4

The essay gives you an opportunity to show how effectively you can read and comprehend a passage and write an essay analyzing the passage. In your essay, you should demonstrate that you have read the passage carefully, present a clear and logical analysis, and use language precisely.

Your essay must be written on the lines provided in your answer booklet; except for the planning page of the answer booklet, you will receive no other paper on which to write. You will have enough space if you write on every line, avoid wide margins, and keep your handwriting to a reasonable size. Remember that people who are not familiar with your handwriting will read what you write. Try to write or print so that what you are writing is legible to those readers.

You have 50 minutes to read the passage and write an essay in response to the prompt provided inside this booklet.

1. Do not write your essay in this booklet. Only what you write on the lined pages of your answer booklet will be evaluated.

2. An off-topic essay will not be evaluated.

As you read the passage below, consider how Royal Dixon uses

- evidence, such as facts or examples, to support claims.

- reasoning to develop ideas and to connect claims and evidence.

- stylistic or persuasive elements, such as word choice or appeals to emotion, to add power to the ideas expressed.

Adapted from Royal Dixon, *The Human Side of Animals*. © 1918 by Frederick A. Stokes Company, New York.

The trouble with science is that too often it leaves out feeling. If you agree that we cannot treat men like machines, why should we put animals in that class? Why should we fall into the colossal ignorance and conceit of cataloging every human-like action of animals under the word "instinct"? Man had to battle with animals for untold ages before he domesticated and made servants of them. He is just beginning to learn that they were not created solely to furnish material for stories, or to serve mankind, but that they also have an existence, a life of their own.

Man has long claimed dominion over animals and a right to assert that dominion without restraint. This anthropocentric conceit is the same thing that causes one nation to think it should rule the world, that the sun and moon were made only for the laudable purpose of giving light unto a chosen few, and that young lambs playing on a grassy hillside, near a cool spring, are just so much mutton allowed to wander over man's domain until its flavor is improved.

It is time to remove the barriers, once believed impassable, which man's egotism has used as a screen to separate him from his lower brothers. Our physical bodies are very similar to theirs except that ours are almost always much inferior. Merely because we have a superior intellect which enables us to rule and enslave the animals, shall we deny them all intellect and all feeling?

It is possible to explain away all the marvelous things the animals do, but after you have finished, there will still remain something over and above which quite defies all mechanistic interpretation. An old war horse, for instance, lives over and over his battles in his dreams. He neighs and paws, just as he did in real battle . . . This is only one of the plethora of animal phenomena which man does not understand. If you are able to explain these things to humanity, you will be classed as wise indeed. Yet the average scientist explains them away, with the ignorance and empty words of the unwise.

By a thorough application of psychological principles, it is possible to show that man himself is merely a machine to be explained in terms of neurons and nervous impulses, heredity and environment and reactions to outside stimuli. But who is there who does not believe that there is more to a man than that?

Animals have demonstrated long ago that they not only have as many talents as human beings but that, under the influence of the same environment, they form the same kinds of combinations to defend themselves against enemies, to shelter themselves against heat and cold, to build homes, to lay up a supply of food for the hard seasons. In fact, all through the ages man has been imitating the animals in burrowing through the earth, penetrating the waters, and now, at last, flying through the air.

There are also numerous signs, sounds and motions by which animals communicate with each other, though to man these symbols of language may not always be understandable. Dogs give barks indicating surprise, pleasure and all other emotions. Cows will bellow for days when mourning for their dead.

In their reading of the weather, animals undoubtedly possess superhuman powers. Even squirrels can predict an unusually long and severe winter and thus make adequate preparations. Some animals act as both barometers and thermometers.

There is no limit to the marvelous things animals do. The ape or baboon who puts a stone in the open oyster to prevent it from closing, or lifts stones to crack nuts, or beats other apes with sticks . . . in all these actions is actual reasoning. Indeed, there is nothing which man makes with all his ingenious use of tools and instruments, of which some suggestion may not be seen in animal creation.

Write an essay in which you explain how Royal Dixon builds an argument to persuade his audience that animals and humans have much in common and humans should treat animals with more respect. In your essay, analyze how Dixon uses one or more of the features listed in the box that precedes the passage (or features of your own choice) to strengthen the logic and persuasiveness of his argument. Be sure that your analysis focuses on the most relevant features of the passage.

Your essay should not explain whether you agree with Dixon's claims, but rather explain how Dixon builds an argument to persuade his audience.

_____

_____

_____

_____

_____

_____

_____

_____

_____

_____

_____

_____

_____

_____

_____

_____

_____

_____

_____

_____

_____

_____

_____

_____

_____

_____

_____

_____

ANSWERS AND EXPLANATIONS

CHAPTER 16

Essay Test Rubric

The Essay Demonstrates. . .

4—Advanced	• **(Reading)** A strong ability to comprehend the source text, including its central ideas and important details and how they interrelate; and effectively use evidence (quotations, paraphrases, or both) from the source text.
	• **(Analysis)** A strong ability to evaluate the author's use of evidence, reasoning, and/or stylistic and persuasive elements, and/or other features of the student's own choosing; make good use of relevant, sufficient, and strategically chosen support for the claims or points made in the student's essay; and focus consistently on features of the source text that are most relevant to addressing the task.
	• **(Writing)** A strong ability to provide a precise central claim; create an effective organization that includes an introduction and conclusion, as well as a clear progression of ideas; successfully employ a variety of sentence structures; use precise word choice; maintain a formal style and objective tone; and show command of the conventions of standard written English so that the essay is free of errors.
3—Proficient	• **(Reading)** Satisfactory ability to comprehend the source text, including its central ideas and important details and how they interrelate; and use evidence (quotations, paraphrases, or both) from the source text.
	• **(Analysis)** Satisfactory ability to evaluate the author's use of evidence, reasoning, and/or stylistic and persuasive elements, and/or other features of the student's own choosing; make use of relevant and sufficient support for the claims or points made in the student's essay; and focus primarily on features of the source text that are most relevant to addressing the task.
	• **(Writing)** Satisfactory ability to provide a central claim; create an organization that includes an introduction and conclusion, as well as a clear progression of ideas; employ a variety of sentence structures; use precise word choice; maintain an appropriate formal style and objective tone; and show control of the conventions of standard written English so that the essay is free of significant errors.

2—Partial	• **(Reading)** Limited ability to comprehend the source text, including its central ideas and important details and how they interrelate; and use evidence (quotations, paraphrases, or both) from the source text.
	• **(Analysis)** Limited ability to evaluate the author's use of evidence, reasoning, and/or stylistic and persuasive elements, and/or other features of the student's own choosing; make use of support for the claims or points made in the student's essay; and focus on relevant features of the source text.
	• **(Writing)** Limited ability to provide a central claim; create an effective organization for ideas; employ a variety of sentence structures; use precise word choice; maintain an appropriate style and tone; or show control of the conventions of standard written English, resulting in certain errors that detract from the quality of the writing.
1—Inadequate	• **(Reading)** Little or no ability to comprehend the source text or use evidence from the source text.
	• **(Analysis)** Little or no ability to evaluate the author's use of evidence, reasoning, and/or stylistic and persuasive elements; choose support for claims or points; or focus on relevant features of the source text.
	• **(Writing)** Little or no ability to provide a central claim, organization, or progression of ideas; employ a variety of sentence structures; use precise word choice; maintain an appropriate style and tone; or show control of the conventions of standard written English, resulting in numerous errors that undermine the quality of the writing.

Essay 1

Sample Essay Response #1 (Advanced Score)

As anyone knows who has had to help their family move house, find a textbook in a cluttered room, or even just clean a crowded apartment, possessions can have a huge amount of power over people. Far from being simply objects that we enjoy or that bring us pleasure, it can sometimes feel that our possessions oppress us. This is the point Morris eloquently makes in her essay "The Tyranny of Things." By using anecdotes, examples, reasoning, and powerful imagery, Morris argues that the very things we cherish are nearly crushing the life out of us.

The author begins by relating an anecdote about two teenagers becoming fast friends over their love of things. It is a touching moment, one to which readers can easily relate; even Morris herself says that we all probably go through this phase. This helps establish her credibility with readers, because her examples make sense to them. Gradually, however, Morris makes it clear that this touching moment has a sinister side—the love of things will only result in resentment.

Morris reasons that while it's natural to go through a phase of wanting objects, it is unhealthy to remain in this state. "Many people never pass out of this phase," she writes ominously. "They never see a flower without wanting to pick it . . . they bring home all their alpenstocks." It begins to sound obsessive, this need to control things. Morris goes on to develop her argument by suggesting that possessions are metaphorically suffocating us. She makes the idea of too many possessions sound repulsive by describing them as "an undigested mass of things." The things almost take on a kind of life force, according to Morris: "they possess us." They "have destroyed" our empty spaces and we feel "stifled."

Another way Morris supports her argument is by giving examples of the unnecessary "tokens" associated with social occasions. She describes how at events, luncheons, and parties, gifts are given and received. She then uses powerful negative imagery to describe the effects of these gifts, comparing the recipient to a "ship encrusted with barnacles" that needs to be "scraped bare again." This language suggests that the gifts are burdensome and even harmful.

By contrast, the imagery Morris uses to describe a simple life filled with fewer things is imagery of ease and relaxation. "We breathe more freely in the clear space that we have made for ourselves," she writes. It is not just that we have literally regained control from our possessions and are now acting rather than being acted upon; it is that we are physically more at ease.

In her conclusion, Morris longs for a day when we can live more simply, with fewer possessions. She describes a "house by the sea" that was simple and empty; it did not "demand care" or "claim attention" or otherwise act upon her. Her wish is that "we could but free ourselves" from the tyranny of things that she feels is draining us of our freedom. And at this point, it is likely the reader's wish, too.

Sample Essay Response #2 (Proficient Score)

Although as people we like to think of ourselves as owners of things, in fact it can sometimes feel like the things we own end up owning us. At least this is what Morris argues in her essay "The Tyranny of Things." Through her use of evidence, reasoning, and word choice, she makes a strong argument that we should own fewer things if we ever want to be truly happy.

Morris tells a story about two teenage girls who instantly know they will be friends because they both like things. They are not happy just to be. They have to own things. It's like their own experiences aren't enough for them. But Morris says that this is bad for people, because they will end up feeling like their possessions own them.

Morris's reasoning is that we can basically get control back over our own lives if we stop needing things so much. If we have too many things, "they possess us." So we have to get rid of things, and then we can feel better. At least these days we aren't buried with our things anymore, like they were in the olden days.

The word choices in the essay are interesting. She talks about the way things become a problem for us: "our books are a burden to us, our pictures have destroyed every restful wall-space, our china is a care." By using a lot of repetition, it shows how powerful things are.

Morris's essay encourages people to free themselves from their things. If they do so, they will be happier. Through her personal anecdotes, reasoning, and repetitive word choices, she makes her essay very powerful.

Essay 2

Essay Response #1 (Advanced Score)

When William Faulkner made his Nobel Prize Acceptance Speech in 1950, he was speaking at the height of the Cold War. The memory of the devastation of the atomic bombs dropped on Japan was still fresh in people's minds, and it's clear from Faulkner's speech that people were afraid more destruction was to come. Faulkner felt strongly that in order for mankind to prevail, writers must write from the heart, rather than writing from fear. In this speech, he uses several techniques to persuade his audience of his claim: he establishes his authority, uses vivid language and imagery, and appeals to his audience's sense of duty.

At the ceremony, Faulkner was speaking from a position of strength and expertise, having just been awarded the Nobel Prize for Literature. In a subtle way, he reminds his audience of this expertise throughout the speech, lending credibility to his claims. In the first paragraph, he redefines the award as an honor for his life's work in mining the human spirit to create great literature. He then reminds the audience of his position as an elder statesman by directing his speech to the "young men and women" who are also engaged in this great work, and goes on to tell them what they must "learn" and "teach themselves" about life and writing. By framing the speech as a lesson for younger writers based on his career-long exploration of the human spirit, Faulkner establishes his authority and commands respect for his ideas.

Faulkner also uses vivid language and imagery to create a vision of a higher purpose to which he would like his audience to aspire. In paragraphs 2 and 3, he paints a picture of the writer as an artist involved in a great struggle, which he characterizes with words like "agony" and "sweat." According to Faulkner, a writer will never succeed if he avoids universal truths, and until the writer realizes this, "he labors under a curse." To Faulkner, a writer who writes from a place of fear instead of compassion creates meaningless work that touches upon "no universal bones, leaving no scars." On the other hand, a writer who writes with pity and compassion lifts the reader's heart and reminds him of his "immortal" nature. This type of vivid language, which is clearly written from Faulkner's heart, helps to support his argument that writing from the heart is the way to create great literature that inspires mankind to prevail.

Finally, in speaking to his audience of younger writers, he calls upon their sense of duty. It's clear earlier in the speech that Faulkner is concerned that younger writers are being defeated by fear, and are failing to explore the rich material of the human heart. He asserts that rather than writing about defeat, they should elevate humans by reminding them of their great capacity for courage, compassion, sacrifice, and other noble qualities. These characteristics are unique to humans and are the "glory" of their past, which Faulkner exhorts them to carry into the future. In the final line, Faulkner calls upon writers to be more than just record-keepers—rather, they should actively inspire humankind to prevail.

In a time of great fear, William Faulkner used his Nobel Prize acceptance speech to express his belief that writers must write from the heart in order to ensure the success of mankind. To convince his audience that they should accept his claim, he first establishes his authority, then uses vivid language and imagery to illustrate the value of writing from the heart, and finally calls upon his audience's sense of duty to elevate the human race. Through skillful use of these features, he constructs a persuasive argument.

Essay Response #2 (Proficient Score)

William Faulkner believed that authors must write from their hearts to make sure that humans prevail on Earth. In his Nobel Prize Acceptance Speech, Faulkner uses his expertise, vivid language, and calls to his audience's sense of responsibility to make his case.

In this speech, Faulkner speaks as both a writer and a teacher. He acknowledges that young writers are listening to him; and he has lessons to give to them. Since he just won the Nobel Prize his listeners believe him to be an expert and this makes them more willing to accept his message. He tells his young listeners that they have lost their way, and they must relearn the "problems of the human heart," which are what make good writing. Faulkner tells his listeners that being afraid is the lowest of human feelings, and they need to put their fears aside and instead explore the higher truths of the human heart. Faulkner knows that his young audience is looking up to him, and so he uses his position of authority to guide them to strive for something greater than their fear.

Faulkner also uses vivid language to enhance his argument. Twice he uses the phrase "agony and sweat" to describe the struggle of the writer who writes from the heart. This type of vivid language makes the writer's struggle seem like a goal worth fighting for. Faulkner describes writing that avoids the problems of the human heart as having no "bones" or "scars." By using words that evoke the human body, Faulkner implies that this type of writing has no weight or depth. Faulkner uses very vivid language to paint a picture of a world after a nuclear apacalypse, which is what his audience fears. In this picture, the evening is "red and dying," the rocks are "worthless" and man's voice is "puny" but still talking. Faulkner then tells his audience he refuses to accept this bleak image—that man will do more than just exist, he will prevail. By using vivid language to describe the defeatist view of mankind, Faulkner makes his audience feel revulsion at this image, and makes the alternative seem much more appealing.

Faulkner wanted writers to write about courage, hope, love, compassion, and pity because these things uplift the human spirit. Faulkner calls upon his listeners' sense of responsibility by telling them that they have a duty to write about these subjects. His implication is that if they don't, mankind will fall back into the bleakness he described previously. He also says that the writer has a responsibility to be a "pillar" holding up mankind. By making his audience feel that they have a responsibility to help mankind, Faulkner strengthens his position.

In this speech, Faulkner makes an effective argument that writers must write from the heart to save mankind and help it prevail. To strengthen his argument, he uses the features of expertise, vivid language, and calls to responsibility.

Essay 3

Essay Response #1 (Advanced Score)

In his speech to the National Union of South African Students in 1966, Robert F. Kennedy makes the claim that the guiding principle of Western societies must be the enhancement of liberty for all individuals. Through appeals to Western values, references to historical evidence, and calls to conscience, Kennedy constructs a powerful and effective argument.

Kennedy begins his speech by praising the core values of Western society—freedom and democracy, and the rights associated with them. In so doing, he both establishes common ground with his South African audience, who viewed themselves as part of Western society, and also highlights the ways in which the repressive government of South Africa in 1966 failed to uphold these values. To Kennedy, the freedom of speech is not merely the right to say whatever one chooses, rather, it allows us to speak up to our governments when they are derelict in their duties, and is a key part of what it means to be an active member of society. Kennedy also insists that the right of individuals to be heard by their government is essential to democracy, because it forces government officials to answer to the people who elected them. Frequently, Kennedy uses heightened language to describe these rights and values, which deepens the impact of his message. The freedom of speech separates us from the "dumb beasts of field and forest." The power to be heard allows people a voice in the decisions that "shape men's lives." Most powerfully, Kennedy states that these rights are "sacred." This kind of elevated language imparts a weight to Kennedy's argument that ordinary language could not.

Kennedy also makes references to historical and current events to bolster his claims. He asserts that the rights he describes are what separate democratic societies from Nazi Germany and Persia, countries known to be extremely repressive. This reference to brutal regimes strengthens his claim that these rights should be the guiding principle of any decent society. He also uses the United States as a model of a society that has been striving for the expansion of liberty and, while failing in some respects, is succeeding overall. Kennedy's father, he says, was barred from many jobs as a young man due to his Irish background, yet several decades later, his son John F. Kennedy became president, proving that conditions can change for the better. Robert Kennedy acknowledges that the United States still has far to go, just like South Africa, yet he cites examples of major progress, such as an African American astronaut and an African American chief justice, as well as Martin Luther King, Jr., who won the Nobel Peace Prize. Kennedy's implication is that the ideals of liberty and justice are worth upholding because they can make a society greater and more inclusive.

Another way Kennedy persuades his audience of the validity of his argument is by making calls to conscience. He states that the most important reason to grant freedom to all is because "it is the right thing to do." He reasons that feelings of compassion are common to all people, as are feelings of outrage when other human beings suffer; therefore, we should all join together in expanding human rights and lessening the suffering of people everywhere. By calling upon his audience's basic sense of right and wrong, Kennedy gives them a personal lens through which to examine his argument, thus making them more likely to embrace its validity.

Robert F. Kennedy passionately believed in the necessity for all Western societies to make the expansion of liberty their guiding principle. To build and support his argument, Kennedy exalts Western values of democracy and freedom, refers to historical examples in which the promotion of liberty made for a better society, and finally calls upon people's conscience to help them see that the expansion of freedom for all is the right thing to do.

Essay Response #2 (Proficient Score)

Robert F. Kennedy's central claim in his speech to the National Union of South African Students is that the guiding principle of Western societies should be the expansion of liberty for all individuals. Kennedy uses several techniques to build his argument, including heightened language, examples of countries that have been improved by the expansion of liberty, and appeals to his audience's sense of right and wrong.

Kennedy was not an ordinary man, nor was he an ordinary writer. His speech contains soaring language that makes his audience feel like they are listening to great literature. When he says that the freedom of speech is what seperates us from "dumb beasts," his vivid language makes that freedom seem even more important. He makes frequent references to God, even calling rights of Western society "sacred." And instead of merely saying that young people must stop racism and injustice, he says that it's there responsibility to "strip the last remnants of that ancient, cruel belief from the civilization of man." This type of language makes the audience feel that they are being called to a higher purpose.

Kennedy also provides examples of ways in which countries that promote liberty fare better than countries that don't. When he contrasts Western societies that value freedom with societies that don't—like Nazi Germany and Persia—he is suggesting that countries that deny people their basic rights eventually fail (in 1966, Nazi Germany and Persia no longer existed, but Western democracies still did). Kennedy then uses America as an example of a country that has been improved by expanding liberties for individuals. He tells a personal anecdote about the prejudice experienced by his Irish father, and acknowledges that the struggle to overcome discrimination can take many years. However he provides evidence that the struggle is worth it as shown by his brother's success in becoming president of the United States, and by the African Americans who at that point had risen to the highest ranks of American society—an astronaut, barristers, and a Nobel Prize winner, Martin Luther King, Jr. These examples support Kennedy's claim that enlarging the liberties of individuals is a worthy goal for Western societies.

Finally, Kennedy appeals to his audience's fundamental sense of right and wrong. He says that expanding liberty is "the right thing to do" and that God commands it. He lists multiple examples of evil in the world—"discrimination in New York, apartheid in South Africa . . ."—and tells his audience of students that they must answer the call to eliminate the suffering of others everywhere in the world. He states that evil is common, therefore it can only be cured by other qualities we all share in common, such as our conscence and determination to make the world a better place.

The argument Kennedy makes in this speech is strengthened by his use of the features mentioned above: heightened language, evidence, and appeals to his audience's sense of what is right and what is wrong.

Essay 4

Essay Response #1 (Advanced Score)

In "The Human Side of Animals," Royal Dixon makes the argument that animals are complex beings with thoughts and feelings that deserve the same respect as humans. When Dixon first makes his argument, he probably realizes that he faces an uphill climb. Most people are meat-eaters, and it is likely that much of Dixon's audience consists of people whose lifestyle depends on the domination and consumption of animals. In order to build a strong argument in the face of such opposition, Dixon effectively uses persuasive techniques that include emotional language and imagery, appeals to his audience's intelligence, and persuasive reasoning and evidence.

Dixon uses emotionally laden language and imagery to persuade his audience of the humanity of animals. First, he conjures the heartwarming image of "young lambs playing on a grassy hillside," only to give his audience an unpleasant jolt when he abruptly turns the lambs into cold, impersonal "mutton." Dixon uses a similarly emotional image later in the passage when he describes cows "[bellowing] for days when mourning for their dead." By including these powerful images that are likely to upset people, Dixon makes it difficult for his audience to maintain the position that humans should have no feeling for animals.

Dixon also uses appeals to his audience's intelligence to sway them to his side. In the first paragraph, he asks the rhetorical question, "Why should we fall into the colossal ignorance and conceit of cataloging every human-like action of animals [as] instinct?" By associating disrespect of animals with ignorance, Dixon leads his audience, who wants to feel intelligent, into agreeing with his views. In the second paragraph, Dixon uses the analogies of fascism and primitive religion to compare dominion over animals to other misguided ideas. Later, he labels the views of the average scientist as ignorant and "empty," encouraging his audience to align themselves with his views instead.

Dixon, however, relies on more than just stylistic elements and emotional appeals to make his case. He also uses persuasive reasoning and evidence to support his point that animals are worthy of the same respect as humans. To critics who would argue that animals' abilities are due to instinct and neurological impulses, Dixon counters that humans, too, are ruled by the same forces, and yet we allow a level of compassion and feeling for humans that we deny to animals. He also makes the point that physically, humans and animals are very similar to each other, and in fact, animals are physically superior to humans in most cases. The major difference, he says, is that we have a superior intellect. By pointing out how much we have in common with animals, Dixon removes the barrier between us and them, making it harder for his opposition to argue that animals have neither intellect nor feeling.

He continues this line of reasoning by pointing out that human and animal behaviors are similar, and that "man has been imitating the animals" by flying, tunneling, and exploring Earth's waters. Dixon uses a variety of examples to provide evidence for his case: animals organizing themselves against enemies, building shelter, storing food, and making and using tools, just like humans. He also cites animal communication as a marker of intelligence and different emotional states, even if humans don't understand what they are hearing. An especially vivid piece of evidence is the example of a dreaming war horse who "lives over and over his battles," just as humans re-live their exploits in their dreams. Time and again, Dixon proves humans and animals share common experiences, and are therefore worthy of mutual respect.

By presenting the evidence of commonalities between humans and animals, as well as evidence of animals' feeling and intellect, Dixon makes an effective case that we should cease our dominion over them. He bolsters his case with appeals to his audience's intelligence and emotional imagery, both of which make his audience less resistant to his claims. While Dixon may not persuade every member of his audience that animals are worthy of respect, his use of these features makes his argument much more effective than it would be without them.

Essay Response #2 (Proficient Score)

Royal Dixon makes the argument in "The Human Side of Animals" that animals and humans should be treated with the same respect. He uses appeals to emotion, rhetorical questions, and evidence of animals' thoughts and feelings to make his case.

Knowing that most people who eat meat would disagree with his claims, Dixon uses emotional language to break down their resistance. It is hard to argue that animals have no feelings when Dixon describes cows mourning for days for their dead. Dixon gives other examples of animals having strong emotions, like when a war horse acts out its former battles in its sleep. These examples remind people of themselves; which is Dixon's goal: to break down the barriers between animals and humans.

He also uses rhetorical questions to persuade his audience to agree with ideas that may be new to them. In the first paragraph he asks, "If you agree that we cannot treat men like machines, why should we put animals in that class?" Since most people would agree with the first part of the statement, they are more likely to agree with the second part as well. The next rhetorical question in the paragraph asks people if they want to "fall into the colossal ignorance" of thinking that all animal behavior is due to instinct, the answer is obviously no. By carefully constructing these questions, Dixon puts his audience in a position in which they will be more likely to agree with his claims.

For readers who still may doubt that animals and humans have much in common, Dixon offers many examples of how animal behavior is like human behavior. Animals build shelter, make tools, and do other things that are just like the things humans do. With these examples, and others, Dixon shows that animals and humans are so similar that it makes no sense for one to dominate the other. In fact, he points out, some animal abilities are superhuman, like their ability to predict the weather. By giving examples of animals' traits and abilities that are similar to and even better than ours, Dixon causes the audience to feel respect for animals.

In conclusion, Dixon uses different ways of getting his audience to agree that animals are worthy of respect in "The Human Side of Animals." The use of emotional appeals, rhetorical questions, and evidence of animals' "humanity" helps him to persuade an audience that may be resistent at first to hearing his ideas.